Citizens for Decency

Antipornography Crusades as Status Defense

Citizens for Decency

Antipornography Crusades
as Status Defense

by Louis A. Zurcher, Jr., and
R. George Kirkpatrick

with the collaboration of Robert G. Cushing,
Charles K. Bowman, Ronald D. Birkelbach, Adreain Ross,
Susan Lee Zurcher, Russell L. Curtis

University of Texas Press, Austin & London

Library of Congress Cataloging in Publication Data

Zurcher, Louis A
  Citizens for decency.

  Bibliography: p.
  Includes index.
  1. Pornography—Social aspects—United States.
I. Kirkpatrick, Robert George, 1943- joint author.
II. Title.
HQ471.Z87 301.2'1 75-22048
ISBN 0-292-71032-1 (cloth)

Printed in the United States of America

Contents

Tables

Preface

We begin this book, as we began the study upon which it is based, by acknowledging our assumption that the term *pornography* is a value judgment. We assume that sexually explicit material can be and is invested with valences by individuals in a manner consistent with their overall network of value orientations, socialization patterns, and self-concepts. We assume that the labeling of sexually explicit materials as "pornographic" can adequately be understood only in the wider context of the sociological structures and processes of the society and the psychological structures and processes of the human personality. At the time of our study (1969–1970), the legal test (determined by the Warren Supreme Court) of whether or not sexually explicit material could be prohibited constitutionally rested on four criteria, all of which reflected the centrality of value judgment. Material was pornographic or obscene if: (*a*) to the average person (*b*) the dominant theme of the material taken as a whole appealed to prurient interest in sex; (*c*) the material was patently offensive because it affronted contemporary community standards relating to the description or representation of sexual matters; and (*d*) the material was utterly without redeeming social value (*Cain*, 1970; *Ginzburg*, 1966; *Hoyt*, 1970; *Jacobellis*, 1964; *Manual Enterprises, Inc.*, 1962; *Memoirs*, 1966; *Mishkin*, 1966; *Redrup*, 1967; *Roth*, 1957; *Stanley*, 1969; *Walker*, 1970). During the writing of this book (1973), the Burger Supreme Court modified the legal test for pornography (*Miller*, 1973; *Paris Adult Theater*, 1973), primarily by removing the "redeeming social value" criterion and by emphasizing the determination of "contemporary community standards." Specifically, the language of the test was changed to read: "whether the average person, applying contemporary community standards, would find the work, taken as a whole, appeals to the prurient interests, whether the work depicts or describes, in a patently offensive way, sexual conduct specifically defined by the applicable state law, and whether the work, taken as a whole, lacks serious literary, artistic, political or scientific value" (*Miller*, 1973). The new test continues to reflect the centrality of value judgment.

Throughout the United States, groups of individuals have been concurring more or less explicitly in their perceptions of what is pornographic, have assessed pornography to be a problem, and have mobilized attempts within their communities to stop or to restrict the commercial availability of various forms of sexually explicit material. How and why those crusades are generated, their evolution, their impact, the satisfaction derived from participation, and relevant characteristics of the participants and their opponents constitute the major issues with which we will be concerned in this book. Our approach to those issues and our interpretations of the data pertinent to them are consistently influenced by our assumption that pornography is a value judgment.

The study and the book are based upon intensive case histories of two antipornography crusades and extensive interviews with their most central participants and opponents. Though Goering, McLaird, and Coates (1969), Elkin (1960), Massey (1971), Wallis (1972), Wasby (1965) and Twomey (1955) have written useful brief accounts of incidents, there has never before been a systematic, comprehensive, comparative, and theory-oriented study of antipornography crusades. Though there are in the literature many studies of social movements which sought to produce change, there are only a few which analyze movements organized to *resist* change. A search of the literature also reveals few studies of small local rather than large national social movements and even fewer studies of two or more like-oriented movements in a comparative framework. Our study helps to fill those lacunae in the literature.

The book provides an in-depth analysis of antipornography efforts as symbolic-status and norm-oriented movements in a context of social change. The analytical approach is sociological and social-psychological, is based on both qualitative and quantitative data, and synthesizes macrolevel data on social structure with microlevel data on individual characteristics. Most studies of social movements have concentrated on the structural *or* the individual level of data and analysis. Within a general setting of social change, we have been able to describe the emergence of symbolic crusades, to determine the characteristics of the crusade organizations, to identify some of the important attitudes, perceptions, and experiences of those who participate in the crusades and those who oppose them, and to isolate some of the conceptual interstices among those entities. Our examination of the social movement organizations which directed the two antipornography crusades is particularly extensive, involving a wide array of structural variables. The comparative analysis of the two social movement organizations allows us to identify which among the variables are the most salient, how the variables interact, and what their relationship is to the symbolic crusade.

At the same time, we have been guided by and thus have been able to test (or at least to illustrate) and conceptually integrate some to-date rarely researched theoretical frameworks concerning social movements, namely: Gusfield's (1963) theory of status politics in symbolic crusades; Smelser's (1962) value-added theory of collective behavior; Zald and Ash's (1966) propositions concerning the growth and transformation of social-movement organizations; assorted propositions concerning the influence of multiorganizational fields upon social movements; and Turner's (1970) propositions specifying the determinants of movement strategy. We are also able to assess assorted hypotheses concerning the social-psychological characteristics of change-resisting individuals and, selectively, other propositions and hypotheses concerning social movements and their participants. At the conclusion of the book, we synthesize the findings which bear upon the total set of hypotheses and propositions into a broad theoretical framework. That framework is cast in a predictive mode, listing a series of "if . . . then" statements concerning the emergence of antipornography crusades specifically and symbolic crusades generally.

Though we have limited our interpretations of the data to those theoretical perspectives which particularly interested us, we believe that the data on natural history and individual characteristics have been presented in sufficient abundance to allow the reader, for pedagogical or research purposes, to substitute alternative interpretations drawn from other theoretical orientations.

Our study of antipornography crusades presents a contemporary example of the processes of citizens' attempts to influence social legislation, a topic which currently is, and increasingly will become, of national concern. Similarly, the study presents an example of citizen voluntarism, another currently increasing phenomenon in our society.

Some of the materials presented in the book have appeared in modified form in journals and research reports (see Acknowledgments). But the book goes beyond those materials and integrates them with other fresh materials into an overall analytical scheme. The full ethnography of the antipornography crusades could not be and was not presented piecemeal in articles. Only book form allows the richness of detail, the depth of process. Only book form provides a vehicle for telling the whole story of the individuals, the organizations, and their interface. Finally, only book form allows the presentation of the complete research design, revealing its multiple approaches, its weaknesses, and its strengths.

We intend the book to be useful for undergraduate and beginning graduate students in the social sciences, particularly for courses in collective behavior, social movements, social change, social problems, political sociology, deviant behavior, and social control.

All names of individuals, organizations, places, and newspapers in this book are pseudonyms, with the exception of a few nationally known public figures, organizations, and publications.

Acknowledgments

The research upon which this book is based was funded by the Commission on Obscenity and Pornography, W. Cody Wilson, executive director, and by a supplemental grant from the Hogg Foundation for Mental Health, Robert Sutherland, director. Dr. Wilson, and commission staff members Bernard Horowitz, Sylvia J. Jacobs, and Anthony Abell continually facilitated our research efforts with their suggestions, criticism, and encouragement.

There was a complex but enjoyable and productive division of labor among the authors of this book. L. Zurcher provided overall direction to the study, coauthored project reports, and wrote the book manuscript from the assorted project materials. Kirkpatrick contributed significantly to the study design, coordinated the interview and data-gathering team in the field, coauthored project reports, and wrote a doctoral dissertation based upon parts of the study. He also shared the travails of preparing the book manuscript. Cushing planned and coordinated the statistical analyses of the data and coauthored a project report. Bowman also coauthored a project report and served as a member of the field team. Birkelbach, Ross, and S. Zurcher helped to prepare the structured questionnaire, served as members of the field team, contributed to the data analyses, and wrote segments of project reports. Curtis saw in the data some potentials for additional and important organizational analysis and followed his interest, much to the benefit of the book.

The following research assistants effectively and importantly contributed to the data-gathering, coding, and analysis phases of the project: Mickey C. Bowman, Marilyn Bidnick, Marilyn Clayton Willis, Rosemary Cooney, Nijole Benokraitis, Paula Miller, Linda Birkelbach, Ralph Nemir, Vicki Watkins, Janine Nussbaum, Malvern Lusky, and Julia Quick.

Would that we could retain this research family for future projects.

The following colleagues read and generously offered helpful comments on working papers and other manuscripts generated by the project: Douglas Wallace, Victor Cline, Roy Wallis, William Gamson, xiv Acknowledgments

Robert Athanasious, Richard Simpson, Gideon Sjoberg, Louis Schneider, Neil Smelser, Mayer Zald, Harold Nelson, Charles Bonjean, John Walton, Sheldon Olson, David Gold, James McCartney, Everett Wilson, James Short, James B. Taylor, Ivan Belknap, Anthony Orum, and Elizabeth Glick. We further gratefully and especially acknowledge the intellectual guidance and counsel of Ralph Turner and Joseph Gusfield.

Typing and clerical assistance for first drafts of chapters were provided by the Western Behavioral Sciences Institute secretarial staff, particularly Patricia Falck, Janis Andrade, Vivian Graham, and Sheila Menaguale. At the University of Texas, Susan Dittmar patiently assembled tables and the reference section and reviewed the manuscript for citation consistency. Natalia Moehle typed the first assembled draft of the manuscript and somehow kept the preparation process (and the authors) organized and relatively on schedule. The final draft of the manuscript was prepared by Pamala Bockoven, a veritable virtuoso of the typewriter. Typing costs for the final draft were funded by a small grant from the University of Texas Research Institute. Denise Cabra assisted and consoled us while the manuscript was in press production.

The leaders of the antipornography crusades we studied consistently and unselfishly cooperated with our research effort. They made their organizational records available to us, helped us gather historical data, facilitated our nonparticipant observation, and provided us with access for formal and informal interviews with their members and even with their opponents. Generosity with their time and energies and a willingness openly to represent their position were typical of the antipornography crusaders. Though some of us began and ended the research project in many ways disagreeing with their goals, we were impressed by, respect, and thankfully acknowledge their sincerity, candidness, and cooperation.

Some of the findings of our study have been published in journals, as follows: Ronald D. Birkelbach and Louis A. Zurcher, "Some Socio-Political Characteristics of Anti-Pornography Campaigners: A Research Note," *Sociological Symposium* 4(Spring 1970):13–23; Louis A. Zurcher, R. George Kirkpatrick, Robert G. Cushing, and Charles K. Bowman, "The Anti-Pornography Campaign: A Symbolic Crusade," *Social Problems* 19(Fall 1971):217–238; Louis A. Zurcher and J. Kenneth Monts, "Political Efficacy, Political Trust, and Anti-Pornography Crusading: A Research Note," *Sociology and Social Research* 56(January

1972):211–220; Louis A. Zurcher and Russell L. Curtis, "A Comparative Analysis of Propositions Describing Social Movement Organizations," *Sociological Quarterly* 14(Winter 1973):175–188; Russell L. Curtis and Louis A. Zurcher, "Stable Resources of Protest Movements: The Multi–Organizational Field," *Social Forces* 52(September 1973):53–61; Louis A. Zurcher, R. George Kirkpatrick, Robert G. Cushing, and Charles K. Bowman, "Ad Hoc Anti-Pornography Organizations and Their Active Members: A Research Summary," *Journal of Social Issues*, special issue on pornography, 29, no. 3(1973):69–94; Russell L. Curtis and Louis A. Zurcher, "Social Movements: An Analytical Exploration of Organizational Forms," *Social Problems* 21, no. 3(1974):356–370; R. George Kirkpatrick, "Moral Indignation and Repressed Sexuality," *Psychoanalytic Review* 61(Spring 1974):141–149; and R. George Kirkpatrick, "Collective Consciousness and Mass Hysteria: Collective Behavior and Anti-Pornography Crusades in Durkheimian Perspective," *Human Relations* (In Press). Our research reports to the Commission on Obscenity and Pornography were titled and are available as follows: Louis A. Zurcher and R. George Kirkpatrick, *"The Natural History of an Ad Hoc Anti-Pornography Organization in Midville, USA"* (Washington, D.C.: Archives of the United States, 1971); Louis A. Zurcher and Charles K. Bowman, *"The Natural History of an Ad Hoc Anti-Pornography Organization in Southtown, USA"* (Washington, D.C.: Archives of the United States, 1971); Louis A. Zurcher and R. George Kirkpatrick, "Collective Dynamics of Ad Hoc Anti-Pornography Organizations," *in Technical Reports of the Commission on Obscenity and Pornography* (Washington, D.C.: Government Printing Office, 1971), V, 83–142; Louis A. Zurcher and Robert G. Cushing, "Some Individual Characteristics of Participants in Ad Hoc Anti-Pornography Organizations," in *Technical Reports of the Commission on Obscenity and Pornography* (Washington, D.C.: Government Printing Office, 1971), V, 143–215. We thank the publishers of the papers and reports for permission to use the materials selectively and in modified form throughout this book.

Citizens for Decency

Antipornography Crusades as Status Defense

Chapter 1

Introduction: Theoretical Aspects of Antipornography Crusades

Concerned citizens in Portland, Oregon, formed a committee to demonstrate for legislators the community's standards concerning unacceptable sexually explicit materials. A massive morality rally was held in the Orange Bowl in Miami, Florida, to affirm publicly and dramatically a defense of decency in America. Groups of citizens in such places as Sioux City, Iowa; Watertown, South Dakota; Littleton, Colorado; Saginaw, Michigan; Houston, Texas; Oklahoma City, Oklahoma; Washington, D.C.; Baltimore, Maryland; Syracuse, New York; and San Diego, California, openly agitated for "tougher" antipornography statutes. Throughout the country, persons participating in antipornography crusades of varying sizes, strategies, and durations observed what they perceived to be the disconcertingly flagrant operation and proliferation of "adult" bookstores and movies, "topless" and "bottomless" entertainment, and "live" sex shows. Angered and intent crusaders energetically held community-wide meetings and rallies; distributed antipornography literature and pamphlets; wrote protest letters and sent petitions to local and national officials and the media; urged, lobbied, and testified on behalf of antipornography statutes; picketed businesses labeled as purveyors of pornography; and in some cases more directly disrupted the operations of such businesses. Occasionally, the efforts of antipornography crusaders became statewide, as in California, where a citizen initiative yielded a proposed antipornography statute (later defeated) so restrictive that John Wayne and other notable conservatives publicly opposed it. The active agendas of national antipornography organizations, such as Citizens for Decent Literature and Morality in Media, Inc., included many requests from local groups for advice on how to conduct antipornography crusades in their communities.

Why do antipornography crusades emerge? Who is actively involved in them? What are the satisfactions gained from participation? What is the organizational structure of the crusades? Who leads them? What do they accomplish? Who opposes them?

The sociological concepts of *collective behavior* and *social movement* are useful devices with which to attempt some answers to those questions. *Collective behavior* designates the study of relatively unstructured, temporary, emotion-laden, and keenly interpersonal social situations, such as crowds, riots, crazes, panics, fads, fashions, publics, and social movements (Broom and Selznick 1968:221). As a form of collective behavior, the *social movement* is considered to be a large-scale, informal but purposive collective effort supported by an ideology and intended to correct, supplement, overthrow, or in some way influence the social order by direct action (Toch 1965:5). Other concepts sometimes included in definitions of the social movement are conscious effort, emergent norms, movement organization, shared value system, sense of community, sense of common problem, noninstitutional or innovative institutional strategy, promotion of or resistance to change, new order of life, and informal leadership.[1] Whatever the definition, it always includes the indication that the social movement reflects the broader processes of social change within a society, either reacting to or purposely stimulating such change.

There are many different varieties of social movements, depending upon the classification scheme of the observer. Lang and Lang noted that "typologies of social movements have been based on four different attributes: 1) some external criterion, such as the area of activity, the interest represented, or the content of its ideology; 2) the type of value orientation; 3) the nature of the goal; and 4) the growth pattern" (1961:497). Turner and Killian (1972:269–405) developed a set of ideal types based upon what they consider to be the essential characteristics of any social movement: a program of reform for society, the establishment of a power relationship favorable to the movement, and the promotion of membership gratification. A threefold typology of social movements—value-oriented, power-oriented, and participation-oriented—emerges for analytical purposes from the relative emphasis a specific social movement is observed to place on each of those essential characteristics. As Wilson explains, "Value-oriented movements are those in which the principal support for the movement is derived from a conviction of the worth of the program for change . . . . Power-oriented movements are those which have as their primary orientation the acquisition of power, status, or recognition for their members . . . . Participation-oriented movements are centered around the provision of membership gratification mainly through self-expression." Participation-oriented movements are further subdivided into "passive reform movements, or those which merely await anticipated changes. . . . Personal-status movements, or those which offer a redefinition of the status system so that the standing of certain groups is enhanced; and . . . limited personal movements, or those which rest their appeal on their exclusiveness" (Wilson 1973:16–17).

Turner and Killian further refined their typology according to "the public definition of the movement's relation to the basic value scheme of the society and upon the consequent general type of opposition evoked and degree of access to legitimate channels of action" (1972: 258–259). Four subtypes of social movements were thus derived: respectable-nonfactional (generally unopposed, meeting with disinterest and token support); respectable-factional (opposed by competing movements advocating the same general objective); peculiar (opposed by ridicule and ostracism); revolutionary (opposed by violent suppression).

Aberle (1966:315–333) offered another typology of social movements, which was based upon the locus and amount of change sought by the movement. As summarized by Wilson, the typology was fourfold: "Transformative movements aim at total change in the social structure. . . . Reformative movements aim at a partial change in supraindividual systems. . . . Redemptive movements aim at total change in individuals. . . . Alternative movements aim at partial change in individuals" (1973:23–26).

Antipornography crusades might be analyzed according to any of those typologies. They can be described as having been primarily power-oriented movements, with a strong undercurrent of participation orientation, particularly at the level of redefinition of personal status. They can be typified as primarily respectable-nonfactional, meeting mostly with disinterest or token support, yet receiving some notable ridicule and ostracism. They might be described as reformative movements, with a strong undercurrent of the alternative-movement goal of partial change in individuals. Both the Turner and Killian and the Aberle frameworks are integrated into broader series of social change and attempt to account for the generation of social movements within that context. These and other schemes for the study of social movements, such as those of Blumer (1951), Cameron (1966), Heberle

(1968), Lang and Lang (1961), Oberschall (1973), Orum (1972), and Toch (1965), would be appropriate for use in analyzing antipornography crusades. We shall employ some of their concepts throughout this book.

However, our analysis of the antipornography crusades and the characteristics of their active participants will be guided mainly by two other major frameworks for studying social movements—Gusfield's (1963) interpretation of the theory of status politics (based on Bell 1961; Hofstadter 1954; 1955; 1967; Lipset 1955; 1959; 1960; Weber 1947) and Smelser's (1962) theory of collective behavior. At the onset of our research, we judged the combination of these two frameworks to be the most useful to us, given our initial impression of antipornography crusades, the kinds of data available to us, and our overall research goals. Gusfield's theory provided the opportunity to analyze antipornography crusades as part of an overall process of social change and also provided a conceptual entry for assessing motivations for crusade participation. Furthermore, Gusfield's theory was based in his research on the temperance crusade—a phenomenon that seemed to parallel antipornography crusades. Smelser's theory offered a conceptual scheme that promised to facilitate our gathering and ordering of crusade natural-history data and was encapsulated within a comprehensive and useful general theory of action.

Gusfield's Theory of Status Politics

The emergence of social movements within a society is not surprising when they develop among segments of the population which are experiencing economic deprivation. However, the reasons for the emergence of social movements among the more affluent segments of the population are less apparent, though no less vital. The social conditions underlying such movements may be only distantly related to their proclaimed foci. A pointed example of that phenomenon was presented by Gusfield (1963) as part of his study of changes in the American temperance movement. He concluded that the temperance crusade, as a social movement, was a way by which members of a status group could strive to preserve, defend, or enhance the prestige of their style of life against threats from individuals or groups whose life style differed from theirs. As the potential crusaders perceived their own claims to prestige increasingly threatened, they sought public acts by which they could reaffirm the acknowledged worth of the life style to which they were committed. Such acts, status politics, were public, so that an overt display of support for their style of life could be gained, preferably at the expense of the challengers.

Gusfield's (1963:13–17) definitions of key terms in the crusade process are useful and will be maintained throughout this book. *Social status* refers to the distribution of prestige among individuals and groups in a social system. *Prestige* means the approval, respect, admiration, and deference a person or group is able to command by virtue of his or its imputed qualities or performances (Johnson 1960:469). As defined thus, the term *prestige* also connotes *power*. *Style of life* refers to the system of values, customs, and habits distinctive to a status group. When the individual's prestige is less than he expects as someone who has pledged himself to a usually prestigious style of life, he becomes a *status discontent*. The public acts in which the status discontent participates in order to raise or maintain his own or his group's status are *status politics*. When acts of status politics reach collective proportions, a *status movement*—a *symbolic crusade*—emerges.

Gusfield (1963:4–8) observed that challenges to life styles are products of social change. As America became more urban and secular around the turn of the century, members of the small-town *old middle class* sensed a threat to the prestige of their life style from the city-dwelling *new middle class*. The members of the old middle class in the nineteenth century, according to Gusfield, were rural, Protestant, and born in America. They espoused value orientations centered on self-control, industriousness, impulse renunciation, and sobriety. Those value orientations were central to their social acceptance and self-esteem. In the cities, which were growing in size and importance as a result of industrialization, members of the new middle class manifested an alternative, urban style of life. That style of life tended to put less emphasis upon the self-control, industriousness, impulse renunciation and sobriety valued by the old middle class. Furthermore, members of the new middle class tended to be Catholic rather than Protestant and recent immigrants rather than native Americans.

Alcohol readily became a summary symbol for the challenging urban life style. Drinking or nondrinking "indicated to what culture the actor was committed and hence what social groups he took as his models of imitation and avoidance and his point of positive and negative reference for judging his behavior" (Gusfield 1963:4). Public and purposive acts which could challenge alcohol as a symbol could simultaneously challenge the life style it symbolized. Thus the temperance movement, a symbolic crusade, provided opportunity for the old-middle-class status discontents to engage in status politics against the new middle class and its prestige-threatening life style.

The passing of the Eighteenth Amendment was the high point of accomplishment for the symbolic crusade of the old middle class, dramatically differentiating the two life styles—that of the rural, traditional, local, native, Protestant nondrinker from that of the urban, modernist, cosmopolitan, foreign, Catholic drinker—and affirming the prestige of the former. At least at first, it did not seem to matter much to temperance crusaders that Prohibition often was not obeyed or enforced. The crusaders had been successful in getting *their* law against the challengers publicly proclaimed, and it was *their* law that drinkers and "such people" had to avoid. Gusfield emphasized the importance of the symbolic nature of status movements. The prestige-enhancing public act tends to be ritualistic and ceremonial and is in itself rewarding and goal-attaining, perhaps even more so than the end result which such activity might bring about. The political victory, for example the passage of a law, is in itself symbolically a victory over the challenging enemy and a public display of the viability, acceptability, and prestige of the victors' life style.

Gusfield observed that life styles "die slowly, leaving their rear guards behind to fight delaying action" (1963:9). He argued that, even though they have ceased to be the dominant economic group, members of the old middle class of America are still searching for some way to restore their weakened prestige. "The dishonoring of their values is a part of the process of cultural and social change. A heightened stress upon the importance of tradition is a major response of such 'doomed classes'" (ibid.). Gusfield suggested that crusades against fluoridation, domestic Communism, school curricula, and the United Nations are among the more recent examples of the continuing efforts of members of the old middle class to restore their lost prestige, to defend tradition against modernity, under conditions of accelerated sociocultural change.

Currently in American society the possibility of alternative institutions and alternative life styles has become passionately popularized in the media and has been actualized by increasing numbers of persons, especially young persons. Epitomized by the now commonplace term *counterculture*, alternative forms of marriage, family, education, religion, and work challenge the traditional forms; an orientation to the present, to the immediate gratification of impulses, to widely assorted sensual experiences, to a negation of achievement motivation, to process rather than product challenges the traditional orientations.[2]

In this book we shall not propose that antipornography crusades are simply a replication of temperance crusades, juxtaposing the old and new middle classes of that era as Gusfield described them. It is now a hundred years later, distinctions between purely rural and purely urban value orientations are less clear; native birth is less an issue; industrialization and urbanization are predominant forms of social organization. Indeed, some members of what might be called the current new middle class are now looking back, romantically and nostalgically, to the possibility of recapturing at least some of the value orientations of rurality (e.g., particularism, closeness to nature, the extended family, the simplification of roles). Yet, though all the specifics may not obtain, we propose that Gusfield was correct in his conclusion that there are important residuals of the value orientations of the old middle class remaining strongly operative in contemporary American society. Those value orientations, encapsulated in the life styles and institutional enactments of significant numbers of Americans, are being challenged by other Americans, who espouse orientations, implement life styles, and enact institutional forms perceived to be alternatives. Though it may not be currently appropriate to typify the conflict as being strictly between the old and the new middle class, it is most certainly appropriate, we argue, to typify it as being between the traditional, or "basic," and the modern, or "deviant," in a context of social change. The processes of status politics, as Gusfield described them, should therefore be identifiable in the case of antipornography crusades.

More specifically, we hypothesize that antipornography efforts will reflect status politics, escalated to the level of symbolic crusades by the concerted activities of status discontents, individuals who perceive as threatened the prestige (and power) of the life style to which they are committed. Those activities will manifest symbolic and public efforts to reassert the prestige of the system of values, customs, and habits embraced by the crusaders.

We shall test this hypothesis by analyzing data from the natural histories of two antipornography crusades and by citing questionnaire data concerning sociodemographic and attitudinal characteristics of the crusaders and of their opponents.[3] The goals, strategies, and tactics of the antipornography crusades and the speeches, actions, responses, attributions, and concerns of the crusaders should reveal status discontent and efforts to resolve it.

Smelser's Theory of Collective Behavior

The master proposition underlying Smelser's theory of collective behavior is that people under strain tend to mobilize action intended to restructure their social environment in the name of some generalized belief (1962:385). The strain is taken to exist within the institutionalized components of the social environment; when the usual institutional means cannot successfully be employed to alleviate the strain, uninstitutionalized action in the form of collective behavior may be undertaken. Following Parsons (1951; Parsons and Shils, eds. 1951), Smelser identified the major components of the social environment (the "components of social action") as values; norms; mobilization of motivation into organized action (organizations, roles, and rewards); and situational facilities. The components are hierarchically ordered from values down to situational facilities, and any restructuring of one of the higher components necessitates changes in those components below it. Smelser (1962:25) defined values as "the most general statements of legitimate ends which guide social action" and quoted Kluckhohn (1951: 411) to elaborate the concept as involving "generalized and organized conception, influencing behavior, or nature, of man's place in it, of man's relation to man, and of the desirable and nondesirable as they may relate to man-environment and interhuman relations." Examples of values would be democracy, free enterprise, Christianity, human equality, and the nuclear family.

Values are at the highest level of conceptual analysis and do not specify how the ends they idealize are to be implemented or reached. Norms, according to Smelser, are more specific than values and indicate "certain regulatory principles which are necessary if these values are to be realized . . . [they] range from formal, explicit regulations found, for instance, in legal systems to informal, sometimes unconscious understandings found, for instance, in neighborhood cliques" (1962:27). Norms implementing the value *free enterprise* would include laws concerning contract, property, and employment and more informal customs concerning such things as market sharing. Norms implementing the value *Christianity* would include the Ten Commandments, fasting, and holy days of obligation.

According to Smelser (1962:27–28), values and norms provide general ends and general rules, but they do not specify who or what will implement them, how the implementation will be structured, or what the rewards for conformity will be. The mobilization of motivation into organized action is the component of the social environment in which values and norms are more sharply detailed. The economic processes of free enterprise are further defined, for example, by what varieties of business organizations (corporations, cottage industry, etc.) will conduct the processes, and what rewards are to be gained by involvement in the process. The processes of Christianity are further defined by what alternative organizations (churches, sects, etc.) conduct religious pursuits and by what rewards are to be gained from religious life. This component of action conceptually includes the broad sociological categories of social organization or social structure (families, churches, armies, schools, unions, friendship groups, etc.), and also includes the rewards (wealth, power, prestige) expected by individuals as a result of their effective enactment of roles in such structures.

The situational-facilities component of the social environment consists of the individual's awareness of the potentials in the social environment and the knowledge, skills, and abilities he or she possesses and feels are useful in influencing that environment. Situational facilities in the free-enterprise example include knowledge of business conditions, the availability of capital, the efficacy of business decisions, and the opportunity to depend upon employees and colleagues. In the religious example, facilities would include the liturgical, sacramental, ecclesiastical, and other knowledges and rituals which lead to sanctity and salvation.

Smelser summarized his argument for the components of action:

> For any instance of action which we wish to analyze, then, we have to pose four basic questions: What are the values that legitimize this action at the most general level? By what kinds of norms is this action coordinated and kept relatively free from conflict? In what ways is the action structured into roles and organizations? What kinds of situational facilities are available? . . . when strain is

> exerted on one or more of these components, *and* when established ways of relieving the strain are not available, various kinds of collective outbursts and movements tend to arise . . . as attempts to reconstitute the component or components under strain. (1962:28)

Smelser identified a central characteristic of collective behavior as the tendency to search for solutions to conditions of strain by moving to a more generalized level of action. If the source of the strain is at the level of facilities, potential solutions may be sought at the level of reconstitution of organized role behaviors, norm systems, or value systems. Once the generalization has taken place and the attempts are made to reconstitute the meaning of the higher-level component, the process of "short-circuiting," unique to collective behavior, takes place. "Having redefined the high-level component, people do not proceed to respecify, step by step, down the line to reconstitute social action. Rather, they develop a belief which 'short-circuits' from a very generalized component *directly* to the focus of strain. The accompanying expectation is that the strain can be relieved by a direct application of a generalized component" (Smelser 1962:71). For example, temperance crusaders believed that the influence (a situational facility) and prestige (a mobilization of motivation) associated with their style of life could be enhanced by the passing of Prohibition (a normative reconstitution).

Smelser specified the forms of collective behavior which can emerge from mobilization to restructure each of the components of the social environment:

1. *Values* (1962:29, 120, 313). An attempt to restore, protect, modify, or create values in the name of a generalized belief yields a value-oriented social movement, such as a political revolution, a utopian movement, a religious revolution, or a nativistic movement. The generalized belief envisions a sweeping reconstitution of self and society—a fundamental modification of conceptions concerning the nature of human individuals, of human interaction, and of society in general. Individual strains supporting the value-oriented social movement are experienced concerning commitment to or faith in the value in question.

2. *Norms* (1962:29, 109, 270). An attempt to restore, protect, modify, or create norms in the name of a generalized belief yields a norm-

oriented social movement, such as the Townsend movement, the temperance movement, the Farmers' Alliance movement, the Dixiecrat movement, the civil rights movement, etc. The generalized belief calls for a new rule, law, or regulatory agency intended to control the inappropriate, irresponsible, or inadequate behavior of others. Individual strains supporting the norm-oriented social movement are experienced concerning conformity or deviation from the current norm or norms. An important aspect of the norm-oriented social movement is that it does not challenge the ongoing societal values; in fact, it refers to those values as a justification for normative reconstitution. The nonviolent civil rights movement, for example, consistently referred to the accepted societal values of equality, opportunity, and the dignity of persons in its quest for legal and procedural changes which would make those values operational for greater numbers of minority Americans.

3. *Roles, Organizations, and Rewards* (1962:29, 101, 226). An attempt to restructure aggressively the patterns of action associated with roles and organizations in the name of a generalized belief yields a hostile outburst, such as riots, scapegoating, lynching, looting, and other forms of mob action. The generalized belief identifies the source, sources, or forces taken to be responsible for an ambiguous but stressful situation and assumes that the ambiguity and strain can be eliminated by killing, injuring, removing, or restricting the individual(s) or group(s) labeled as culpable. Individual strains supporting the hostile outburst are experienced concerning responsibility or lack of responsibility in organized role behavior, loyalty to the role or roles, and the expectations of rewards for role enactment.

4. *Situational Facilities* (1962:29, 94, 131, 170). An attempt to restructure ambiguity in situational facilities or to act in the perceived absence of those facilities, in the name of a generalized belief, yields panic, typified by collective flight, or a craze, typified by manias, booms, fads, and fashion. The generalized belief in panic is hysterical, imputing to some ambiguous entity both the power and the intention to threaten or destroy. In panic, persons abandon their usual patterns of social interaction in order to protect their lives, property, or power. The generalized belief in the craze is wish-fulfilling and assures the believer that some powerful force, object, or behavior can successfully neutralize or defeat a frustrating, dangerous, or destructive agent of some kind. Individuals flee toward a potential source of protective gratifica-

tion. Individual strains supporting panic or a craze are experienced concerning competence or a lack of competence in the ability to predict and control the environment.

As mentioned earlier, in the Smelser framework the components of social action are conceptually arranged in a hierarchy of abstraction, from values at the top to situational facilities at the bottom. The hierarchy is taken by Smelser to be empirically demonstrable for the various forms of collective behavior. Attempts to restructure values in the value-oriented social movement include the restructuring of norms, social organizations, roles and reward distributions, and situational facilities. Attempts to restructure norms through the norm-oriented social movement include the restructuring of social organizations, roles and reward distributions, and situational facilities. And so on, down the hierarchy.

We hypothesize that the antipornography crusades are norm-oriented social movements and, consequently, that our data will fit with and will support Smelser's outline of the characteristics of such movements. The antipornography crusaders will cite acceptance of, commitment to, and concern over "basic" societal values and will act collectively to restore, protect, modify, or create norms in the name of a generalized belief. That generalized belief will call for new laws and regulatory devices concerning pornography, which will be intended to control the "irresponsible" behavior of others, who will be seen to be deviating from "established" patterns of behavior and thereby to be threatening "social order" and "basic values." As pointed out earlier, the implementation of a norm-oriented movement involves components of social action lower than norms. Consequently, we hypothesize that the antipornography crusaders will express and attempt to resolve strains—concerning the stability of traditional social institutions (e.g., family, religion, education, work); concerning the rewards (prestige) they receive from enacting roles in those institutions; and concerning the usefulness of their knowledge, skills, and perspectives in predicting the consequences of their own behavior and in controlling significant aspects of the social environment which impinge upon their everyday lives. Similarly, the antipornography crusades as norm-oriented movements will involve elements of panic (flight from existing norms or impending normative change), craze (plunge to establish new means), and hostility (eradication of someone or something responsible for evils) (Smelser 1962:271). Varying strains on different components of action will yield variation in the operations of the antipornography crusades (e.g., more or less hostility, more or less craze, more or less panic). Finally, we hypothesize that the process of "short-circuiting," as described by Smelser (1962:111) will be apparent in the operations of the antipornography crusades. That is, the antipornography crusaders, experiencing strain concerning their ability to predict and control their social environment and concerning the prestige they feel should be associated with their enactment of traditional social roles in traditional institutions, will perceive the general source of the strain to be the challenge to basic values and traditions by the enactors of alternative life styles. Pornography—and, more concretely, certain "adult" bookstores and theaters—will be perceived as symbolic representations of the alternative and challenging life styles and will be specifically and dramatically labeled as sources of evil. The generalized belief will emerge that laws pertaining to pornography, to "adult" bookstores and theaters, are inadequate. If the old laws can be strengthened or made more operational, or if new ones can be introduced, pornography, the bookstores and theaters, and the alternative life styles they represent will be punished, immobilized, damaged, or destroyed. The short-circuiting process will be completed with the belief that the normative changes will once and for all sweepingly remove or in some way neutralize or offset the original source of strain, the alternative life styles.

While applying data to these hypotheses, we intend to demonstrate some points of articulation between Gusfield's theory of status politics and Smelser's theory of collective behavior (although in our analysis we are using only parts of each of those scholars' elegant frameworks). We shall illustrate with the antipornography data that symbolic crusades are norm-oriented movements. We shall further illustrate that status discontent is a conceptually useful explanation of strain and that challenges to life style introduce an array of strain touching upon all of the components of action. We shall demonstrate that the symbolic crusades involve norm-oriented beliefs, hysterical beliefs, and wish-fulfillment beliefs. Consequently, antipornography crusaders will manifest concerns with: belief in and commitment to broad values concerning self and society; conformity to and deviation from norm systems; responsibility-irresponsibility and loyalty-disloyalty regarding organized social roles and the rewards associated with such roles; and confidence or lack of it in predicting and controlling elements of the social environment. Finally, we shall demonstrate the role of symbolism in the short-circuiting process for generalized beliefs and show that under some circumstances norm-oriented crusaders will resolve status discontent with a more symbolic than utilitarian restructuring of norms. If, however, the crusade does not yield satisfactory results in either a symbolic or a utilitarian manner, the antipornography crusade will continue and shift its strategies in the direction of hostility, craze, or panic. Throughout our selected synthesis of those Gusfield and Smelser concepts, we shall also introduce, where relevant, some concepts and observations of other collective-behavior scholars.

We shall test the hypotheses, provide the illustrations or assessments, and articulate the different theories with comparative data from the natural histories of the two antipornography crusades.

Drawing from his conceptualization of the components of social action, Smelser suggested an "intellectual apparatus" with which the assorted and complex determinants of collective behavior, including social movements, might be analyzed. He described the intellectual apparatus as being based upon the logic of "value-added," and argued that it offered "a way of ordering determinants in a scale from general to specific. Each determinant is seen as logically—though not necessarily temporally—prior to the next. Each determinant is seen as operating within the scope established by the prior, more general determinant" (1969:91).

Smelser ordered the determinants of collective behavior as value-added stages, each stage being a necessary but not sufficient prerequisite to the next and, ultimately, to the emergence of collective behavior. The value-added stages are (a) structural conduciveness (the form of collective behavior must be physically and socially possible); (b) structural strain (within the context of the conduciveness there must be some social or social-psychological disequilibrium, inconsistency, or conflict); (c) growth and spread of a generalized belief (the strain must be articulated and its source identified and labeled); (d) precipitating factors (an event or situation must focus the generalized belief more clearly and give evidence that the source of the strain is correctly identified and labeled; (e) mobilization of participants for action (events and/or the leader[s] must develop and implement a course of action based on the generalized belief—that is, a course seen to be able to alleviate the strain); (f) the operation of social control (counterdeterminants to the first five stages must be activated which shape the form, direction, and intensity of the collective behavior). In a later work (1972), Smelser dropped precipitating factors as a stage because he felt it introduced a misleading temporal factor. We have chosen to retain that stage for our analytical purposes.

We shall present, in the value-added sequence suggested by Smelser, the natural-history data from the two antipornography crusades we studied.[4] It must be emphatically noted that Smelser (1972) clearly indicated that the value-added stages were intended for logical rather than empirical-temporal relationships among the determinants of collective behavior, and thus the value-added model is not a natural history. We elect to impose a natural-history function upon the value-added paradigm because the sequence is a convenient way to order the natural-history data and because at the same time we will be able to assess the usefulness of the stages for that purpose. Furthermore, the value-added sequence provides a good context in which to examine the hypotheses we have derived concerning status discontent, symbolic crusades, and norm-oriented movements. Smelser (1962:270–312) outlined in detail what he felt to be the key factors of the value-added stages as they applied to norm-oriented movements. Throughout our analysis, we shall present those conceptualized factors and assess their empirical utility.

Individual Characteristics of Conporns and Proporns

The antipornography crusader typically and popularly has been stereotyped as a little old lady in tennis shoes and a print dress, who, with a shopping bag hanging over one arm, in her free hand wields an umbrella with which she prods and pummels a smut dealer. We choose to base our hypotheses about the individual characteristics of antipornography crusaders upon a somewhat broader perspective. Our review of the literature encourages us to hypothesize differences, in selected individual characteristics, between those persons who were actively and centrally involved as members of the crusades and those persons who were actively and publicly opposed to the crusades. Hereafter, we shall refer to the active and central crusaders as "Conporns"; we shall refer to their opponents as "Proporns." (Proporns were not always in favor of pornography as such but always were against censorship and opposed to the activities of the crusaders.)

First, we shall demonstrate characteristic differences between Conporns and Proporns generally, with a set of hypotheses drawn from the literature on status discontent and change-promoting or change-resisting individuals or groups. We then shall test a set of hypotheses concerning differences between Conporns and Proporns in status inconsistency. Finally, we shall test hypothesized differences in political trust and political efficacy between greater- and lesser-constraint–oriented Conporns.

General Characteristics

We hypothesize that, when compared with Proporns, Conporns will: be older; more often be affiliated with organized religions; be more religiously oriented and religiously active; more often be reared in smaller towns and cities; less often be in professional occupations; have less formal education; be more family oriented; have more children; be more politically conservative; be more authoritarian; be more alienated; have a more traditional view of the family and of heterosexual activity; be less politically tolerant; be more dogmatic; be more favorable toward censorship; more often associate pornography with correlates of social and individual pathology; and have had less formal sex education.[5] We shall test these hypotheses with data from formal, structured questionnaires administered to Conporns and Proporns. A detailed description of the questionnaire and the sample will be presented below. The findings concerning the individual characteristics of Conporns as compared with Proporns will be interpreted as they apply to Gusfield's depiction of persons who were status discontents in the temperance crusade he studied.

Status Inconsistency

Earlier in this chapter we accepted Gusfield's definition of social status as the distribution of prestige among individuals and groups in a social system. For our purposes, Eitzen provided a useful transitional statement concerning social status as it relates to the concept *status inconsistency* (also called status incongruence or status discrepancy): "Status is accorded to individuals. People evaluate and rate others on a number of dimensions (e.g., possessions, life style, income, extent of education, race or ethnic background, and type of occupation) and this evaluation constitutes an individual's status in a social system. It is possible that an individual may rate high on some dimensions by which status is judged, but low on others. Such variations in status have been conceptualized by sociologists as status inconsistency" (1970a:493).

Geschwender (1967) noted three assumptions implicit within status inconsistency as a concept: the person is aware of the inconsistencies in status; inconsistency results in stress for the person; and the person will attempt to reduce the stress by such behaviors as social mobility, restructuring the status system by deliberate change, or isolating himself from the social system.

The trend-setting research on status inconsistency was conducted by Lenski, who concluded from his empirical investigation that "the more frequently acute status inconsistencies occur within a population, the greater would be the proportion of that population willing to support programs of social change" (1954:411). Since the publication of Lenski's research in 1954, there has been a flood of published studies on the antecedents, types, consequences, correlates, and theoretical/methodological difficulties of status inconsistency (the status factors usually considered in the studies are education, occupation, income, and ethnicity). Among the substantive topics examined as dependent variables which might or might not be related to the independent variable of status inconsistency have been liberal or leftist political orientation or behavior, preference for political change,[6] conservative or rightist political orientation or behavior, preference for the political status quo,[7] prejudice,[8] upward social mobility,[9] religious orientation,[10] psychological stress, psychosomatic symptoms,[11] political apathy,[12] participation in social movements,[13] civil rights militancy,[14] and small group behavior.[15]

The findings concerning the relation of status inconsistency to the assorted substantive dependent variables listed above have been unclear. Some authors have tended to reject the status-inconsistency proposition.[16] Other authors have reported partial support for the proposition, limited by such factors as (a) the specific configuration of status rank (e.g., which among the variables, education, income, occupation, and ethnicity, are high or low; the relation of ascribed to achieved statuses);[17] (b) the operation of significant intervening variables (e.g., perception of status inconsistency, socialization factors, subcultural values, satisfaction with public visibility, interpersonal attachment),[18] (c) the operation of status variables (e.g., socioeconomic status, ethnic status) independently or under conditions of cross-pressures;[19] (d) significant methodological flaws.[20]

Conporns and Proporns have definite perceptions of and opinions concerning the processes and content of contemporary social change. If status inconsistency is related to such perceptions and opinions, what patterns of inconsistency might be found among Conporns and Proporns? Some of the refinements of the status-inconsistency concept, based upon the research reports and critiques listed above, seem pertinent to that question.

One of the conceptual and empirical evolutions of the status-inconsistency paradigm has been the distinction between "over-rewarded" and "under-rewarded" inconsistents. Over-rewarded inconsistents manifest, for example, high-status income combined with low-status education and/or occupation. Under-rewarded inconsistents manifest, for example, low-status income combined with high-status education and/or occupation. Geschwender (1967; 1968) found that under-rewarded inconsistents were prone to participate in change-inducing social movements, while over-rewarded inconsistents were not. Chiricos, Pearson, and Fendrich (1970) found some support for Geschwender's hypothesis concerning under-rewarded inconsistents, if the under-rewarded condition was perceived to be such by the respondent. Hunt and Cushing (1970) and Eitzen (1970a) reported the presence of a significant number of over-rewarded status inconsistents among members of the John Birch Society and supporters of George Wallace. Their findings suggest that, expanding upon Geschwender's hypothesis, over-rewarded inconsistents will participate in social movements or political action, but the movements or action are likely to be change-resisting in character (see also Lipset and Raab 1969; Rush 1967; Trow 1958). Hunt and Cushing observed, regarding the over-rewarded status inconsistent, that "acceptance of the John Birch Society . . . seems to be linked with status discrepancies where people are potentially threatened or displaced by the increasing complexity and centralization of national life." On the other hand, the under-rewarded status inconsistent "is likely to be favorably disposed toward the recent structural changes in American society and to seek continuation of the political reforms begun during the New Deal era" (1970: 600).

If one accepts the premise that American society includes a strong value orientation for material acquisition, then in a very real sense the over-rewarded status inconsistent "has it made" in the status quo. The structure of the social environment and the distribution of rewards, prestige, and power are such that the over-rewarded status

inconsistent is benefiting beyond what he or she might ordinarily expect—status level of income significantly exceeds status level of occupation and/or education. Over-rewarded status inconsistents, therefore, could be expected to resist planned or unplanned changes in the
social environment which might threaten their somewhat precarious
over-rewarded situation. Lenski (1954) commented in passing that if
a person was happy with a specific pattern of status inconsistency, he
would not at all be interested in social change. Bradburn and Caplovitz
(1965) found in a national survey that over-rewarded status inconsistents tended to be relatively content individuals. Curtis (1970) has contrasted stressful and change-motivating "negative" (under-rewarded)
status inconsistency with rewarding and maintenance-oriented "positive" status inconsistency. Robinson and Shaver (1969) have wondered
about the different consequences of "desirable" and "undesirable"
status inconsistency.

We now suggest that an important component of the Conporns'
life-style constellation is over-rewarded status inconsistency, which
they actively work to defend. Thus, we suggest that there is another
reaction to status inconsistency beyond the three generally described.
That reaction is not social mobility, not encouragement of innovations
in the social environment, and not withdrawal from the social environment. Rather, the reaction, in the form of a symbolic crusade, is
intended to maintain a societal status quo which supports the life style
of the Conporns and which sustains the benefits of their over-rewarded status inconsistency. On the other hand, again assuming the
materialistic bias, we suggest that under-rewarded status inconsistency is part of the profile of Proporns. Consequently, they tend to
support innovations in the social environment broadly and generally,
in line with their general attempts to reconstitute their under-rewarded
status inconsistency.

More specifically, we hypothesize that Conporns will tend toward
an over-rewarded status-inconsistency pattern of high income with
lower education and/or lower occupation. In contrast, Proporns will
tend toward an under-rewarded status-inconsistency pattern of low
income with higher education and/or higher occupation. We shall test
these hypotheses with data from the structured questionnaire.

As we test these hypotheses, we intend to integrate the findings
with some observations and theoretical perspectives of other authors.
Orum has written, "No one has yet shown the explicit links between
status inconsistency, psychological strain, and belief in or participation

in movements" (1974:185). Given the composite framework and multiple data base of our study, we are encouraged to illustrate such links.

Olsen and Tully, in their critique of the status-inconsistency concept and research, suggested that a more productive approach to understanding preferences for or resistances to change "would be to study further the separate effects of a variety of independent variables, such as one's social power, privilege, and prestige" (1972:572). Several other authors commented on the crucial role of perception of status or threat to status in the inconsistency process.[21] Perceived status inconsistency was even more important than objective status inconsistency in the generation of unrest and the intention to act. We shall demonstrate that Gusfield's concept of status discontent can be used conceptually to represent the operation of perceived status inconsistency, to represent concern with social power, privilege, and prestige, and to relate those factors directly to participation in symbolic crusades.

In his discussion of the relation of status inconsistency to social unrest and social movements, Geschwender argued: "It must be emphasized that propinquity to participate in social movements is not the same as joining them. It is a necessary but not sufficient condition for membership" (1968:483). He advised that status inconsistency might usefully be considered one of the elements of structural strain among the value-added stages described by Smelser. To summarize his point, Geschwender transposed the hypothesis "status inconsistency predisposes one toward participation in social movements" to read "status inconsistency is a type of structural strain which predisposes symptoms of individual unrest in status inconsistents" (1968:478). We shall demonstrate, with the antipornography data, the role of status inconsistency as an element of structural strain in the development of a norm-oriented social movement.

Geschwender (1967) described the status-inconsistency/social-unrest process as being motivated by the need to resolve cognitive dissonance (Festinger 1957; 1964). The status inconsistent attempts to resolve dissonance first by social mobility (by moving up the status hierarchy in the lower of his status factors). If the mobility is blocked or unsuccessful, "then the individual will shift to more complex forms of dissonance reduction" (Geschwender 1967:169). With antipornography data, we shall relate that shifting process to Smelser's conceptualizations concerning movement up and down the components of action as a means of restructuring the social environment and relieving structural strain.

We shall test the hypotheses and provide the illustrations and demonstrations with both natural-history and structured-questionnaire data.

Political Efficacy and Political Trust

Gamson (1968; 1969) has argued for the general proposition that when, in a neighborhood, community, or society, citizens manifest a high degree of political efficacy and a low degree of political trust, the optimum conditions exist for the mobilization of citizen political action oriented toward constraint. He defines political efficacy as the ability to influence or make significant inputs to the political system. Political trust is "a differentiated attitude toward different levels of the political system—toward the public philosophy which justifies a regime, its political institutions, or the authorities who hold office at a particular time" (1969:2). Constraint, according to Gamson, is a form of political influence in which the citizens strategically add "new disadvantages to the situation or the threat to do so, regardless of the particular resources used" (1969:10). To support his proposition, Gamson cited data (Paige 1968) which suggest that respondents' reports of high political efficacy with low political trust were associated with their participation in the constraining actions of civil rights activity or rioting. Since Gamson's examples referred to actions and orientations left of political center, it seemed appropriate to test, with data from the antipornography crusades, the viability of Gamson's proposition as it might apply to actions and orientations right of political center.

Furthermore, since we have comparative data on two cases of citizen political action, we can test the relation of relative degrees of political efficacy and trust to relative degrees of strategy for constraint. Specifically, we hypothesize that Conporns in the antipornography crusade which employed the greater degree of constraint as a strategy will report a higher degree of political efficacy and a lower degree of political trust than Conporns in the antipornography crusade which employed the lesser degree of constraint as a strategy. We shall relate this finding to Gusfield's (1963:6–7) distinction between assimilative reform and coercive reform in symbolic crusades, to Smelser's (1962: 271) observations concerning the operation of hostility in norm-oriented social movements, and to Turner's (1970:147–149) identification of the alternative social movements' strategies of persuasion, bargaining, and coercion.

Gamson (1968) suggested that low political trust probably is associated with alienation. Powerlessness and normlessness are considered to be two of the components of alienation (Dean 1961). If powerlessness conceptually can be taken to subsume, or at least to be related to, a lack of political efficacy, and if normlessness can be taken similarly to be related to a lack of political trust, then we can formulate two further hypotheses concerning the antipornography crusades. The Conporns in the antipornography crusade implementing the greater constraint will report a lower degree of powerlessness and a higher degree of normlessness than the Conporns in the crusade implementing less constraint.

We shall test these hypotheses with both natural-history and structured-questionnaire data.

Organizational Characteristics of the Antipornography Crusades

Smelser reported that a norm-oriented movement "often is carried out by an organization, such as a political party, a pressure group, or a club" whose participants attempt to affect economic, educational, political, religious, or other norm systems "directly, or induce some constituted authority to do so" (1962:274–275). The organization can be established (existing before the movement begins) or new (forming as the movement develops); formal (constituted with a charter, title, by-laws, etc.) or informal (consisting of a gathering of interested citizens); and general (committed to issues broader than those of concern to the movement) or specific (agitating for a single type of measure).

We shall demonstrate that the organizational characteristics outlined by Smelser as being associated with a norm-oriented movement are systematically interrelated with each other and can influence or be influenced by other organizational variables (e.g., leadership styles, reactions of the community, membership satisfactions). To accomplish this demonstration, we shall examine as hypotheses some of the propositions developed by Zald and Ash (1966) concerning the growth, decay, and change of social movement organizations. We shall also test a set of hypotheses drawn from the literature on multiorganizational fields and attempt to reveal that the structure and operations of the antipornography organizations are related to the degree that the organizations are integrated with other voluntary associations and agencies in the community. Finally, we shall test with antipornography data a set of hypotheses drawn from Turner's (1970) propositions concerning the determinants of social movement strategies.

Organizational Growth, Decay, and Change

Relatively few studies have given more than brief attention to the characteristics and the dynamics of social movement organizations as such.[22] In his recent text, Wilson observed that "few models have been constructed which place primary emphasis on organizational constraints on the emergence and growth of social movements" (1973: 29).[23] Zald and Ash (1966) represent one of those few attempts. After an extensive review of the literature, Zald and Ash derived a stimulating set of propositions concerning the growth, decay, and change of social movement organizations. At the conclusion of their theoretical essay, they called for a systematic examination of the propositions with data from empirical and preferably comparative studies.

Zald and Ash intended their propositions to be applied primarily to large-scale, national social movements and organizations. Each of the antipornography crusades we studied was based in a single community. However, we do not consider the antipornography organization data to be inappropriate for use in assessing the Zald-Ash propositions. Nor do we consider the propositions to be inappropriate as another device for analyzing the antipornography crusade. We believe that the structure and processes of smaller, local social movements and organizations are at least qualitatively illustrative of, if not qualitatively identical to, the structure and processes of the larger cases.

Nine of the seventeen Zald-Ash (1966) propositions are for our purposes the most theoretically important and are the ones for which we had relevant data. The propositions, rewritten as hypotheses concerning the antipornography organizations and renumbered, are as follows:

1. The more insulated the antipornography organization is by exclusive membership requirements and goals aimed at changing individuals, the less susceptible it is to pressures for organizational maintenance or general goal transformation.

2. The antipornography organization created by another organization is more likely to go out of existence following success than the antipornography organization with its own linkages to individual supporters.

3. The antipornography organization with relatively specific goals is more likely to vanish following success than the organization with broad general goals.

4. The antipornography organization which aims to change individuals and employ solidary incentives is less likely to vanish than the organization with goals aimed at changing society and employing mainly purposive incentives.

✗ 5. The inclusive antipornography organization is likely to fade away faster than the exclusive organization; the latter is more likely to take on new goals.

6. The inclusive antipornography organization is more likely than the exclusive organization to participate in coalitions and mergers.

7. The exclusive antipornography organization is more likely than the inclusive organization to be beset by schisms.

8. Routinization of charisma is likely to conservatize the dominant core of the antipornography organization while simultaneously producing increasingly radical splinter groups.

9. The exclusive antipornography organization is almost certain to have a leadership which focuses on mobilizing membership for tasks, while the inclusive organization is readier to accept an articulating leadership style.

A combination of natural-history and questionnaire data will be used to assess these hypotheses. Drawing upon the findings, we shall if appropriate modify the Zald-Ash propositions as they bear upon the small or emergent social movement organization.

The Multiorganizational Field

The concept *multiorganizational field* suggests that organizations in a community setting approximate an ordered, coordinated system. A broad use of the term would refer to the multiorganizational environment of the focal organization, the total possible number of organizations with which it might or might not establish specific linkages. A narrower usage would refer to those organizations among the universe of organizations with which the focal organization did in fact establish specific linkages. We shall use the term in the first, larger sense.

Interorganizational processes within the multiorganization field can be identified on two levels, which conceptually overlap: the *organizational* level, where networks are established by joint activities, staff, boards of directors, target clientele, resources, etc., and the *individual* level, where networks are established by multiple affiliations of members. We are aware of no research which focuses upon the multiorganizational fields of social movements, either at the organizational or the individual level. A few studies, as part of their broader concerns, do present information relevant to the multiorganizational field at the organizational level.[24] Similarly, a few studies as part of their broader concerns do present information relevant to the multiorganizational field at the individual level.[25] Research relevant to the organizational level has reported the commonality of community political and organizational textures (Greer and Orleans 1962); the representation of the community as an ecology of games (Long 1958); the interpenetration of organizational representation (Turk and Lefcowitz 1962; Warren 1967; Zald 1969); and the interface between local urban structures and the larger society (Turk 1970; Walton 1967). Research relevant to the individual level has reported a pattern of multiple memberships in voluntary associations (Babchuk and Booth 1969); the existence of moral "entrepreneurs" for whom moral issues become a central life interest to be pursued in varieties of organizational settings (Becker 1963); and a number of findings concerning the characteristics of persons whose membership in complex organizations tended to be firm and integrated.[26]

Multiorganizational fields should operate significantly, on both the organizational and the individual levels, in the emergence and maintenance of antipornography organizations. From the literature on multiorganizational fields we can hypothesize generally that: the antipornography organizations will be enmeshed in a network of other community organizations (voluntary associations) in the larger multiorganizational fields; those interorganizational linkages will be based upon common interests, ideologies, audiences, or other shared characteristics; participants in the antipornography organizations will share memberships in other voluntary associations within the multiorganizational field; differences between the two antipornography organizations in the kinds of alignments they have within the field will be associated with differences in their goals, strategies, member recruitment patterns, member characteristics, goal achievements, and life span.

More specifically, we hypothesize that the antipornography organization that has the closer and more ordered interaction and integration with its multiorganizational field will have greater: homogeneity of membership (age, education, and income); member satisfaction with work; member political interest; member sense of political trust; member sense of organizational identity; member knowledge of organizational name, goals, and strategies; member degree of outreach; integrity of organizational boundary; member optimism about organizational goal accomplishment, about community support for antipornography activities, and about the future diminishing distribution of pornography; organizational success; specificity of organizational goals and strategies; and tendency to disband following goal attainment.

We shall test these hypotheses with natural-history and questionnaire data and attempt to integrate the findings with those concerning the Zald-Ash propositions.

The Determinants of Crusade Strategy

Turner (1970:146) has argued that most social movement theory has been concerned with predicting support for the movement. Little attention has been given to how a movement acts upon the larger society to promote the changes with which it is identified. Research focusing upon the choice of power strategies elected by a social movement in its confrontation with a target group would provide such information.

Turner suggested that there were three alternative strategies available to social movements: persuasion, bargaining, and coercion. He defined the strategies as follows:

Bargaining takes place when the movement has control over some exchangeable value that the target group wants and offers some of that value in return for compliance with its demands. One of the commonest forms of bargaining in a democratic society is the offer of votes or other support to the target group . . . or one movement offers to form a coalition with another movement in which each movement supports the aims of the other movement. . . .

Coercion is the manipulation of the target group's situation in such a fashion that the pursuit of any course of action other than that sought by the movement will be met by considerable cost of punishment. The extreme form of coercion is the threat of total destruction

. . . lesser forms of coercion involve weakening or inconveniencing or embarrassing the target group. Terrorism is one of the most highly coercive strategies. A less intense form of coercive strategy is illustrated in organized civil disobedience when there is no obstructive activity. . . . Coercion can be viewed as negative bargaining. . . . The essence of coercion is usually the *threat* of harm. . . .

Persuasion is the use of strictly symbolic manipulation, without substantial rewards or punishments under the control of the movement. The basic procedure of persuasion is to identify the proposed course of action with values held by the target group . . . calling attention to potential rewards and penalties that are not manipulated by the movement distinguishes persuasion from bargaining or coercion. (1970:148–149)

The choice of movement strategies is determined, according to Turner, by the movement's strategic or expressive consideration, by its concern for constituency values, by its pursuit of support from external publics, and by the degree of its involvement with the target group.

Strategic considerations are those having to do with the judgment of which strategy is likely to contribute toward the attainment of the movement goals. *Expressive* considerations are those involving the gratifications that come with the exercise and display of power. People gain satisfaction just from the act of wielding power, and conspicuous and dramatic displays of power give more personal satisfaction than behind-the-scenes or restrained maneuvering. (1970:154)

Turner suggested that the movement guided primarily by strategic considerations generally has a more sophisticated leadership than the movement guided by expressive considerations. The membership is under a greater degree of organizational discipline, the movement exercises only the minimum power needed to attain the goal at hand, and the preferred movement strategy is persuasion, with bargaining and coercion following, in that order. The movement guided primarily by expressive considerations generally has a less sophisticated leadership, the membership is less disciplined, the movement wields maximum power for display, and the preferred movement strategy is coercion, with bargaining and persuasion following, in that order.

The kinds of values generally espoused by the movement constituency, according to Turner, can limit the choice of strategy. Pacifistic values, for example, preclude the use of coercion. The strategy is also limited by the kind and amount of support the movement needs from various external publics. This is particularly the case if the movement needs to increase its numbers by coalition; the strategy is decided by agreement among the coalescing groups. Turner points out that the movement's choice of strategy must not alienate the "bystander" public, since those usually uninvolved individuals, if angered, can significantly affect the movement's potential for accomplishing its goals. Turner observed that it is "characteristic of small, weak, and inexperienced movements that they are especially fearful of opposition from these publics and hopeful of support from a humanitarian public. Consequently, there are strong inhibitions against the use of coercion and great reliance on persuasion" (1970:152–153). The choice of strategy is also limited by the degree to which the movement has a dependent or interpenetrating relationship with the target group.

Based upon Turner's observations and conclusions we can derive a set of hypotheses concerning the organizational strategies of the antipornography crusades. Specifically, we hypothesize:

1. The antipornography organization guided by the greater degree of strategic consideration will have greater leader control; have greater member discipline; exercise minimum needed power; elect and maintain persuasion as a movement strategy.

2. The antipornography organization with the most interpenetrating relationship with the target group will tend to elect persuasion as a strategy. As a corollary, the antipornography organization with the most interpenetrating relationship with its multiorganizational field will tend to elect persuasion as a strategy.

3. The antipornography organization most concerned about negative reactions from the public will tend to elect persuasion as a strategy.

4. The smaller, weaker, and less experienced antipornography organization will manifest inhibitions against coercion and a greater reliance on persuasion as a strategy.

5. The antipornography organization most committed to a value for the political process will tend to elect persuasion as a strategy.

We shall test these hypotheses with natural-history data. We shall attempt to articulate the findings with those pertaining to the Zald-Ash propositions concerning social movement organizations and with those concerning the operation of the multiorganizational field in anti-pornography crusades. We shall also attempt to integrate the findings with Gusfield's analysis of the generation of assimilative versus coercive reform, with Smelser's specifications for the generation of hostile outbursts, and with Gamson's arguments concerning the emergence of political constraint. Finally, we shall demonstrate, as Turner suggested, that, although one strategy may predominate at a given time (perhaps even for the life of the movement), the other two strategies also operate, situationally, to a lesser degree.

Research Setting and Procedure

The antipornography crusades we studied were the Interdenominational Citizens' Council for Decency, Inc. (ICCD) in a city that we will call Midville, U.S.A., and the Uprising for Decency (UFD) in a city that we will call Southtown, U.S.A.[27] Midville is a rather heavily industrialized city in the northern Midwest and has a population of approximately 100,000 persons. Southtown, with a population of nearly 250,000 persons is the capital of one of the Southwestern states. Detailed descriptions of the Midville and Southtown communities will be presented in Chapter 2. The two crusades that were chosen for this study were selected because they were operating and available for research at the time the Commission on Obscenity and Pornography was contracting for such data. The Southtown crusade literally grew up around us, in our city of residence. The opportunity to study the Midville crusade came upon the recommendation of the commission, whose staff had learned about its existence from other sources. All names of individuals, organizations, places, and newspapers in this book are pseudonyms, with the exception of a few nationally known public figures, organizations, and publications.

Our study of the crusades, the Conporns, and the Proporns utilized four basic field research techniques: nonparticipant observation; document search; informal, unstructured interviews; and formal, structured interviews. The natural histories of the crusades were assembled from data obtained from observation, document search, and informal interviews. The individual characteristics of the Conporns and Proporns were assembled from data obtained from formal, structured interviews. The structured interviews contained items which assessed respondents' demographic, political, membership, and social-psychological characteristics; history of sex education and contact with pornography; perception of and participation in the antipornography organization; perception and definitions of pornography and its assumed correlates.[28]

We were able to maintain close observation of the emergence of the Southtown antipornography crusade from its beginning in February, 1969, until its termination in June, 1969. Six of the seven major meetings of Uprising for Decency were attended by at least four investigators; three of the meetings were tape-recorded. We also had access to smaller, informal meetings of the Southtown leadership and to the organization's records, memos, newsletters, and other relevant documents. Over 150 unstructured interviews were conducted with Conporns, city officials, police officers, theater managers, and other citizens knowledgeable about the antipornography crusade. Structured questionnaires were administered (by ten interviewers) to forty-nine Conporns, twenty-six Proporns, and thirty-eight control respondents. Conporns and Proporns were identified by our observation of their relevant activities, reports of such activities, and by snowball sampling. The snowball sampling was continued until respondents were renominated and no new names were being added to the list, with resulting confidence that nearly the entire universe of leaders and most active participants had been interviewed. Control respondents were sampled randomly from the city blocks on which Conporns resided, thus providing at least a rough matching on socioeconomic and ethnic characteristics.

Near the end of June, 1969, we had the opportunity to collect data in Midville. For seventeen days, six investigators visited the city and gathered organizational documents, newspaper accounts, and over fifty unstructured interviews with Conporns, city officials, bookstore employees, and other citizens knowledgeable about the antipornography crusade. The task was more difficult than in Southtown, not only because of the briefer period of study, but also because the Interdenominational Citizens' Council for Decency, Inc., had been in operation formally for over five years. The formal, structured questionnaire was administered (by five interviewers) to thirty-six Conporns, twenty-five Proporns, and twelve Controls. The Midville respondents were sampled and interviewed according to the same procedure as the Southtown respondents.

More details about the questionnaire, the research procedure, and attendant problems are presented in Chapter 8 and in the appendix.

Some of us on the project were from the outset opposed to most of the perspectives and goals of the Conporns. We were divided about the issue of pornography as such. Some of us felt that all restrictions should be removed from the availability of sexually explicit materials; some agreed that the materials ought to be limited to adults and that stern penalties ought to be affixed to unsolicited mailings; some called for action against what they perceived to be the real danger of pornography, the perpetuation and exploitation of stereotypical and degrading sex roles. Throughout the life of the research project, we regularly and at length talked in staff meetings about our individual biases and by doing so worked to minimize their impact on what would at best still be data gathered under considerably less than ideal conditions and controls. The degree to which our subjectivity and value orientations, advertent or inadvertent, influenced our interpretations is most appropriately judged by the reader.

Our comparative analysis of the Midville and Southtown crusades may seem to reflect a "managerial" or "establishment" bias.[29] The Southtown crusade will consistently be interpreted to have been the more orderly, systematic, controlled, and system-linked of the two crusades. That interpretation may suggest that we viewed the strategy and tactics of the Southtown crusade as more "appropriate" than those of the Midville crusade. Actually, some of us on the research project were inclined toward that view (to the extent that we "preferred" either of the crusades). However, some of us thought that the more free-swinging Midville crusade strategy and tactics were more "appropriate." Our differences in opinions concerning the crusade styles were also a topic for thorough discussion during research staff meetings. In the final analysis, both the Midville and Southtown crusades were interpreted as having operated primarily as symbolic protests, whether they were more or less "establishment" oriented or "orderly" in nature. The Southtown crusade, the more "managed" of the two crusades, did, as will be shown, appear to bring about more systematic structural change regarding the control of pornography.

Structure of the Book

This introductory chapter has presented the theoretical foci of the study and a brief description of the research design. Chapters 2–7 will present the natural histories of the Midville and Southtown antipornography crusades. Each of those chapters is structured around one of Smelser's value-added stages for the development of a norm-oriented social movement. For example, Chapter 2 presents those natural-history data pertinent to structural conduciveness; Chapter 3, those pertinent to structural strain; Chapter 4, growth and spread of a generalized belief; Chapter 5, precipitating factors; Chapter 6, mobilization of participants for action; and Chapter 7, the operation of social control. Within each chapter, data from Midville are presented first, then data from Southtown, followed by a comparative and analytical discussion. Interpretations and applications of, and hypotheses drawn from, Gusfield's theory of status politics and Smelser's theory of collective behavior, along with aspects of other relevant theories, are woven throughout the discussions.

Chapter 8 presents data on individual characteristics of the Conporns, Proporns, and Controls, drawn from the structured questionnaires. Those data are analyzed comparatively as they bear upon the hypotheses derived from Gusfield's depiction of status discontents, the literature on change-resisting or change-promoting individuals or groups, the theory of status inconsistency, and Gamson's formulations concerning political efficacy and political trust.

Chapter 9 focuses on the structural and functional characteristics of the antipornography organizations which directed the crusades. Natural-history and interview data are merged to analyze comparatively the hypotheses drawn from Zald and Ash's propositions concerning social movement organizations, from the literature on multiorganizational fields, and from Turner's formulations concerning the determinants of social movement strategies.

Chapter 10 summarizes the hypotheses set for assessment at the outset of the study and the findings as they related to the hypotheses. The various individual and organizational characteristics introduced as variables for analysis are inserted among the value-added stages, in order to expand the conceptual and empirical boundaries of the stages and to integrate the theoretical perspectives we have used throughout the study. The value-added stages and associated variables are then outlined and integrated with the findings, in an attempt to provide an analytical overview and a set of predictive hypotheses for further research on antipornography crusades or, more broadly, on symbolic crusades in general. The generality of the findings and the hypotheses are discussed.

In Chapter 11, a summary is presented of the major findings and recommendations in the Report of the Commission on Obscenity and Pornography. Some of the counterarguments of the six dissenting commissioners are noted, as are the reactions of Former President Nixon, his staff, the Senate, and several Conporns. Those reactions are placed in the context of the findings and interpretations of our research. The recent modifications of the legal test for pornography, decided by the Burger Supreme Court, are discussed as they bear upon the future of antipornography crusades. Some speculations are offered concerning the future emergence of other types of symbolic crusades.

A reproduction of the structured questionnaire employed in our study is provided as an appendix, with items labeled to identify the scales or item sets they comprised.

Chapter 2

Structural Conduciveness: "A Little Slice of Real America"

Midville

Community Setting

Citizens in Midville liked to illustrate the location of their city to visitors in a unique but rather effective way. They would hold up the right hand vertically with the palm toward the speaker and the thumb jutting diagonally upward, thus graphically depicting an outline of the state. Pointing to the edge of the fleshy part of the palm, between the thumb and index finger, they indicated Midville's location in the state, often suggesting that it was "right near the beginning of the life line."

More formally described, Midville was in the east-central portion of one of the northern states and was located fifteen miles from a large bay that was part of one of the Great Lakes. The city was ninety miles north of Major City, the largest city in the state. With a population of 103,600, Midville was one of the few cities of substantial size between the northern regions of the state and its more densely populated south-central and eastern portions.

Midville had a relatively recent frontier history. According to local historians, the town traced its beginnings to a fur trading post established in 1816. A group of settlers surrounding the trading post created the community of Midville City in 1819. A fort was established in 1822, and in 1857 the trade center of Midville City was incorporated.

By 1969, there were over three hundred manufacturers represented in Midville, producing such diversified items as bottled beverages, caskets, mobile homes, plastic products, machine tools, fertilizer, mattresses, window shades, laundry equipment, and wheat germ. Several nationwide businesses had their home offices in Midville. The largest manufacturing complex in the city was General Motors, whose opera-

tions included a massive iron foundry, six steering gear plants, a trans-
mission plant, laboratories, and administration centers. According to
the Midville Chamber of Commerce, the General Motors aggregate of
plants was responsible for the employment of more people than any
other single industry in the region.

Agriculture, especially the growing of beans, was also an important
industry for the city. Midville boasted having one of the world's largest
bean elevators, and there was a large complex of bean processing
plants located in and around the city.

Seventeen percent of Midville's population was non-White, as compared with 11 percent nationally. Other relevant Midville population
characteristics included: females, 52 percent; birth rate, 28 per thousand; median age 28 years; median family income, $5,921; median
years of school completed, 10.3; median value of owner-occupied
housing units, $10,500. Midville's birth rate was slightly higher than
that of the United States as a whole (23.7 per thousand). The median
family income in Midville was slightly higher than the national average ($5,660). The Midville median level of formal education was lower
than the national average (10.6 years). The median age in the city was
slightly lower than the national average (29.5 years).[1]

Forty percent of Midville's employed civilian labor force fell within
the "manufacturing" category, in contrast to the national figure of 27
percent. Twenty-five percent of Midville's occupations were cate-
gorized as "operatives and kindred," considerably higher than the national 18 percent. As compared with the national figure of 75 percent,
84 percent of Midville's citizens reported "private wage and salary"
type of employment. Clearly, Midville was an industrial city, and
many of its citizens depended upon industry for employment.

Midville was a politically active city. Eighty-two percent of the eligible voters cast votes in the national election of 1968; 56 percent of
their votes were for the Republican Party. Sixty-eight percent of those
eligible voted in the 1966 local election.

In 1969, Midville was chosen by a national magazine as an "All-
America City." The citizens were quite proud of that choice, considered it to be a great honor, and took the award as a responsibility.
All-America City shields and pennants, colorfully bedecked with red,
white, and blue stars and stripes, adorned public buildings, public
vehicles, parks, policemen, and official correspondence and publications.

Midville citizens, however, were not altogether happy with the descriptive magazine article. The report labeled Midville as "insular, provincial, and undisturbed." Furthermore, the article reported that Midville's Blacks and Chicanos were maintained in a relatively subordinate condition by the Anglo majority and that Midville's approach to ethnic problems was "typical tokenism." Midville citizens argued that their City Council in 1967 had elected a Black mayor. The magazine concluded that the Black mayor was really a figurehead and that the real power was held by the Anglo city manager. The article also observed that, Midville citizens' claims to the contrary, not everyone who was looking for work in the city could find it.

The west side of Midville was almost exclusively an Anglo residential area. East of the Midville River, less affluent Anglos, Chicanos, and Blacks lived in integrated neighborhoods. On many blocks all three ethnic groups were represented in adjoining residences.

The Chamber of Commerce represented Midville as a religiously oriented community. The current telephone book listed 145 churches representing 36 denominations. Along with 30 Lutheran, 28 Baptist, 13 Catholic, 13 Methodist, and 7 Presbyterian churches, there were numerous smaller groups, including an Islamic mosque, a Baha'i temple, and a Buddhist temple.

Public education within the city limits was provided by twenty-six elementary schools, five junior high schools, three high schools, a special education school, and a business institute. Omicron College (a two-year junior college) and Midville Valley College (a four-year college) were the institutions of higher education in the area. Both colleges were considered by many of the Midvillians interviewed to be the seats of liberalism in the community.

Midville was a curious mixture of city and small town, and some of the citizens seemed to reflect this status confusion. Several of the respondents felt that Midville was definitely urban and that, for example, "you could walk all over the downtown streets without meeting familiar people, even if you have lived here for a good length of time." Other respondents disagreed with that point of view and, for example, observed that it was "impossible for a person to be anonymous in this community. Everywhere you go, you meet someone you know."

Midville was a city where, as one respondent indicated, "the taxi drivers ask the visitors where the action is," and "it's a nice place to live, but you wouldn't want to visit here." After 9 P.M. on weekday evenings, the "sidewalks are rolled up." Saturday night in downtown Midville showed some pedestrian activity until about 11 P.M., when again there seemed to be imposition of an informal curfew on walking traffic. However, after 11 P.M. there seemed to be considerable automobile traffic, much of it young people riding around in cars or on motorcycles. Many of the young persons' cars were lowered in the front, in the style of the West Coast during the 1950's. Also, much of the popular music on the local radio stations reflected the fashion of the 1950's "rock-and-roll." Young people tended to accumulate around drive-in food stands and restaurants, often touring by vehicle from one to another. For older persons, there were numerous taverns, but very few nightclubs.

There was a very small enclave of what might have been considered "hippies" centering around the Cinnamon-Green Coffee House and the Zeppelin Shop, both in the old town section of Midville. A draft information center was located in the basement of an Episcopal church, in another part of town. The "hippies" in Midville appeared to be what are sometimes labeled the "plastic" or "week-end" variety. That is, most of those individuals interviewed were not ideologically committed to any particular social movement. Rather, they seemed to congregate at the coffee house and the Zeppelin Shop for socializing. The draft information center was not action oriented, but an information source.

As a Chamber of Commerce bulletin indicated, Midville was indeed a very friendly city, with the "latch string always out and visitors always welcome." We had no trouble, for example, cashing our out-of-town checks at places whose management was unfamiliar with us. Continually and impressively, the citizens of Midville with whom we interacted were courteous, cooperative, and even generous in their dealings with us. Those characteristics were typical not only of private citizens, but of businessmen and tradesmen as well.

In sum, Midville appeared to be very much as the national magazine had described it—that is, insular, provincial, and undisturbed. Though industrialized and relatively affluent, Midville was nonetheless small-townish in life style. Modally, its image was reflected by the city's All-America label, in the sense that it reflected identification with Americanism in a traditional and conservative manner.

Precrusade Antipornography Activity in Midville

Prior to the mobilization of the antipornography crusade in late 1968 and early 1969, Midville had a considerable but relatively quiet history of antipornography activity. A series of controls of "sexually objectionable material" had been conducted since 1950, through the interrelation of three official agencies: the police department, the city attorney's office, and the Censorship Advisory Board, with the latter agency being pivotal.

The Censorship Advisory Board was established by a city ordinance and was composed of six citizens appointed by the city manager for a three-year term. The board was charged with advising the police chief "in all matters pertaining to the safeguarding of the public welfare and morals through censorship of publications and amusements." The board reviewed publications that came to it, on a voluntary basis, either from private citizens or from the police department. The assessment of the appropriateness of a given publication was based upon a four-point code, which asked: (a) Does the publication glorify crime or criminals? (b) Is it sexy, or does it feature illicit love? (c) Does it contain illustrations which are suggestive or indecent? (d) Does it carry disreputable advertising? If the board determined that the answer to one or more of the code questions was "yes," the publication was turned over to the city attorney's office for judgment concerning possible violation of the state law or city ordinance pertaining to obscene materials. If the city attorney concluded that the publication violated a law, prosecution would result.

The Censorship Advisory Board regularly referred for guidance to a list of "questionable publications" periodically distributed by the police department of nearby Major City. Representatives of the Midville police department also occasionally checked the local newsstands and bookstores, both to insure that objectionable publications had in fact been removed from sale and to determine whether publications other than those appearing on the Major City list were available in Midville and should be reviewed by the board. Interested citizens were encouraged to submit to the police department or to the board examples of materials which they felt to be objectionable.

According to a Midville assistant city attorney, in nearly all cases those publications deemed objectionable by the board were voluntarily withdrawn from sale by local businessmen. Only rarely was prosecution necessary. Some examples of books and periodicals voluntarily removed from the racks by retailers, at the urging of the board, were Havlock Ellis's *Psychology of Sex* (removed in 1954), Evan Hunter's *Blackboard Jungle* (removed in 1955), selected issues of *Sexology* magazine (removed in 1950 and 1955), two portfolios of the photographs of

Serge Jacques and Andre DeDienes (removed in 1956), De Sade's *Justine* (removed in 1955), Schiddel's *Girl With the Golden Yo-Yo* (removed in 1955), and selected issues of *Caberet* and *Pin-up Photography* (removed in 1955 and 1956).

There was evidence that from the early through the late 1950's citizens were becoming increasingly concerned with the problem of pornography in Midville and increasingly were expressing appreciation for the efforts of the police department and the Censorship Advisory Board. Some of this evidence appeared in the form of letters to relevant agencies and to the *Midville News* (e.g., a letter to the editor of the *Midville News* in 1955 asked, "Do we have to find one of our little girls murdered before we act?"). Simultaneously, however, there was some growing expression of concern with freedom of the press. For example, another 1955 letter to the editor of the *Midville News* warned that "some of the world's greatest gems of literature were subjected to onslaughts such as we are now witnessing in Midville, and if it were not for an alert vigilant court safeguarding the right of freedom of speech, those masterpieces would have been laid to the book burners."

In the mid-1950's there appeared in Midville also to be some concern with other than published sexually explicit materials. In 1955, for example, a citizen who had purchased an "obscene ashtray" at a local "trick shop" offered it as evidence to the Midville police department. The ashtray was decorated with a picture of two dogs, allegedly suggestively posed. Acting on the complaint, the police obtained a warrant, and the case record was marked "cleared by arrest" (of the proprietor of the "trick shop"). There were from 1950 to 1955 a sprinkling of additional complaints, including objection to a high school play in which a girl danced "bare-legged" while males on stage "observed her." However, most of the antipornography activity during this period was focused on books and magazines.

In 1957, just four months before its modification of the definition of pornography in the landmark *Roth* case, the Warren Supreme Court struck down as unconstitutional the obscenity statutes of the state in which Midville was a city. The court held that the state statute was so sweepingly restrictive that it served to "burn the house to roast the pig," and that it reduced the adult population of the state "to reading only what is fit for children," arbitrarily curtailing "one of those liberties of the individual, now enshrined in the Due Process Clause of the Fourteenth Amendment, that history has attested as the indispensable conditions for the maintenance of progress of a free society" (*Butler*,

1957; see also Bender 1971; Clor 1969; Murphy 1963). The court ruling rendered Midville's own city ordinance concerning obscenity and the role of the Censorship Advisory Board somewhat ambiguous. Yet apparently the board and the police continued their relatively quiet antipornography activities much as before. When the Major City police department, as a result of the court decision, stopped distributing lists of objectionable publications to local communities, the Midville police department began to compile its own list and continued to spot-check newsstands. In 1958, an issue of *Playboy* magazine was removed from sale, as was Rocky Graziano's *Somebody Up There Likes Me*. However, according to police officials, business owners were no longer quite so willing to comply voluntarily with the complaints of the Censorship Advisory Board. The voluntary compliance became even more difficult to obtain after the *Roth* decision and subsequent Supreme Court decisions or interpretations which increasingly liberalized definitions of pornography and obscenity with such tests as "taken as a whole," "prurient interest," "community standards," and "redeeming social value" (see Preface).

The Evolution of Crusade Leadership

Mrs. Marjorie Roberts was an articulate, engaging, college-educated, middle-class housewife in her fifties, who had for many years actively held membership in several community voluntary associations, generally associated with religious activities. As early as 1961, Mrs. Roberts had taken actions intended to meet what she perceived to be national and local challenges to decency. From 1961 through 1963, Mrs. Roberts conducted an extensive letter-writing campaign concerning a number of decency issues. In a letter to Mrs. Jacqueline Kennedy (which was referred to J. Edgar Hoover), she urged intensified federal action concerning sexual offenses against children. She addressed a series of letters to producers and sponsors of various television programs, protesting program themes that she interpreted as justifying such topics as atheism, the demeaning of patriotism, unchecked liberalism, the weakening of controls on sexual behavior, and unrestricted license to publish objectionable materials under protection of freedom of the press. Several of her letters were signed by eleven other Midvillians, whom she considered to be colleagues in her corrective efforts.

In April, 1963, Mrs. Roberts and her eleven colleagues, all of whom were affiliated with religious organizations, devised a tentative plan for a decency organization which was given the working title Unity for Social Action (USA). The "proposed prayer" of the organization was to be as follows:

> O Lord, Master of all created things, we beg of You to use us as Your Instruments to rid our Country of the moral decay which is endangering its survival. Grant us the Grace to be persevering in our campaign against indecency, so that our young men and women may realize the sacredness of virtue. We realize that we cannot succeed in our efforts to change the cold lustful hearts of the mercenaries, motivated by selfish ambitions without Your divine assistance. Therefore, we implore You to give us the strength and determination to proceed with this battle against corruption. Dear God, grant us that they may repent the wrong they have been doing the innocent. Please God, forgive them for their greed and us for sitting idly by while our young people and our Country have been so misused. Amen.

The "Areas of Interest for Study and Action" by the organization were to be "Literature, Education, Patriotism, Health, Safety, Entertainment, Recreation, Advertising, Manufacturing."

According to Mrs. Roberts, Unity for Social Action never became a viable organization under that name. She reflected that "it was difficult to get a lot of people involved at this time, because they really didn't know how bad the problem was." However, she and her colleagues continued their letter-writing campaign, directing protests or plaudits to business organizations, the media, and numerous government officials. During 1963, Mrs. Roberts made contact with Citizens for Decent Literature (CDL), the national antipornography organization, and requested information concerning ways and means to deal with the problem of pornography in Midville.

In May, 1964, Mrs. Roberts, her eleven colleagues, and an unrecorded number of community leaders met to discuss the topic of objectionable literature. During that meeting, the participants discussed the problem as it existed in Midville, shared concerns about the dangers of pornography, and speculated about possible courses of action.

In September, 1964, Mrs. Roberts and her colleagues, now with co-sponsorship by representatives from a broader group of Midville churches, sponsored a public symposium, generally on community decency, but more specifically concerned with pornography. At that meeting, the Citizens for Decent Literature film *Perversion for Profit* was shown, and presentations were made by a panel consisting of a state legislator, a medical doctor, and a lawyer.

The action resulting from these meetings continued to be a campaign of letter writing, but the content of the letters was increasingly narrowed to deal specifically with pornography. Letters were sent to the Midville postal inspector, calling attention to questionable advertisements in magazines; to the owners or managers of chain drug and grocery stores, regarding objectionable reading material on magazine racks; to the advertising manager of the *Midville News*, concerning objectionable advertisements for local movies; to the chairman of the State Fair Commission, calling for the elimination of "girlie shows" from the midway; and to a book publisher, complimenting him for the healthy quality of publications produced by that company for young people. Several of those letters carried the typed letterhead "Interdenominational Council on Indecent Literature," representing the growing concerted action of Mrs. Roberts and her colleagues.

The letters began to produce some tangible results. The executive vice president of a drug company responded with congratulations and a statement of agreement to cooperate in "cleaning up the news racks." The *Midville News* agreed to modify its advertising policy for movies and to eliminate depictions of "couples in compromising positions, couples in bed, horizontal embrace, suggestive dress or undress, nude figures or silhouettes, etc." The chairman of the State Fair Commission promised continued scrutiny of the midway shows and commended Mrs. Roberts for her efforts. In retrospect, Mrs. Roberts considered these responses to be "the most important early accomplishments" of her group.

In June, 1965, after several months of sporadic but increasingly concerted activity (including deliberate efforts toward organizing, attempts to "spread the word," and the letter-writing campaigns), Mrs. Roberts and her colleagues formally and legally structured their group as the Interdenominational Citizens' Council for Decency, Inc. (ICCD). According to one respondent who was instrumental in the evolution of the organization, legal incorporation was effected so that ICCD could solicit funds which would be tax deductible for the donor.

Mrs. Roberts named the following individuals as being instrumental during the several months of discussion leading to the establishment of ICCD: the Reverend Mr. White (member of the Midville Council of Churches and pastor of the Brittany Avenue Baptist Church); Father Johnson (director of the National Organization for Decent Literature for the Catholic diocese of Midville); Father Wilson (director of the National Catholic Office for Motion Pictures of the Midville diocese); Captain Walker (of the juvenile division of the Midville police department and chairman of the Midville Censorship Advisory Board); the Reverend Mr. Lewis (pastor of the Bethlehem Lutheran Church and representative for the Missouri Synod Lutheran Pastors of the Midville district); Dr. Stewart (director of secondary education, Midville public school administration); Rabbi Stone (of Temple B'nai Israel); the Reverend Mr. Jackson (of the Evangelical Ministerial Association). At the June incorporation meeting, three of these persons were elected to positions as executive officers of ICCD: Mr. White (chairman); Father Johnson (vice-chairman); and Mrs. Roberts (secretary-treasurer). Mrs. Roberts continued to be the most active leader of the group —the chairman and vice-chairman of ICCD tended to be more in the nature of figureheads. At a subsequent ICCD meeting, held in September, 1965, advisory board members were elected, including some of those individuals named by Mrs. Roberts as having been instrumental in the formation of ICCD (Mr. Lewis, Mr. Jackson, and Captain Walker) and three new persons: Mrs. Stephens (of Church Women United); Mr. Russell (of the Youth Protection Agency); and Mrs. Park (of the Midville City PTA Council).

The June, 1965, incorporation meeting yielded an ICCD constitution, two articles of which were particularly important in the formation of the antipornography crusade. The purpose of the organization was stated as being (a) to safeguard the standards of decency in the community in the field of entertainment and (b) to establish a community conscience concerning decency. The methods to be used by the organization to accomplish its purpose were stated to be (a) education on the many-faceted problems of decency; (b) moral persuasion for decency; (c) encouragement of the legal enforcement of present laws and those laws which might be enacted to further decency.

Immediately following ICCD incorporation, Mrs. Roberts and the other executive officers set out to acquire representatives to ICCD from other community voluntary associations. Mrs. Roberts reported that, within three months after its incorporation, ICCD had acquired at least nominal representation from thirty-one such associations, including the First Baptist Church of Midville, the First Congregational Church, the Midville Council of Catholic Women, the Midville High School PTA, St. George's Altar Society, and the Weber Junior High PTA. Most of the associations were church-related, youth-serving, or fraternal-service groups (an analysis of the aligned groups is presented in Chapter 9). Among the churches, the Roman Catholic denomination was dominant. Mrs. Roberts had a quite active history of involvement with Catholic church groups.

Throughout the balance of 1965 and into the middle of 1966 Mrs. Roberts and ICCD continued their letter-writing activities. A series of letters were sent to program directors of local television stations, calling their attention to assorted movie rating lists (enclosed with the letters), and asking that those movies objectionable for young persons be moved to later hours. One of the television stations complied with the request, at least for those movies over which the local station (and not the network) had control. Mrs. Roberts's correspondence with Citizens for Decent Literature increased during this period. She also inaugurated correspondence with another national antipornography organization, Morality In Media (Operation Yorkville). Her correspondence reported to both organizations, especially CDL, the growing activities of ICCD and requested film and printed materials which might be useful in dealing with "our local problem." The published materials received from the national antipornography organizations and other materials selected and reproduced from articles in *Reader's Digest* and religious periodicals were distributed by ICCD to several community voluntary associations (usually those who had ICCD representatives). The CDL film *Printed Poison* was shown by ICCD at some of their own meetings and at meetings of some other community organizations. Significantly, that film describes in detail a decency campaign which can be conducted by local communities against pornography.

The *Midville News*, in part as a result of the urging of ICCD, decided to refuse to carry the advertising for a new "girlie" theater which was to open in Midville. Mrs. Roberts and ICCD were concerned about the opening of the theater, the first of its kind in Midville. Previously the antipornography activities of Mrs. Roberts and her colleagues had been directed toward "cleaning up the news racks" in drug and grocery stores. Now, in mid-1966, a business which dealt specifically with objectionable materials was entering the scene.

In May, 1966, again at the urging of ICCD, the mayor of Midville issued a proclamation for "Action for Decency Day." Mrs. Roberts felt that the proclamation was a "wonderful accomplishment" for ICCD. Executive officers and advisory board members of ICCD wrote a joint letter to all of the clergymen in Midville urging them to announce the event from the pulpit and to participate in it.

Though the leaders of ICCD felt that Action for Decency Day was a great success, there seemed to be relatively little response to it throughout the community of Midville. It did, however, very much encourage ICCD leaders in their efforts and no doubt was one of a series of events and activities which began to sensitize the community to the "problem" of pornography.

Throughout late 1966 and early 1967 Mrs. Roberts and ICCD continued passing out pamphlets, holding meetings, and writing letters. Most of the correspondence now was directed to legislators and government officials, including Mrs. Pat Nixon, urging stronger statutes for the control of pornography. Complimentary letters were sent to such public figures as Art Linkletter, Groucho Marx, and Bennett Cerf, concerning their stand on the issue. Letters were typed on official ICCD letterhead stationery. ICCD distributed one thousand copies of a "Citizens Media Ballot," which was printed on a postcard to facilitate the expression of opinions concerning products of the media. The ballot was to be returned to its designer, the Center of American Living, which would tabulate the results in the form of opinion polls. During this period, ICCD also urged citizen referral of questionable materials to Midville's Censorship Advisory Board.

According to Mrs. Roberts, she and her colleagues continued to have interest in some community decency problems other than pornography. Some information came to her regarding a homosexual, and that information was relayed to the vice squad. Similarly, knowledge of a case of venereal disease in a local school was given to the Midville Public Health Department, and information regarding a family whose children were becoming involved with moral problems was relayed to the Midville public school administration. Mrs. Roberts and her colleagues also asked the city of Midville to provide better lighting in areas of high crime incidence. Finally, ICCD assisted the Midville Deanery Council of Catholic Women in sponsoring a day-long seminar on narcotics, venereal disease, and pornography.

In July, 1967, members of the vice squad of the Midville police department entered the "adult" bookstore section of the recently opened "girlie" theater. The police officers purchased materials which they assessed to be pornographic, formally lodged a complaint, and subsequently arrested Mr. Baker, the alleged bookstore manager (according to a later review of events in the *Midville News*, December 29, 1967). According to police officers, the action of the vice squad had been precipitated by the activity and appeal of Mrs. Roberts and the ICCD.

In September, 1967, three persons operating an "adult" bookstore in Hamilton (near Midville), Mr. Martin, Mr. Kelley, and Miss Hall, were arrested for having sold obscene material to a plain-clothes policeman. Mr. Martin was the leasee of the building in which the Midville "girlie" theater and its "adult" bookstore facility were situated (*Midville News*, September 10, 1967).

In December, 1967, Mr. Hunter, a clerk in a newly opened "adult" bookstore in Midville, the Midwestern Bookstore, was arrested by police officers who had followed the same procedure described above. The bookstore materials were confiscated (*Midville News*, December 29, 1967). In January, 1968, Mr. Evans, another clerk in the Midwestern Bookstore, was arrested on the same charges (*Midville News*, January 25, 1968). In March, 1968, a Midville city assistant prosecutor asked for an injunction to close the Midwestern Bookstore, which by then had moved from its first location to a location in the center of downtown Midville. The prosecutor asked the court to declare thirty-eight books and magazines which had been purchased from the Midwestern Bookstore by Midville police officers as obscene, lewd, and indecent, and thereby to close the store (*Midville News*, March 16, 1968). No injunction was ordered by the court.

Mrs. Roberts and ICCD were heartened by the actions of the Midville police department and joyous when the three persons who had been arrested in Hamilton were found guilty of the sale of obscene literature by the Hamilton circuit court. Mr. Martin was given a ten-day jail sentence and a $1,000 fine, ordered to pay $500 in court costs, and put on two years' probation. Mr. Kelley was fined $100, ordered to pay $200 in court costs, and placed on probation for one year. Miss Hall was directed to pay $100 in court costs and put on six months' probation (*Midville News*, May 10, 1968). But ICCD enthusiasm was dampened when in July, 1968, the Midville circuit court ordered that charges against Mr. Baker and Mr. Evans of the Midwestern Bookstore be dismissed and that all confiscated materials be returned. The Midville assistant prosecutor handling the case had indicated that the defense counsels had cited a multitude of recent U.S. Supreme Court cases dealing with obscenity, and that had led to the dismissals (*Midville News*, July 9, 1968). Several of the ICCD leaders complained bitterly about the U.S. Supreme Court decisions, led by the *Roth* decision of

1957, and the impact that they were having upon the lower courts. Mrs. Roberts herself had, in 1967, written a long letter to the Supreme Court registering her disapproval of such leniency.

In July, 1968, a coordinated effort by the Midville police department vice squad, the state police intelligence division, the Midville prosecuting attorney, and an assistant prosecutor resulted in the arrests of Mr. Edwards, a Midwestern Bookstore clerk, Mr. Baker (for a second time, while picking up the confiscated materials released following his first dismissal), the operator of a drive-in movie theater (showing an "adult" film) in nearby Rogers, and, in their home, a Midville school teacher and his wife. All ultimately were charged with the sale of obscene materials, Mr. Baker in connection with the drive-in theater (*Midville News*, July 12 and 13, 1968). The school teacher pleaded guilty and was sentenced accordingly. Later in July, charges against the other persons were dismissed by the court, and confiscated materials were ordered to be returned. In addition, the charges against the Midwestern Bookstore clerk arrested earlier, Mr. Hunter, were dismissed (*Midville News*, July 17, 1968).

Again Mrs. Roberts and her ICCD cadre were deeply disappointed by the court actions. Thinking that a change in the Midville obscenity statute might facilitate convictions, Mrs. Roberts and ICCD undertook to influence the city council to make such changes. Modifications to the statute were made and approved by the council in August, 1968. However, the changes dealt specifically with establishing limitations on the availability of defined "pornographic" materials to minors. The issue of to whom antipornography legislation should pertain was controversial within ICCD itself. Some of the leaders thought that such laws should forbid the use of pornographic materials by all citizens, regardless of age. Others felt that the laws should be written only to protect children. The third and winning faction of the ICCD leadership argued that it didn't make any difference what one's opinion was concerning the adult use of pornographic materials, since any ordinance that was too restrictive of adults would probably be struck down in both higher and lower courts. Consequently, the ICCD leadership concurred that the revision in the Midville ordinance should be specifically oriented to restrict the availability of pornographic materials to minors.

In October, 1968, Mrs. Roberts (representing ICCD) wrote a letter to all Midville dealers in magazines and books, all exhibitors of films, and all major civic organizations apprising those persons of the changes in the Midville city antipornography ordinance. She enclosed a copy of the ordinance in each of the letters and admonished the recipients to write legislators and representatives demanding stronger laws governing obscenity. The letter also indicated that Mrs. Roberts and her colleagues were appealing to citizens living outside the Midville city limits, urging them to convince their own local governing boards to adopt a similar ordinance.

The owners of the "adult" theater under scrutiny of ICCD decided to close the business in 1968. The owners reported that they were going out of business because of lack of patronage. ICCD, however, felt that it had been influential initially in getting the theater to modify the kinds of films it showed and finally in contributing to factors which resulted in its closing. When the theater was operating, Mrs. Roberts was reported to have occasionally stood outside the theater, across the street in a parking lot, and to have attempted to assess the ages of individuals entering the movie. Supposedly she had checked the identification of some persons whom she thought to be under age. But ICCD had difficulty finding legal ways to stop the showing of the "girlie" or "nudie" films at the theater. They were, however, able to get the police department to initiate charges of false advertising against the management. Apparently it was the theater's practice to show one full-length feature and a long series of "trailers." ICCD had discovered that in order to show trailers or previews legally, a theater must have a contract for the films being advertised. The "adult" theater apparently was showing some trailers for films which it did not have under contract. The false-advertising action was successful, and the "adult" theater was forced to use only trailers for which it had contracted films. ICCD considered this to be a notable success and was delighted when the theater management decided to close, for whatever reason.

Up to this point (fall, 1968), Mrs. Roberts and her colleagues in ICCD were quite pleased with the development of their organization and with what it had accomplished, although Mrs. Roberts continued to refer to ICCD organizationally as a "toddler." ICCD members were chagrined by the Supreme Court decisions which, according to Mrs. Roberts, "played into the hands of the smut peddlers." However, they were proud of having urged into existence the revised obscenity ordinance and of having curtailed the obscene films that had been shown at the "adult" theater. In several of her letters, Mrs. Roberts catalogued other ICCD successes: cleaning up drugstore and grocery-store publication racks; modification of movie schedules on local television stations; banning of burlesque shows from the county fair; restrictions on advertising copy in the *Midville News*, influencing Action for Decency Day in Midville; distributing numerous antipornography pamphlets and films to assorted voluntary associations; influencing the police to act against "smut sellers"; and conducting an extensive letter-writing campaign to government officials, well-known personalities, and "anybody else who would listen to us."

However, Mrs. Roberts and her ICCD cadre were somewhat disappointed with the level of community involvement in antipornography endeavors. Thus far, the community remained relatively indifferent to the activities of ICCD. Mrs. Roberts repeated, time and time again, that the citizens of Midville simply "did not know how serious the problem was." She puzzled over ways that she and her colleagues "might get more people involved."

As mentioned above, the Midwestern Bookstore had in March, 1968, moved to its new location in the center of downtown Midville. Mrs. Roberts and her closest friend in ICCD, Mrs. Nelson, had become particularly concerned, since a number of Midville Valley College students had temporarily been housed in a hotel in downtown Midville, while they waited for on-campus dormitory facilities to be completed. The hotel was across the street from the Midwestern Bookstore. Mrs. Roberts had wondered about the natural curiosity of youth and students and feared it would lead them to the bookstore. Subsequent rumors she had heard confirmed her fears—apparently some of the students had been frequenting the bookstore and had been sold "so-called 'adult' books." Mrs. Roberts and Mrs. Nelson decided to take a closer look at the Midwestern Bookstore.

Southtown

Community Setting

Southtown was the seat of Central County and the capital city of one of the Southwestern states. It was situated almost exactly in the middle of that state, eighty miles northeast of the state's third largest city. Located on a major river, which was used as a navigable commercial waterway in the middle and late nineteenth century, most of Southtown was on a prairie, with its western residential areas and three dormitory suburbs rising up into a hilly plateau. Having a population of 245,295 persons, Southtown was the sixth largest city in the state.

Southtown had a relatively recent frontier history. The area that is now downtown Southtown had been purchased by the republic of which it became a part as the location of the permanent capitol building in 1839. Since that time, Southtown had remained primarily a governmental center, with republic and later state legislative, executive, and judicial offices and state welfare and service organizations (such as the state schools for the blind, the deaf, and the mentally retarded). A considerable portion of the land area of Southtown was devoted to 224 international, national, regional, district, and state associations and to assorted governmental and service institutions.

Southtown's primary commercial activities, therefore, were governmental, service oriented, and educational, rather than industrial or agricultural. There were, however, several light industries located in or near the city, including a chemical plant, a mattress and bedding plant, a business machine assembly plant, a school bus factory, and a vanilla factory.

The agricultural importance of the city was limited in scope. There were meat-processing, chili-making, and several small-scale food-preparation companies located near the outskirts of Southtown. The prairies east of the city were primarily devoted to cattle and cotton, while the hills of the plateau were largely semiarid and stony, utilized for grazing some beef cattle, but mainly for sheep and goats.

Thirteen percent of Southtown's population was non-White, as compared with 11 percent nationally. Other relevant Southtown population characteristics included: females, 51 percent; birth rate, 27 per thousand; median age, 25.6 years; median family income, $5,119; median years of school completed, 11.9; median value of owner-occupied housing units, $10,800. Southtown's birth rate was slightly higher than that of the United States as a whole (23.7 per thousand). The median family income in the city was slightly lower than the national average ($5,660), and Southtown's median age was somewhat younger than that of the nation as a whole (29.5 years). The Southtown median level of formal education was higher than the national average (10.6 years).[2] Thirteen percent of Southtown's employed civilian labor force fell within the "educational services" category, in contrast to the national figure of 5.2 percent; 10.8 percent worked in public administration, as compared with 5.0 percent nationally; and 8.7 percent in construction, as compared with 5.9 percent nationally. Only 7.5 percent of the Southtown labor force was in manufacturing, as compared with 27 percent for the nation as a whole.

Though Southtown was a capital city, its citizens were not particularly politically active. Only 66 percent of the eligible voters cast votes in the national election of 1968; 55 percent of their votes were for the Democratic party. Only 43 percent of those eligible voted in the 1966 county and state election.

As is typical of capital cities, Southtown had many apartment complexes, which served a large segment of the Southtown population—particularly the transient middle-to-high-income student and government population. Dwelling unit construction had increased in step with the population boom—from 132,459 persons in 1950, the city had grown to nearly a quarter of a million in 1969. Though urban in appearance, Southtown nonetheless gave the impression of a smaller town that had grown up very rapidly. The business area was small, with the bulk of the city devoted to residential and service-facility uses. There were no industrial parks, and industry was not evident as one drove about the city. The impression was one of relative cleanliness and prosperity, primarily because the east-side Black and Chicano poverty areas were not easily accessible or visible to those who utilized the main arterial traffic routes to and from the business district. The low-income areas were, however, present and extensive. Southtown ranked near the top among American cities in per capita prevalence of poverty. The city was largely residentially segregated according to the three main population groups—Anglo, Black and Chicano.

The Chamber of Commerce represented Southtown as a religiously oriented community. There were approximately 275 churches in the city in 1969, representing 32 denominations. Baptists (53 churches) and Southern Baptists (46 churches) were the most numerous in the listings. There were 16 Catholic parishes and 2 synagogues.

The State University was founded at Southtown in 1883, having become by 1969 a major regional state university with an enrollment of more than 37,000 students. State University was considered by several of the Southtowners interviewed to be the most liberally oriented educational institution, not only in Southtown, but in the state and even in the Southwest. Actually, the faculty and student body tended toward a moderate political or ideological stance but were liberal when compared with most Southtowners. The great majority of the students were born and raised in the state. State University did have a lively, vocal, and visible presence of "hippies" and "street people," many of whom congregated (to sell their wares or for recreation) in the business districts adjacent to campus. The University also had a small but active cluster of on-campus radical students and a few overtly radical professors. In contrast, the citizens of Southtown were primarily conservative and traditional, in the pattern of Southern Democratic politics. The influence of the Baptist religion upon state and local government was still considered to be significant, and a fundamentalist perspective was not uncommon.

Several of the Southtowners interviewed expressed pride that there had been no major or sustained ethnic or university violence in their city. Often that relatively stable condition was attributed to the ability of citizens of the state in general, and Southtowners in particular, to keep things under control—as one respondent phrased it, "to keep our problems reined in." It was generally accepted that a "frontier mentality" remained widespread among the older citizens of Southtown— the view that one's hostile environment must be firmly and if necessary forcibly "whipped into shape" and kept that way.

Southtown was known to be a relatively "jumping" city. Automobile traffic and pedestrian activity were present in the downtown and especially the university areas nearly twenty-four hours a day. There were numerous private clubs, hotel clubs, and other sources of evening entertainment. The presence of the university and governmental population demanded a wide variety of recreational diversions.

"Southern hospitality," meaning general openness and friendliness extended even to strangers, was publicized by the Chamber of Commerce as being a fact in Southtown. It was also touted that, though Southtowners generally tended to demonstrate primary allegiance to their state, they nonetheless manifested zealous national patriotism and were inclined to consider themselves to be among the "real Americans."

Precrusade Antipornography Activity in Southtown

There was no evidence of any large-scale formal or informal Southtown antipornography activity in recent years except for that associated with the 1969 crusade. A mimeographed list of state and local censorship organizations prepared by the Commission on Obscenity and Pornography noted the existence, in 1959, of a "Southtown Advisory Committee On Newsstand Displays." None of the respondents interviewed remembered the existence of such a committee or what it might have accomplished.

Representatives of two local church groups (Church of Christ and Baptist) reported in interviews that their churches had "kept an eye" on the sale of alleged pornography in Southtown and sometimes had established committees "to talk to the retailers." Apparently any action taken by the church groups did not go beyond visits to owners or managers of drugstores, grocery stores, and other retailers with requests that they remove selected publications from the sales racks. According to the respondents, the local retailers without exception complied with the citizens' requests.

The vice squad of the Southtown city police had in recent years maintained a rather efficient control over the availability of sexually explicit materials in Southtown. There were no "adult" bookstores as such in Southtown, nor was there much over- or under-the-counter sale of sexually explicit materials. The shopper could find a few of the Traveler's Companion or Bee-Line books among the publications for sale in small convenience grocery stores. However, the availability of such books was irregular.

Southtown did have two "skin-flick" theaters. Mr. Mason, the manager of one of the theaters (the Bijou) reported in an interview that he had over the last six years maintained an informal relationship with the Southtown vice squad. Members of the vice squad would periodically "drop in" to review the films shown at his theater and might suggest that certain films, or certain portions of films, be removed from presentation. Mr. Mason reported that he had complied with the suggestions and had maintained good relations with the police.

The Evolution of Crusade Leadership

In early January, 1969, one of the Southtown councils of the Knights of Columbus, during their regularly scheduled evening meeting, decided to do something about the lack of "family film entertainment" and "the abundance of lewd movies" in Southtown. Antipornography activity had for several years been part of the action platform of the Knights of Columbus at the national and state level. Prior to 1969, Knights of Columbus local councils in a few other cities in the state had successfully brought public pressure to bear upon newsstand, drugstore, and grocery-store managements to "clean up their racks." The Southtown local chapter which had at this time decided to do something about the "movie situation" was particularly close, geographically, formally, and informally to the Knights of Columbus state headquarters (whose offices were situated about one hundred yards from the local council's meeting hall). The state secretary of the Knights of Columbus was particularly active in the local chapter. (Southtown had four Knights of Columbus councils, but only one was to take active leadership in antipornography activities.)

The issue of lewd films had been placed on the January meeting agenda by Mr. Edward King, one of the council officers. Mr. King reported that there was "no single reason" why he had brought the "problem of lewd films" to the attention of the Knights of Columbus council. He stated that in the last few years, influenced by impromptu discussions with others and by his own observations, he had come to the conclusion that such films had become a social problem in Southtown. Although he was concerned about Southtown's two "skin-flick" theaters, he felt the problem was considerably broader. That is, he felt that families and young people had little decent film entertainment from which to choose in Southtown. Mr. King argued that "people don't have a free choice. They can't choose from a wide selection of films. Most of the pictures shown during any week in Southtown are not the kind you can bring your whole family to, or you would want to let your children go to." He felt strongly that many of the films shown at Southtown theaters would have a negative effect on young people. Mr. King cited several instances where young people had complained to him that "they had no movies that they would want to take their dates to on weekends." He further indicated that his wife and several of her friends had complained to him about the problem and had asked him what he thought could be done about it.

Mr. King did not think that "hard-core" pornography was a problem in Southtown. In his opinion, the Southtown police "were doing a very good job of keeping that kind of thing under control." The unavailability of decent films in the city could not be attributed to lack of police efficiency. Mr. King felt that the police were "unable to do anything because the laws were not good enough." Those laws "had significantly been weakened" by the recent Supreme Court decisions. Furthermore Mr. King thought that Southtown citizens had not made their dissatisfaction clear enough to the legislators, movie producers, or local theater management.

Mr. King was a tall, clean-cut, religious, intelligent, and soft-spoken man in his thirties. He was an insurance agent by profession, a college graduate, and had for many years been extremely active in local civic organizations—especially the Knights of Columbus. In the latter organization he had held major official positions and had won several awards for outstanding service. During the period of time when Mr. King had lived in another part of the state, he had as an active member of the Knights of Columbus led a small but successful action toward "cleaning up publication racks." Thus he had brought with him to Southtown some experience in antipornography activity. Now as chairman of a KC-council action program committee, and stimulated by his discussions with others and his observations of the local situation, Mr. King felt that the issue of lewd films was most appropriate for council focus.

During the January, 1969, council meeting, Mr. King was commissioned by his fellow members to approach State Senator Welles, who was known to be concerned with the problem of pornography, and to discuss with him what could be done about it. In the last week of January, Mr. King did consult with Senator Welles, and sought his advice. The senator strongly agreed that there was a problem of "pornographic and obscene films" in Southtown and generally in the state. The senator apprised Mr. King of the importance of "tighter and tougher laws" concerning the availability of "questionable" films. He further advised Mr. King that nothing could effectively be done until adequate community support was demonstrated for legislative change. Senator Welles then suggested that Mr. King consult with Mr. Tarran, the local district attorney, concerning the matter.

During the last week of January, Mr. King met with Mr. Tarran and asked what could be done about the problem of lewd films. The district attorney showed him the present statute concerning such films and demonstrated that the authorities were unable to act except in those cases where the films had been produced in the state. Films brought across state lines were exempt from legal action or control. He felt that the law was inadequate and told Mr. King that the grand jury was "at this time looking into the problem of filthy films in the city." The "filthy films" in question were those being shown at Southtown's two "skin-flick" theaters. The district attorney, as had Senator Welles, told Mr. King of the importance of gathering and publicizing community support for legislative change.

After his discussion with Senator Welles and Mr. Tarran, Mr. King was convinced that the course of action was clear. It would be necessary to demonstrate community support for legislative change pertinent to the commercial and public showing of films. In addition, Mr. King thought it important for citizens to make their opinions known to the producers and retailers of films. What remained to be determined, according to Mr. King, was "the best way to demonstrate community support" and "the most efficient and effective way of getting legislators to react."

Mr. King reported to his fellow Knights the outcome of his consultation with Senator Welles and the district attorney. The members discussed, at informal meetings, the possibility of structuring a community meeting, in which the problem of lewd films could be publicly aired and a plan of action developed. Mr. King and his colleagues agreed that community representation at such a gathering should be broad and that important legislators and public officials should be in attendance, hopefully to speak. Mr. King was charged with the responsibility for arranging the public meeting, inviting public officials and representatives of other groups, and choosing the appropriate meeting hall.

Mr. King invited the participation of three state representatives, the Southtown chief of police, District Attorney Tarran, and State Senator Welles. He formally asked only two local groups to send representatives (the Southtown Baptist Association and the Michael Road Church of Christ). The two church groups had earlier made attempts to do something about pornography (reading materials, specifically) but had not in Mr. King's view been successful. He thought the church groups spent too much time "crusading and speech making" and not enough time "taking specific action." He also felt their approaches had been too "religious oriented" and "did not involve enough of the diverse groups in the community." Finally, Mr. King thought the church groups had been "too broad in their purpose." In his opinion, the appropriate strategy for dealing with the problem of lewd films was to concentrate on "specific legal change" and "to keep hammering at that."

Other local groups were informally invited to the public meeting by Knights of Columbus members' "putting out the word" about the forthcoming meeting, which had been scheduled for February 17, 1969, in the auditorium of the Knights of Columbus council.

Mr. King commented that the February 17 meeting "was an experiment." He was not at all certain what kind of community response there might be to such a meeting, or whether "the idea would go anywhere at all." The February *KC Knight Letter*, published by the council, announced:

> On February 17, 1969, at 8:00 p.m. at the Knights of Columbus Hall there will be a meeting to form a group to fight the selling of books of obscene material to juveniles. That *must be* and *can be* stopped— We will also try to have a law passed to stop movies of this type from being shown to youngsters under eighteen. Let's be specific— this is a problem that many American families are facing right now and we all need some kind of guidance—So come out on February 17th—put a circle around that date. Senator Welles will be the principal speaker.

The announcement of the meeting implied that the major purpose was "to form a group to fight the selling of obscene materials to juveniles." Only secondarily was the issue of films mentioned. This was contrary to the original intention of Mr. King, and he was not happy about what he considered to be a "misleading statement of purpose." He was not opposed to action against the selling of pornographic materials, but, as mentioned above, he insisted upon "one thing at a time," and the first thing was to be an effort to provide more "family film entertainment." Several other members of the council, however, had been particularly concerned about paperback books that were occasionally available in Southtown stores. Continually, there was pressure to include books with films as the target for action. Gradually, Mr. King became tolerant of those urgings, though he himself never wavered from his focus upon films.

By February of 1969, several antipornography bills had already been introduced into the house and senate of the state legislature. Those bills, at that time under committee consideration, variously recommended changes in the definitions of obscenity and pornography, modifications to the penalties for offenses against the statute, extensions or restrictions of the statute, and so on. It was clear that as early as February, 1969, at the same time that Mr. King and his colleagues were determining a course of action, the legislature was more or less actively concerned with the issues of pornography and obscenity in the state. The legislators were not agreed as to what the most basic flaws of the current state antipornography statute were. Some argued that the statute's provision for allowing films produced out of state to be shown with impunity, regardless of content, was the major flaw.

Others felt that the fines were not large enough (maximum of $1,000 and/or one year imprisonment in the county jail). Some legislators argued that the definition of *minor*, taken to be under the age of twenty-one years, was inappropriate—that is, the age level should be lower. Still others felt that the definitions of obscenity and pornography were not detailed enough and hampered prosecution.

On the evening of February 7, 1969, according to a front-page article in the *Southtown Globe* (February 7, 1969), "amid charges of nudity and counter charges of political suppression, a controversial theatrical production came to an abrupt end . . . on the University campus." The play, *Now the Revolution*, was produced by university students and was described as a rock musical with political satire.

Newspaper reports and interviews with persons in attendance often conflicted about the degree of nudity that allegedly took place during the presentation of the play. According to the newspaper article, "two girls in the cast stripped off their blouses and one exposed her breasts during a climactic revolution scene near the end of the show"; there was also a scene "depicting a girl giving birth to a naked man" (*Southtown Globe*, February 7, 1969). Interview respondents indicated that there had also been three cast members (two females and one male) totally nude for a short period of time and one female cast member who "took off her slacks, wearing only net hosiery underneath, revealing her entire pubic region."

During the first performance of the play, a Southtown police lieutenant had telephoned a university vice president, Dr. Jackson, and reported that he had "seen a girl back stage naked from the waist up," which event was in violation of the state penal code.

Later in the day of February 7, the police department reportedly received from four to seven calls from women complaining about nudity in the matinee performance of the university play. The county attorney was informed and stated that he was prepared to accept complaints, since actions in the play, in his judgment, were clearly in violation of state statutes. The county attorney then went to the university campus, but the police lieutenant and Dr. Jackson had already stopped the matinee and apparently had reached an agreement not to file charges. The play had been stopped in the middle of a performance. By the afternoon of Friday, February 7, the university ban on the production was rescinded, because the cast had agreed not to break the law. That evening the play did reopen, and all the cast members remained clothed throughout the performance. However, it was rumored that after the closing on Saturday night, several of the cast members led an exuberant crowd outside the theater and across the campus, and that amid frenetic dancing and singing a few of them completely disrobed.

Mr. King and his colleagues had not been involved in complaints made concerning the university play. There was no way to discover the identification of the women who had phoned complaints to the Southtown police. One responding official felt he had "more than just a hunch" that female members of the cast themselves phoned in order to get more publicity for the production.

Though less than a dozen persons were involved in actions to restrict the university play, the publicity associated with the event served to call public attention to a specific decency activity. Both the county attorney and the owner of one of the Southtown "skin-flick" theaters reported in interviews their belief that the action concerning the play significantly helped to stimulate subsequent action against both of Southtown's "skin-flicks."

On the evening of February 10, 1969, Mr. Davis, the manager of one of Southtown's two "skin-flick" theaters (the Avalon) was arrested by Southtown vice-squad officers on the charge of displaying lewd motion-picture films. The theater's current main attraction, *The Excited*, was described in the *Southtown Gazette* (February 11, 1969) as showing erotic sexual acts and "male and female pubic areas" and was confiscated.

Two days later, on the evening of February 12, 1969, Mr. Mason, the owner-manager of the Bijou Theater, was arrested and also charged with displaying lewd motion-picture films. The main attraction, *Dominique*, described in the *Southtown Gazette* (February 13, 1969) as being about "lesbianism," was confiscated.

Mr. Mason was particularly disturbed by the action of the Southtown police. As mentioned earlier, representatives of the vice squad had occasionally reviewed his films at the theater and suggested that certain productions or certain portions of productions be removed from presentation—suggestions with which he had always complied. However, Mr. Mason reported in an interview that during recent weeks his relationship with local authorities had deteriorated. He could not understand what had brought *Dominique* to the attention of the vice squad. He repeatedly expressed his willingness to cooperate with the authorities, or even with "citizen's groups, if any should get organized." He complimented the Southtown police on "the tremendous job" they were doing with "the narcotic and theft problems of a city such as Southtown." But he felt he was clearly within his rights, "according to federal law," in showing *Dominique*. He said he would in any event cooperate with the police department, although he knew "there is no local law for them to enforce about these films." He suggested that some of the problems might be solved by forming a local "censorship board" which "ideally would be made up by theater managers and art people only." "But," he admitted, "such a board would probably have to have business representatives, church representatives, *and* theater manager representatives on it." He stated that he would be quite willing to support such a "censorship board, so long as it is applied to *all* the theaters in Southtown, including the big ones who show films almost like mine but don't get into any trouble for it."

Mr. Mason considered himself to be a good citizen. He was a graduate of a religiously oriented university and had a brother who was a missionary. He expressed concern that his children "might read about me and wonder what kind of a criminal their father is." Mr. Mason had not seen the film *Dominique*, even though it had been confiscated from his theater. In fact, he stated that he "seldom saw the movies shown at the theater." He reported that he ordered them by title from "the larger organization with which I am affiliated, that has its headquarters in Sterling City." He stressed that he would "rather go to a good movie or drink beer with my friends, if I had an evening's entertainment to plan." Yet he argued that "anyone that has reached the age of discretion and wants to look at 'skin-flicks' or their contents should not be denied the right to do so."

Mr. Mason appeared to be a confused and angry man, who could not quite understand why suddenly police action had been instigated against him. He closed the interview by stating, concerning the Bijou Theater, "It's my living. I don't make much at it, but I am comfortable. I am not particularly proud of it, but it's a living."

Mr. Davis, the manager of the Avalon Theater, took more immediate and direct action following his arrest than Mr. Mason. Mr. Davis notified the distributors of the film *The Excited* that the police had confiscated it. On February 13, 1969, the *Southtown Globe* received what was supposed to have been a copy of a telegram sent by Canyon Productions, Inc., of Hollywood, California, to the Southtown police department. The telegram stated that the film *The Excited* had been "legally transported in interstate commerce by a federally licensed and bonded carrier" (*Southtown Globe*, February 14, 1969). Consequently, the film was exempt from prosecution under the state penal code. The letter then ordered the police to return the film immediately and said that otherwise further legal action would be forthcoming. The Southtown police indicated that they had not yet received such a telegram and that they felt it to be a publicity stunt. Mr. Davis, however, thought it was an indication that the "movie people" were fighting back.

When interviewed about the action against the Southtown "skinflicks," Captain Thomas, the head of the Southtown police vice squad, reported that the movies themselves prompted police action. Captain Thomas admitted that the existing statute made it virtually impossible to prosecute "in cases like this." He stated that he would not "make a routine" out of "moving against the theaters" and that he would "not be a censor," but when someone "made a complaint, he would institute the same action again." When asked why the vice squad had chosen to act in the case of *The Excited* and *Dominique*, Captain Thomas responded that those two films had been "more pornographic than the other movies that had been showing." Apparently some citizen or citizens had directly or indirectly complained to the vice squad concerning the "skin-flicks." It was not possible to determine who the complaining persons were, except that they were *not* Mr. King or any of his cadre.

Mr. Hill, the county attorney, felt that the movies *The Excited* and *Dominique* were of a quality such that "most everyone would agree that they constituted pornography." He added that they were "as raunchy movies as I have ever seen." He compared them with "stag" movies, "except there was no actual penetration." He reported considerable favorable community support for police action concerning the Avalon and the Bijou theaters. He stated, "I have gotten more mail on this than anything since I have been county attorney—about twenty letters, and all favorable." He agreed with Captain Thomas that the present statute provided an escape for many objectionable films. However, he outlined a specific plan of action aimed at making up for inadequacies in the law: "What we plan to do is follow the same procedure we followed in this case—to file a complaint, to get an injunction, to confiscate the films, and then to dismiss the case—and to continue to do this over and over again until these people stop showing the films." He added that by this tactic "we can show the theater owners that we will take it to court, and if we continue to harass them, perhaps they will back down." He felt that this tactic was a "Mexican stand-off" but "served to call the community's attention to the problem." Mr. Hill stressed that he would not initiate any such action but would so act when and if he received other citizen complaints.

The police action had an immediate impact upon the kinds of films that were being shown at the Avalon and the Bijou theaters. The management of the Avalon Theater visited County Attorney Hill, in order to determine what kinds of films could be shown without arrest. Mr. Mason indicated that he was "booking milder prints, older ones, not like the new ones coming out any more." Furthermore, he was watching the age limit of eighteen years much more closely than before.

During the week of February 17, 1969, the grand jury, which, as indicated above, had previously been investigating the Avalon and Bijou theaters, subpoenaed *Dominique* and *The Excited* for a private showing. Both films were to be reviewed by the grand jury on the morning of February 18, in one of Southtown's large "legitimate" movie theaters.

Mr. King and his colleagues followed these activities with great interest. Mr. King did not feel that his visits with Senator Welles and particularly with District Attorney Tarran two weeks earlier had directly influenced the police action. The grand-jury investigation of the problem of lewd films had begun before he visited the district attorney. He admitted, however, that "the timing was just right on this. We started our interest while Mr. Tarran and the grand jury were busy with their end of it. It may be that things just got to a point here in town. But it was a lucky break for us, even if it was just a coincidence. . . . We're real pleased at the way things have gone." Mr. King added that, although his visit probably had no direct impact on the district attorney, "perhaps it was important to him to see that there were people in the community interested in doing something about the problem. He did tell me he was going to tell the grand jury about that."

Candidates for city council election were actively campaigning during February and March. Some respondents felt that the lewd-film issue was raised by a few politicians as a vote-getter. Many of the respondents, including Mr. King, disagreed with that interpretation. They felt simply that the time was ripe and that the citizens of Southtown had had enough.

Mr. King was pleasantly surprised with the turnout at the February 17 public meeting, which he had felt would be only experimental and which would determine the possibility of mobilizing community support for legislative change concerning pornography and obscenity. Approximately two hundred persons attended the meeting and heard speeches by Senator Welles, State Representative Randolph, State Representative Owens, District Attorney Tarran, and Captain Thomas of the Southtown police department. Among the community groups represented at the meeting were the Boys' Club of Southtown, the Junior Chamber of Commerce, the Michael Road Church of Christ, the Southtown Baptist Association, the Hilltop Baptist Church, the Southtown Catholic Youth Association, the Masons, the American Legion, the Central Christian Church, the Valley Church of Christ, and the Knights of Columbus. Mr. King commented that he was surprised not only by the number of people that turned out but also by the participants' diversity. He interpreted the attendance to be an indication of the potential for community support and decided at that time to "really get going" in establishing an antipornography effort.

During the meeting, the speakers made the Avalon and the Bijou theaters the focus of their attention. They reiterated that the movies confiscated from the theaters had been produced outside the state and had been brought across the border legally. Thus, the state obscenity statute did not apply. The speakers, with much support from the audience, talked about the necessity for tighter restrictions on such films. Representative Randolph, during his speech, told the audience that he would prepare legislation modifying the statute so that "none of the exemptions shall apply when the violation involves the exhibiting to a minor." He described the two films which had been confiscated as being "plain, flat filth" and urged that "effective legislation be passed."

The participants in the meeting wholeheartedly agreed with the speakers, and several of them urged that somebody do something to get the legislation underway. Many members of the audience expressed the feeling that they were frustrated with now knowing about a problem and not being able to do anything about it right away. Mr. King reported that he keenly felt the audience's frustration and hoped to be able to channel their eagerness into constructive effort.

One of the church ministers in attendance suggested to the meeting participants that a "massive rally" be held to show legislators that the community was concerned about the problem of "filthy films" and that they wanted to do something about it. Mr. King, as chairman, considered that suggestion, which had unanimous support from the participants, to have been a key factor in the development of the subsequent antipornography crusade. Mr. King notified the press that he, his colleagues, and members of the public meeting would meet again within ten days to make plans for a demonstration of public sentiment.

The following morning, February 18, 1969, the grand jury viewed the confiscated films *The Excited* and *Dominique*. Present, in addition to members of the grand jury, were Representative Randolph and staff members of both the county attorney's and the district attorney's offices. The *Southtown Globe* (February 18, 1969) reported that those attending the screening of the film were "shocked" and "disgusted." Representative Randolph was quoted as saying that he would intensify pursuit of modifications in the state antipornography statute, specifically eliminating the out-of-state–production exemption when the violation involved exhibiting the film to a minor. Furthermore, he intended to pursue an amendment to the statute which would make bringing a minor to such a theater an act of contributing to the delinquency of a minor. Representative Randolph stated, "I've never considered myself to be a prude, but I honestly can say that those two films are not by any stretch of the imagination artistic . . . the sole emphasis in the two films is on fornication" (*Southtown Globe*, February 19, 1969). With regard to changes in the statutes, he added that he was "interested in getting effective legislation passed, rather than something broader that, because of Constitutional questions and resistance of the film industry, would probably never make it to the floor of the House" (*Southtown Globe*, February 19, 1969). Representative Randolph compared his bill to others presently in committee. He felt his had a chance of getting through and that it was liberal. Other bills, he commented, were "shotgun" in nature, and were quite conservative—even smacking of censorship. He felt that there would be considerable community support for changes in the legislation, even though "Southtown is the most liberal town in the state. The University liberalizes it." He was aware of Mr. King and the "citizens' group" that had organized the public meeting of February 17, 1969. He was impressed by Mr. King, referring to him as "a very active individual." A brief report of the public meeting and an announcement that Mr. King and his group soon would be holding a planning meeting were included in the article (*Southtown Globe*, February 19, 1969).

In his February 22 "Capitol Report," Senator Welles commented that among the bills he was sponsoring he felt "particularly strong about one to control the flow of obscene movies in the state." He added that he and another senator were "pushing legislation to block the legal loophole that exempts virtually all movies produced outside the state from control within the state, thus allowing pornographic films to reach state audiences." Senator Welles's bills were distinct from the one introduced by Mr. Randolph.

On February 25, a Southtown district judge ordered the Southtown police vice squad to return the movies *The Excited* and *Dominique* to the management of the Avalon and Bijou theaters. It was indicated that the state obscenity statutes did in fact exempt the films from legal action because they had been produced out of state and legally transported in interstate commerce. However, the district judge at the same time enjoined the Avalon and Bijou theaters from showing the two "lewd, obscene, lascivious and immoral" movies, declaring them to be a "nuisance." All parties, including the defendants, agreed to the injunction without a hearing. The two films were then, as scheduled by the distributors, sent to another part of the state for commercial presentation. The injunction was specific only to the films *Dominique* and *The Excited*, and did not apply to any other films.

Mr. King, having heard about the reaction of the grand jury and the officials who had viewed the two films, was more convinced than ever that he and his group were "on the right path" and that orderly public action carefully organized by a group of "reasonable" persons would be an effective vehicle for influencing legislative change. Considerable publicity had, by this time, been given to the lewd-film situation in Southtown, and at least a minimum of community opinion was crystallizing. Mr. King and some of his colleagues had established solid contacts with significant members of the legislature and local law-enforcement authorities. Now, according to Mr. King, it was time to put together an organization and to "do more than just give speeches."

On the evening of February 27, 1969, eight men, all central and active members of the Knights of Columbus council, met at the Knights of Columbus hall to discuss a specific course of action for influencing the changing of the state antipornography statutes. In particular, they were intent upon (a) setting up an organizational framework which would facilitate "getting the legislation done"; (b) finding ways of getting more community support; and (c) determining a strategy for exerting pressure on the movie industry to produce more films which were appropriate for family entertainment.

For about ten minutes before the meeting was scheduled to begin, the men who had already arrived informally discussed the problem of pornography and its correlates. One of the participants suggested that all young people who went to "smutty" movies were "sick." He discussed in detail what he perceived to be the relationship between "fonography" [sic] and mental illness. During the discussion he attributed the "large percent of youth who were not qualified for the draft because they were mentally unfit" to the use of pornography, and was convinced that "insanity is caused by using fonography." In conclusion, he summarized that it was possible that both the use of pornography and mental illness "had something to do with low blood or low blood sugar. Who knows, the problem might be solved if people are more careful about what they eat."

After he had finished his rather lengthy statement, one of his colleagues teased him: "Say, does that mean you were sick when you went to see that strip show in Sterling City last year?" The group laughed, and the challenged participant responded, "Well that was different. That was not the same thing. I was just doing that for fun. Besides, I wouldn't want my daughter to see that. It's a different thing entirely." Somewhat sheepishly, he fell silent.

Another group member complained to his colleagues about the general film fare in Southtown: "Do you know that this week there is only one picture in town that has a G rating? That means there's only one picture in town that a family could go to see together—out of all the theaters we've got!" The group agreed with him and concurred again that something should be done about the situation. One of the members cited, as an example, a "pornographic movie that was now showing, called *Johanna*." Another group member asked him to explain why the film was pornographic. He responded that he did not "know the plot" because "I have not seen the film; but I have heard about it, and I don't like the idea at all." Another member cited *Bullitt* as being "obscene, too. They used the word *bullshit* in there, and they had no need to use that word in there at all. It doesn't even fit with the rest of the plot. It's just thrown in there for I don't know what. Also, the guy and the girl are shown in bed together, and they aren't even married."

Mr. King arrived at the Knights of Columbus hall and called the meeting to order. Immediately, under his leadership, the group became quite task oriented. He began to focus his colleagues' attention on the idea of the rally proposed during the public meeting of February 17. He suggested that such a rally should provide the opportunity to circulate a petition, which would be presented in support of legislation, and to distribute to the participants printed postcards (addressed to Jack Valenti, president of the Motion Picture Association). The postcards would protest the lewd quality of commercial films and would request more family-entertainment films. Mr. King suggested an attendance goal of five thousand persons for the rally, and he thought it would be quite possible to get a turnout that large. He stated that he had been in personal and telephone contact with representatives from several community organizations and that "at least twenty of them are now behind us." Those organizations included the American Legion, Parent-Teacher Associations, the Catholic Laity, the Church of Christ, Rotary Clubs, the Baptist Association of Southtown, the Masons, the Boys' Club, and the Catholic Daughters. (A Presbyterian organization, a Methodist organization, and the Optimists were reported as having indicated that they did not want to be involved with the rally because "they felt we were going about it the wrong way." The three groups objected to the public display that the rally would encourage.) If each of those twenty voluntary associations were assigned a quota, he suggested, the audience figure of five thousand could "easily be reached."

Mr. King urged the strategy of "organizing, contacting, and turning out people for the rally." He told the group that the rally would have to include "a broad range of speakers and perhaps some entertainment," but more importantly, it would be necessary "to keep the action moving at the rally."

Mr. King then turned to the task of structuring the organization. He straightforwardly stated, "The Knights of Columbus is going to take the lead" in developing the action. Consistent with that intention, he established a "steering committee," consisting of six subcommittees, all of which would be chaired by active Knights of Columbus members. The six subcommittees were to be called Publicity, Legal, Speakers, Security, Program, and Coordinating. Mr. King would be chairman of the steering committee.

Each of the subcommittees had been carefully and deliberately chosen by Mr. King. The Publicity and the Legal subcommittees were to work in tandem determining the best methods to publicize the forthcoming rally, in line with the ultimate goals of influencing legislative change and informing the Motion Picture Association of Southtown community opinion. The chairman of the Legal Subcommittee was to be a local judge, who would make certain that no public statements made by the antipornography organization were libelous or in conflict with standing federal, state, or local laws. The Speakers Subcommittee was responsible for making certain that the Southtown clergy would announce the proposed rally in their churches and urge parishioners to attend. The Security Subcommittee was to watch over the proceedings of the other subcommittees prior to the rally and prevent any activity or information leakage which would allow a countermovement to develop. Mr. King and his colleagues were concerned that an opposition might coalesce and interfere with the anticipated phased progress toward legislative change. Mr. King further encouraged group members to keep their activities more or less "under wraps" until the appropriate time for publicity. He especially warned the participants not to talk with newspaper reporters. At the rally, the Security Subcommittee members would serve as sergeants-at-arms and "keep order" during the proceedings. The Program Subcommittee would be in charge of "lining up" speakers and providing a proper balance of information and entertainment on the program. Finally, the Coordinating Subcommittee would serve to integrate the activities of the other five subcommittees.

Mr. King neatly drew the organizational structure of the steering committee, including the six subcommittees, on a blackboard in the meeting room. As he described the functions of each committee, he would point to the appropriate box on his organizational chart. He speculated that "in order to be effective, fifty men would be needed" to staff the steering committee. He indicated that he intended to recruit the men from among Southtown Knights of Columbus members at a forthcoming meeting. Most of the subcommittee chairmanships were filled, by Mr. King's appointment, from the ranks of the eight men present at the meeting.

During the meeting, one of the participants passed around a copy of what he called an "antipornography kit" distributed by the Knights of Columbus at the state level. The kit actually was a mimeographed pamphlet with several sections. The cover sheet was a memo from the chairman of the Knights of Columbus State Social Action Committee, advising each KC council to start "on its way to victory over indecent literature." The reader was further advised, first, to read the enclosed general plan; second, to appoint a chairman ("one of your brother Knights") and to set up a decent-literature committee; third, to "pass the torch" (let the community operate on its own); and, fourth, to stay informed. The manual also advised the council to expand in the campaign so that the "entire community is encompassed in this unified civic project." The kit detailed specifically, step by step, the procedures for putting together an antipornography effort. The last three pages of the manual offer the reader a sample letter to merchants concerning the removal of undesirable literature from the news racks; a form for reporting the activities of the KC antipornography campaign to the KC decent-literature chairman; and an order blank for the Knights' own copy of the Citizens for Decent Literature film *Printed Poison*. The influence of CDL upon the Knights of Columbus kit was quite apparent; in fact the memo advised the councils to affiliate themselves with CDL.

The state secretary of the Knights of Columbus reported that the kit had been widely used by KC councils throughout the state and the nation. In his opinion, sixty-four local communities had "cleaned up their book problems over the past five or six years" by following the advice in the pamphlet.

The pamphlet concentrated primarily upon reading materials alleged to be pornographic and made no mention of films. The general plan for the antipornography activity carefully advised the councils to avoid other activities which might be construed to be illegal or inappropriate —such as boycotting or other kinds of threats to individual freedom. The memo gave the impression that a sweeping antipornography movement had been taking place in the state—an impression that could not be substantiated. Certainly Knights of Columbus local councils had been involved in antipornography activity in various locations. However, most of those activities involved relatively quiet requests, on the part of Knights of Columbus members, for merchants to police their newsstands.

Mr. King was aware of the KC antipornography kit; however, he was unimpressed with it. He criticized the pamphlet as being "not specific enough and trying to deal with too much at one time." Furthermore, he concluded that the pamphlet was concerned with published material, rather than films, and suggested citizen pressure on merchants, rather than stimulating legislative change. Mr. King felt that the pamphlet had been of little influence in the way that he structured the Southtown antipornography effort. He thought his choice of actions had been influenced primarily by his "business and civic club experience." The kit appeared to him to be too much of a crusade, and he considered himself not to be a crusader.

Mr. King continued to direct the meeting, and discussion continued concerning the structure and the function of the proposed rally. The group agreed that "people were disgusted with us at our last meeting (the public meeting) because we could not provide action for them. We talked about the problem, and everybody got mad, but we couldn't give them any action." One of the participants suggested a boycott of the movies, but Mr. King quickly discouraged him, reminding him of their goals—legislative change and generally expressing community opinions to the movie industry. Another of the eight participants recommended that "we invite theater owners to attend the rally, so that they will know what they are up against." The other participants agreed. Mr. King listened quietly to these other suggestions but gently continued to redirect any shifts of emphasis to the notion of marches, boycotts, and so on, back again to a concentration upon orderly public statements which, through the medium of the rally, would ultimately aim toward legislative change.

Mr. King announced to the group that the newspapers and local television stations had offered to "do what they could" to publicize the rally. He again emphasized the importance of the proper timing of publicity and reminded the Publicity and Legal subcommittees of their important responsibility in handling the timing and content of such publicity. He spoke of the importance of a "gradual but steady build-up" in community interest, and advised that the movement must "avoid delays, but still not peak too soon."

Mr. King stated that he had received many phone calls from people during the past week, indicating that they were behind him and supported his position. He added that most of the support had come to him spontaneously. Nevertheless, he counseled the other members that "personal contact is irreplaceable. We have got to draw on our friends and contacts in the neighborhood and community and get people going." The members then began discussing their various contacts throughout the city—and the number and complexity of the contacts was impressive. The participants ranged widely through both formal contacts with dozens of community voluntary associations and official agencies and a wealth of informal, particularistic contacts with relatives, friends, acquaintances, and colleagues.

The participants discussed possible sites for the rally. One of the members suggested that the university might contribute an auditorium for the meeting. Mr. King responded, "The university? We might be asking for trouble at the university, with a topic like this." The other members agreed. The group decided that the rally should be held at the Southtown Municipal Auditorium because that was "neutral ground" and because one of the members had a friend who was the manager of the auditorium and they could get a good price on the rental. Furthermore, the auditorium was one of the few buildings in the city which could accommodate the expected five thousand people.

The chairman of the Security subcommittee, one of the eight men present at the meeting, was officially named "Sergeant-at-Arms." He laughed as he accepted the appointment and, seemingly embarrassed, said: "That's okay! I took karate one time and I will fix those long-haired guys. I have a good eye for that kind of thing. I can spot those instigators real soon. All of us on the Security Committee will be wearing red Knights of Columbus jackets; so we will be identified easy in the group." The participants were frankly concerned about the possibility of a counterdemonstration during the rally and hoped to prevent, or at least to control, such an occurrence.

The funding of the potential rally was discussed, and Mr. King reported that the Knights of Columbus council had voted to pay all the expenses, with the hope that participating community groups subsequently would, through contributions, help pay back some of the money.

The members again agreed that the internal organization of the rally was to be handled by the Knights of Columbus. The various other community groups who affiliated themselves with the antipornography effort were to "turn out their own people" for the rally.

The format of the rally was discussed briefly by the members, one of whom suggested that "we get a drum and bugle corps or a band to lend some excitement to the rally." The members agreed, further discussed the program, and finally decided that the rally would include perhaps six "moving" speakers, a band, a color guard, and "plenty of action to get the people there and to keep them interested." Committee subchairmen were commissioned to "line up" program components and to involve representatives of other community groups in subsequent meetings of the developing antipornography organization.

Mr. King set a second meeting of the steering committee, "involving more representatives from other organizations," for March 13, in the Knights of Columbus auditorium. He then adjourned the meeting and left. The group quickly fractionated, and the discussion returned to emotional comments about the dangers of pornography and its causal relations to various forms of social maladies.

Discussion

The cities of Midville and Southtown manifested a demographic profile indicative of potential support for a symbolic crusade, as typified by Gusfield. Both Midville and Southtown had relatively recent frontier histories and were continuing to experience the conflicts of rural-to-urban transition. The citizens tended to be religiously fundamentalist, politically conservative, vigorously patriotic, local rather than cosmopolitan in orientation, and traditionalists in their views of social institutions. Both communities represented, in the traditional sense, what a Southtowner proclaimed to be "a little slice of real America." The modal style of life represented values, customs, and habits centered around traditionalism and conservatism.

Evidence for the growing popularity of alternative life styles and social institutions, particularly among the young, was impressed upon both communities by the media and by the actions of students associated with local campuses. Like alcohol in Gusfield's analysis of the temperance movement (1963:24), pornography had the potential to become an item the consumption or support of which indicated the social status of the user or approver. Pornography could become a symbol differentiating between life styles, a possibility contributing to the conduciveness for a symbolic crusade.

Smelser (1962:278) indicated that the most general condition of conduciveness for a norm-oriented movement was the opportunity for the participants to urge modifications in norms without simultaneously challenging values. Pornography as an issue clearly is conducive to demands for normative change (in pornography laws, for example) without challenging (in fact, by serving) traditional and conservative values concerning religion, sexual behavior, and other life-style components.

There must be some way or ways by which potential participants in the norm-oriented social movement can affect the normative order— for example, petitions, elections, initiatives, letters to congressmen, letters to editors, demonstrations, request for court injunctions, and so on (Smelser 1962:282). By such procedures citizens can, through contact with authorities, influence the changing of laws and other kinds of normative procedures. The citizens of both Midville and Southtown had opportunity to affect the normative order in this fashion. In fact, the early activities of Conporns in both Midville and Southtown (especially Midville) employed some of the methods listed by Smelser.

Drawing upon the work of Almond (1960), Smelser stated that "interest-articulation" must be differentiated from "interest-aggregation" if citizens are to be able to channel dissatisfaction into norm-oriented movements. *Interest-articulation* refers to the structures through which interests, grievances, and desires are made explicit. Such structures include "lobbies, pressure groups, armies, bureaucracies, churches, kinship, and lineage groups, ethnic groups and status and class groups" (Smelser 1962:278). *Interest-aggregation* "refers to the structures in which these articulated interests are combined, weighed, and forged into policy. Examples of structures for the aggregation of interests are legislatures, bureaucracies, political blocs, and coalitions" (ibid. 278). In the cases of both Midville and Southtown, the structures of interest-articulation (the emerging antipornography groups) were separate from the structures of interest-aggregation (legislatures, law-enforcement agencies, the movie industry, the businesses) they were trying to influence.

Though it is important for the purposes of structural conduciveness that avenues for influencing the normative order be open, it is also necessary for the potential participants to perceive some avenues for change to be closing or closed (Smelser 1962:284). Further, it is necessary that the citizens perceive a teetering balance of power between themselves and the opposition (however vaguely defined that opposition might be at the time). The conduciveness for development of a norm-oriented movement is facilitated by ambiguity concerning power. "This ambiguity is created by an event or a series of events which signifies a new chance for success in overcoming opposition or a new danger of being defeated by the opposition" (Smelser 1962:284). The relatively tentative nature of the early antipornography activity of Mrs. Roberts, Mr. King, and their colleagues reflected what they perceived to be a precarious balance between the power of those who opposed and the power of those who proposed pornography. Both Mrs. Roberts and Mr. King experienced minor successes and setbacks in their efforts, which events heightened the conduciveness for the development of a norm-oriented social movement. They also perceived some channels for normative change to be open, some to be closed or closing. Still open were the processes for systematically bringing about legislative change and for filing complaints against "smut dealers" with the police. As a result of the Supreme Court decisions, the opportunity for gaining informal compliance from businessmen and the opportunity to get convictions for violations against present antipornography statutes were closing.

Smelser commented that a communication network has to be available among the potential participants as an element of conduciveness for the development of a norm-oriented movement (1962:286; see also

Killian 1964:443; Turner and Killian 1972:36). Mrs. Roberts, Mr. King, and their colleagues amply demonstrated the availability of a communication network—through voluntary-association ties, through the local media, through personal contact with friends, and through the church "pulpit system."

Smelser observed that a norm-oriented movement frequently is conducted by some sort of organization (1962:274). Antipornography organizations, more rudimentary in Southtown than in Midville, had emerged in both cities. The presence of those organizations contributed to conduciveness for the development of a norm-oriented social movement against pornography. The presence of the organizations meant also the presence of leaders and a cadre who could be influential in the development of the movement. Smelser (1962:17), Lang and Lang (1961:522–523), and others have commented on the importance of potential leaders and cadre as elements of conduciveness for movement emergence. Mrs. Roberts, Mr. King, and their colleagues had in their respective cities clearly demonstrated antipornography leadership potential.

Both Midville and Southtown (Southtown less so) had some history of antipornography activity. Both cities also had businesses presenting or selling sexually explicit materials which could be defined as pornographic (in Midville, "adult" bookstores; in Southtown "skin-flicks"). Both of those factors contributed to structural conduciveness—the former as a strategy, the latter as the target.

On the basis of these indices of structural conduciveness, it could be expected that the antipornography crusade would, if other of the Smelser value-added stages were present, be considerably more intense and perhaps more coercive in Midville than in Southtown. Southtown was to some extent subject to the greater liberalizing influences of a major university and the cosmopolitanizing presence of state and federal agencies. Southtown's population generally was not subject to the industry-related economic fluctuations in the work force that occurred in Midville. Barton and Lazarsfeld (1969:191) have reported that economic fluctuation was, in the communities they studied, one of the key variables associated with a high level of participation in public affairs. As noted earlier, the citizens of Midville recorded a considerably higher percentage of voting participation than the citizens of Southtown. Midville was a smaller city than Southtown, with a consequent greater facility for communication and personal contact with a larger percentage of the citizens. Furthermore, Midville had

· been labeled an All-America City—a label which certainly contributed to conduciveness for the development of an antipornography crusade. Midville had a considerably longer and more intense history of antipornography activity than Southtown, both officially and unofficially. Mrs. Roberts and her colleagues had been engaging in antipornography activities and had been forming their decency organizations far longer than Mr. King and his colleagues. Consequently, the Midville cadre had considerably more opportunity to experience the dislocations of successes and failures than the Southtown cadre.

It may seem that some of the factors presented as structural conduciveness, especially in Midville, actually already represented the operation of a symbolic crusade, the mobilization for action of a norm-oriented social movement. Some of the early activities of Mrs. Roberts and Mr. King could (and will) be considered precipitating factors for the emergence of the crusades. The sorting of events from the natural histories of the two antipornography crusades into the Smelser stages must be arbitrary. Smelser indicated that the same events or factors might be interpreted as operating in different value-added stages, depending upon the chronological point from which the analyst viewed the movement. We have decided to consider the mobilization for action of the Midville and Southtown crusades to have begun at that point in their histories when significant numbers of citizens other than the cadre became involved in the concerted antipornography effort. In addition to an increase in the scope of the antipornography activities, the mobilization-for-action stage will be marked by a significant increase in their intensity. Those antipornography activities we have reported in this chapter as elements of structural conduciveness for the subsequent development of the crusades were noticeably tentative, fractionated, and experimental. Mrs. Roberts and Mr. King were not yet quite certain how best to go about accomplishing their "decency" tasks. Both leaders were not yet certain how best to involve larger numbers of community citizens in their efforts. There were not yet antipornography crusades in Midville or Southtown; but the structural conduciveness for them clearly was present.

Chapter 3

Structural Strain: "Changes Are Raging out of Control!"

Midville

Many of the Midvillians interviewed, not a few of whom were in key community positions, were concerned about the possibility of a national recession, which would have a drastic impact upon the economic health of industrialized Midville. Several respondents and the local media reported the negative impact of inflation upon the local wage earner and bemoaned the fact that their hard-earned dollars did not seem to have much buying power. Some of the respondents were concerned that ultimately, particularly if the war in Viet Nam ended, economic imbalance might lead to a large number of "lay-offs" by the local factories and plants.

There also was evidence of community concern, from interviews and the local media, about the possibility of ethnic conflict in Midville. A few of the larger cities in the state had recently experienced severe rioting, and although Midville had, as yet, experienced no marked conflict, there was some anxiety that the 17 percent non-White population was becoming more militant.

The fact that Midville had been named an All-America City was in itself a structural strain. It was, as one respondent put it, "a hard image to live up to." "All-America" denoted a multitude of basic values that Midville was supposed to possess and to manifest in citizen behavior. Several of the Midvillians interviewed saw their community as being one of those which had the responsibility to resist the sources of social change which might undermine the "American way."

According to Conporns, several other respondents, and editorials in the local media, challenges to the conservative and traditional life style representative of the Midville image were apparent everywhere.

The national mass media ("people like that Cronkite fellow") daily reminded the citizens of, and even seemed to give approval to, the possibility that the "now generation" or the "counterculture" was becoming more widespread, more forceful, more prestigeful. Traditional attitudes toward sexual behavior, work, religion, education, authority, patriotism, war, child-parent relations, and marriage were seen to be eroding, especially among young people. More than a few reputable legislators, theologians, doctors, entertainers, and educators were perceived to be contributing to the legitimacy of life styles different from, even opposed to, that of "right-thinking" and "solid" Americans. Most disconcerting of all to Conporns, the federal government (under Presidents Kennedy and Johnson) had taken various actions felt to be weakening normative support for the traditional life style. Under the "misguided" leadership of Chief Justice Warren, the Supreme Court, that most revered and powerful guardian of traditional American values, had legislated against, as one Conporn stated, "all that I have stood for all of my life." The "no prayer in public schools," the "freedom for pornography," and, to a lesser extent, the civil rights and rights-of-arrestee decisions were viewed by Conporns as grievous errors which enormously complicated their expectations for human behavior.

An important source of strain reflected in the local media and by Conporns was the growing feeling that citizens were either unable or unwilling to reverse trends which threatened their traditional and accustomed life style. The continuing and increasing presence of pornography in Midville, combined with the inconclusive nature of assorted though not markedly concerted actions to restrict that presence, was itself not only a source of strain but also a symbolic representation of loss of control.[1] An increasing amount of unsolicited "smut mail" was being received by the citizens of the All-America City. The citizens' inability to control receipt of such unsolicited mail or to control conclusively the unsavory programs, stories, films, and advertisements in the mass media contributed to the sources of strain. The informal arrangements between the local police department and the community businesses which sold books and magazines or showed films had broken down. In general, legal sanctions against pornography had been rendered ineffective by Supreme Court decisions. Indeed, the state antipornography statute after which Midville's antipornography ordinance had been modeled had been declared unconstitutional. Thus, in the opinion of Conporns, the local governmental structure was unable or unwilling to act with regard to the "blight of pornography," the "cancer," in the middle of their All-America City. In downtown Midville, across the street from the *Midville News*, the city's most prestigeful hotel, a college dormitory, and other respectable businesses, the Midwestern Bookstore, summarized a Conporn, "thumbed its nose at the community."

At another level of structural strain, Mrs. Roberts and her colleagues in ICCD had declared themselves to be protectors of decency in Midville and increasingly felt pressure to implement their intentions. The challenge of the Midwestern Bookstore had to be met by someone or some group who understood the dangers it posed, and ICCD by charter was under obligation to respond.

The Midwestern Bookstore

At 122 South Paine Street in downtown Midville, the Midwestern Bookstore was among the usual diversified downtown businesses, including department stores, taverns, specialty shops, restaurants, and travel agencies. One block down and across the street was a recently constructed building housing the *Midville News*, the city's major newspaper. Directly opposite the bookstore was the weathered but nonetheless popular Tisdale Hotel. The area contained predominantly old buildings but was well maintained.

Situated within a row of small shops, the Midwestern Bookstore did not stand out during the day; unless one knew where to look, it could easily be missed. However, at night, until it closed at 10:30 P.M., it was one of the few places open on that side of the street and was easily identified by a red neon sign which exhibited the word *Bookstore*. The entrance to the store was between two small display windows, in which an assortment of popular (not sexually explicit) magazines and books were displayed. Affixed to the window on the right was a poster of a blindfolded man with the caption "Who should decide what you should read?" Halfway up the left display window were the words *Adult Bookstore* spelled out with red tape. This was meant to be more of a description of the materials for sale within the store than its proper name. However, very few individuals in Midville with whom we talked used the proper name of the bookstore (the Midwestern Bookstore); instead, most called it the Adult Bookstore.

The visitor entering the front door noticed immediately that the store was clean and carpeted and that the material was well organized. The visitor first saw a room a little larger than the average living room, fitted with two long wall racks and a two-sided center rack. The racks in that room were for a wide range of popular magazines, paperbacks, and newspapers. The paperbacks included best sellers, westerns, science fiction, murder mysteries, and nonfiction. The magazines ran the gamut from titles like *Boating* to *Playboy*. None of the materials in this front room (other than *Playboy* and its kind) were considered to be pornographic by respondents.

On the back wall of the front room was a door and next to it a small window through which one could see a back room. From within the back room, a clerk, sitting at a counter, peered out in order to view customers seeking entrance from the front. On the door to the back room there was a sign warning that a person must be at least eighteen years old to enter and that identification would be required. Following that notification was a statement advising "If you are offended by nudity you should not enter." An admission charge of one dollar was routinely required, though permanent memberships could be acquired. Any money spent on admission could be redeemed as a deduction from the price of books, photographs, films, or other materials offered for sale.

Immediately inside the door and to the right in the back room were a glass display counter and a cash register. On the top shelf of the glass counter was a small array of "french ticklers," phallic earrings, and other jewelry, and various sizes and kinds of dildos and vibrators. The bottom shelf of that counter contained cellophane-wrapped sets of four-by-five-inch black-and-white or color photographs of male and female models with genitals in a state of excitation. These photos sold for $3.50 (black and white) and $5.00 (color) a set. Next to the photograph sets were packaged reels of eight-millimeter black-and-white and color films. Each film package had a photograph of one frame on the outside, which indicated the contents and whether the film involved one or more persons and heterosexual or homosexual activity. According to the clerk, none of the films contained pictures of actual physical contact; the actors only "seemed to be doing it." The black-and-white films sold for $15.00, color films for $25.00.

On top of the display counter were copies of *Screw* (a New York sex tabloid) and "classified-ad" magazines containing advertisements from individuals who were looking for varieties of sexual partners. *Screw*, like everything else in the back room, was marked up considerably—from thirty-five cents to one dollar. At one end of the glass counter was a small rack of calendars with photographs of nude men and women.

The wall of the back room was completely covered with a floor-to-ceiling rack of paperback books. Selling for two to four dollars apiece, the majority of books in that section were from diversified publishers and contained different degrees of sexual content and explicitness. Some of the books compiled one sexual incident after another, with no thought to plot, while others presented a story line with verbal descriptions of sexual scenes integrated with the text. Subjects for those books that attempted storylines ran from the supernatural to the world of big business. Most of the books in this particular section presented a range of sexual activities including fellatio, cunnilingus, group intercourse, anal intercourse, sadomasochism, and genital intercourse all within the same cover. Completing the wall section was a smaller display of yellow-covered Bee-Line books, with a price tag of three dollars.

The back wall contained racks of magazines and paperbacks oriented toward the theme of male homosexuality. The magazines were packaged in cellophane, but both front and back covers illustrated male nudes, in sexual poses, with genitals fully exposed. The homosexual magazines tended to be the highest-priced publications in the store, ranging from five to seven dollars per copy. None of the photographs showed penises in a state of full erection, but some photos showed semierection. A small subsection of that set of racks contained books and magazines depicting photographs of nude male children.

Running diagonally across the center of the back room there was a two-sided rack of paperback books. On one side was a large selection of illustrated paperbacks, almost all by the same publisher. Those books sold for four to five dollars each. The print was rather poor, and the photographs placed intermittently throughout the books illustrating female poses were somewhat blurred. Little or no attempt was made at a story line, and both grammar and syntax were quite elementary. The sexual activities portrayed covered the full range of physical possibilities. The left end of that side of the rack had a smaller section of the same type of book.

The opposite side of the center rack had three main sections. A small subsection was devoted to the green-covered Traveler's Companion series. Paperbacks from two other publishers took up the majority of the space on that side of the rack. Each of the publishers had a distinct cover format which was the same for all books in the line. As with the other paperback books already mentioned, these included a variety of sexual acts, but they seemed to make some attempt to keep up with the contemporary social scene by incorporating into the plot marijuana, LSD, psychedelic settings, and trips to India to study yoga. The third section of that side, at the end of the center rack, was dominated by the "specialty" paperbacks. Those were books whose subject was predominantly a single type of sexual behavior. The behaviors depicted included fellatio, cunnilingus, anal intercourse, incest, sadomasochism, degradation, and necrophilia. The titles almost always indicated what particular practice was detailed behind the cover—for example, *Rear Entrance*, *Mary the Mouth*, *The Paths of Incest*. Scattered among that section were a few sexual documentaries and classics of erotica such as the *Autobiography of a Flea*. The books in that section ranged in price from two to four dollars.

With the exception of a small stand of Greenleaf Classics in the left rear corner of the back room, all of the left wall from the floor to the ceiling held racks of pictorial magazines, termed "naturalist" magazines by the bookstore clerk. The majority of the magazines were wrapped in cellophane, but at the bottom of the rack the shopper could find assorted unwrapped copies to peruse. The magazines were about the size of *Newsweek* or *Time*, sold for three to five dollars, and contained mostly full-page black-and-white or color photographs. They had very little text. The magazines presented photographs of individuals representing various ethnic groups, younger and older persons, and individuals in various combinations of numbers. As did the paperback books, some of the magazines catered to particular varieties of sexual behavior or to fetishes. For example, some of the magazines specialized in photographs of girls wearing leather, latex, garter belts, stockings and shoes, and so on, generally with a common denominator of exposed genitals, some in a state of excitation. Those photographs which contained pairs or groups of individuals only suggested copulatory and other kinds of sexual contact. No actual contact was depicted. As with the homosexual magazines, no full erections of the penises were noted in photographs of male models. Some of the magazine titles reflected the major themes of the photographs, for instance, *Bizarre Taste*, *Leather Action*, *Naked Femme*, *Lesbiana*.

To the left of the magazine rack was a medium-sized rack of "adult party" records. Around the corner from the party-record racks stood another medium-sized wall rack about six feet high, which was directly opposite the glass display counter. The shelves contained a variety of magazines and paperbacks, including Swedish, Danish, and other imported photograph portfolios, more classified-ad booklets, and a few copies of pictorial magazines dealing with sexually oriented commercial and underground films. The paperback books in that section were predominantly pseudo-scientific treatises of sexual practices—for instance, *The Techniques of Oral Sex* and *The Variations of Anal Intercourse*. A few sexual documentaries and some "legitimate" sexual-technique books completed the display.

The back room had no windows, and the lighting, though modern, was only adequate. The room was clean, and the material was extremely well organized and displayed.

Visitors could browse and read as long as they wished with no interference from the clerk. The clerk would not approach the visitor; the visitor had to initiate contact in order to gain more information or to make a purchase.

The clientele of the Midwestern Bookstore seemed quite diverse. For example, during one period of research observation, the customers included a male of senior high school age; a male about twenty years old with long hair, sideburns, and sandals, carrying some college textbooks; a man about fifty years old, wearing a well-tailored business suit; a gray-haired middle-aged man wearing a sport coat and slacks; another man about fifty years old wearing neat but casual clothes; two young men about twenty-five years old, one of them in Western dress; and a middle-aged woman wearing rather ill-fitting and worn clothing.

The salesclerks in the bookstore all were young (the oldest was perhaps in his late twenties) and were casually dressed. Only rarely were there more than two salesclerks—one in the front section of the store, another in the back room. There were both male and female salesclerks, but there seemed to be no rigid assignment of one sex or the other to the front or to the back room. According to the clerks, the Midwestern Bookstore did "a hell of a good business"; one estimated the store's average monthly gross to be approximately ten thousand dollars.

The Midwestern Bookstore was not unlike other "adult" bookstores throughout the country, with the exception that it did not present for sale materials which pictorially depicted actual sexual contact (such contact was described in the verbal texts of paperbacks). The patrons of the bookstore appeared to be not unlike those described as patrons of other such stores—that is, predominantly Anglo, middle-class, middle-aged, married males, dressed in business suits or neat casual attire, shopping alone.[2]

As pointed out in Chapter 2, Mrs. Roberts and her colleagues in ICCD had directed their antipornography efforts toward "cleaning up the news racks" in drugstores and grocery stores. The most explicit sexual materials contained on those news racks were "girlie" magazines, which showed at most bare breasts, bare buttocks, and occasionally "suggestive" poses. The materials offered for sale by the Midwestern Bookstore were in comparison far more sexually explicit, even though they did not pictorially display actual sexual contact as did some bookstores in other cities.

Southtown

In Southtown, there seemed to be relatively less structural strain concerning economic factors than in Midville. Although several of the respondents and the local media expressed concern about inflation, a large percentage of Southtowners held government or service-related jobs which were less vulnerable to a possible recession than the industrial jobs in Midville. Furthermore Southtown had one of the lowest costs of living among United States standard metropolitan areas. The possibility of ethnic conflict did not seem to be of much concern to Southtown residents. Although Blacks and Chicanos accounted for nearly 25 percent of the total Southtown population, little overt ethnic strife had been encountered. Southtown respondents generally felt that ethnic minority groups were quite controlled by formal and informal aspects of the social structure.

Like Midville, the All-America City, Southtown, the state capital, was presented in promotional materials as a stronghold of traditional Americanism. As in Midville, the Conporns in Southtown, several other respondents, and the local media noted with alarm the breakdown of basic values manifest in the actions of young persons, the operations of the federal government, and the decisions of the Supreme Court. Several of the respondents and local editorials expressed concern that changes in the fabric of American society were taking place too quickly and that those changes brought with them threats to the accustomed and traditional style of life. As one Conporn summarized the problem: "Change is raging out of control, and something ought to be done about it!"

Contrasts between traditional and alternative life styles were manifested daily for Southtown citizens on the campus of the large state university located in the heart of the city. At one level of abstraction there was structural strain between the behavioral perspectives of the conservative state legislators (and regents) and the university as a whole. At another level, within the university itself, relatively liberal staff and students engaged in activities which conflicted with life-style expectations of relatively conservative staff and students. Controversies about those activities, disagreement about student participation in and control over administrative decisions, controversies about academic freedom, and so on were publicized in the local media and reminded the Southtown citizens of the contrasting life styles and the competition among them. A most dramatic representation of that competition was the campus chapter of the Students for a Democratic Society. Virtually everything that the members of SDS represented was considered by the local press and the Conporns to be destructive of basic American values. Though violence on campus had been rare, the university had over the last two years experienced, in concert with other universities throughout the nation, numerous large-scale peace rallies, marches, student strikes, and other events perceived by some Southtowners to be evidence of disruption and disrespect.

There had been, as reported by one of the local newspapers, a noticeable increase in unsolicited "smut mail" in the community, over which, as an irate Conporn observed, "the post office seems to have no control." Local "legitimate" movie theaters, competing for the patronage of the large and affluent university population, tended to program films which were not considered by the Conporns to be suitable for families as a group or children as individuals. "Why should the college-types dictate the kind of pictures available in this community; what about our rights, too?" reflected a Conporn. The two Southtown "adult" theaters, emboldened by the Supreme Court decision, the weakened role of the local police, and the apparent national trend toward softness on pornography, were showing more and more daring films—according to Conporns, in disregard of the standards of the community.

Mr. King and his colleagues in the Knights of Columbus were charged by organizational raison d'être to inaugurate and implement action projects of religious and moral service to the community. Mr. King's choice of action to encourage more family film entertainment was escalated by his colleagues and others in the community to include action against pornography in general and what pornography symbolically represented in the processes of change and the threats to tradition. The two Southtown "skin-flicks" were clear and present examples of those changes and those threats.

The "Skin-Flicks"

The two "skin-flick" theaters were located on opposite sides of the same east-west downtown street, which crossed Southtown's major business avenue. The theaters were, therefore, located in central downtown Southtown. The Avalon Theater was two blocks east and the Bijou Theater five blocks east of the major business avenue. The area along the street on which they were situated was exclusively devoted to various business enterprises. Nearly all those businesses, particularly those proceeding further east, tended to cater to lower-middle and lower socioeconomic-class customers. In the first block east of the major business avenue were several small specialty shops for middle-income clientele—jewelry stores, a pipe shop, and the city's oldest, formerly exclusive, hotel. The hotel was, however, scheduled to be vacated and torn down because of its age. The second block east was lined with bargain department stores, credit furniture stores, small credit and loan companies, and a few "outlet" and "discount" stores. Continuing east, the number of cafés, taverns, and pool halls increased. Pawn shops, used clothing and furniture stores, junk shops, and warehouses increased in number. Several blocks further, across an interstate freeway, Blacks and Chicanos populated one of Southtown's poverty pockets.

The Bijou Theater was located at what is essentially the beginning of the city's "skid row," where typically groups of disabled, elderly, unemployed or otherwise stigmatized individuals patronized the cafés, businesses, and pool halls along the street. Many Southtown citizens equated the entire street with the term *skid row* and referred to its habitués as "riff-raff."

The Avalon Theater was for a number of years a movie house showing second-run Hollywood films and Spanish-language pictures. Toward the end of 1968, new management extensively renovated the theater and limited it to the exhibition of so called "skin-flicks." The titles of films shown there included such features as *The Excited*, *For Single Swingers Only*, *Fanny Hill and the Red Baron*, *The Bushwhacker*, *Lady Godiva's Ride*, *Babbette*, and other commercially available and widely distributed "sexploitation" films. The films showed female breasts, male and female buttocks, and female pubic hair. No excited genitalia were shown, nor were oral-genital or genital-genital contact actually depicted, although those activities were suggested by poses, camera angles, body movement, vocal utterances, and gestures.

The Avalon Theater's entrance was virtually a storefront and consisted of a small box office and entrance and exit doors. The marquee displayed photographs reproduced from the films being shown and/or colored posters advertising the films. The price of entry was $1.75, but escorted women were admitted free. The advertisements for the theater, regularly appearing in the Southtown and university daily newspapers, specifically welcomed military personnel and college students.

The theater was long and narrow, and its lobby and aisles were carpeted. There was no lobby concession counter, but popcorn, candy, soft drinks, and cigarettes were available from vending machines. Smoking was not permitted in the viewing section of the theater.

The patron entered the auditorium in the middle of one side. To the left was a major front section of the theater, to the right a smaller back section, to which led a small flight of stairs. Directly across from the point of entry was a fire exit. The projection room was to the rear of the viewing area and elevated somewhat. The lighting in the theater was adequate, and sound and visual equipment seemed considerably better than in many theaters of this type. The advertisements for the Avalon announced "super-stereo sound." The total patron capacity of the theater was approximately 250 persons.

The Bijou Theater was located in an older building than the Avalon Theater, but like the latter it initially featured second-run Hollywood films and Spanish-language pictures. In 1961, the present owner-manager bought the theater and changed its film fare exclusively to one similar to that described for the Avalon.

The outside of the Bijou Theater had a more "movie-house" appearance than that of the Avalon. A small box office was centrally located, and doors on either side led to the theater's interior. There was no lobby, as such. The patron bought a ticket, and entered directly into a short hallway with left and right entrances into the rear of the auditorium. Candy and soft-drink machines were placed in the hallway.

The viewing area itself was very poorly lit (even prior to film showing) and slanted slightly downward to a screen that appeared to be much too large for the stage on which it was situated—one side of the screen was closer to the audience than the other because it would not fit evenly across the stage. Uncushioned folding wooden seats were arranged in the left, center, and right sections of the auditorium, divided by two aisles. There was no carpeting on the concrete floor. In general, the Bijou appeared to be considerably dilapidated and both looked and smelled of considerable age. The total patron capacity of the theater was approximately 150 persons.

Like the Avalon, the Bijou advertised in the local and the university newspapers. Both the Avalon and the Bijou usually had only two employees working at any given time—the box-office attendant and the projectionist.

The patrons at both the Avalon and the Bijou tended to be male university students and local businessmen. Both theater owners reported that approximately 85 percent of their patronage fell into these categories—the rest were military personnel, senior high school students, "drop-outs," and a few "dirty old men." The weekly attendance at the Bijou was reported by the owner-manager to be around three hundred persons. The Avalon's weekly attendance was considerably higher than that. Weekend evening showings sometimes played to nearly full houses, when college students took their dates to the theaters (particularly to the Avalon, which was more modern and admitted escorted women free).

During the weekday afternoon showings, usually only males attended the theaters. For example, the Avalon attendance on a Wednesday between 3:30 and 5:30 P.M. included a total of forty-two men, described by attending staff members as nine Anglo males dressed in business suits and ties (three in their twenties, six middle-aged); eight Anglo males wearing button-down-collar shirts and sweaters (in their late teens or early twenties); eight Anglo males with crew cuts and wearing spread-collared sport shirts (in their late teens or early twenties); seven Anglo males with long hair, mustaches, beards, and "hip" clothing (six in their middle or late twenties, one middle-aged); two Chicano males dressed in business suits and ties (middle-aged); three Chicano males wearing button-down-collar shirts and sweaters (in their late teens or early twenties); four Chicano males wearing work clothes (middle-aged); one Black male wearing a business suit and tie (middle-aged). There were four sets of two and one set of three male

companions, all among the younger patrons and involving both Anglos and Chicanos (no sets were integrated).

On a Saturday afternoon during which Mr. King and his colleagues
were organizing the antipornography activity, the Avalon Theater was
showing a double feature, *The Bushwacker* and *Sex for Sale*. Both of those
films were of the "sexploitation" variety, involving complete nudity,
camera close-ups of buttocks, breasts, and pubic hair (but not genitals).
There were long love-making scenes, with extensive kissing, caress-
ing, and dubbed moaning, sighing, gasping, and panting. Cunnilingus
and fellatio were implied by body positioning and camera angle, but
never were actually shown. Coitus, both genital-genital and genital-
anal (from a variety of body positions) were simulated, but no penetration was shown and no genitals displayed. Both films had scenes
involving heterosexual, homosexual (female only), and group sexual
activity. *The Bushwacker* also had scenes depicting sadomasochistic
sexual activity and necrophilia.

The twenty-five patrons of the Avalon Theater on that Saturday,
between 4:30 and 6:45 P.M., were described by attending research staff
members as being quite similar in physical characteristics and proportion of solo patrons to the Wednesday afternoon crowd described
above, with the exception that there were two male-female couples in
the audience. At the Saturday evening showing, between 9:00 and
11 :15 P.M, there were seventy-four patrons, similarly diverse in physical characteristics. However, there were twelve male-female couples
(including two sets of two couples sitting together), six sets of two male
companions, three sets of three male companions, and two sets of four
male companions. The proportion of solo patrons was lower, and the
average patron age was lower.

Other observations made at varying times and on varying days by
research staff members yielded similar descriptions of the audiences
of both the Avalon and the Bijou theaters.[3]

The audience reaction to films at both the Avalon and Bijou theaters generally was more disorderly than one might find in other
"non–skin-flick" commercial movie theaters. That is, there was generally some more or less quiet conversation taking place throughout
the showing of the features, and several audience members often loud-
ly commented or joked about specific sequences of the films. However,
the audience usually would become quite still during the intense love-
making scenes.

The Southtown telephone directory listed, in addition to the Avalon and Bijou, eleven "walk-in" theaters and seven "drive-in" theaters. Two of the "walk-in" theaters were situated near the university campus and frequently showed domestic or imported "art" and "hip" films, such as *Camille 2000*, *All the Loving Couples*, *Easy Rider*, *The Sterile Cuckoo*, *Belle de Jour*, *The Prisoner*, and *The Libertine*. Several of the drive-in theaters regularly showed "adult-only" features, such as *The Goddess*, *Suddenly a Woman*, *The Fountain of Love*, and *Man and Temptation*. Other commercial movie theaters often showed films that were X-rated, according to the Motion Picture Code, such as *The Killing of Sister George* and *Succubus*.

The management of the Avalon and Bijou theaters in interviews both complained that many of the films shown at other "straight" Southtown theaters were just as "raunchy" as those shown at their own theaters. There were, of course, some quite noticeable differences. The "art" and "hip" films shown at the theaters near the university more often than not presented sexual encounters only as a minor part of an overall theme. The "adult" features shown at the drive-in theaters infrequently showed total nudity and rarely showed pubic areas or symbolic though explicit copulatory action, as did the films shown at the Avalon and Bijou.

Mr. King and his colleagues in the Knights of Columbus were just as concerned with the showing of X-rated and "adult" films at the walk-in and drive-in theaters in Southtown as they were with the features at the "skin-flicks." In fact, Mr. King was more concerned with the former than with the latter, since he felt that families would not be prone to attend the Avalon and Bijou but would like to be able to attend other of the theaters in Southtown. Mr. King had never attended the Avalon or Bijou, nor had any of his colleagues in the Knights of Columbus.

Discussion

Gusfield pointed out that the life style enacted by temperance crusaders was a model of the legitimate, traditional, and dominant definition of respectability (1963:84–85). For the crusaders, abstinence from alcoholic beverages was a symbol of that respectability. However, according to Gusfield, middle-class respectability was at that time undergoing considerable challenge. Temperance crusaders had realized that alternative middle-class norms were increasing in power, and those who adhered to the old norms were becoming objects of ridicule and contempt and were being relegated to inferior status. Those who had abstained from alcoholic beverages, rather than those who drank them, were beginning to be perceived by some as deviates. The kinds of social changes (including an increased acceptance of drinking) which were taking place throughout the country impinged upon the chosen and previously rewarded life style of those who subsequently chose to become temperance crusaders (1963:133–134). The temperance crusade itself became a battle of traditionalists and localites against modernists and urbanized cosmopolitans (1963:177). The status conflict profoundly disturbed those who from an early period of socialization had internalized traditional values, norms, and roles, the implementation of which provided the core of a claim to status and respectability. Gusfield (1963:143) suggested that participation in the crusade, a fundamentalist reaction, was an attempt to reassert the challenged life style and to denigrate the threatening modern life styles as illegitimate and not worthy of cultural domination. The traditionalists evolved to become status discontents, threatened by the character of social change, and in defense became preoccupied with those groups which were seen in status opposition.

Gusfield (1963:110) noted the powerful impact upon those adhering to traditions of a political victory, even if only symbolic, by the challengers to tradition. It was a blow to the traditionalist's belief in the domination, in the leadership position, and in the legitimacy and veracity of his or her world view. The government served a key role in assigning prestige to specific life styles. Gusfield suggested that the government could influence the hierarchy of prestige not only through its instrumental acts, but through its symbolic acts as well (1963:166–167). Public figures and political individuals could, by expressing their opinions, reinforce or demean specific societal value clusters and, by doing so, enhance, maintain or threaten the life styles of those who adhered to the values. Generally, the individuals whose status had been threatened in one way or another could call upon the government, or upon important and visible representatives of it, to make pronouncements or take acts which would instrumentally or symbolically support the life style they implemented, or help to remove threats to it.

As hypothesized, the status discontent experienced by the Conporns was not unlike that experienced by the temperance crusaders. Their life styles were being threatened by what they perceived to be dangerous and relatively unchecked social change. Alternative life styles were emerging which seemed to be receiving more prestige and reinforcement from status distributors (i.e., the Supreme Court, the mass media, and respected others) than they deserved. As a result, the Conporns' own tradition-based and tradition-oriented life styles were suffering status degradation. The status discontent they experienced was a significant strain, the resolution of which they could determine by actively engaging in status politics.

In his discussion of structural strain,[4] Smelser observed that "the history of social movements abounds with agitations on the part of groups who experience a real or apparent loss of wealth, power, or prestige" (1962:287). That real or apparent loss is a source of strain for individuals in the same sense as the experience of status discontent described by Gusfield. Smelser further commented that "any disharmony between normative standards and actual social conditions can provide the basis for a movement whose objective is to modify the norms. This is particularly true when either norms or social conditions undergo rapid change in a relatively short time" (1962:288; see also Klapp 1972:15; Turner and Killian 1972:46–47). Clearly there was a discontinuity between the normative standards accepted and expected by those who adhered to a traditional life style and their perceptions of the actual social conditions (which included the growing prominence of alternative life styles). Those changes and challenges were perceived by Conporns and reported in the local media of both Midville and Southtown to have accelerated dramatically in the late sixties —a relatively short time.

Smelser noted that "sometimes new legislation creates strains on existing normative arrangements" (1962:289). The decisions of the liberal Supreme Court under Chief Justice Warren had broad repercussions upon formal and informal normative arrangements, societywide. Those repercussions dislocated the expectations that Conporns in Midville and Southtown had for the manner in which decent persons conducted themselves. The normative restructuring was perceived to support values which were at odds with those embraced by the crusaders, a situation which Smelser felt "creates bases for defining certain social conditions as 'evils'—social conditions which previously had passed less noticed" (1962:289). It has been said that pornography, like poverty and prostitution, has always been with us. Yet under certain conditions of strain the presence of pornography can become particularly and painfully noticed, not so much for what it is as for the range of structural strains it is made to symbolize by status discontents.

The fear of recession or ethnic conflict and the perception of the community as one of the last bastions of Americanism were other elements of structural strain shared by Midville and Southtown, though their presence in Midville was considerably more severe. Each of those strains contributed to the potential for status discontent in that they all reflected, at least in part, fears of status dislocation.

For the communities of Midville and Southtown and for the Conporns in both cities, pornography was present and increasingly noticeable as a structural strain. Formal and informal measures for controlling pornography and the range of strains and alternative life styles it symbolized had broken down. The bookstore in Midville and the "skin-flicks" in Southtown were concrete, physical, and tangible strains, representatives of the threats to decency, of the threats to a traditional and conservative life style.

Smelser argued that the kinds of strains providing the basis for some form of collective behavior may exist in any one or more of the four components of action: values; norms; roles, social organizations, and reward contribution; and situational facilities. The actual form the resulting collective behavior takes depends upon the characteristics of the other value-added stages, especially the kind of generalized belief which evolves concerning the most appropriate way to ameliorate the strain.

Conceptually, the condition of status discontent as described by Gusfield represents a strain which, since it is concerned with style of life (values, customs, and habits), touches upon all four of the Smelser components of action. The status discontent is concerned about prestige losses to his or her value system, the efficacy of norms which implement and protect those values, the rewards he or she gets as a result of enacting roles in keeping with the values and their protecting norms, and the control he or she has over maintaining a status quo in which those value, norm, and role specifics continue unambiguously to function.

Midville and Southtown Conporns, other respondents, and the local media in both cities evidenced structural strain at the value level concerning the challenge to what has been called the "old culture" by the value orientations of the "counterculture." Slater (1970:31) typified the value-orientation conflict by citing the counterculture (when compared with the old-culture) preferences for personal rights over property rights, human needs over technological requirements, cooperation over competition, sexuality over violence, distribution over concentration, the consumer over the producer, ends over means, openness over secrecy, personal expression over social reforms, gratification over striving, and communal love over Oedipal love. The traditional emphases upon self-control, industriousness, impulse renunciation, and general conservatism were under challenge. Alternative interpretations of religious, educational, philosophical, and political values were being introduced—"modernism," "revisionism," and "situation ethics" increasingly were being introduced by representatives of the "now generation." More importantly, those contextually novel value orientations seemed to be growing in popularity. Turner and Killian (1972:28) noted that when alien values from deviant subcultures are introduced into conflict with older, dominant values, a prime condition for the emergence of collective behavior is present.

The norm systems, both formal (e.g., laws, social control agencies) and informal (e.g., folkways, mores, implicit undertandings between individuals and groups for specific behaviors), were perceived by Conporns to be weakening. That weakening and the concomitant structural strain were felt to be due in part to broad trends which were challenging basic values (including values associated with law and order), in part to disruptions in the traditional, more disciplined, socialization processes for young people, and in part to some specific acts of government and legal bodies (e.g., the Supreme Court decisions).

The Conporns had been accustomed to enacting social roles considered by them to be "appropriate," "right-thinking," "decent," "God-fearing," and typical of the best features of "real Americanism." Those roles articulated with their value orientations for self-control, industriousness, impulse renunciation, and general conservatism. (A detailed social-psychological portrait of the Conporns is presented in Chapter 8). Furthermore, they had been accustomed to receiving the reward of prestige for such role enactment and had been comfortable with the perception that the traditional social role they enacted was powerful in American society. Moreover, they had been comfortable with a perception that the traditional social roles they enacted were rooted in stable and accepted forms of traditional societal institutions (e.g., traditional forms of family, education, political arrangements, recreation, marriage, and occupation). The configurations of social change, particularly the increasing popularity of alternative institutions, alternative social roles, and alternative hierarchies of prestige and other forms of social reward confronted the Conporns with a threat to the viability of their own roles, their own rewards, and their own institutional ties. The possible devaluation of their own life style, as it was operationalized by enactment of social roles, was not only a structural strain but also a challenge to self-concept (to the degree that perceptions of the self reflected identification with the challenged roles, rewards, and institutions). Turner and Killian (1972:45–46) observed that if role incumbents were perceived not to be carrying out their role prescriptions, social unrest and disorganization would result and encourage collective behavior. That condition would be particularly intense if persons were perceived not to be enacting roles in which social control was vested.

Finally, the Conporns were experiencing strain in the situational-facilities components of social action. Their ability to influence and control the environment, specifically to arrest change which threatened the viability and prestige of their life style, had been called into question. The mechanism of citing basic values as an automatic means for regulating the behavior of others had become less effective. Some of the norm systems upon which they ordinarily would have called in order to resist changes perceived to be dangerous to them had been weakened. The power of the traditional social roles they enacted had become problematical.

Smelser (1962:51–52) noted that a condition of ambiguity is central to and characteristic of structural strain. The status discontent experiences more or less ambiguity in each of the four components of action. The clarity and certainty (arbitrary, to be sure) he or she has earlier experienced in the sanctity of specific values, the efficacy of specific norms, the prestige associated with enacting specific social roles, and the predictability of specific acts to influence and control the environment have become somewhat blurred. Some sort of action is needed to correct the situation. What kind of action that will be depends upon the kind of generalized belief the status discontent evolves concerning who or what is to blame for the strain and upon what are perceived to be the restrictions on alternative forms of action. In Midville and Southtown, pornography, and more specifically the Midwestern Bookstore and the "skin-flicks", were readily available not only as sources or reminders of strain, but as targets for blame and action.

According to Smelser (1962:49–50), strain in a component of social action is first experienced at lower rather than higher levels of abstraction. That is, the strain is first apparent to the individual, for values, at the level of commitment to personal values; for norms, at the level of operative rules of behavior; for the mobilization of motivation, at the level of deprivation in role performance; and for situational facilities, at the level of ambiguity in facilities to attain goals. The natural histories of Midville and Southtown and the comments of the Conporns and other respondents indicated the presence of strain experienced at those concrete levels. The natural histories and respondent observations (some noted earlier as structural conduciveness) also indicated that Midville and the Midvillians manifested more intense degrees of structural strain than Southtown and the Southtowners. Because of the city's industrialization, Midvillians were more concerned about economic vagaries; also, they were more fearful of the possibility of ethnic conflict. Midville's image, more than that of Southtown, had been pronounced to be a paragon of Americanism. The Midvillians were situationally made more sensitive to the impact of social change, the impact of alternative life styles upon the prestige of their own life style. Mrs. Roberts and her colleagues in ICCD had a much longer history of decency activities than Mr. King and his colleagues in the Knights of Columbus. Consequently, Mrs. Roberts and her colleagues had experienced considerably more disillusionment with the efficacy of the usual norm systems for controlling assaults upon decency (translated as life style). The greater experience of structural strain by Midvillians created the possibility that, the other value-added stages being implemented, the antipornography crusade in Midville would be greater in scope and intensity than that in Southtown.

In summary, the hypothesized element of structural strain and the social and psychological processes of that strain were present and operating in Midville and Southtown. This is not to say that the Conporns were homogeneous in all experiencing the same *specific* element of social discontinuity and the same *specific* motivating factor of stress. "Life style" incorporates a complex of variables. Many people can enact the same life style, perceive similar threats to it, concur on a course of defense, and yet be heterogeneous in the specifics of motivation. At the very least they may differ in the degree of emphasis placed on the specifics.

Smelser cautioned that "a condition of structural strain must combine with appropriate conditions of structural conduciveness" (1962:

292) if it is to become a determinant of some form of collective behavior. The natural histories of Midville and Southtown indicated that elements of conduciveness and of strain articulated strikingly well. The conditions in both communities were set for the evolution of a generalized belief which, in the context of conduciveness and sharpened by precipitating factors, would label specifically the attackable sources of strain and crystallize a particular course of remedial action.

Chapter 4

Generalized Beliefs: "Pornography Is Leading Us to the Fall of Rome!"

Midville

A number of consistent and integrated generalized beliefs cut across and emerged from the Midville field and interview data (especially the public speeches, protest letters, charter, records, and newsletters of ICCD). A presentation of selections from among those materials, ranging chronologically from early 1963 until early 1969, reveals the character of the beliefs.

The March, 1963, letter written by Mrs. Roberts and her eleven colleagues protesting an episode of a network television series was an early illustration of some generalized beliefs. The writers' complaint read, in part:

> This was the most blatant piece of brainwashing or propaganda that we have ever seen. The atheist is portrayed as martyr and a good guy, while the conscientious moral citizen is depicted in the role of a villain or to say the least self-righteous hypocrite. The atheist's halo was almost visible.
>
> We will agree that each person as an individual has a right to his own convictions, but in as much as this country is largely made up of "Believers" in God and in as much as our founding fathers saw fit to recognize the existence of God in drawing up the Constitution, it is no more than right that every effort and safeguard be taken to preserve that concept and that can only be done by seeing to it that the atheist or communist does not get the chance to plant the seeds of their convictions in the minds of our young citizens, via the classroom.
>
> We have become alarmingly aware of far too much liberalism being tolerated in our public high schools and colleges and univer-

sities in the name of education and knowledge and now we are to have foisted upon us via our T.V. screens such propaganda in the name of entertainment. Many young people and weak-kneed adults accept the philosophy and argument offered in such portrayal. An intelligent person can refute the pat suggestions and poorly veiled arguments, but we Americans are getting less and less able to think for ourselves. Krushchev will be able to take over this country without a shot being fired unless we wake up.

This up-coming episode dealing with the license of creative arts and the rights of authors, artists, etc., to unbridled rule in the name of creative genius sounds like another of the same ilk, if we can judge by the trailer. These may not be the opinions of your firm, but it is up to you to know what is going on the air under your sponsorship. Moral consciences of the communities must not be invaded and violated and our democratic system must not be jeopardized to serve these special interests. If this up-coming show is aired and is what it appears to be, we will be forced to withdraw our patronage of your products and look elsewhere at that time slot for entertainment.

. . . We have heard so much this past few days about the effort being made to locate the poison tuna but we complacently allow the minds of our young citizens to be poisoned by such propaganda and false advertising with practically no protest. Are the lives of our citizens more precious than their souls?

In April, 1963, some of the letters of protest written by Mrs. Roberts and her colleagues included a summary statement about the national antipornography organization, Citizens for Decent Literature, which they considered to be "rendering an inestimable service to our community." They concluded that "no one with a love of decency can remain detached from this movement." The advice and example of CDL were to be influential in the evolution of the Midville crusade.

In May, 1964, Mrs. Roberts and her cadre attempted a summary statement of the problem of pornography, which read in part as follows:

There is no question. When one sees the "hard core" pornography, it is just that. It generally shows sexual acts and related matter.

Grey matter is that which to some would be obscene but to others might be called art. It does not go to the actual portrayal of immorality, but it is highly suggestive, leaving the remainder to the imagination.

Do we have a right to inflict on someone else our opinions as to what is pornography or grey matter?

How can we stop it?

1. Legally.

2. Bringing up the moral standards of the community. . . . We can protest to the dealer who sells the material. . . .

The best thing we can do is to influence the people in our churches as to the danger involved here and to have them speak out if they do not like it. . . .

. . . The most insidious effect of all this material is the constant portrayal of abnormal sexual behavior as normal. Perversion for profit thus wrecks the chance for impressionable adolescents to achieve a normal healthy relationship upon their maturity.

One marriage ran into difficulty because of the participants' thinking that the presentation of sexual matter in books, magazines and on television was the normal manner when it actually was far from it. Pastoral counseling made the marriage return to a solid foundation and it lasted.

. . . Is not a cooperative effort called for?

How would we go about it legally and morally, to establish a community conscience?

. . . A constant protestation of the seller to the type of literature sold which is objectionable would at least have a nuisance value, if not a beneficial value, in getting rid of this material.

A positive program of united objection would be of value, a united statement is not sufficient.

Special use of the mass media of communication should be used to present this problem to the community as well as to provide them some education as to this literature and its dangers.

In September, 1964, some of Mrs. Roberts' ministerial colleagues wrote a letter to community leaders which included a statement of the belief that, "if such a book as *Das Kapital* and the *Communist Manifesto* can shake the world into revolution, so the indecent literature which appears regularly upon many of our newsstands can contribute to the rapes and the breakdown of moral standards. . . . We believe that much of the increase in crime in the Midville area is the result of this kind of literature." In November of the same year, Mrs. Roberts, representing her colleagues, wrote a letter to a corporation official which referred approvingly to a psychiatrist's opinion that there was a causal relationship between the reading of "lurid magazines" and lawlessness, antisocial behavior, delinquency, and criminal activity. She concurred that, as a result of the need to obtain gratification from "abnormal stimulation, girls and boys run away from home and become generally incorrigible." A March, 1965, letter written by Mrs. Roberts to a corporation official, again representing her colleagues, observed that publications "glorifying crime, criminals, and giving detailed directions for committing henious [sic] sex perversions, the pseudo-medical case histories of all manner of irregular immoral conduct, expose of cases, the scandal sheets (Tabloid Newspapers) which are now enjoying a real revival, paperbacks with lurid escapades, often in vulgar language, are presented to the immature mind which because of natural curiosity falls easy prey to it."

Three of Mrs. Roberts's fellow crusaders, clergymen, now as members of ICCD, wrote a joint letter in May, 1966, to all Midville clergymen, urging them to participate in Action for Decency Day and to announce it from the pulpit. In their letter, the three men noted:
"There are those, including some in the Clergy, who say that unsavory literature does not affect the people who read it. If that be true, could we not save a considerable amount of money in our Christian Education budget by refraining from the purchase of Christian literature? Obviously, we believe that good literature does affect people in a good way. Evil, erotic, smutty literature likewise affects people, but in the opposite direction."

In October, 1967, Mrs. Roberts wrote a protest letter, on official ICCD stationery, to the Supreme Court of the United States. That letter read, in part:

Having just read of the decision of the U.S. Supreme Court regarding the admission of Danish Nudist Magazines clearly intended for homosexual consumption in the *Midville News*, on October 24, 1967, we wish to register our disapproval of such leniency.

Those persons and organizations working in the field of indecent literature, movies, etc. are aware of the moral corruption engendered by such material falling into the hands of children, perverts, and those of unstable mental health. Numerous cases of young boys have been documented as being led into homosexuality by stimulation by a homosexual adult. In fact, it stands to reason that every homosexual adult was at some time led into that perverted activity by an adult. Nudist magazines are bait.

In July, 1968, a Midvillian (not an official member of ICCD) wrote a very strong letter to the editor of the *Midville News*, condemning the judges and the courts who were dismissing the charges against Midvillians who had been arrested for allegedly selling pornography. The letter proclaimed: "The emotional cripples, with hang-ups on perversions who become the child-molestors and rapers of old women as well as beautiful young girls, the murderers and sadists in our midst have free access to enter such establishments . . . . This opinion has been formed by eminent authorities who have found such materials in the possession of offenders. It is documented in numerous treatises on crime and juvenile behavior."

Mrs. Roberts in January, 1969, wrote on ICCD stationery a lengthy letter to the editor of the *Major City News*, telling him about the activities of ICCD and urging antipornography activity in Major City. In that letter, Mrs. Roberts presented an updated and perhaps the most thorough presentation of the generalized beliefs held by herself and shared by her colleagues in ICCD. That letter read, in part:

> There is a mania with sex-oriented literature, perversions, etc. in the U.S. today, even more than the rest of the world. Other nations with years of war tearing the fabric of their society have an excuse for some of their low standards, but America does not. There is an obsession with the scandalous. . . . We have progressed step-by-step from one level to another until today there is practically no place left to go down the ladder—we have reached the bottom—we have turned over every rock to peek at the crawly things in the slime beneath them. We have wallowed in the filth until we are almost mired beyond escape. We are the Sodom and Gomorrah of this age. Won't you please join with those of us who are trying desperately to roll back this trend—by making a New Year's resolution to weigh carefully statements and reporting of sensational news. What ever happened to that old slogan prevalent in the newspaper world, "All the news that's fit to print." Why not remember that young children read the newspaper today, even as young as those who want to buy *Playboy*. . . . We know that sin has always been with us since Adam and Eve (some religious authorities question this) and that it will be with us until the end of time, but we must

not wallow in it, we must set higher and higher sights as desirable goals for adults as well as children and perhaps some day, even publishers like Hugh Hefner will accept the challenge and expend his talents in a truly artistic area of the field of journalism. It is possible that some may have a twinge of conscience and a spurt of patriotism and even find that money can be made in other than evil channels. Let us turn our eyes and the eyes of the communications media upward with the Apollo 8 crew and see and concentrate on what is good, wholesome and beautiful in this wonderful world that God has given us. . . .

Like drugs or alcohol, pornography is especially harmful to the young. It is an established fact that such crimes as arson, rape, child molesting, theft, purse-snatching, mugging, etc. are used as an outlet by youth too young for normal outlets for the stimulation of pornographic material. . . .

. . . Society must be constantly uplifted for the good of all. We do no one a service by taking the attitude that what they do is their own concern and none of his neighbor's business. . . . Civilization requires curbs for its very survival and the good of society.

In January, the *Midville News* undertook an exposé of the Midwestern Bookstore (to be described in detail in Chapter 5 as a precipitating factor contributing to the antipornography crusade). The exposé incited a number of Midvillians (not all members of ICCD) to write letters to the editor of the *Midville News*. Several of those letters, as indicated by the following, manifested generalized beliefs:

I wonder if the people who promote this literature like to eat off dirty dishes and find contaminated and decaying food an important part of their diet. (January 20, 1969)

If you would study history carefully, you would find that the great civilizations of the past fell apart because their people lost their ability to control themselves in maintaining basic moral standards. (January 21, 1969)

Let us hope now that Warren either removes himself at once or gets removed so that this foul stuff can get cleaned up and Christian Americans can recover their dignity. (January 23, 1969)

Pornography, in all its forms, is one of the major causes of sex crimes, sexual aberrations and perversion. (January 26, 1969)

What can we expect when one woman atheist is allowed to censor the Bible and prayer in our schools, and, on the other hand, our children are being brainwashed with evolution as fact rather than unproven theory all through their formal education so that our schools are turning out atheists, agnostics, communists and far out what-have-you's by the thousands every year. (January 26, 1969)

Just as narcotics and dope can affect the minds of both adults and children and are illegal for both, so, too, it should be with obscenity and pornography. These, too, are narcotic, in that both adults and children can become addicted to them and be destroyed in both soul and mind. (January 31, 1969)

We could have a swing back toward a more balanced level of guidelines in many areas from literature to sensible legal regulations for the conviction of Communists, traitors, criminals of all kinds, etc. (February 25, 1969)

The generalized beliefs among the Midvillian letter writers included a common theme of the need for action of some sort, usually norm-oriented, to rectify dangerous erosions taking place as a result of social change. The sensible controls on individual behaviors were consensually believed to be weakening, and not enough people in the community were aware of the dangers. It was up to the "right-thinking" Midvillians to re-establish those controls. As one ICCD respondent summarized, "we let the long-hairs and the pinkos do all the talking and get all the T.V. publicity, and that's got to stop!" Another argued that he and his "neighbors" had not taken enough action to demonstrate what the "community standards" were, but "the pendulum is swinging our way now here and all over the nation." In Midville the belief had clearly evolved that pornography and what it represented constituted the source of strain, the source of the threat. In a context of additional precipitating factors (Chapter 5), the Midwestern Bookstore would become an even more specific and attackable symbol of the dangers.

Southtown

The Southtown field and interview data (especially public speeches, petitions, newsletters, and records of antipornography meetings) revealed a number of consistent and integrated generalized beliefs. A presentation of selections from among those materials ranging chronologically from January until April, 1969, indicates the character of the beliefs.

During the formative January and February meetings, Mr. King and his fellow Knights of Columbus often commented on the general decline of moral values in American society. Pornography was seen variously to be one of the major components of that decline, the predominant symbol of the decline, one of the causes of the decline, or the major cause of the decline. As the meetings and discussions progressed toward the emergence of the antipornography crusade, the generalized belief increasingly narrowed to seeing pornography as one of the major causes of societal erosion, if not the major cause. That belief was supported by the comments of other individuals with whom Mr. King and his colleagues talked. For example, the Southtown county attorney had observed that pornography, and specifically the kinds of films available in Southtown, unduly aroused persons, gave an inappropriate view of sexual relations, taught perversion, and very probably contributed to the prevalence of rape and other sex crimes. Representative Randolph had stated that such films "distorted values concerning sex . . . were related to the kinds of over-stimulation that leads to rape . . . encouraged sex mistakes such as unmarried girls getting pregnant . . . and made the viewer feel inadequate because of the hypersexuality displayed on the screen." A current Knights of Columbus newsletter recommended that local councils show their members the Citizens for Decent Literature film *Pages of Death*, because it "dramatizes an actual sex crime committed by a sixteen year old boy and traces the stimulation of his act to exposure to obscene magazines and paperbacks."

In the March, 1969, public meeting sponsored by Mr. King and the Knights of Columbus (to be discussed in detail in Chapter 5 as a precipitating factor), one of the participants (a Church of Christ minister) read a sample antipornography petition which he had used in another city. The petition was illustrative of generalized beliefs concerning society and pornography and read in part: "We are sick and tired of the peddlers of filth having free course in saturating our nation with that which helps destroy the moral fiber of our people. We believe that stringent laws should be enacted to stop the production and sale of such obscenity whether in the movies, in magazines, and books and that the Courts should stand firm in convicting and handing out stiff sentences to those who are guilty of breaking the laws enacted."

During the same meeting, a second petition was read as a draft. That petition also contained some relevant aspects of generalized beliefs, and read in part:

> We citizens of our State wish to commend our President, Richard M. Nixon, who has encouraged effective antipornography measures since he pledged this so vividly in his election campaign to "initiate an immediate program to protect our young boys and girls from the twisted minds trying to seduce them with pornographic literature."
>
> . . . We heartily endorse measures to stamp out this "plain, flat filth" which is through the media of films that are enticing our youth away from the family atmosphere that they are entitled to.
>
> We further feel that our social, economic, cultural and spiritual values of the citizens of our State will be exemplified only when films are made available for our people which are accessible to everyone through the thousands of theaters throughout our great state. We are speaking of a mushrooming of wholesome family entertainment for our civilization; not the flood of works which have been viewed as not being of any value and which have degraded the individuals who view them. For the most part these indecent films are directed at our youth, and too often the apathy of citizens has contributed to its incidence. Oftentimes certain unscrupulous movie producers maneuver many of our good citizens and the theater owners unwittingly to provide circulation for these salacious productions.

A mimeographed "Capitol Report" issued by Senator Welles in March was mailed to Southtowners and particularly appealed to Mr. King and his colleagues. The report contained the following statements, which affirmed the trend of generalized beliefs concerning pornography:

> Psychologists and psychiatrists with whom I have discussed this legislation tell me that exposure to obscenity can trigger a sensitive young mind, particularly in the case of children who have some emotional problem to begin with. They may be influenced to perform acts their normal judgment would not allow.

We are, in this state and nation, spending large sums of money to protect our children from polio, measles and diphtheria. We slow down traffic around their schools, provide school lunches, write welfare checks for the dependent, go to court to aid the neglected, support training schools and juvenile centers. We are doing great things for the material well-being of our young people.

Can we expect them to grow up healthy when their minds have been filled with dirt?

The most eloquent manifestations of generalized belief were the speeches made by the invited presenters at the decency rally, which marked the high point of the antipornography crusade (the rally will be fully described in Chapter 6 as part of the mobilization for action). The first speech of the rally, the keynote address (presented by a minister of the Church of Christ), was so illustrative of the consensually validated generalized beliefs that it will be quoted at length:

It is a fortunate privilege indeed to be allowed to meet in an assembly like this to express our feelings and to share with those in positions of authority our views on community subjects and subjects that affect our nation. We have since World War II experienced a rapid acceleration. The knowledge explosion has been beyond our comprehension. The scientific explosion has been beyond anything that we at this moment can conceive. The educational explosion has been terrific, and the moral explosion of this nation has really been an explosion and disintegration.

We are lovers of liberty and are champions of every man's rights, but when we reach the point where respect for decency and morality has disintegrated and really atomized, we have reached a low point in American progress. . . .

I think historians possibly could resurrect out of the dust of past centuries four great governments of men; the Greek, the Roman, possibly the British, and the American. Each has had its moment of glory, and at the moment we are in the center stage. Whether this glory will continue or end, or whether it will vanish as a vapor, can well depend on what groups like this one may choose to do.

. . . We have reached the place in our history where the emphasis is no longer upon the clean and the good and the decent and the moral. We are undergoing a stage in our history where the thing to do is to be dirty and unshaven, and even to march for some cause, and to skirt the edge of violence if possible, and to ruffle the feathers of most of us.

But there is still a worse angle to our society, I think. That's the fact that within recent times about all the moral restraint has broken down. This is an age of permissiveness. This is an age in which under the guise of the exercise of personal liberty just about anything goes. Even religious circles have felt the pressure of an existential ethic and a situational morality, and a loosening of mores that leaves us without an anchor, without a rock of ages to which we can cling, which allows every man to play God, and which allows him to set his own standards and to be his own determinator.

. . . We live in a time in which a man who runs for President runs the risk of being shot down in the hall, and a man who leads a crusade for better things for his race can't walk out on his private balcony without endangering his life. We live in a kind of society where people have decided that they will choose which laws they will respect and which laws they will ignore and disregard.

. . . When any citizenry takes the law into its own hands, to be judge and jury over what it will and will not obey in the way of law, anarchy and chaos is the only result.

(Applause)

If this be true of the simple laws of our land, it's far more true in our moral ethics. When we reach the place where we repudiate any divine system of morals, when God is dead as far as the average man is concerned, and we have decided for ourselves which moral laws we will obey and which we will not obey, we have really reached the low ebb.

If the voice of the people is the voice of God in civil affairs, certainly, then the man is no better than a hog or a dog if he doesn't choose to be on his own initiative. And this seems to be the morass into which our society has sunken. Taking refuge in the loopholes in the law and taking comfort from decisions of the Supreme Court in their efforts to guarantee every man his individual rights.

Certain interests have become vulturous in nature, to prey upon of all things the flower of the land—its youth. . . .

A young man said to me the other night, "I tried to pick a show that I could take my date to. I searched the paper, and every ad in the paper was a show that was not decent for me to take my friend to see. I would have felt embarrassed. I have tried it time and time again, only to be embarrassed at what I have to look at on the screen."

Neighborhood stores and magazine racks have become of such nature that the magazines for young people especially, out in the open, not under the counter, but on top of the counter, have become of such a nature that parents are even having to boycott the stores in order to make an impression upon the store keepers to keep this filth off the magazine racks, and out of the general public market.

Our society is reaching the point—it isn't sick, we don't have a sick society, but we have a society doing some sick things. . . . If we don't do something about it, if we don't take a constructive step, then the next funeral may not be for a Kennedy or a King, the next funeral may be that of our own great American government, and our own moral American society, and there in the casket, wrapped in the American flag, will be the remains of the greatest government history has ever known, and the future of the greatest body of people that this world now knows.

(Applause)

I am pleading on behalf of those tens of thousands who could not be here. That on the city level, that on the State and even on the national level, the loop-holes be plugged, that good laws be enacted and ordinances be put on the books that will give the young people of this country a chance to grow up with a healthy wholesome attitude toward morals. . . .

I believe there is an Uprising for Decency. It was noticed in Florida a few days ago in a meeting like this. It has been noticed in Washington. In recent days certain television shows have been cancelled on the air because they were too dirty to look at.

(Applause)

This is a step in the right direction. This is an Uprising for Decency. We've had marches for other things. Let's have a march for decency! Let's fill the streets with it!

(Applause)

Let's fill the legislative halls with it!

(Applause)

Let's fill the newspapers with it! Let's put it on television! Let's put it where it will tell and give America something to live for as well as something to die for!

(Lengthy applause)

The keynote speech was particularly indicative of generalized beliefs concerning sweeping and threatening changes in society, the relations of those changes to the disruption of basic values and the role of pornography in the changes. Another of the rally speakers (a Baptist minister) expressed the generalized beliefs which more specifically related pornography causally to incidences of social pathology. The speaker's presentation included the following statements:

My first few weeks in Southtown were sad. Do you remember back in August of 1965, the headlines read about two girls, college students, who were murdered and their bodies were found in the North part of the city? I can never forget the newscast on the TV screen of the young man's apartment who committed the crime— and I shall never forget the magazines that were lying on his coffee table! . . .

. . . In 1963, the editor of the *Southtown Globe-Times* reported the capture of a sixteen-year-old youth who admitted molesting four younger boys. He told the police that the idea for his crime came from a book he had read in which a man took two small boys to a park and molested them in the same manner. And so the scope of obscenity sweeps across the mass media.

. . . The first danger I think we have to be aware of is the perversion of the minds of young people and adults. The various societies for mental health view obscenity as a social ill that will wreck the well-being of the members. The second peril is seen in the insatiable desire for stimulation following reading materials. That is, some of the publications tend to start excitement and want the reader to finish up on it.

. . . Once initiated into a knowledge of the unnatural, the impressionable young mind with an insatiable curiosity characteristic of those reaching for maturity inevitably hunts for something stronger —something with more jolts—something imparting a greater kick.

The dealer in pornography is acutely aware of this progressive passage. His array of materials to feed this growing hunger is carefully geared to the successive stages. Like the peddler of narcotics his only interest is to insure that his customers are hooked. . . .

A third particular danger is in the creation of the appeal for a philosophy of life completely devoid of ethical and moral principles. This kind of literature is not only disruptive of the morals in terms of sexual values, but it is destroying the morals in terms of parental control and respect for authority. . . .

A fourth fast-growing problem is the establishment of a growing market for the sale of pornographic pictures and writings bent on filling the pockets of unscrupulous publishers. . . .

Finally, the correlation between crime and obscenity is another major one that means much to me. . . . Case workers, law enforcers, and anyone who has contact with juvenile delinquents cite salacious literature as a contributing factor to the rise in juvenile crime. . . . The National Council of Juvenile Judges at their convention in 1956 . . . held that the characteristics of juvenile delinquency had changed as a result of the stimulation of these publications, as reflected in acts of violence, rape, torture, robbery, and even homicide.

. . . J. Edgar Hoover has stated that this is no time to hold a scholarly debate concerning the exact cause/effect relationship between obscenity and sex crimes. What we do know is that, in an overwhelming number of cases, the crime is associated with pornography. We know that sex criminals read it and are influenced by it. "I believe," he says, "that pornography is a major cause of sex violence. I believe if we can eliminate the distribution of such items from impressionable school-age children, we shall greatly reduce our frightening sex crime rate."

. . . Why is there growing concern, not only here, but in many communities throughout the nation? . . . why are we concerned, you and I? Are we seeking to be sensational, to capture the headlines, to feed some ego-inflated desires within our own bosom? I doubt that this is the reason.

(Applause)

For as you will soon discover, if you have not already, this is no popular cause. And some will venture to say as I've heard one academic person say, that we are all victims of a repressed sexual desire, and this is the way of satisfying libidinal drives, and our superegos protect us. Well, to believe this is to out-Freud Freud. Let me share with you what I believe to be my main reason for concern, and I hope yours. Pure and simple, it is this: the love for people.

(Applause)

We believe in the dignity and worth of every person. And we are diametrically opposed to any force or factor that maims, harms, hurts, manipulates that most valuable quantity, the human personality.

(Applause)

There is no doubt in my mind that this misuse of the most sacred and wonderful gift which we call our sexual nature, what that misuse does to people. That gift through which life is entrusted into this world; that gift through which American love is expressed; that gift which symbolizes the unity and fidelity and commitment two people make to each other for a lifetime, when that gift is taken and used for lucrative profits, when that gift is taken and used for insatiable self-application, when that gift is taken and used for personal exploitation and personal gain, when that gift is taken and used for satisfaction of perverse desires; then that use is wrong. . . .

. . . Air and water pollution must be dealt with by our generation. But there is a most precious commodity even more important than air and water, and that commodity is the lives, the spirits, the emotions of your youth. What about mind pollution? How long are we going to sit in the rocking chair of apathy while our youth are being brainwashed with the garbage of obscenity?

(Applause)

. . . For the sake of our children, for the sake of our nation and for the sake of our way of life, the flood of filth must be stopped.

(Lengthy applause)

The decency rally in which the speeches quoted above were presented took place during the mobilization-for-action stage of Smelser's value-added scheme (see Chapter 6). The speeches themselves, therefore, were given after key precipitating factors (Chapter 5) had incited the mobilization for action. But the generalized beliefs represented in the speeches were manifested in a consistent and integrated fashion by Mr. King, his Knights of Columbus colleagues, crusade participants, and other respondents. Early in the development of the Southtown antipornography crusade, Mr. King and his Knights of Columbus colleagues had expressed the beliefs that the problem in Southtown was lack of "family film entertainment." During the months in which the crusade evolved, that belief expanded in proportion, redefining the problem more broadly to be pornography and its correlates in a context of erosive social change. "Pornography," as one of Mr. King's colleagues summarized, "is leading us to the fall of Rome and the pit of hell."

Discussion

The generalized beliefs manifested among the assorted Midville and Southtown sources contained several significant themes.

Belief in God was explicitly stated to be not only exemplary, but based in the very roots of America and patriotism. Atheists implicitly were equated with Communists, and there were strong opinions that a Communist conspiracy was focused upon education and entertainment, among other social institutions.

Liberalism was construed as being dangerous and as having its well-springs in secondary schools, colleges, and universities. Adults who tended to accept a liberal philosophy were held to be weak-kneed, and Americans in general were perceived to be growing less and less able to think for themselves. This sort of weakness was presented as providing Russia with the opportunity to take over the United States without a shot being fired. Citizens were admonished to wake up.

Young people in particular were cited as being vulnerable to the influence of liberal propaganda, and the obligation to protect them against such messages was stressed. A conflict was described between freedom of the press and the invasion of the community moral conscience. That invasion was construed as jeopardizing the democratic system and serving only special-interest groups.

Human nature was seen as essentially weak and easy prey to temptation. Those who had not fallen to temptation were presented as having an obligation to protect those who might fall. Confusing and detrimental acceleration of change had taken place in the United States, led by outright conspirators or by those who naïvely counseled change.

The United States was depicted as being in a state of moral disintegration, with basic values being eroded ever more rapidly. Law and order were seen as breaking down, and comparisons were drawn with the fall of other great civilizations. The prevalence of pornography was a clear manifestation of a general moral decline; it was seen to be either a tool of those conspirators who would destroy the nation from within or a tool of ruthless profiteers who did not care about the nation and its young people. The use of pornographic material was associated, causally or correlatively, with venereal disease, drug usage, sex crimes of all sorts, the failure of marriages, juvenile delinquency, failure in school, loss of religion, disrespect for authority, parent-child difficulties, arson, theft, purse-snatching, mugging, and murder. At the highest level of abstraction, pornography was seen as causally related to the general decline of basic values in American society.

The Conporns saw themselves not as censors or vigilantes but as individuals who were concerned about freedom—their freedom and the freedom of their children. They described their actions as the result not of pettiness or irrationality but of a sense of responsibility for the greater good of society. It was argued that citizens must take a stand, lest they have their own freedoms and style of life restricted or devalued by purveyors of pornography. Antipornography activity itself was equated with patriotism, with religion, with virtue, and with respect for the dignity of human beings.

It was indicated that those who opposed pornography and were willing to take action against it were not alone. A momentum was observed to be sweeping the nation—a momentum of righteous individuals who were no longer going to stand by passively while all they respected and valued was challenged by individuals and events urging or stimulating dangerous alternatives. Those comments hinted at the dynamics which some months later would be illustrative of the awakening of the "silent majority."

It was agreed that local government and law enforcement officials were unable to do anything about the problem of pornography because their hands had been tied by ineffective laws and by Supreme Court decisions favorable to "smut peddlers." It was felt that individuals or groups had to do something on their own to rectify the situation —specifically, they would need to bring attention to the problem and thus arouse the citizenry; they would have to bring what law there was to bear upon "smut peddlers," even if it was not totally effective; they would have to work to inaugurate new legislation and establish it in the existing city ordinances and state statutes; they would have to join together with other like-minded individuals in a demonstration of strength; they would have to take action which would result in informing local merchants and law-enforcement officials about the "real" level of community standards. It was thought that to engage in such activities successfully would reaffirm and bolster flagging American basic values, would reaffirm the life style of genuine Americans, would protect young people and vulnerable adults from being corrupted, and would punish or destroy the efficacy of those individuals ("smut peddlers") who were generating and profiting from the problem.

Smelser stated that "generalized norm-oriented beliefs may build up in various ways. They may develop gradually over decades in a 'literature'; they may crystallize in the mind of a single man or woman; they may be hammered out in a manifesto or party platform, they may be imported from one cultural setting into another" (1962:293). The generalized beliefs expressed by the Conporns had many sources, several of them lodged in networks of social interaction involving the Conporns and generating emergent norms for belief and for behavior (Turner and Killian 1957; 1972). Such sources included: newspaper and magazine stories and editorials; speeches and statements by prestige-ful individuals; conservative political tracts; personal observation; conversations with associates; religious sermons; PTA speeches; pres-entations made in meetings of other voluntary association; bulletins and pamphlets from assorted national or regional religious and anti-pornography organizations; and personal interpretations of the prob-lem by leaders and cadre of the local antipornography crusades.

According to Gusfield (1963:79), temperance crusaders, like Con-porns, believed their own life style to be a model of right-thinking de-cency and to be representative of that of the majority of American citi-zens. The temperance crusaders very much wanted other individuals to be like themselves. Furthermore, they, like the Conporns, tended to view human nature (especially in young persons) as "weak" and high-ly temptable.

The temperance crusaders felt that power, prestige, and even in-come were legitimately tied to the values of the sober, industrious, middle-class citizen (Gusfield 1963:85). In the generalized beliefs dis-cussed above, the antipornography crusaders also associated decency with reward structures inherent in the traditional American way of life. Some of the Conporns, in fact, became particularly agitated when they learned that the local "smut peddlers" were earning rather large sums of money.

Gusfield drew on Hofstadter's (1954) analysis, according to which Populist appeals were based essentially upon a theory of conspiracy. According to the theory, heinous individuals in the industrialized cities of the East had manipulated currency, taxes, and government policy for their own advantage. Legislatures and governmental sys-tems were bribed, gerrymandered, and rigged. "Ordinary people" were preyed upon and cheated by the "Easterners." Gusfield sug-gested that Populist and Prohibitionist ideologies were bridged by impressions of conspiracy. The Populist assumption of malevolence and profiteering could easily be extrapolated to the impact of "liquor trusts" upon "good people's" attempts to stop immoral trade in alcohol (Gusfield 1963:97). The Conporns' generalized beliefs, at the higher level of abstraction, included perceptions of conspiracies. The conspiracies, however, were those in which individuals and groups of individuals advertently or inadvertently were causing the moral ruin of the nation. The crusaders felt cheated, not financially but culturally—they were being robbed of the prestige frequently associated with their chosen style of life, which they perceived to be *the* American style of life.

Gusfield observed that moral indignation often indicates threatened status. The injured party must demonstrate that the deviates have violated not only the crusaders' expectations but also the expectations of other citizens. Thus the threatened party takes steps to show publicly, and perhaps dramatically, that his or her expectations are in fact societally widespread and legitimate.

According to Gusfield, attempts to maintain or enhance status against challenge more often than not have become fundamentalist reactions. There was a revivalistic tone to the activities of the temperance crusaders and a preoccupation with the regeneration of values in such areas as family life, child training, and religion. Gusfield reported that the temperance crusaders depicted American life as having fallen from its earlier position of virtue, very much after the fashion of Rome or Greece (and possibly with the same ultimate consequences). The crusaders called for restoration of such basic values as truth, honesty, recognition of authority, morality, and respect for age (Gusfield 1963:144). That sort of fundamentalist action, with revivalistic and regenerative tones, was apparent among the generalized beliefs of both Midville and Southtown Conporns.

Summarizing some aspects of status interest and conflict, Gusfield reflected upon the operation of generalized beliefs:

> Precisely because prestige is far from stable in a changing society, specific issues can become structured as tests of status when they are construed as symbols of group moralities and life styles. A civil liberties issue, such as domestic Communism, takes much of its affect and meaning from the clashes between traditionalized and modernist groups in American culture. Elements of educational sophistication, religious secularism, or political liberalism may appear as alien, foreign, and in direct contradiction to the localistic ways of life of the traditional oriented culture. Issues of civil liberties

become fields on which such cultural and educational groups fight to establish their claims to public recognition and prestige.

In his analysis of McCarthyism, Peter Vierick [1955:91–116] has referred to just this kind of process in characterizing the attack on officials in the State Department. Vierick placed one source of this attack in the feeling of degradation which the Midwestern, agricultural middle class felt at political domination by the aristocracy of the Eastern Seaboard, educated at Ivy League schools and so prominent in State Department affairs. They symbolized the State Department personnel as "striped-pants diplomats" and "cookie pushers." "Against the latter . . . the old Populist and LaFollette weapon against diplomats of 'you internationalist Anglo-phile snob' was replaced by 'you egghead security risk'."

In the struggle between groups for prestige and social position, the demands for deference and the protection from degradation are channeled into government and into such institutions of cultural formation as schools, churches, and media of communication. Because these institutions have power to affect public recognition, they are arenas of conflict between opposing status groups. Their ceremonial, ritual, and policy are matters of interest for status groups as well as for economic classes. (Gusfield 1963:175).

The generalized beliefs of the Conporns in Midville and Southtown contrasted their life style with those of persons educationally sophisticated, religiously secular, politically liberal, modernist, and associated with the "now generation" and with those of the users, supporters, or passive tolerators of pornography. The modernists were believed to be getting too much attention from the media and too much prestige from significant individuals at the expense of the Conporns.

The temperance crusaders believed that the use of alcohol was associated with all kinds of social pathology (Gusfield 1963:30–35). The Conporns in Midville and Southtown held a similar belief about the correlates of pornography.

Smelser (1962:111–112) suggested that the generalized belief in a norm-oriented movement associates the frustrations of structural strain with a specific source and holds that a particular kind of normative reorganization, such as passage of a law or establishment of a regulatory agency, will immobilize, damage, remove, or destroy the source. The broader concerns of the strain "short-circuit" to a labeled enemy and remedy. Smelser added: "Those who adhere to normative beliefs endow themselves and the envisioned reconstitution of norms with enormous power, conceived as the ability to overcome that array of threats and obstacles which constitute the negative side of the adherents' world-picture. The proposed reform will render opponents helpless, and will be effective immediately . . . . Because of this exaggerated potency, adherents often see unlimited bliss in the future if only the reforms are adopted. For if they are adopted, they argue, the basis for threat, frustration, and discomfort will disappear" (1962:117).

Thus the generalized beliefs in norm-oriented movements promise "extraordinary results . . . if only certain reforms are adopted, and (on the negative side) gloomy predictions of decay and collapse if the sources of strain are not attacked quickly and vigorously. Adherents to such movements exaggerate reality because their action is based on beliefs which are both generalized and short-circuited" (1962:72). Smelser further observed that "normative movements frequently display the world-view of conflicting forces of good and evil which characterize many types of generalized beliefs—two omnipotent forces locked in combat" (1962:118).

The generalized beliefs manifested by Conporns in Midville and Southtown clearly match the characteristics of generalized beliefs described by Smelser as being typical of norm-oriented movements. The Conporns diagnosed a malaise in American society, an erosion in basic values, engendered both by inadvertent but accelerating social change and by deliberate conspiratorial social change. Pornography was taken to typify the changes, to symbolize the erosion, and to represent (or to *be*) the source of the changes. The crusaders described a battle of good and evil, predicting the victory of good but also predicting dire consequences if action was not taken by those whose life style exemplified the good. The action urged by the Conporns centered on norm modification (the development of new antipornography laws, the modification of old ones) or on norm validation (engaging in action which would force antipornography laws to a test and which would involve the "smut peddlers"). It was believed that such action would control, damage, or punish the responsible agents, the "smut peddlers," and would reaffirm the life style of the crusaders (thus easing the structural strain). Also, it was believed that such action would have remarkable impact upon the societal malaise, making well again the state of the nation and soundly re-establishing the basic values.

The expressions of intended action were more specific among

Southtowners than among Midvillians. The Southtowners, Mr. King and his colleagues, very specifically incorporated into their generalized beliefs the determination that the state antipornography statutes should be changed, should be "toughened." They believed that no other form of action, norm-oriented or otherwise, would be as effective or as appropriate. Subsequent precipitating factors (Chapter 5) would reaffirm that belief. Mrs. Roberts and her ICCD colleagues, on the other hand, were less certain what kind of action should be taken, except that it should somehow make more effective the imposition of normative controls upon pornography and what it represented. The idea of "toughening" antipornography statutes was part of that broad but somewhat vague belief concerning normative action. Subsequent precipitating factors would sharpen that belief and delimit a specific strategy. The differences between the Midville and the Southtown Conporns in specificity of the action among their generalized beliefs was to contribute to the greater volatility of the Midville antipornography crusade (as did the greater degree of Midville structural conduciveness and structural strain).

Smelser noted that in the early stages of a norm-oriented social movement the generalized beliefs "are marked by diffuse discontent, informal methods—random verbal statements, scattered protest meetings, rumors, speculations, etc., predominate. As the beliefs crystallize, more formal methods of pamphleteering, advertising, publicizing, and arranging mass lectures and demonstrations receive more emphasis" (1962:293). That pattern of development was apparent in both the Midville and the Southtown antipornography crusades—from smaller, informal meetings to larger; formal meetings; from exploratory, relatively uncoordinated protest (letters, proclamations, etc.) to intentional, coordinated strategies; from word-of-mouth communication processes to structured advertising, systematic use of the media, and coordinated use of communication channels in formal voluntary associations.

Turner (1964) analyzed the interactive and emergent process of generalized beliefs (conceptualized as rumor) in forms of collective behavior.[1] He noted that, in the process, "conceptions are developed, tested, selected, and rounded out as part of a preparation for action or as a support for action already under way" (1964:404). The belief tended to use ambiguity and situations where "traditional understandings fail to supply a basis for definition, and institutional arrangements do not adequately coordinate action" (1964:403). Emergent beliefs are particularly important if "events occur which threaten the normal understandings underlying daily action" (1964:405). Turner observed that generalized beliefs became sharpened by the mechanisms of keynoting, symbolization, and coordination. *Keynoting* "refers to the phenomenon in which a gesture or symbolic utterance made to an undecided and ambivalent audience crystallizes sentiment" (1964: 407). *Symbolization* is that part of the process which "serves to bring symbols into selective salience and to reconstitute their meanings in relation to shared requirements for action" (1964:407). The symbol "must have applicability to the situation and must formulate the situation in such a fashion as to simplify and clarify action. Aside from referring to the situation at hand in some crucial sense, the symbol must be nonspecific in character. Words like 'liberty,' 'peace,' and 'states' rights' have sufficiently vague referents that they can be fitted to many different situations—sometimes even with contradictory implications—and people with rather different viewpoints can join in their use" (1964:407). The symbols serve to legitimate the emerging collective behavior, and to identify the target for action. The mechanism for *coordination* sharpens the participants' perception of their concerted (rather than independent) action. It "enhances its [participant's] sense of power, and whatever conveys a sense of strength reinforces the sense of rightness. Symbolic references to invincibility shade imperceptibly into legitimating symbols of manifest destiny, the wave of the future" (1964:409). (Keynoting, symbolization, and coordination will also be seen operating in the emergence and impact of precipitating factors, in Chapter 5.)

The generalized beliefs expressed by Midville and Southtown Conporns fit well with those processes described by Turner. The content of the beliefs included the weakening or failing of institutions and traditional understandings for behavior and indicated some confusion about expectations concerning the routines of day-to-day life. The mechanism of keynoting, in the form of speeches and specific events, sharpened the beliefs concerning societal malaise, undue change, and the role of pornography in those processes. Feelings of invincibility, rightness, power, strength, duty, and ultimate victory manifested the mechanism of coordination. Symbolization was markedly present among the generalized beliefs of Conporns. In fact, the beliefs represented a veritable orgy of symbolizing—patriotic, religious, moral, and political. The symbols were sufficiently vague to serve as conceptual umbrellas for participants with a wide diversity of interests and motives.

The generation of symbols as a vocabulary for action was central to Gusfield's (1963) analysis of temperance crusades. Status discontent evolved, communicated, and then rallied around highly abstract moral catchwords and legitimated the symbolic crusade in those terms. Similarly, the Conporns established their vocabulary for action around such abstract symbols as basic values—their erosion, the specific threats to them, the sources of the threats, and the obligations for defense. Status is in and of itself a symbolic process. It is not surprising, therefore, that the defense of challenge to status (by status discontents) could as one option be conducted with symbolic justifications and manipulations (see also Klapp 1972:91–110, 146–161).

Smelser (1962:119) stated that, because of the hierarchical nature of the components of action, intentions to restructure or defend norms include the intention to restructure or defend roles, social organizations, reward distributions, and situational facilities; the norm-oriented generalized beliefs also would incorporate beliefs relevant to components of action lower on the hierarchy. Following Smelser, we hypothesized earlier (Chapter 1) that the antipornography crusaders would, in their generalized beliefs, cite the acceptance of, commitment to, and concern over basic societal values, and that they would act collectively to restore, protect, modify, or create norms in the name of a generalized belief. We hypothesized that the generalized belief (or beliefs) would call for new laws or regulatory devices concerning pornography, which would be intended to control the "irresponsible" behavior of others. Those "others" would be believed to be deviating from established patterns of behavior and thereby to be threatening social order and basic values. We hypothesized that the generalized beliefs would include concerns about the stability of traditional social institutions, about the continuity of prestige received as a reward for enacting roles in those institutions, and about the usefulness of one's knowledges, skills, and perspectives for predicting the consequence of one's own behavior and for controlling significant aspects of the environment which impinge upon everyday life. Those hypotheses concerning the content of the generalized belief are taken to be supported. Thus, it can be seen that the generalized beliefs (Smelser 1962) espoused by and in ICCD and UFD contained (*a*) norm-oriented beliefs (a call for a new rule, law, or regulatory agency intended to control the inappropriate behavior of others); (b) hostile beliefs (an identification of the source taken to be responsible for an ambiguous but stressful situation and the assumption that the ambiguity and strain can be eliminated by removing or restricting the group[s] labeled as culpable); (c) hysterical beliefs (an assignment to some ambiguous entity of both the power and the intention to threaten or destroy); and (d) wish-fulfilling beliefs (an assumption that some powerful force, object, or behavior can successfully neutralize or defeat a frustrating, dangerous, or destructive agent of some kind). As the natural histories reveal, the generalized beliefs in ICCD manifested more intense hostility, hysteria, and wish-fulfillment than those in UFD.

Again following Smelser, we hypothesized that the generalized beliefs would manifest the "short-circuiting" process, skipping from a very generalized belief component directly to a concrete focus of strain (a target). The content of the generalized beliefs expressed by Conporns in Midville and Southtown is taken to support that hypothesis. That is, the antipornography crusaders, having expressed a feeling of strain concerning their ability to predict and control their social environment and concerning the prestige they felt should have been associated with their enactment of traditional social roles, perceived the general source of the strain to be the challenge to basic values and traditions by the enactors of alternative life styles. Pornography and, more concretely, certain "adult" bookstores and theaters were perceived to be symbolic representations of the alternative and challenging life styles and were specifically and dramatically labeled as sources of evil. The generalized belief held that laws pertaining to pornography, to "adult" bookstores and theaters, were inadequate. If the old laws were strengthened or made operational, or if new laws were introduced, pornography, the bookstores and the theaters, and the alternative life styles they represented would be punished, immobilized, damaged, or destroyed. The short-circuiting process was completed with the belief that the normative changes would once and for all sweepingly remove or in some way neutralize or offset the original source of strain, the alternative and challenging life styles.[2]

Some significant precipitating factors were perceived to verify the generalized beliefs, and these prepared the antipornography crusades for mobilization. Those precipitating factors will be discussed in Chapter 5. In Chapter 8, questionnaire data will be presented which further support the interpretations made concerning the content of the generalized beliefs.

Chapter 5

Precipitating Factors: "Dung in Our

Own Nest, As It Were!"

Midville

As discussed in Chapter 2, ICCD has been incorporated and operating more or less actively since late 1965. Though none of the initial efforts approached the level of mobilization which was to burst forth in 1969, the summation of those efforts could be interpreted to have served as a precipitating factor. A number of the early efforts convinced ICCD participants and observers that some success could be achieved toward "stamping out smut." Before and after incorporation of ICCD, Mrs. Roberts and the cadre were instrumental in effecting, at least temporarily, the following successes: "cleaner" newsracks in some drugstores; removal of a "girlie show" from the local fair; prohibition of objectionable advertisements for objectionable movies in the *Midville News*; scheduling of "mature" movies at later times on television; better street lighting in a problem area of Midville; closing of an "adult" theater after charges of false advertising; modification of the Midville antipornography ordinance; increased police action concerning pornography; getting Action for Decency Day proclaimed in Midville. The summation of some of the early failures could also be interpreted to have served as a precipitating factor: the Supreme Court judgment that the Midville antipornography statute was unconstitutional; other Supreme Court decisions concerning pornography and decency-related issues; the inability of Midville police and courts to convict "smut peddlers" against whom charges had been filed.

In late 1968 and early 1969, however, three major events took place in Midville which were clearly precipitating factors and not part of the earlier components of structural conduciveness. Those three events were the Midville speech of Raymond P. Gauer, Mrs. Roberts' visit to the Midwestern Bookstore, and the *Midville News* exposé of the Midwestern Bookstore.

The Midville Speech of Raymond P. Gauer

Late in the summer of 1968, Dr. Henry, director of the Midville Public Health Department and a member of ICCD, planned a seminar on the social problems of venereal disease and illegitimacy. In connection with that seminar, Dr. Henry contacted Mrs. Roberts and asked her for the name of someone, preferably a psychologist, who could "prove that pornography causes V.D." Mrs. Roberts gave Dr. Henry the name of Raymond P. Gauer, the executive director of Citizens for Decent Literature. Dr. Henry called Mr. Gauer and invited him to come to Midville and speak. Mr. Gauer agreed, and on October 23, 1968, jointly sponsored by ICCD and the Midville Public Health Department, Mr. Gauer visited Midville. On the afternoon of October 23, he gave a luncheon speech to twenty-five members of local law-enforcement agencies. That evening he spoke at a public meeting.

The entire transcripts of Mr. Gauer's two speeches in Midville were not available. ICCD did have, however, a mimeographed Gauer speech, which was headed "Typical CDL Speech." The following selected quotes illustrate some of the major points concerning the problem of pornography emphasized by Mr. Gauer during his Midville presentations:

> The average decent adults in our society are just not aware of the serious nature of the problem. . . .
> . . . [CDL] set out with a two-pronged attack . . . number one, to educate the public to the serious nature of the problem . . . number two, to direct this educated public opinion to a solution to this problem through the law. . . . We say there are laws on the books and we as citizens have not only the right but actually the responsibility to participate in the enforcement of these laws. . . . I have stressed the responsibility of individual *citizen participation* in the enforcement of obscenity laws. . . . As a result of this concentrated effort, there are today more arrests, more prosecutions and more convictions being achieved in this area of law than ever before in the history of this country. A real indication of this is the fact that a law suit was filed recently in the Federal District Court in Los Angeles against CDL by one of the largest smut publishers

for $3,000,000. He claims his business has been severely hampered and is on the verge of destruction, as a result of our activity on a national scale. We consider this to be the best news we've had. A direct indication that these people can be reached and are being reached and will be reached, even more effectively, if enough citizens will speak out and demand this kind of action.

Mr. Gauer, in his "typical speech," then proceeded to discuss the terms *average person*, *applying contemporary community standards*, *material to be considered as a whole*, and *prurient interests*, as they were relevant to Supreme Court decisions. In discussing the average person, he argued that a jury may be most representative and that it is not up to a policeman, not up to a judge, but up to the average person as best measured by a jury to determine what is pornographic and what is not. He considered that the citizens of the community have the right to establish what their contemporary community standards are and when those standards have been violated. Both of those definitions emphasized very clearly Mr. Gauer's urging for community action, for citizen participation. In his review of the major Supreme Court decisions, Mr. Gauer commented: "That's one of the problems with decisions from the high court that are favorable to the industry [pornography]. They immediately stand ready to go far beyond that which had previously been proscribed." He added that many of the lesser court decisions were reversed by the Supreme Court with "five-four decisions, to which they just signed their name, with no written explanation. So, in effect, we have five men in Washington, who can't even agree among themselves as to the reason for so doing, imposing their own standards on all fifty states of the Union, whether we like it or not."

Mr. Gauer expressed what "prosecutors throughout the country" felt concerning Supreme Court decisions. They "threw their hands up and said, 'What's the use?' We can get a conviction in our own community, it will be upheld in our State Courts and our State Supreme Courts, but the U.S. Supreme Court will kick it out, so *why bother?*" As a result, Mr. Gauer reported, the publication of pornography had increased markedly, as had its distribution, throughout the United States. Consequently, Mr. Gauer introduced "the issue of whether or not the jurisdiction should be removed from the Supreme Court in this area of law." He suggested that "obscenity cases should be left with the State courts, and not subject to appeal to the Supreme Court."

Perhaps as a way of showing the strength of CDL, or the efficacy of direct action, Mr. Gauer reported the influence that CDL had, in Washington, by direct contact with senators, in the defeat of Abe Fortas's appointment as Chief Justice of the Supreme Court. (CDL's primary objection to Fortas was that he, in 1957, had been defense attorney for a publisher of a "girlie" magazine. Subsequently, Fortas was "sitting on the bench where he was to rule in behalf of his former client.")

Mr. Gauer then outlined, in his "typical speech," what action a person might take "in this day and age of big government" when the "individual sometimes wonders, 'What can I possibly do?'" He stated, "I might tell you I've been involved in this work for a long time and I know lots of things that don't work. One thing that doesn't work is to go around and talk to the guys in the community selling this kind of stuff and say, 'How about being a nice guy and get rid of your dirty books.'" He continued, "If you see material in your community that you consider to be below the standards of the community, the most effective thing you can do is report the situation to those responsible for enforcing the law. That is your local police, your city prosecutor or district attorney." Mr. Gauer stated that citizen complaints accomplish at least four important things:

1. Every complaint indicates that the standards of the community are being violated. . . .
2. Every complaint indicates that there will be support for any action taken by law enforcement or prosecution in this area.
3. And probably most important of all—every complaint must be investigated. Just the fact that the vice squad officers are checking on outlets in the community, as a result of citizen complaints, can go a long way to discourage the display and sale of such material. . . .
4. And of course most important of all is that the complaint by you as a concerned citizen can trigger the whole mechanism that can result in the arrest, the prosecution and the conviction of the criminal who is producing, distributing or selling the material in your community.

Mr. Gauer closed his "typical speech" by quoting Edmund Burke as having said, "All that is required for the triumph of evil is for good men to do nothing." Mr. Gauer added, "All that's required for pornographers to take over completely our newsstands, our United States mail, our theaters, is for you, the good people of the community, who are concerned, to do nothing. So if you agree that there is a problem and that a workable solution has been offered, I say, for God's sake, make your voice heard and do something."

Some of the quotes from Mr. Gauer's afternoon speech in Midville appeared in the *Midville News* (October 24, 1969) and were quite similar to statements made in his "typical speech." His evening speech also contained similar material. However, the evening speech, in part because of an experience he had that afternoon, contained several important and pointed references to the Midville "pornography problem."

According to Mrs. Roberts and Mrs. Nelson, after Mr. Gauer had completed his luncheon speech, members of ICCD asked him to go to the Midwestern Bookstore and see for himself what they were selling. Mr. Gauer was reported to have replied that he had seen such bookstores before and it was not necessary for him to see others. However, the ICCD leaders were adamant, and Mr. Gauer agreed to go. That night, at his dinner speech, after he had viewed the contents of the Midwestern Bookstore, he proclaimed: "The Midwestern Bookstore at 122 South Paine Street has one of the worst displays of obscene literature in the country. In seventy major cities I have never seen a worse display of material—it is unbelievable." Mr. Gauer advised the group of citizens to "complain to their law enforcement authorities and get the owner arrested—he has no legitimate leg to stand on."

Mr. Gauer's statement, reproduced in the *Midville News* (October 24, 1968), electrified the ICCD members and, according to their report, "the entire community of Midville." The All-America City had "one of the worst displays of obscene literature in the country." As one ICCD member proclaimed in disgust, "We have discovered dung in our own nest, as it were!"

Mrs. Roberts, Mrs. Nelson, and others of the ICCD cadre asked Mr. Gauer what specifically they could do in order to take action against the Midwestern Bookstore. He was reported to have told them they could best take action by going into the bookstore and buying two copies of a book that was clearly "hardcore pornography." They should give one copy of the book to the vice squad and hand carry (to avoid legal difficulties with the public mail) the other copy to a group of community leaders.

Mrs. Roberts's Visit to the Midwestern Bookstore

Mrs. Roberts, Mrs. Nelson, and their colleagues in ICCD thought about and discussed Mr. Gauer's advice for over a month. In November, 1968, Mrs. Roberts and Mrs. Nelson decided to visit the Midwestern Bookstore, to purchase some books, and to pass them on to the vice squad and to selected community leaders.

According to Mrs. Nelson, "At first we were apprehensive about entering the bookstore; so we dressed up in old clothes so we wouldn't look out of place." On the morning of their intended visit to the bookstore, Mrs. Roberts went to Mrs. Nelson's house, where they knelt and prayed together. According to Mrs. Nelson, "We normally pray individually each morning, but this morning we decided to pray together." The two women concluded that, if they could not find a convenient parking place near the Midwestern Bookstore, they would not go in, for that would be an indication that "God did not approve of our actions." They drove from Mrs. Nelson's home to the downtown area and, as reported by Mrs. Nelson, "It was hard to believe that on a busy day in downtown Midville, where there is never any parking place, there was a parking place right in front of the bookstore." Somewhat hesitantly and quite nervously, the two women went into the front part of the bookstore, walked to the door against the back wall, and entered the back room. The women took a few minutes to look around the store, "to make sure we got a copy of a book which was hard-core pornography." They purchased two copies of the book *Bitches in Heat*, by Carson Davis (1968), and two copies of a photograph portfolio. After making the purchases, the women immediately returned home.

The emotional experience of entering the Midwestern Bookstore and buying the materials was quite intense for both of the women. Mrs. Nelson reflected, "We could not eat, we wept, we felt dirty, and as we read our Bible we couldn't get the other books out of our mind."

The following day Mrs. Roberts and Mrs. Nelson took a copy of *Bitches in Heat* to the Midville police department vice squad. Mrs. Roberts then contacted the Chamber of Commerce and obtained a list of the presidents of all the clubs and civic organizations in Midville. From that list, they compiled a shorter list of sixteen community leaders, using mentions in newspaper articles as criteria to determine which leaders would be most likely to favor their cause and which leaders "had expressed interest in the welfare of Midville in the past."

The sixteen persons chosen included Mr. Wallace, editor of the *Midville News*; Mr. Vance, president of the Second National Bank; Mayor Tucker, mayor of Midville; Mr. Parker, head of the Midville Youth Protection Services; Mr. Morton, owner of the Morton Insurance Agency; Mrs. Thompson, an active leader in community and state affairs; Mr. Gilbert, president of the Gilbert Grocery Company; Dr. Sullivan, superintendent of the Midville Public School System; Mrs. Wright, dean of students at Central Junior High School; and seven other prominent business or agency men and women. The selections made by Mrs. Roberts and Mrs. Nelson were a fairly adequate representation of the Midville community power structure.

Mrs. Roberts and Mrs. Nelson spent the day after they had visited the Midwestern Bookstore preparing their distribution list and tearing up *Bitches in Heat* into four-page sections, making sure that each excerpt contained what in their view was "hard-core pornography." They also prepared a memo to accompany the material which was to be distributed among community leaders. The memo, suggested to them by Mr. Gauer and by members of the vice squad, read as follows:

MEMO

The enclosed pages have been torn from a paperback book purchased at the Midwestern Bookstore, 122 South Paine Street. You are one of sixteen prominent persons from this area to be sent similar material from the same book. A second copy of this has been taken to the Midville County Prosecutor's Office with a request that it be inspected to determine if it is in violation of the State Laws on obscenity. The complaint was signed by a number of persons.

We are following the procedure recommended by Mr. Raymond P. Gauer, National Executive Secretary for Citizens for Decent Literature, to arouse the indignation of the community and to get action to remove this blight from our downtown area. It is of considerable concern that it is located on one of our main streets and across from the Tisdale Hotel where Midville Valley College students are being housed.

The contents of almost every page of this book, and hundreds of other books, are equally vile—or worse! An entire wall—top to bottom—several rows deep—is lined with magazines of the most disgusting nude poses imaginable, not artistic . . . but the "sick" and perverse approach. Mr. Gauer said "in seventy major cities,

I have never seen as large or a worse display of obscene materials—
it's unbelievable! Get the owner arrested. He has no legitimate leg
to stand on."

Obscenity has been defined by the U.S. Supreme Court in 1957
as material below the standards set by the community. Do you
consider this material below *your* standards? Or is it acceptable for
our community? To date, the arrests made have not resulted in
convictions because no community standards have been expressed
by the citizens. Would you express your opinion so that together
we may define community standards? Send a note at once to either
the County Prosecutor, Midville County Courthouse, or to Inter-
Denominational Citizens Council for Decency, Incorporated.

The memo was signed by Mrs. Nelson and Mrs. Roberts, representing
ICCD.

Bitches in Heat was typical of the "generalist" sexually explicit paperbacks available in the Midwestern Bookstore. The pages described
episodes of cunnilingus, fellatio, oral and anal intercourse, group sex
acts, some sadomasochism, and some homosexuality. It had a very
weak story line, with a "girls should be careful" and "young girls
should be protected" morality message. The portfolio of photographs,
which had been divided into one-page segments by Mrs. Roberts and
Mrs. Nelson, contained pictures of females, with exposed genitalia in a
state of excitation. Mrs. Roberts and Mrs. Nelson prepared sixteen
brown-envelope packets, each containing the memo, four pages from
Bitches in Heat, and one photograph from the portfolio.

Mrs. Roberts and Mrs. Nelson then decided that, if they were able
to gain access to the "big and important men" with relative ease, then
"God approved of their actions." Mrs. Nelson reported that "the first
man we went to see, a big, busy man who didn't even know us, let us
right in. We walked up to his secretary and told her we wanted to hand
the envelope to him, and to our surprise we were immediately allowed
to see him." In fact, according to Mrs. Roberts and Mrs. Nelson, all
sixteen of the persons to whom they distributed the materials made
arrangements to see them immediately. The women interpreted this
as clear evidence of God's approval of their efforts.

Mrs. Nelson indicated that, after the pages of the books had been
delivered to the community leaders, "the lid blew off." Some of the
community leaders immediately wrote to the public prosecutor, and
others wrote to ICCD. Mr. Wallace, the editor of the *Midville News*, and

Mr. Young, a business executive, were particularly incensed. Mr. Wallace indicated that at first he had not even looked at the material that Mrs. Roberts and Mrs. Nelson had brought to him. He felt that they were probably just some "girlie magazines" similar to those that Mrs. Roberts had been concerned about in the past. However, he happened to have lunch with Mr. Young, who expressed his concern about the material and advised Mr. Wallace to look at it. Mr. Wallace went back to his office after lunch, looked at the material, and was "aghast." He then decided to have his paper do a series of articles on pornography and obscenity in Midville. Immediately, he sent two newspaper reporters to the Midwestern Bookstore, instructing them to gather information for the exposé. According to Mr. Wallace and Mrs. Nelson, one of the two reporters was accosted by a homosexual during his first visit to the Midwestern Bookstore.

The *Midville News* reporters called Mrs. Roberts and Mrs. Nelson to interview them about ICCD. The reporters indicated that several other persons they had interviewed had mentioned ICCD as being central in getting the sample material to influential persons in the community. Mrs. Roberts and Mrs. Nelson arranged interview appointments for the reporters with additional members of ICCD. According to one of the ICCD respondents, active ICCD members were asked to help prepare the series of articles, which with enthusiasm they did.

The Midville News Exposé of the Midwestern Bookstore

The January 13, 1969, issue of the *Midville News* carried two articles on pornography and obscenity in Midville, specifically about the Midwestern Bookstore. The first of those articles, headlined "Sex Bookstore Offers Something for Everyone," was the opening article in a series intended to call the Midwestern Bookstore to the attention of citizens. The second article, headlined "Public Reaction: Shock, Disbelief," reported the impact of the material circulated by Mrs. Roberts and Mrs. Nelson among the community leaders.

The "Sex Bookstore" article described in detail the physical setting of the Midwestern Bookstore and the general range of material available to the visitor. The first few paragraphs of the article read:

> Pay a buck and get your ticket: Then, step inside—there's no time limit.

Women, incidentally, are admitted free.

You can spend hours browsing through a variety of magazines or reading paperbacks with titles ranging from "Bitches in Heat" to "Hustling Homo."

Ashtrays, easy chairs, and even a sofa are provided. Some say a vomit receptacle also should be furnished.

Don't think about ordinary nudie or girlie magazines in connection with this place, the Midwestern Bookstore, 122 South Paine. Exhibited there is some of the rawest, vilest material found in print. . . .

The Midwestern Bookstore may well be the most advanced of its kind in the state. Experts have said it is the worst in the country for pornographic literature. . . .

It's all part of the Midwestern Bookstore's business philosophy of tantalizing the customer's sex buds with a wide selection of adult merchandise. (*Midville News*, January 13, 1969)

The "Public Reaction" article cited verbatim comments from some of the community leaders who had viewed the material. Among the quotes were the following:

"This is the most vile, vulgar, obscene literature I have ever read."

"You have no way of knowing how bad it is until someone shows you the materials. It was very shocking. There is no place for such a store and such literature in any city."

"A blight on the community."

"I was shocked and amazed that this type of material was being sold on the open market where it would be available to anyone. With this type of material, I don't think a store like this has a place anywhere. It can only serve to bring down the level of society's morals." (*Midville News*, January 13, 1969)

According to Mrs. Roberts, Mrs. Nelson, Mr. Wallace, and several members of ICCD, the articles in the *Midville News* had a dramatic impact on Midville citizens. Mrs. Roberts reported that "everybody began to talk about the Midwestern Bookstore and wonder what to do about it."

On the next day, January 14, 1969, another article in the *Midville News* series described the characteristics of the paperback books available at the bookstore. The title of the article was "Book Appeal Similar:

Buy Me, I'm about Sex." A second article appeared in the same issue, entitled, "Supreme Court, Key in Obscenity." Both of the articles began on page 1 of the newspaper.

The "Book Appeal" article read, in part:

> Tad went to the weekend cottage to seduce his brother's hot-bodied wife. But suddenly two desperate, thrill hungry fugitives crashed the scene with their nympho moll, and the party soon turned into an orgy.
>
> So reads the blurb on the cover of the "Copulation Explosion," on sale at the Midwestern Bookstore.
>
> This book is but one of hundreds of "documentaries," novels, and illustrated manuals that deal exclusively on the theme of sex, sex, and more sex.
>
> Other paperback titles and their cover blurbs include:
>
> "The Variations of Anal Intercourse: Often ridiculed as the practice indulged in only by homosexuals or farm boys, this frank study shows how this deviation is finding favor among people from every walk of life, in every income bracket at every age."
>
> "Lesbian Ward: An incisive analysis of the women who are trapped in a world of abnormal lust and who must bow to their unnatural cravings to survive."
>
> "Rape Me Lover: The increasing number of women who seek and need brutal treatment to arouse their sexuality."
>
> "Take My Tool, The Revelations of a Sex Switch."
>
> "Bull Nuts: He was hard as nails and as gay as they come."
>
> "The Demi-Wang. By Peter Long: Hilarious tale of Egbert, half a man physically, but all man in desire; . . ."
>
> The paperbacks deal with virtually every aspect of sex and the sex act between man and woman, man and man, woman and woman—even man and beast.
>
> There is something for every pervert—from the man who likes pictures of lesbians making love, to the homosexual who seeks out illustrated novels which leave little to the imagination.
>
> . . . A list of selected titles from the paperbacks includes: "Tit for Tat," "Only Do It Nude," "The Hairy Queens," "Rubber-mania," "Orgasmus," "Come Again," "Queers and Quickies," "Up the Groove," "Action Piece," "King Size," "Field Whore," "Sex on the Beach." (*Midville News*, January 14, 1969)

The "Supreme Court" article indicated that local and state courts had done little to prevent the sale or possession of obscene materials, because of the effect of the Warren Supreme Court decisions. It was reported that since 1967 eight charges involving six persons had been lodged by the Midville County prosecutor's office for violations of selling or offering for sale obscene literature, photographs, or film. Five of those cases had been dismissed, two were still pending, and one person had pleaded guilty. The article suggested that, unless the material was presented to a jury, convictions were virtually impossible.

In the January 15, 1969, issue of the *Midville News*, two more articles on pornography and obscenity appeared, again both on page 1. The first was headlined "Magazine Nude Photos Not Artistic Endeavor." The second, headlined "Intent Justifies Sex in Literature," discussed the difference between literature and pornography.

The "Magazine Nude Photos" article was particularly response-provoking in Midville, and read:

> It has a full-color cover.
>
> Pictured is a young nude female.
>
> She sits with her legs spread. Her arms rest on her knees. One hand reaches up to cover a pouting mouth. Her eyes glare. Wisps of stringy brown hair fall on her sagging breasts.
>
> "Susy" is the name of this magazine, one of the many stocked by the Midwestern Bookstore. . . .
>
> The female sex organs, pubic hair, bellies and breasts are pictured throughout the magazine, which bills itself as "for adults only," with "exciting stories," and "full color photos."
>
> The photos are taken from unusual angles and could hardly be classified as an artistic endeavor. The female nudes are flabby and sagging—but all-revealing.
>
> "Susy" is only one of over 100 girlie magazines sold at the store for $3 to $5. They differ only in their choice of nude female camera angles and poses.
>
> The magazine, however, isn't quite like "Lesbiana." . . .
>
> As its title suggests, the 66-page magazine depicts females cavorting with females. Some of them wrestle with each other in unusual poses. Some of them appear to be in the act of spanking each other.

Others are lying with legs draped around each other.

A blurb introducing a picture sequence of wrestling nude females reads:

"One of our models didn't show up for shooting so we talked our secretary (the blond) into standing in. The model is a local hooker here in Hollywood and she knew how to handle herself pretty well. Marty, our secretary, held out for about an hour of fighting and although she wasn't able to get a hold on the girl she did pretty good getting out of all the holds the other girl got on her. Even though some of the holds hurt like hell, Marty was too proud to admit defeat. The hooker finally pinned her shoulders to the mat with her knees and we counted Marty out. SOME FIGHT." . . .

In "Husky" there are 49 pictures of nude men, 11 in color. On one page two nude men sit looking at a magazine. One is perched on the other's leg. On other pages nude men are posed reclining, lying, sitting or standing. On many pages the male sex organs are the focal point of the camera. . . .

Family nude publications also are sold. These sport pictures of men, women and children in various at-home or recreation activities.

Sadism is a frequent theme in many of the magazines. Spanking, supposed sex murders are pictured.

All of them fall into one category however.

They exploit sex to make a buck. (*Midville News*, January 15, 1969)

The "Intent Justifies Sex" article of the January 15 issue presented a discussion of the current constitutional definition of obscenity and pornography. In particular, the article emphasized the "contemporary standards" issue and implied that the citizens of Midville ought to do something to demonstrate what those standards were.

Instead of further articles in the pornography series, there appeared in the *Midville News* on January 16, 1969, the following first-page editorial:

In this space since Monday, the *News* has been detailing the type of material on sale at the Midwestern Bookstore.

We have just scratched the surface.

Stories of perversion, sensuality, deterioration . . . we could fill all this space again today, and tomorrow, and tomorrow . . . and tomorrow . . . and tomorrow!

We are stopping now, not because the problem is solved, but because the point is made. No one in Midville who has read these stories can say that this "adult" bookstore is simply a harmless spot where girlie magazines are sold.

Whether it continues to operate will depend upon what you—the people of Midville—do now. (*Midville News*, January 16, 1969)

The earlier articles and editorials had indicated that there were to be further descriptive articles of the materials in the Midwestern Bookstore; the January 16 editorial indicated that no further such articles would be forthcoming. At least one of the reasons (and perhaps the most significant reason) why the series ceased was an unexpected aspect of reader response.

One hundred and forty-one letters to the editor were written concerning the *Midville News* series on the Midwestern Bookstore. Ninety-six of the letters favored the newspaper's series and opposed pornography for various expressed reasons. Twenty-eight letters opposed the series, primarily citing civil-libertarian reasons. Seventeen letters, although reflecting an opposition to pornography, also opposed the newspaper's series, on the basis that it was too vivid and was in itself pornographic. According to Mr. Wallace, the newspaper editor, sixty-two other persons canceled their subscriptions (the unexpected aspect) following the first two articles of the series. Some of the comments in the letters of cancellation were as follows:

If the *News* has the right to print vile, vulgar, and obscene words and book titles, they should not condemn a bookstore for selling such things . . . . Let me ask you, how would you answer a seven-year-old child asking "Mama, what is a *Hustling Homo?*" . . . What do you say to a twelve-year-old when he asks "What does *Humpers Wild* mean?" . . . I say to you, *Midville News*, you have carried the "freedom of the press" a bit too far. (January 19, 1969)

I have never in all my life read so much trash published in the *Midville News* as I have read in the last two days . . . . Why don't you editors start printing some of the truths found in God? (January 19, 1969)

Without even trying, not costing a cent, your *Midville News* has given those who run the Midwestern Bookstore a $1,000,000 advertising campaign. (January 20, 1969)

I am writing to you in regards to the filthy sex column you had in your paper. It made me sick to my stomach, dirtied my eyes and my mind, nauseated me. . . . Any good Christian could not read that without dirtying his or her mind and a guilty conscience. (January 21, 1969)

Mr. Wallace reported that he felt uncomfortable about those letters, understood the point of the persons so writing, and "felt unjustified in printing any more articles in the series."

As indicated, some of the letters to the editor opposed the series for its intent, rather than for its content:

Nothing in the adult bookstore is nearly as sick, or as sickening, as the sight of an editorial against freedom of the press by the one editor in the Midville Valley for whom I have any journalistic respect. . . . Why should you have the power to decide what I read? (January 16, 1969)

Your breed is typical of the hypocrite that will buy a book, read it from cover to cover, and then complain afterwards that it is obscene —after having enjoyed each word thoroughly. Your guilt complex takes over and you are repulsed by yourself for having enjoyed such material. . . . You who are doing all the complaining, obviously have read some of the material, therefore, I contend that your morals have been corrupted and that you are not competent to judge or censor anything. (January 19, 1969)

They are the same passions which would burn a "witch" at the stake or drive a "Communist" from the country. (January 21, 1969)

I would expect you to lead a crusade against anything sexier than the Immaculate Conception! (March 19, 1969)

. . . the use of this issue as a public scapegoat to avoid confronting the immorality of hunger, war, and white racism. (March 19, 1969)

The large majority of the letters to the editor, however, wholeheartedly supported the series. Several of the letters, as indicated below, called for action against the Midwestern Bookstore:

I believe that today we citizens of Midville should do everything in our power to remove the Midwestern Bookstore, 122 South Paine, and any others like it from our community. (January 15, 1969)

But, I am appalled that this so-called 'adult bookstore' should be allowed to sell to and expose the young people of Midville to such "pure trash"! . . . Our Lord has not created the human body to be used in such an obnoxious, distasteful manner as found in this material. . . . I intend to contact the Interdenominational Citizens Council for Decency. . . . What will you do? (January 21, 1969)

Perhaps the tide can be turned and wouldn't it be wonderful if it all started here in Midville and only because the *Midville News* had the courage to start it! (January 21, 1969)

Too many people in and around Midville were not aware that the old "filth peddler" had set up shop in our own home town. (January 24, 1969)

We've had enough of words. Pages of them. Now it's time for action. Good, solid, American PEOPLE action. Legal action. Mere letters to the editor, resolutions, marching, picketing, demonstrating, will not do the job. People will.
    Let the people of Midville and its suburbs—we're all concerned—draw together through our churches, service clubs, labor unions, professional organizations, and other groups, to form a united force powerful enough to clean this vice, this ugliness this repugnant cancer from our community. (January 24, 1969)

The *Midville News* continued editorial comments on the Midwestern Bookstore and what might be done about it. In a January 26, 1969, editorial the *News* observed, in part:

Frankly, we wish that there were a blueprint we could lay down, that we could report a simple means to solve this problem. But there isn't. And we, no more than others, really are not sure how to move.
    But basic to our belief in the American democracy is the idea that, given full information, the people will find a way to do what should be done. . . .
    . . . Thus, on this issue, we strongly believe that a vicious evil was afoot in our town. We reported the evil. Whether we went beyond the bounds of good taste or not, many have disputed, but no one denies that the Midville community now knows what is being purveyed to its youth and its degenerates.
    The responsibility now, therefore, is squarely on the conscience of the public.

Many possible avenues of action exist.

It seems to us, for example, that the Supreme Court decisions under which the store has continued to do business do not totally rule out the possibility of pornography. Each individual piece, perhaps, should be tested legally. "This one is worse than the last one judged; it should be tried." In addition the county should not hesitate to appeal if that be possible.

The letter of the law, all laws, should be applied to the hilt to the store's operator. Petitions, letters and personal contacts certainly will have an impact on elected political officials, including legislators, Congressmen and Senators.

A massive wave of public indignation will make itself felt. If nothing else, the idea that pornography is wrong—providing the community truthfully feels it is wrong—can be transmitted directly to the new President of the United States with the request that he question any future appointees to the Supreme Court on their feelings about this matter before he appoints them. . . .

. . . An informed public opinion is the basic strength of America . . . for, in the pursuit of the right, the country will find good and proper answers.

But if all we do is fuss, fume, and forget, then the Midwestern Bookstore will survive in Midville. And if it does survive, and if you do believe in the validity of the democratic ideal, then you simply have to accept the idea that the material it sells does have a rightful place in our community and our society.

We do not believe this. We hope and pray that the community will prove it is not so. (*Midville News*, January 26, 1969)

The precipitating factors had, in the context of structural conduciveness and structural strain, substantiated and sharpened the generalized beliefs. Those beliefs had short-circuited to a concrete target, the Midwestern Bookstore. Midville and Midvillians were ready for mobilization for action, were ready for a norm-oriented symbolic crusade. Indeed, Mrs. Roberts and her colleagues had already begun the mobilization by arranging for the emergence of specific precipitating factors.

Southtown

Some of the early activities and experiences of Mr. King and his Knights of Columbus colleagues, described in Chapter 2 as contributing to structural conduciveness, could also be interpreted as having been precipitating factors: the police action concerning the "nude" play on the State University campus; the confiscation of films from the two "skin-flick" theaters and the arrest of the theater managers; the grand jury's reaction to the films; the subsequent injunction against the showing of the two films; the successful experimental public meeting sponsored by Mr. King and the Knights of Columbus; the suggestion at that meeting that a rally be held to demonstrate community concern and the statement by Representative Randolph that the films shown at the two "skin-flick" theaters were "plain, flat filth"; the number of antipornography bills currently under consideration by the state legislature; and the generally supportive statements by legislators and by individuals who were candidates for public office in the current election. Each of those events or activities had received some newspaper publicity. A few of them had received enough such publicity and had been instrumental enough in influencing Mr. King and his colleagues that they not only could but should be considered precipitating factors. Those events or activities were included in Chapter 2 as elements of structural conduciveness primarily to provide the reader with an early and chronologically sequential introduction to the potential for an antipornography crusade in Southtown. The police raids on the "nude" play on the university campus and the Southtown "skin-flicks" and the attendant newspaper publicity were precipitating factors. Similarly, the widely publicized negative comments (e.g., "shocked" and "disgusted") from members of the Southtown grand jury and other officials following their review of the two confiscated films constituted a precipitating factor. The publicity concerning the raids and the grand jury's comments provided opportunities for Southtowners to become sensitized to the presence of "smut" within their community.

The success of the experimental public meeting sponsored by Mr. King and his fellow Knights was also a precipitating factor. The meeting was reported in a Southtown newspaper; more importantly, it was reported as part of an article that described the reaction of the grand jury to the viewing of the confiscated "skin-flick" films. Consequently, the early activities of Mr. King, his colleagues, and others at the experimental antipornography meeting were linked, in print, with a declaration of the presence and problem of pornography in Southtown. During the experimental meeting, the Avalon and Bijou theaters were specified as the epitome of pornography in Southtown. The narrowing of the definition of the problem to refer specifically to the two theaters precipitated the possibility that they could become discrete targets for antipornography action. (They did not become discrete targets, for reasons which will be outlined later.) During the meeting, Representative Randolph described the "skin-flick" films as "plain, flat filth." That phrase served as a keynoting and precipitating epithet, which would be referred to numerous times during the mobilization of the Southtown antipornography crusade. Finally, during the experimental meeting, the actual form that the antipornography crusade was to take, a decency rally, was precipitated by the suggestion of one of the ministers who was present as a participant.

But Mr. King still reported that, at the current stage of the proceedings, it was not yet entirely certain whether significant numbers of individuals in Southtown could be mobilized, in a rally or otherwise, to support change in the state antipornography statutes. Even though there had been ample opportunity for the community to be sensitized to the "plain, flat filth" present in Southtown, even though he had perceived the experimental antipornography meeting to be a success, even though he had "sort of pledges" of the interest of twenty community voluntary associations in the antipornography endeavor, and even though he had (as described in Chapter 2) already met with his Knights of Columbus cadre and prepared a skeleton structure for the decency rally, Mr. King was worried about the possibility of mobilizing for action. He and his colleagues would not be reasonably confident that their tentative plans would work until after two additional and crucial public planning meetings had been held. Both of those meetings and events which transpired during them were significant precipitating factors leading to the mobilization of participants for the symbolic crusade. In addition, a publicity campaign concerning the decency rally, which was to be evolved by Mr. King, would serve as a precipitating factor and would markedly broaden the potential for the involvement of Southtowners in the antipornography activity.

The Public Planning Meetings

On March 3, 1969, Mr. King's Knights of Columbus council as a group formally passed a resolution calling for statewide KC action against pornography. The resolution read as follows: "Be it resolved that the Knights of Columbus Councils of this State through the State Officers should undertake as a state-wide project the forming of public opinion against lewd and indecent movies; and ultimately cause to be enacted state legislation which would prevent these movies from being shown to those persons under the age of eighteen (18)."

As representatives of the statewide organization of the Knights of Columbus, Mr. King and his colleagues at least symbolically spoke for thirty-three thousand potential votes. He straightforwardly advised his colleagues, "We should not be bashful about letting legislators know that we have a lot of vote power behind us."

During the first two weeks of March, at least three more antipornography bills were introduced into the state legislature. One of the bills was submitted by Representative Randolph, as promised. He stated, in an article in the *Southtown Globe* (February 27, 1969) that his obscene-movie bill was receiving strong support in the legislature, even from individuals who were members of the opposing political party. He further reported that mail being sent to him was running seventy to one in favor of the bill.

On the evening of March 13, 1969, as scheduled by Mr. King, a public planning meeting of the developing antipornography organization was held in the Knights of Columbus auditorium. Besides the Knights of Columbus, thirteen other community groups were represented, including, for example: Parent-Teacher Associations, the Southwood Church of Christ, the Witness Rural Baptist Church, the Catholic Youth Organization, and the Civitan Club. A total of thirty-nine persons attended the meeting.

Mr. King opened the meeting and introduced the representatives from various community organizations who were in attendance. He then posted an organizational chart on the wall and explained the steering committee and the six subcommittees to the group, stating: "We have organized our council to act as the coordinator of the rally for all these groups, because some of the work had to be done before we could hold this meeting tonight. So we have set up our organization this way, and as you can see from the chart, we think it will work pretty well this way." All of the persons attending the meeting agreed to the organization as structured.

Mr. King then outlined the suggested format for the decency rally. He first explained that the date had tentatively been set for April 7, 1969, and that arrangements had been made for renting the Southtown Municipal Auditorium. He told the group that:

eight bills had been introduced into the Legislature for the purpose of controlling lewd films. We want to carry it a little further, and that is the purpose of our rally. We want to take a two pronged approach. First, we want to display our support to the legislators, and in that regard we are going to circulate a petition throughout the auditorium. Second, we want to circulate postcards, addressed to Jack Valenti, President of the Motion Picture Association, on which each person will write in his own words, asking for more wholesome film entertainment. . . . I know that we can't clean up pornographic movies—that is not going to solve the problem. What we want to do is provide more wholesome entertainment for our families and for our young people.

According to Mr. King, the rally was to start at 7:30 P.M. but to be preceded by twenty minutes of band music. At 7:30 P.M., an American Legion color guard would post the colors. Then there would be a pledge of allegiance to the flag, a singing of the national anthem, an invocation, and the introduction of guests and speakers. Included among the guests were to be as many senators, representatives, and city officials as possible. Those legislators who currently were guiding bills toward approval would be asked to give brief progress reports. The introductions would then be followed by three speakers, two of whom were ministers "known for their good speaking" and one an active Catholic layman, also "known for his speaking ability." After the speeches, the petitions would be circulated and the postcards handed out.

Mr. King suggested that "any group who wishes to contribute ten dollars, a maximum of ten dollars, to the expense fund is invited to do so. If we can get at least twenty groups contributing, that would just about meet all of the expenses. The ten dollars is not a prerequisite for participation. We don't want to imply that because your group doesn't feel like contributing it cannot participate." He told the participants that, as presently estimated, the bill for the rally would be approximately $550: $174 for the rental of the auditorium; $225 for the printing of postcards, petitions, and posters and the purchase of flowers; $150 for newspaper advertisements.

One of the participants, a minister, asked whether or not "the organization had a name." Mr. King responded that it did not have a definite name, but "we thought of calling it the Southtown Committee

on Objectionable Movies." Most of the participants expressed disagreement with that title, and another minister told the participants
about a petition that his church had circulated concerning indecent
literature in another part of the state. The minister explained:

> . . . those of us who are members of the Church of Christ had an
> annual gathering of the flock in White Falls, here a while back. . . .
> There were about ten thousand persons at least there, and about
> fifteen hundred copies of the petition were passed out. There was
> room on each petition for about one hundred names, and people
> all over the state signed it, and I think we struck a real blow there.
> Anyway, we called our movement "Uprising for Decency!" I would
> like you to consider that as a name, not just because we have done
> it, but because it worked well.

He then proceeded to read his petition (parts of which are presented
in Chapter 4 as an example of generalized beliefs). The group seemed
quite pleased with the name. Mr. King commented, "I think that is ex-
cellent, and I would, barring any objections, suggest that we do identify ourselves as the 'Uprising for Decency' group and that we call the
rally to be held on April 7 the 'Uprising for Decency Rally.' Is this acceptable to you?" The response from the audience was a unanimous
and excited affirmative.

Mr. King had asked one of the Knights of Columbus officers, who
was familiar with the legislators at the capitol, to prepare a petition
draft for the evening. Mr. King called on that officer, Mr. Highsmith,
and asked him to read the draft. Mr. Highsmith read a very long petition (parts of which are printed in Chapter 4 as an example of generalized beliefs). A female participant, who was a secretary in the state
house of representatives, suggested that the petition was so long it
would never be read by legislators. Mr. King appointed the woman,
the minister who had contributed the name Uprising for Decency, Mr.
Highsmith, and the minister who had asked originally whether or not
the effort had a name, to be a petition subcommittee. The subcommittee agreed to meet the next day and to have the final draft of the
petition ready for the group by the next public meeting.

Another of the ministers in attendance, this one representing the
Church of Christ, warned that, "if our rally at the auditorium is just
a meeting, and everyone signs a petition and goes home, it won't be

a success." He wondered if it would be possible that "out of this auditorium movement we might get two thousand or three thousand or five thousand of these young people, who are the pawns in this battle, to really become concerned about it." He then proposed "a march from the River to the Southtown capital steps, right down Main Avenue, of five thousand teenage youngsters who are asking adults to give them a better bill up there, and let the governor and the legislature see them. Let them present themselves in such a way that they would have a real point to make, and this would be a march for decency instead of the type of marches that have made the national news. We might make the national news media with an action of this sort."

The minister was calling for more direct action, in the form of a public march and for the involvement of more young people. Although he did not say so overtly during the meeting, Mr. King did not favor either of those tactics. He continued to feel that "marches were in this case a waste of time" and that "the most important people to get involved were voting adults. They are the ones who have an impact upon legislatures." Mr. King suggested to the minister: "We would be very pleased if this rally was not the last effort on behalf of this group. Possibly it won't be. Maybe after the rally, you can generate this youth group that you speak of."

Mr. King then asked all the persons attending the meeting to

> get people from your respective groups interested and organize your people to turn out to the rally. No one here is qualified to work in your own group except you. The whole success of the program is going to depend on how well we individually go back and motivate and turn out people in our groups.
>
> I'll give you an example of how we're going to try to do it, and we don't have a final answer, but this is our way of approaching the problem. It would be ideal if we could get every Catholic family in Southtown to come to the rally, but we know we can't do that. In order to turn out as many as possible, we're going to ask our bishop to write each parish and ask that his letter be read at each service on the Sunday morning before the rally. The letter will ask the parishioners to come to the meeting, to "do something about decency." Whether or not that approach will work remains to be seen. We don't know either, but we do want to work with you if we can, in an advisory capacity, to help you set up your own com-

mittee. If you don't need our help, that's fine too. But we are depending on you to motivate and turn out your own group.

The participants discussed their intention to have legislators and public attorneys at the rally, "not only to talk, but to listen as well." A representative of the PTA informed the group that a notification of the rally would be put in the monthly PTA magazine, and that information "would go into fourteen thousand homes in the northeast part of Southtown."

A male participant suggested to the group "another way of fighting pornography." He explained in considerable detail the action of a number of young persons in San Lorenzo, who had purchased alleged pornographic books and pictures from retailers and then had taken them to the district attorney and to members of the legislature. Their actions subsequently resulted in arrests of some retailers.

Mr. King listened patiently to the story and then steered the meeting back to what he considered to be the task at hand. Consistently he had opposed direct action against businesses, even the "skin-flick" theaters. Steadfastly he refused to let those theaters become the single targets for the antipornography activities—the goal was to change the state antipornography statutes, not, in Mr. King's words, "to harrass the movies." Information concerning the purchase-complaint-arrest strategy (similar to that advised by Mr. Gauer in Midville and by Citizens for Decent Literature in general) had been made available to Mr. King in the Knights of Columbus antipornography kit and by such law-enforcement officials as the county attorney, who had specifically suggested the procedure (see Chapter 2).

Mr. King explained to the group the plans to publicize the rally in the media. He informed them that "this evening's meeting will be reported briefly in the paper," elaborated on the importance of "timing" publicity, and advised the participants about "being careful that the material does not defeat our purpose." He noted that the Publicity and Legal subcommittees and all the committee personnel were available to the participants and the organizations they represented for "clearing and screening" any public announcements they wished to make concerning the rally.

The chairman of the Publicity Subcommittee reported to the group that several local television stations were interested in reporting the rally and its preparations and that two local "talk" shows wanted to interview principals involved in the rally. Fifty thousand flyers and five thousand posters were being printed for distribution throughout the city. Five thousand postcards were also being prepared, and enough petitions for eight thousand signatures were being printed. The local newspapers were to be informed about the planning activities "when appropriate," so that they could "time" their stories for "maximum impact." Shortly before the scheduled date of the rally, a large advertisement was to be placed in the paper.

Several other items of business were then offered to the group for discussion—decorations for the rally, the kind of band that would be used, the placing of flowers, and so on. The group discussed an appropriate time for the next meeting, and it was set for March 27. Mr. King and the subcommittee chairmen of Uprising for Decency were to meet, however, on the evening of March 20 for another organizing session. After some closing comments to the participants, Mr. King adjourned the meeting.

On the evening of March 20, 1969, Mr. King and the subcommittee chairmen of UFD met, as scheduled, in the Knights of Columbus hall. At that meeting they discussed further the details of the rally, including the progress of printing the petitions, postcards, and posters, the methods of distribution, the speakers being lined up, and various other topics relevant to the division of labor. According to Mr. King, they spent "nearly an hour trying to decide which councilmen and political candidates to invite. Finally we devised a form letter to be sent to all of them. That way none of them could complain that they weren't invited or didn't know about it."

Mr. King was quite pleased with "the way things are going." He was gratified by the cooperation of other community organizations, whose total number represented had now reached twenty-six. He felt that the last public meeting had been an extremely important one, and it made him feel more confident about the decency rally's potential for being a success. He was particularly enthusiastic about the generation of a name, Uprising for Decency, for the antipornography effort. But he was still somewhat concerned about the rally, reflecting: "All this preparation is leading up to the rally. If it falls though, everything may fall flat. We've got to make a good showing on the rally in order to support the legislation. Also, the events there will determine where we go from there."

The subcommittee chairmen discussed the advisability of having a "question-and-answer period" following the major speeches in the rally. They finally ruled out such a period because "it would give the disturbers too much of a chance to disturb things."

Mr. King congratulated the subcommittee chairmen on their progress and urged them to keep up the good work. Every committee chairman was putting in, according to Mr. King, forty hours a week just on rally preparation. As each subcommittee chairman gave his report, he ran through a litany of persons and organizations with which he had formal or informal contact. The meeting lasted less than an hour, because everyone had so much to do.

On March 14, 1969, Senator Welles introduced two bills, Senate Bills 660 and 661, both concerned with pornography, which would be the only two such bills to clear all the committees in both the senate and the house of representatives. These would be bills that UFD would support from their inception through to their signing into law. Senate Bill 660 amended the state penal code to bring "skin-flick" theaters into the definition of "disorderly houses," thereby applying to the theaters the possibility of heavier penalties. Senate Bill 661 was a general antipornography bill which, according to Senator Welles, was intended to "stop the sale or distribution of harmful materials to any person under the age of sixteen" (later amended to seventeen). This included the materials not produced in, but transported into, the state. According to Senator Welles, the "bills have been drawn carefully, with thought for their constitutionality. While the U.S. Supreme Court maintains liberal safeguards for press freedom, it has indicated an understanding of the need to protect young minds from harmful influences. I believe my legislation can stand the constitutional test." Since the bill was aimed specifically at minors, there was little danger of constitutionality being an issue.

After the March 13 meeting of UFD, Mr. King, as mentioned above, was wondering whether or not the organization had yet gained any visibility with the legislature. He visited with Senator Welles, to "sound him out" about the impact of UFD. According to Mr. King, Senator Welles had seen UFD's activities as influential. Mr. King reported that Senator Welles had concluded that "we had enough support, and he decided to draw up Senate Bills 660 and 661. I feel that those bills were drawn up as a result of our meeting. They clearly were the result of our activity." Mr. King was quite pleased with this outcome and commented that he was increasingly convinced of the feasibility of UFD's plans. Senator Welles's comment was an important precipitating factor, having provided the leader of UFD with increased courage of his convictions. Mr. King commented specifically:

> This was the way to work. I am no vigilante and no militant, just an interested citizen. I wanted to work with little fanfare and not a lot of publicity yet, so that the movie people could not organize against us. I thought it was important to get the bills going *before* we had the rally, and then use the petitions we'd gather at the rally to help push the bill through. A whole bunch of bills had been started, but they had different weaknesses. We figured that it would work out all right in the long run. If there were a whole bunch of bills in there, at least one or two of them would get through.

Mr. King called the scheduled March 27, 1969, meeting of UFD to order in the auditorium of the College Street Church of Christ. The meeting was attended by forty-seven people, representing twenty-nine community groups, including, for example, two American Legion posts; the Greenwood Baptist Church; the Catholic Daughters; the four Knights of Columbus councils of Southtown; Sertoma; the Michael Road Church of Christ; the Ben Hur Shrine-Masons; the Civitan Club; three PTA chapters; the Holy Cross Parents' Club; the Boys' Club of Southtown; the Catholic Youth Organization; and the Independent Auto Repair Shop Association.

At the beginning of the meeting, some of the candidates in the city council election made brief presentations, declaring themselves against pornography and in favor of more severe state statutes.

Mr. King then informed the participants that he was to give a report to the local newspaper "before 10 A.M. tomorrow morning, so we can begin our hot and heavy publicity campaign." He read telegrams from two persons who had been invited to attend the planning session but could not attend. The first telegram was from the mayor of Southtown, who declined the invitation, without essential comment, because of other commitments. The second was from a city councilman, who also declined, but with a statement of support. Mr. King commented about the wide support the efforts of UFD seemed to be getting from local and regional government officials.

The participants reviewed the agenda for the UFD rally. The postcards, flyers, and posters had been printed, and samples were distributed. The posters were six by twelve inches, made of white cardboard, and announced in bold red and blue type:

Uprising for Decency

What can you do to help stop
dirt—filth—obscenity
in movies and publications?

Attend huge rally
of concerned citizens

Municipal Auditorium
April 7—7:30 p.m.

Sponsored by twenty-seven Civic, Religious,
and Educational Organizations in Southtown

Let your voice be heard!

The flyers were six by twelve inches, made of white paper with bold black print; they stated the same message as the poster. Five thousand posters and fifty thousand flyers had been printed.

The postcards were addressed to Mr. Jack Valenti, President, Motion Picture Association of America, in Washington, D.C. The cards, five thousand of which had been printed, read:

Dear Mr. Valenti:

Thanks to you and Mr. Eugene Dougherty for the film-code classification system.

I heartily endorse measures to stamp out "plain, flat filth" that entices our youth away from the family atmosphere; let us promote a mushrooming of wholesome family entertainment for our civilization.

Sincerely,

Citizen for an Uprising for Decency

Mr. King pointed to large boxes of the materials and advised the participants to "take whatever you need." He announced to the group that the "Southtown Baptist Association has taken twenty-five thousand flyers for distribution to their members!"

Holding up a sample of the petition and passing around a few other copies for persons to see, Mr. King read the final version of the Petition for an Uprising for Decency:

We the undersigned citizens of Southtown, U.S.A., hereby dedi-
cate ourselves for a more concentrated effort in supporting and
regulating more stringent laws which will curb the production and
sale of materials which are obscene in the form of lewd films and
pornographic materials. The moral strength of our nation is at
stake, and we pledge ourselves to support our lawmakers and law
enforcement agencies and courts in doing something about this
NOW!

We citizens of Southtown for an UPRISING FOR DECENCY wish to
commend our President of these United States in his pledge to
initiate an immediate program to protect our young boys and girls
from the twisted minds trying to seduce them with pornographic materials. President Nixon has stated, "The most dangerous threat to the psychic health of young people goes relatively
unregulated. This is the business of dealing in obscene and pornographic materials, a lucrative industry with sales estimated at up to
two billion dollars a year. There is no difficulty in setting up
standards of obscenity for children because the Supreme Court has
held that laws could be drawn to establish differing standards of
obscenity for minors. We can constitutionally restrict from children
matter that would not be objectionable for adults."

We citizens of Southtown for an UPRISING FOR DECENCY
are determined to press for more effective legislation against obscenity, both in films and in printed matter. We heartily endorse
measures to stamp out this "plain, flat filth" that entices our youth
away from the family atmosphere that they are entitled to—and we
trust that our voices will be heard by men of responsible position
who receive this petition. PLEASE DO NOT TURN A DEAF EAR TO THE
VAST MAJORITY OF AMERICANS WHO ARE SICK AND TIRED OF THE TRAF-
FIC IN OBSCENITY, AND WHO PLEAD FOR RETURN TO MORAL DECENCY
AND UPRIGHTNESS.

The petition then provided space for the petitioner's name, street
address, city, state, and zip code. It was a combination of the draft
petitions read at the earlier public planning meeting and suggestions
from the members of the Petition Subcommittee which had been appointed by Mr. King.

Mr. King advised the group, "The bishop will circulate a letter to be
read at all pulpits of all parishes in Southtown, on two successive Sun-
days—this Sunday and Easter Sunday—asking every Catholic in at-

tendance to make a point of attending the rally." He added, "We think that should do some good, but we also are going to use the posters on the bulletin boards." He asked the participants to "make it your personal objective to get the posters and flyers into the hands of the membership of your respective organizations. We must do it if the rally is to be a success. And I think that between now and the rally this is the most important thing that each of us can do, because what remains is simply to firm the program up and have it ready for presentation."

Mr. King reported that he had talked personally with Senator Welles, Representative Randolph, Representative Owens, and the district attorney, all of whom had agreed to be in attendance at the rally. The city council members had been invited and would attend. All the candidates in the current city council elections had been invited, and many would be at the rally.

In order to get a "rough estimate about how many people would be at the rally from among those represented here tonight," Mr. King asked each participant to give some idea of how many persons had committed themselves to attend. Each member of the audience responded when called upon, and the total pledged by the organizations represented totaled over two thousand persons. Mr. King stated that was "fine, but we've got to make sure we get more than that. We are aiming for seven thousand."

The chairman of the Publicity Subcommittee, at Mr. King's request, made a report to the group. He told them about an ad, identical to the posters and flyers, that was to appear on Easter Sunday in the local newspaper. Three television stations, several radio stations, and twelve newspapers had been notified and had indicated that they were going to cooperate with publicity. The governor's office had been notified, and a letter of support supposedly was forthcoming. The publicity chairman had sent a registered letter, through one of the U.S. Senators from the state, to President Nixon, and "a letter of support is expected from the President."

Pausing for a moment in his agenda, Mr. King wondered out loud with the audience about "the way this organization has fallen into place so quickly. We got some people to attend the sessions, but most of the delegates made themselves known to us, and we just followed up to keep you apprised of the dates. We really haven't done much soliciting, and the kind of support that has come in confirms that this really is a hot issue with the people, and all you have to do is give them an opportunity to make their feelings known and heard."

The expectation of UFD participants was that Municipal Auditorium would "overflow with people who were interested." Mr. King specifically stated, "I think we'll have a packed house down there. I'll be disappointed if we don't."

A participant asked whether there would be "any objections to letters to the editor of the newspaper, supporting Uprising for Decency." Mr. King answered: "No, not now. I think we should move into full swing on our publicity campaign." He added that the editor of one of the local newspapers "has, since the grand jury and the confiscation of the films and so forth, been getting a lot of mail on the issue. He would welcome letters to the editor. In fact, I am sure he would publish them. I can assure you that he has assured me that the support of the newspaper means editorial support and news reporting support as well. So I think we will start seeing, this week-end, a pickup on the publicity." He continued, "The editor discussed with me the timetable, and there are certain things that he called to my attention about the reporting. In particular, he said that you don't want to have too much publicity too early, because you will lose momentum. That's why, although we've met several times before, he does not want to come out with any stories until the week-end just before the rally. I think that's a good idea."

Some details were discussed concerning the method of distributing the petitions and the postcards efficiently and gathering up the petitions again, once signed. Getting additional signatures from fellow employees, friends, and neighbors was discussed and felt to be a good idea. However, Mr. King insisted that all petitions be returned directly to him within ten days after the rally. He explained his reason for the timing: "As you may or may not know, we plan to hold these petitions until such time as the committee hearing is conducted on Senate Bill 660 and 661. So I can't tell you exactly when I will need the petitions, because the date of the committee hearings is not yet set. But I think ten days' leeway would be sufficient at this point, and I would rather not have the petitions out longer than that."

A participant asked whether it might not be "advisable that we get on the phone and contact everybody from the different organizations again and let them know where the hearings arc, so that we all can have representation there." Mr. King agreed: "That's going to be another project. Yes, definitely, we should have some organized representation at the committee hearings, and we'll make sure that we do. But I don't want to get into that before we get the rally conducted.

That's the most important point right now, and we should concentrate on the rally."

A participant at the meeting suggested: "Why don't we raise the problem of drugs in Southtown at the rally, too? It seems that that would be a good place to do it, because drugs are just as big a—if not bigger—problem as pornography." Mr. King answered quickly, "No, ma'am. The approach of our particular interest here, in the petition and on the postcards and at the rally, will be on two things: on obscene movies and printed matter. And that's not to say that we don't have other problems, but these are the only two that we are going to attempt to do something about at this time."

In a subsequent interview Mr. King commented: "It sometimes was difficult to keep people locked in on just the issue of pornography and obscenity. I really didn't want to go beyond the issue of films and had to give a little on the printed-matter problem, but that was as far as I wanted to go. If we added a whole range of problems, then we wouldn't be able to focus accurately on the legislation, the legislators would become confused and disinterested, and all we could do would be shout and give speeches and nothing would be changed."

Some concern was expressed by members of the group about retaliation from the movie industry. One participant wanted to know "what they are doing in retaliation now. Is it something similar to what we are doing? Are they getting their lawyers ready?" Mr. King answered: "I honestly don't know. . . . There no doubt will be some opposition, and who knows, it may be insurmountable opposition, but at least we should expect it, and we should be resolved in our effort to obtain some solution to it."

Some of the participants commented about how easy it was going to be to get signatures on the petition. One individual, who had received advance copies of the petition, told the group that he had left one in his office at his place of work. He was called away from his office for about an hour, and when he returned, he reported, "I found it completely signed, and someone had attached a blank sheet to the back, and it was signed clear down to the bottom of the blank sheet." Mr. King was pleased, and exclaimed: "Is that right! Well, that's encouraging. We hope that we will have quite a weapon here with these signatures, when the petitions are assembled."

Some smaller details were discussed, including the distribution of pencils for signing the petitions and the photographing of events. When the details were agreed upon, Mr. King prepared to close the meeting. He informed the group: "This will be, unless further notice is given, the last planning session. We will keep you informed by telephone, and if a need arises for another called meeting, we will get in touch with you. But we plan to devote our time on the subcommittees from here on to putting the program together, setting up the publicity, and letting the rest of the chips fall where they may."

A representative of the Church of Christ interrupted Mr. King:

> I would like to say one other word here. . . . I would like to let you know that the plan of the Michael Road Church of Christ is to have a youth march, sometime before school is out, up Main Avenue . . . Our members are just thrilled to death about this, and they said that they could send three or four busloads of young people, even from out of town, here to Southtown. . . . So our plans are to contact all the Churches of Christ and, of course, everyone else who is interested. But we will contact the ones we know first. And to have this youth march before school is out, will let us move while this thing is at its peak so to speak. So if any of you folks are interested in helping with this, please contact us over at the Michael Road Church of Christ, because we would like to have your name, if you would like to enter this. . . . We are not trying to take the lead away from you in this. It's just that someone has to take the initial step, and I want to thank you for the great job that you have done. I know that it has taken a lot of time.

Mr. King calmly commented, "Very good. Well, I'm sure that many of our groups will want to participate, and I can assure you that we will help in any way we can. I think that to be effective, Uprising for Decency has to have a cross-section of organizations, and that is what we have had so far and what we would like to continue to have."

He then thanked the people in the audience for attending and adjourned the meeting.

Mr. King was not happy with the sudden introduction of the youth march by the church group. He thought he had successfully squelched discussion of such a march at earlier meetings. His view of such marches, as represented several times above, was that they were "a waste of time and didn't accomplish anything." Further, he was interested in getting qualified voters to sign the petition, and "a bunch of kids who can't vote can't sign the petition." Mr. King informally managed to discourage the Church of Christ from holding the march.

The Publicity Campaign

As planned by Mr. King, the publicity for the UFD rally peaked during the week before the rally was scheduled to be held.

A bulletin sent to all Southtown members of the Knights of Columbus and intended to be shared with other citizens, read:

CITIZENS OF SOUTHTOWN ARE CONCERNED ABOUT LEWD FILMS (SLICK FLICKS)

JOIN SOME 25 GROUPS, COMPRISED OF THOUSANDS OF CITIZENS FROM OUR COMMUNITY, WHO WILL BE OUR GUESTS IN THE CITY AUDITORIUM, 7:30 P.M., Monday, April 7, 1969. THIS WILL SERVE AS NOTICE THAT OUR COUNCIL MEETING, FIRST MONDAY IN APRIL, WILL BE THE OPEN MEETING IN THE CITY AUDITORIUM. What better way to serve than to take steps to stamp out this "plain, flat filth" through the media of films that are enticing our youth away from the family atmosphere that they are entitled to.

Remember, all faiths and societies will be our guests to push for legislation against obscene films.

The Knights of Columbus state magazine, which reached all KC members in the state, informed the readers about the Uprising for Decency in Southtown and the imminent rally.

On Friday, March 28, the State University newspaper carried an article announcing the UFD rally, without editorial comment.

In the Saturday, March 29, edition of the *Southtown Globe-Gazette* (on week-ends, the *Southtown Globe* and the *Southtown Gazette*, owned by the same corporation, merged into a single edition), an article was printed under the heading "'Uprising for Decency' Rally Set To Combat Pornography." The article, placed on page 7, described the rally as being "sponsored by a large number of Southtown civic, religious, fraternal, educational and veterans groups" and said it "had been definitely booked for April 7th at the Southtown Municipal Auditorium." The article quoted Mr. King as saying that the "purpose of the rally is to display public support for the legislation which attempts to regulate and curb production and sale of lewd films and pornographic material." The list of organizational participants was presented, and the text of the petition was reprinted. Mr. King was quoted in the article as saying: "The group is strictly local in origin, and has nothing to do with similar movements elsewhere in the country. . . .

The group was formed at a February 17 meeting at the Knights of Columbus Council. . . . The group is aimed at the 'family unit,' and the April 7 rally will consist of a flag ceremony, an invocation, three religious speakers, and a mass signing of a petition calling for more stringent pornography laws." The article reported that Mr. King anticipated that 4,500 persons would come to the auditorium for the rally.

An article in the *Southtown Globe* (Tuesday, April 1, 1969) was headed "Decency Boost Told." The article (on page 3) reported that five more organizations had been added to the list of participants in UFD. According to Mr. King, this article was part of a deliberate strategy, worked out by the editor of the *Southtown Globe* and himself, to give the reader the indication that the "movement was gaining ground."

On Thursday, April 3, the *Southtown Globe* published an article (page 21) listing the speakers scheduled for the UFD rally, and repeating the details of the petition and the purposes of the gathering. The speakers included a Church of Christ minister who was also the editor of a religious news publication; an attorney who was also the executive director of a Catholic action layman's organization; and the pastor of a local Baptist church. The article announced, "There is no admission charge and all interested persons are invited to attend."

The following day, Friday, April 4, the *Southtown Gazette* (page 31) predicted "Valenti Due 'Decency' Postcards." The text of the postcards to be distributed at the rally was specified, the petition strategy reviewed again, and the speakers again announced.

On Sunday, April 6, the day before the rally, the *Southtown Globe-Gazette* (page A9) printed an article headed "Large Crowd Seen for Decency Rally." The article read, in part:

> Thousands of teenagers and adults are expected to turn out in full support of the "Uprising for Decency" rally at 7:30 p.m. Monday in Municipal Auditorium.
>
> The rally, open to the public and free of charge, supports legislation to regulate and curb production and sale of lewd films and pornographic material. (*Southtown Globe-Gazette*, April 6, 1969)

The article reviewed the plan of the rally, the participants, the petitions and postcards, and the fact that invitations had been extended "to all City Councilmen, to candidates in last Saturday's council race, to the Central County legislative delegation, and to County officials." On the same day a large advertisement, an exact duplicate of one of the posters, was published in the *Southtown Globe-Gazette* (on page A27). The advertisement was indicated as being sponsored by the Independent Auto Repair Shop Association of Southtown and carried its official seal. Mr. King had negotiated with that organization, which had sent representatives to UFD, to pay the $150 cost.

On April 7, 1969, both the *Southtown Globe* and the *Southtown Gazette* carried page 1 articles announcing the UFD rally to be held that night. The morning paper announced, "Protest Rally Attacks Smut Here Tonight," and read, in part:

> Municipal Auditorium is expected to be packed Monday night with teenagers on the warpath—not against teachers, "cops" or even the "establishment"—but rather against obscenity and profanity in films and books.
>
> The rally, set to begin at 7:30 p.m., is free to the public and is being sponsored by Southtown civic and church groups. (*Southtown Globe*, April 7, 1969)

The evening paper reported, "Decency Rally Slated Tonight," and stated, in part:

> Southtown area teenagers will rally Monday night in Municipal Auditorium to protest obscenity and profanity in films and books.
>
> Sponsored by local church and civic groups, the "Uprising for Decency" rally will begin at 7:30 p.m.
>
> Ministers and church leaders will speak to the teens at the rally where petitions will be distributed urging a return to moral decency and righteousness. . . .
>
> . . . Mr. King said the petitions "will effectively demonstrate to our legislators the public sentiment in support of this movement." (*Southtown Gazette*, April 7, 1969)

Both articles explained in detail again the petition procedure, the postcards, who was invited, and who the speakers would be. Those were the first articles concerning the Uprising for Decency rally which had appeared on page 1 of the local newspapers.

Mr. King was pleased with the phasing of the newspaper publicity. That phasing had gone, he stated, as he had planned with the newspapers. Mr. King was also pleased with the widespread distribution of the flyers and posters, with the mention of the rally on local radio and television "talk" shows, and with the degree to which local clergy had cooperated in announcing the rally from their pulpits. But he was not completely pleased with the content of the newspaper articles in the *Southtown Globe* and the *Southtown Gazette*. Those articles, he felt, "gave the misleading picture that the rally was just for teenagers or kids. I wanted to avoid that. That's exactly what I didn't want to have happen. We need adult signatures, not the signatures of kids." He commented worriedly: "I don't know what's going to happen now. I sure hope that this doesn't mean that we won't get a lot of adults at the rally. After all this work, we better be able to fill out those petitions. But," he added, "we're committed now; everybody's fired up. We've got a lot of support, and we're going to *go!*"

Discussion

Gusfield (1963:16, 185) observed that those events which had served to differentiate status groups, the traditionalist from the modernist, were crucial in the development, maintenance, and intensification of the temperance crusade. Several of the precipitating factors in Midville and Southtown dramatically illustrated the differences between traditionalist and modernist, exemplified symbolically by orientation toward pornography. For example, in Midville, Mr. Gauer's comments and the newspaper exposé of the Midwestern Bookstore focused a distinction between the "corrupt" and those who would fight "corruption," with those potentially "corruptible" being in need of protection. The issue became a question of good versus evil, and there was no middle road. Either persons were for good or they were for evil. Either they were against pornography and what or whom it represented, or they were for pornography and what or whom it represented. Being tolerant of or indifferent to pornography was essentially the same as being for it. Decent citizens were under obligation to declare themselves for decency; precipitating factors had drawn the battle line. In Southtown, the "shocking" acceptance of nudity on the university campus and the discovery of "disgusting" films at the "skin-flicks" similarly sharpened differences between life styles, again symbolically represented by orientation toward pornography. The perception had emerged of "us" versus "them" with regard to the maintaining of basic values. The precipitating factors had confirmed the fact that there *was* a tangible and concrete threat to the prestige and power of the traditional life style to which the respondents, indeed to which all right-thinking persons, were committed. It had been confirmed that there *was* reason to be a status discontent.

The context and impact of the precipitating factors in Midville and Southtown are taken to support the hypothesis, following Gusfield, that the processes of status discontent were in operation and that the emergence of acts of status politics was feasible and imminent.

In his discussion of the role of precipitating factors as they relate to generalized beliefs, Smelser noted: "They mark the sudden establishment or symbolization of one of the conditions of conduciveness or strain. In this way precipitating factors focus the belief on a particular person, event, or situation. In addition, precipitating factors create a sense of urgency and hasten mobilization for action" (1962:294). He further commented that precipitating factors: "may confirm or justify existing generalized fears or hatreds" (p. 249); may provide "adherents of a belief with more evidence of the workings of evil forces, or a greater promise of success" (p. 352); "constitute 'evidence' for anxious persons that the terrible and unknown forces implicit in anxiety are manifesting themselves in concrete ways" (p. 133); provide "'evidence' that the worst which has been feared is now manifesting itself" (p. 150); reveal "the insidious character of an enemy" (p. 295); and "provide a concrete setting toward which collective action can be directed" (p. 17). (See also Turner and Killian 1957:307.)

As hypothesized, events interpreted as precipitating factors in Midville and Southtown concretely identified an enemy (the Midwestern Bookstore and the Avalon and Bijou theaters) against which specific action could be taken. The precipitating factors also identified the nature of that action—in Midville, direct action against the bookstore, using the purchase-complaint-arrest strategy advised by Mr. Gauer and local law-enforcement officers; in Southtown, the holding of a rally and the gathering of petition signatures in support of "tougher" antipornography laws, as advised by Senator Welles and other local legislators. Furthermore, the dramatic and highly publicized qualities of the exposés readily symbolized the broader conditions of conduciveness and strain and "proved" the nature of the generalized beliefs extant in both cities. Henceforward, not only could somewhat vague or highly abstract fears or concerns, ambiguous status misgivings, and broadly stated worries about undue changes be more narrowly and symbolically redefined as concern with the dangers of pornography, but the targets of concern could be specifically identified (with more precise symbolic representation) as bookstores or theaters. The threatening "they" could be delimited to refer to tangible and reachable places and persons. Most of this process operated within the network of social interaction, yielding emergent norms for behavior (Turner and Killian 1957; 1972) through a dialectic exchange.

Summary catchwords, indeed crusade slogans, emerged from the exposés and themselves became precipitating factors—in Midville, Mr. Gauer's depicting of the Midwestern Bookstore as "one of the worst displays of obscene literature in the country;" in Southtown, Representative Randolph's description of the confiscated films as "plain, flat filth." Those catchwords and other such symbolic representations in the context of precipitating factors, crystallized the short-circuiting of generalized beliefs: If the Midwestern Bookstore was eliminated, if the "skin-flicks" were restricted (by changes in the antipornography laws or by stringent applications of current laws), the dangers of pornography would be neutralized, the threats to traditional life style would be removed. Those patterns and processes of precipitating factors are taken to support the hypotheses, following Smelser, concerning the operation of precipitating factors in the evolution of a norm-oriented movement as manifested in antipornography crusades. The symbolic nature of the action engendered by the precipitating factors will be illustrated more completely in Chapter 6.

Smelser (1962:354) wrote, "One of the most important kinds of precipitating factors—which often heightens enthusiasm and participation in the movement—is any event which gives evidence of a sudden change in the movement's fortune." He further stated, "Many precipitating factors are interpreted as signs, either of the opponents' power or the proponents' chances of success" (1962:294), and "limited successes of a movement, especially unanticipated successes, often "prove" the efficacy of a given method of agitation, and stimulate more agitation of this type" (1962:295).

The early successes of Mrs. Roberts and her ICCD colleagues served as precipitating factors in this fashion, as did her and her colleagues' successes in getting Mr. Gauer to speak in Midville, in getting the materials from the Midwestern Bookstore, and in receiving access to and support from the community leaders (especially the press) to whom they brought the bookstore materials. Mr. King's and his UFD colleagues' successes in gaining support from local politicians and officials, in getting good turnouts at planning meetings for the decency rally, and in acquiring press exposure similarly served as precipitating factors. Turner and Killian (1957:307) noted the importance of the success of early minor or symbolic acts of protest as crystallizing events for subsequent larger-scale acts of collective behavior.

As was mentioned in Chapter 2, the characteristics and orientations of the key leaders in social movements are most significant in determining the characteristics and orientations of the movements themselves. With regard to the shape of precipitating factors in collective behavior, Smelser (1962:295) indicated that "any given precipitating factor may appear unexpectedly or it may be arranged by some party interested in the outcome of the movement." More specifically, he stated, "A leader, by a series of planned actions, may deliberately 'arrange' for the occurrence of a precipitating event" (1962:203). Mrs. Roberts, with the support of her colleagues, arranged the precipitating factor of Mr. Gauer's visit to Midville and his subsequent speeches. She and Mrs. Nelson deliberately purchased materials from the Midwestern Bookstore and distributed them to prominent citizens in the hope of generating response from them as a precipitating factor to further action. Mr. King, with the support of his colleagues, arranged public planning meetings, with the hope that the resulting attendance would serve as a factor precipitating the realization of the decency rally. He calculatingly devised a schedule of publicity with the editors of local newspapers and with officials of local radio and television stations in order to maximize the precipitating quality of the publicity. At least some of the precipitating factors associated with the emergence of the antipornography crusades in Midville and Southtown were intentionally planned by crusade leadership.

There was an important difference between Mrs. Roberts and Mr. King regarding their reaction to one key precipitating factor—the advice offered by significant individuals concerning the appropriate action to take in the mobilization of the antipornography crusades. Mrs. Roberts and her ICCD colleagues elected to follow the advice of Mr. Gauer and local police officials in taking direct action against the Midwestern Bookstore. That action involved purchasing materials at the bookstore, filing a complaint with the police concerning its pornographic nature, causing the arrest of bookstore employees, and then testifying at the subsequent hearings or trials. Mr. Gauer had advised that, though convictions might not be possible under the current law, every complaint would reaffirm community standards, would indicate support for law enforcement and prosecution, and in general would discourage the display and sale of such material by immobilizing the bookstore. The purchase-complaint-arrest strategy was still an attempt to reconstitute norms, by testing the viability of antipornography statutes and by forcing their operation with direct citizen action. (At the same time, Mrs. Roberts and her ICCD colleagues were planning to work for actual modifications in the antipornography statutes.) However, the direct-action form of normative reconstitution elected by ICCD contained an element of hostility (in the Smelser sense of the term) and more than just a hint of harrassment. There was a precedent for that strategy; it had been used by some Midvillians a few years earlier (as described in Chapter 2). Furthermore, Mrs. Roberts and her ICCD colleagues had experienced several disappointments and frustrations in their attempts to control pornography in Midville. Compared with Mr. King and his UFD colleagues, they were angrier, more volatile, and readier to take direct rather than indirect action. As discussed above, the structural conduciveness, structural strain, and character of the generalized beliefs were more severe in Midville than in Southtown. Similarly, the character of precipitating factors in Midville had been significantly more dramatic, more publicized, and more intense than in Southtown. It was therefore very probable that the mobilization for action and the form that such action would take would be more severe in Midville than in Southtown.

In addition to the advice he received from Senator Welles and others concerning a strategy of petitions in support of legislative change and attempts to influence the movie industry, Mr. King had been exposed to advice concerning the purchase-complaint-arrest strategy. The county attorney had straightforwardly recommended that plan of action as a means to harrass the owners of the Avalon and Bijou theaters. Similarly, one of the participants in a UFD planning meeting recommended the strategy. The publicity concerning the Avalon and the Bijou theaters created a situation in which those two businesses could easily have become specific targets for direct action. Mr. King, however, flatly refused to allow such action, and maintained the orientation of the Southtown antipornography crusade toward legislative change. He accepted the fact that the Avalon and Bijou theaters had become symbols for the mobilization toward such change, and he thought that happenstance to be useful. But he was unwavering in his conviction that those businesses, or any individual businesses, should not be approached directly. Most of his UFD colleagues supported him in that position. (The contrasting leadership styles and goal orientations of ICCD and UFD had significant implications for other structural characteristics of the two antipornography organizations. Those organizational characteristics will be discussed in detail in Chapter 9.)

The events interpreted as precipitating factors in Midville and Southtown had, as hypothesized, affirmed the conditions of structural strain and structural conduciveness and had focused and "proven" the generalized beliefs. Mrs. Roberts and Mr. King, ICCD and UFD, Midville and Southtown were mobilizing for action. The precipitating factors had already begun shading over into the operation of full-scale norm-oriented movements, of full-scale symbolic crusades.

Chapter 6

Mobilization for Action: "We Showed Them Where We Stand!"

Midville

On January 16, 1969, the Midville prosecuting attorney gave a talk on pornography and the law at a meeting of ICCD (at the organization's invitation). During his talk, the prosecutor passed out "complaint forms" for action against alleged pornographic materials and suggested that ICCD members fill them out and submit them to his office. At the top of the complaint form was the statement, "We bring to your attention that the enclosed publication [followed by blanks for date of purchase, title, author, and publisher] is being sold, offered for sale, and distributed in this jurisdiction." Next followed a blank for the name and address of the store selling the material. The form also stated, "After examination of the contents of the above publication, we feel there is probably cause to believe that the same is in violation of the obscenity laws of the State." The form concluded with the statement, "We ask you to conduct an investigation of this matter, and if, in your judgment, a violation of aforesaid laws exists, we then ask that you take whatever police action is necessary to enforce those laws." Blanks were then provided for the signature and address of the complainant. According to respondents in the Midville police department, the complaint form was prepared by ICCD itself.

The *Midville News* (January 17, 1969) reported the meeting at which the prosecutor spoke to ICCD. In the article, which was entitled "Anti-Pornography Campaign Starts," readers were informed that "citizens concerned with ridding Midville of pornographic literature, may contact the Interdenominational Citizen's Council for Decency." The article also reported, significantly, that, "at its Thursday meeting, the Council (ICCD) appealed for interested citizens to join with it to lay 'battle plans' for forcing the Midwestern Bookstore, 122 South Paine, out of business." The article also indicated that Raymond P. Gauer was to be invited to return to Midville for the March, 1969, meeting of ICCD.

The series of articles in the *Midville News* about the Midwestern Bookstore elicited proclamations and declarations from several Midville civic groups and organizations. Those proclamations and declarations were part of the mobilization of the antipornography crusade. On January 16, 1969, for example, the Midville Education Association publicly condemned the Midwestern Bookstore (*Midville News*, January 17, 1969). On Sunday, January 19, the Midville post office blocked mail-order sales from a California firm and denied the firm the right to receive funds from the Midville area (*Midville News*, January 19, 1969). The decision was made by the post office on the basis of evidence that the firm had been mailing obscene and pornographic materials. The customer-relations representative of the post office indicated that he now was getting "dozens of requests a day for prohibitory orders from Midville area residents" (*Midville News*, January 17, 1969). The representative attributed the increase in requests for prohibitory orders to the "recent heavy mailing" to Midville residents and the fact that "many would have thrown it in the wastebasket, but since the *News* articles, they want to do something about it" (*Midville News*, January 17, 1969).

On January 21, 1969, the *Midville News* printed an article that reported that ICCD "had been deluged with telephone calls and mail from citizens concerned with eliminating pornographic literature in Midville." The *News* advised that "the Council will not have time to answer all requests individually but does suggest a plan of action to 'eradicate the blight in the Midville downtown area—namely the Midwestern Bookstore.'" That advice was to write the Midville city council and the Midville County board of supervisors, urging action against the bookstore. It was further advised that citizens write letters of protest urging action on the problem of pornographic material, in general, to the Midville county prosecutor and to senators and representatives from the state. Organizations and associations in Midville were urged to take a public stand "on the issue of pornography and the presence of the Bookstore by presenting resolutions to the City Council."

On January 23, 1969, the Midville city council made a public pronouncement which supported the opponents of pornography in Midville and praised the work they were doing to fight it. The mayor told the overflow crowd of visitors that action against the Midwestern Bookstore "lies with you." He added, "It's encouraging to see citizens pursue this matter along legal lines" (*Midville News*, January 28, 1969). During the meeting, the council received a petition signed by eighty-four Midvillians, stating opposition to the existence of the Midwestern Bookstore. In the same meeting, the Parent-Teacher Association of Saint Mary's Cathedral School presented a resolution in opposition to pornography. The principals of seven Lutheran schools asked the city council to eliminate pornographic materials from Midville. Representatives of the First Christian Church asked all civic, social, and religious groups in Midville to pass resolutions as an attempt to "rid the community of smut peddlers" (*Midville News*, January 28, 1969).

Direct Action against the Midwestern Bookstore

On January 23, 1969, a complaint was filed against Mr. Smith, a salesclerk in the Midwestern Bookstore, by a Mrs. Wyatt. Mr. Smith was arrested and charged with "Knowing Sale of Obscene Literature"—specifically, that he did "knowingly sell a certain obscene, sadistic, lewd, lascivious, filthy and indecent magazine, containing, obscene, sadistic, lewd, lascivious, filthy and indecent pictures, said magazine being entitled '*Venus*, Volume 1, Number 3'." (Information Sheet, Circuit Court, January 23, 1969). Mr. Smith's bail was placed at $10,000. (The charge against him was punishable by a maximum of one year in prison and a maximum $1,000 fine.) He was remanded to jail pending a pretrial examination when he was unable to post bond immediately (*Midville News*, January 27, 1969). According to interview data, $10,000 was the largest bond ever set for an offense in the history of the Midville circuit court—the largest bond prior to the mobilization of the anti-pornography crusade was $2,500. (Bills, supported by ICCD, were currently being considered in the state legislature to raise fines for the sale of pornography to a maximum of $10,000.)

On January 28, 1969, a Midville citizen, Mr. Morgan, filed a complaint against another Midwestern Bookstore salesclerk, Mr. Thomas. Mr. Thomas was arrested, charged as Mr. Smith had been, and released on bond.

The action against the Midwestern Bookstore followed the purchase-complaint-arrest strategy suggested by Mr. Gauer and the Midville prosecutor. The ICCD bulletin of January, 1969, specifically mentioned that a report would be given on the progress made by Mrs.

Nelson and Mrs. Roberts "in following Mr. Gauer's recommendation in taking legal steps to have this blight (the Midwestern Bookstore) removed."

A January 28, 1969, article in the *Midville News* reported the purchase-complaint-arrest tactic in operation: "Citizens are signing the complaints, rather than the police as was done in the past. Vice Squad detectives were assisting the citizens in making identification of the sellers." The article also indicated that the Midwestern Bookstore, apparently as a way of making it more difficult for the purchase-complaint-arrest tactic to work, had stopped admitting women customers to the back room without charge.

On the next day, January 29, a third salesclerk of the Midwestern Bookstore, Miss Strong, was charged with the selling of obscene literature, arrested, and freed on $10,000 bond (*Midville News*, January 29, 1969). The same day, Mr. Smith had a second complaint filed against him, was arrested again for allegedly selling pornographic materials, and was released on a bond of $10,000, making him liable for a total of $20,000 bond. A private citizen, after having purchased materials from the bookstore, had lodged the complaints. That evening, the management of the Midwestern Bookstore put a sign on the rear wall of the front room, which notified patrons that they must show proof of age before admittance to the bookstore backroom and that women were not allowed in the back room. A *Midville News* story of January 30, 1969, reported:

> In a related development, the State Civil Rights Commission Wednesday refused to take the case of two Midville women who told commission workers the bookstore (the Midwestern Bookstore) was discriminating against women by refusing to admit them to the rear section of the store. The women contend that section contains obscene literature. The store began barring women after several complaints were signed by women.
>
> The commission worker said he felt the case was not made in good faith and was not intended to rectify a case of discrimination. (*Midville News*, January 30, 1969)

The two women, said to be affiliated with ICCD, apparently were attempting to reopen opportunities for Midville women to continue the purchase-complaint-arrest tactic.

Mr. Baker, the alleged owner of the Midwestern Bookstore (against whom selling-of-pornography charges had been lodged and dismissed in 1967), surrendered himself to court authorities on January 30, 1969, to face charges that he had failed to pay city withholding tax for employees of the bookstore. According to an article in the *Midville News*, January 31, 1969, "The amount of tax in question amounted to $15.00," and Mr. Baker "had paid approximately two-thirds of the tax for the period charged in the warrant." City attorneys and city tax officials are reported in the article to have stated that "the warrant was issued" because Mr. Baker "did not appear after two requests for an examination of the withholding records." Interview data revealed that the tax action against Mr. Baker probably was more a part of the overall antipornography effort against the bookstore than an isolated case of minor tax delinquency.

The *Midville News* (January 31, 1969) mentioned the possibility of a countersuit being undertaken by the Midwestern Bookstore. The Midville chief assistant prosecutor was cited as stating that "there was a possibility the Prosecutor's Office, the City Police and the complainant would be involved in a suit brought by Baker's attorneys. 'I can't see how they will be successful with such a suit but I guess they can try. I think it will be a bluff tactic. The people have a right to complain, the police must investigate and the Prosecutor's Office must issue warrants if the complaint is valid,' the Assistant Prosecutor said."

The Midwestern Bookstore lawsuit was to become a reality and was to have a significant impact upon ICCD and the antipornography crusade in Midville. (The lawsuit will be discussed in detail, as a component of social control, in Chapter 7.)

The January 31 *Midville News* article reported more official protests against the Midwestern Bookstore from community organizations (e.g., PTA, First Free Methodist Church, Reynolds Women's Temperance Union, and State Avenue United Methodist Church), and commented that more petitions calling for the closing of the bookstore were being circulated. Letters and petitions were reported as pouring into the city clerk's office, and those protests were being forwarded to "President Richard M. Nixon, the U.S. Supreme Court, Congressman James Pool, R-Midville, Senator Philip A. Glass, Governor William C. Wynn, and State legislators Jerome T. Marshall, James E. Travis, Jr., and Bert C. Vincent."

A February 4, 1969, article in the *Midville News* reported that a fifth obscene-literature warrant had been issued by the Midville police (again based upon citizen complaint) and that the salesclerk could not be found. The back room in the Midwestern Bookstore had been closed, apparently because there were not enough employees to run it.

Resolutions and objections against the Midwestern Bookstore continued to be filed with city officials. The Midville Censorship Advisory Board urged "the Chief of Police and County Prosecutor to take action to eliminate the Bookstore." The board added that it "supports any legal actions to close the operation." The Midville County Farm Bureau passed a resolution indicating that it had "committed its organization towards the elimination of obscenity such as the Midwestern Bookstore" (*Midville News*, February 4, 1969).

Rep. James Pool was reported (*Midville News*, February 5, 1969) to have sent letters he had received concerning pornographic literature to the "Federal Commission on Obscenity and Pornography." He described the commission as "established in late 1967 to study the area of 'pornography' and recommend to Congress what action is necessary to cut down the problem." In the same issue (February 5) of the *Midville News*, a more extensive article concerning the Commission on Obscenity and Pornography, under the title "Pornography Commission Considers Midville Visit," stated:

> Midville may eventually be a "case history" for the Federal Commission on Obscenity and Pornography.
> The Commission, in response to a recent communication from Rep. James Pool, R-Midville, has indicated that it probably will be "sending representatives of the Commission to Midville to interview the various participants in the conflict that has been occurring these past weeks." (*Midville News*, February 5, 1969)[1]

On February 6, 1969, the *Midville News* reported that the back room of the Midwestern Bookstore was still closed. On the same day, Mr. Smith was charged for the third time with the sale of obscene literature and was released again on $10,000 bond (giving him a total of $30,000 bond to date).

Suspicions again were aroused concerning preparations for a bookstore retaliatory lawsuit:

> Police are investigating at least two reports of a man posing as a member of the State Bar Association who has called people who have signed the obscene literature warrants.
> Police said the man secured the names from a woman active in

the anti-smut campaign when he told her he was attempting to compile information surrounding the cases.

In a call Wednesday to another woman who had signed a complaint, the caller said he had the books she had bought and would like to come to her home and discuss the case. He did not appear. Police are holding all material purchased at the Bookstore as evidence in the five cases. (*Midville News*, February 6, 1969)

Some of the ICCD members felt that the man posing as a member of the State Bar Association was actually a lawyer for the Midwestern Bookstore, who was preparing a possible lawsuit.

Letters and petitions continued to be sent to the Midville County board of supervisors and to the Midville city council calling for action against the Midwestern Bookstore. In a February 11, 1969, *Midville News* article, it was reported that the board of supervisors had received "seventy-eight names on eight letters and two petitions" and that the Taylor Methodist and Stewart United Methodist Churches had sent resolutions to the council objecting to the store's operation. The article also announced a debate on the issue of pornography, scheduled by the American Civil Liberties Union, to be held on February 18. This was the first mention anywhere, other than a few letters to the editor of the *Midville News*, indicating opposition to the antipornography crusade.

Miss Strong, the salesclerk of the Midwestern Bookstore who had already been freed on $10,000 bail after being charged for the sale of obscene literature, was charged a second time for an identical alleged offense (*Midville News*, February 12, 1969). The complaint was filed by a citizen, following the purchase-complaint-arrest tactic.

The debate on censorship, between the national executive director of the American Civil Liberties Union and the arts editor of the *Midville News*, was held as scheduled. The debate took place at Saint Paul's Episcopal Church in Midville. (Several Episcopal ministers had indicated in interviews that they were opposed to the principle of censorship and the tactics of the antipornography crusade.) Among the arguments of the ACLU representative were these:

Reading standards should be set by each individual, not imposed or enforced by the community. . . .

. . . Businesses which sell pornographic literature should be allowed into the marketplace of the community.

Their business success or failure should determine whether they will continue operating—that is their right.

. . . "Smut crusaders" concerned with stores selling pornographic literature should go after the dirty old men who buy it rather than try to close down the store. (*Midville News*, February 19, 1969)

The newspaper reported that the ACLU representative referred to the *Midville News* article dealing with the Midwestern Bookstore "as part of a campaign of harrassment." He cited "the Supreme Court decisions to support his argument that the individual was guaranteed the right to read anything he wanted to under the First Amendment" and said "he was tired of people who put themselves on the side of God, country, motherhood, and righteousness in their attack on obscenity."

The *Midville News* arts editor argued that:

The publication and distribution of pornographic literature should be restrained. . . .
. . . Pornographic literature is a public problem requiring community judgment. . . .
. . . Pornographic literature is not in the better interest of the community because it does not promote purity of mind, spirit or body. . . .
. . . That youngster into whose nervous hands come evocations, bestiality, perversions, ungoverned lust and the depictions of the most bizarre and twisted behavior . . . will he be helped to regard his sister, his mother, or his girl friend with pure and benevolent respect? . . . As a devotee of Judeo-Christian concepts of God and Man, I am driven by the inability to conceive of Moses, Abraham, Isaiah or Jesus of Nazareth advocating the pornography we have herein.

. . . If that limits me . . . if . . . that puts me on the side of God, the angels and righteousness, so be it—I think I prefer that side to any other. (*Midville News*, February 19, 1969)

Over two hundred persons attended the debate, and ICCD members felt that the ACLU man had been soundly defeated. One letter sent to the editor of the *Midville News* stated, as a compliment, that the Midville newsman debator "did Midville real proud" (*Midville News*, February 25, 1969). The writer of the same letter suggested, "It might be good to write to Mr. W. Cody Wilson, executive director of the President's Commission on Obscenity and Pornography, . . . asking him for a list of the names and addresses of the members and write to them, urging them to get on with the job and come up with a conclusion."

Mr. Smith, on February 25, 1969, was charged for the fourth time with the sale of obscene literature and was again freed on $10,000 bond (totaling to date $40,000 bond) (*Midville News*, February 26, 1969). On February 27, 1969, the *Midville News* reported that a $1,000,000 civil suit had been filed in Coast Town federal court by Mr. Baker, owner (now admitted) of the Midwestern Bookstore in Midville, charging violations against his constitutional rights. Those being sued included city officials, citizens who had filed complaints against the bookstore, and members of community organizations, including Mrs. Roberts of ICCD. The bookstore legal action caused the actions of the antipornography crusade to be, as an ICCD respondent indicated, "more cautious." However, the mobilization of the crusade continued.

Earlier in the week, on February 22, Mr. Russell and Mrs. Roberts, representing ICCD, wrote a letter to Mrs. Pat Nixon at the White House. The letter read in part:

> Dear Mrs. Nixon:
>
> In September, 1967, Congress enacted legislation authorizing the President to appoint "a Commission on Obscenity and Pornography." Mr. W. Cody Wilson . . . is executive director. It is gratifying to note that President Nixon has voiced his concern over many problems presented today—increasing crime, lawlessness, degenerating moral standards and the breakdown in communications, all of which have contributed to the serious unrest on college campuses, in urban areas, etc. and have even interfered with the democratic processes, which built our country.
>
> Because there is such a need for a more wholesome atmosphere in order to challenge, motivate and uplift our younger generation, we can envision you as a catalyst or stimulating spark which could unite the efforts of many groups which have been separately striving toward a common goal.
>
> . . . The strong moral fiber of your family has been an inspiration to many, but there is need for an even greater expression. Time is of the essence, if our youth are to be rescued. They are our most precious possession. Your voice raised in their defense will be most valuable.

On the evening of March 3, 1969, a "Concerned Citizens" petition, signed by 8,022 Midville adults, condemning the Midwestern Bookstore and urging that it be closed, was presented to the Midville city council. The wording of the petition was as follows: "We, the undersigned, hereby express our condemnation of the Midwestern Bookstore, 122 South Paine, Midville, [state]. We join with others in requesting action on any and all levels of government to make it possible to remove from this and other communities those establishments which produce, distribute and sell debased and ethically unsound materials. We believe the excessive preoccupation with sordid sex and violence, in magazines, papers, books, television and motion pictures is detrimental to children, youths and some adults" (*Midville News*, March 4, 1969).

According to the *Midville News* article, "The petition prompted the Council to direct the City Attorney to investigate whether the city could adopt a constitutional law prohibiting the sale of obscene literature. A study on the possibility of such action is to be made."

Mrs. Ray, who was cited in the *Midville News* article as one of the women who circulated the petition, explained that no club or organization began the petition drive. Rather, "It's just a bunch of citizens." She indicated that one of the major purposes of the petition was to demonstrate contemporary community standards as they applied in Midville, thus increasing the possibility of local convictions concerning the sale of pornographic materials. Mrs. Ray had stated: "We have here more than eight thousand signatures of people from the Midville area who are eighteen or older. This goes to prove the high standards of Midville." She "asked that the petition be sent to President Richard M. Nixon, the judges of the U.S. Supreme Court, federal and state legislators from the Midville area, Governor William Wynn, the U.S. Commission on Obscenity and Pornography, local judges, the Midville County Board of Supervisors, and the Midville Prosecuting Attorney" (*Midville News*, March 4, 1969). In addition, thirty-one community voluntary associations had independently presented petitions or resolutions to the city council. Those associations included Saint Mary's Cathedral PTA, the Midville branch of the Association of Childhood Education, Hope Memorial Baptist Church, First Free Methodist Church, Peace Lutheran Church Ladies' Guild, Midville County Farm Bureau, Midville Junior Women's Club, and the Optimist Clubs of Midville.

The petitions and resolutions which had been forwarded to federal and state judges and legislators resulted in considerable response from those officials, most of whom encouraged the efforts of the Midville citizens. Particularly gratifying to ICCD participants was the following letter from Vice President Spiro T. Agnew, sent to the Midville city clerk: "President Nixon has asked me to thank you for sending him the petitions and communications filed with the City Council. The distribution of obscene literature must be stopped and therefore is receiving top priority attention from officials of this administration" (*Midville News*, March 4, 1969).

Amid the reports of official approval of the antipornography crusade, there appeared one negative remark. One of the Midville city councilmen, Mr. Wood, was reported as stating:

> As a Councilman, I feel these communications [petitions and letters] are directed at us, but we have explored every possibility of legislating and I would hope people realize our position.
>
> We are a legislative body and we've done as much as we can.
>
> As a lawyer, I can't sluff aside questions of free speech and free press. I feel the courts will have to struggle with these rights as opposed to obscenity. We can't work to close the Bookstore just because we don't like it.
>
> As an individual, I feel that each of us has a right to decide what we want to read and what we don't want to read. (*Midville News*, March 4, 1969)

The councilman's comment brought an immediate response from the *Midville News*. On March 5, 1969, the *News* printed the following editorial comment:

> Councilman Wood, whether he intended it that way or not, left a number of those involved in the fight against the Midwestern Bookstore with the feeling that he was telling them—"You've made your case, now quit bothering us"—in his statement at Monday's Council meeting. We hope neither he nor any councilmen really mean that. When 11,000 persons are deeply concerned about a problem, it is the Council's place not only to listen but to lead. If all present avenues have been exhausted, then it owes it to the community to explore new ones. (*Midville News*, March 5, 1969)

The "11,000 persons" who were cited as being concerned about the problem of pornography in Midville, included 8,022 "concerned citizens" petitioners and the approximately 3,000 other individuals who, by petition, letter, or group resolution, had, in February and March of 1969, protested the operation of the Midwestern Bookstore. Furthermore, according to Mrs. Roberts, nearly 8,000 persons had by that time applied for and received cards indicating their "auxiliary membership" in ICCD.[2]

According to interviews, the "concerned citizens" petition, signed by the 8,022 persons, had primarily been organized by Mrs. Ray. She earlier had made her opposition to the Midwestern Bookstore known by a letter to the editor of the *Midville News*. Mrs. Roberts, representing ICCD, had been contacting everyone who had signed letters of objection printed in the newspaper, and, after reading Mrs. Ray's letter, she contacted her. As a result of the conversation between Mrs. Roberts and Mrs. Ray, the latter, according to Mrs. Roberts, "singlehandedly obtained 8,000 signatures on the petition." Mrs. Ray admitted that she herself "got 8,000 signatures." She further reported that she originally had been motivated to start the petition drive by her contact with Mr. Smith, the salesclerk at the Midwestern Bookstore. Mrs. Ray apparently had been attending a city council meeting at which the issue of pornography and obscenity was being discussed. Mr. Smith, also in attendance, was reported by her to have overheard a conversation in which she was engaged. As Mrs. Ray recollected, he interrupted the conversation and ridiculed her. She then asked herself, "What can I do as a citizen?" She discussed the issue with Mrs. Roberts, decided to start a petition, and for two months delivered copies of the petition to all of her friends and to all of the churches in Midville. She gave a speech to the city council, urging antipornography efforts. After she had delivered the 8,022 signatures to the Midville city council, and after the publicity concerning the petition in the *Midville News* and on local radio and television stations, she reported that she was "deluged with phone calls at the frequency of one every five minutes all night long." Mrs. Ray stated that three of the phone calls were from men who "addressed improper comments towards her." She notified the police of the improper calls, and subsequently they investigated.

Some of the citizens of Midville, particularly the most active members of ICCD, were becoming impatient with the fact that the Midwestern Bookstore was still operating in the same manner, as the following news story, under the title "Inaction by City Officials Frustrates Bookstore Foes," indicated:

"Why should we have to do what our elected officials fail to do for us?"

That is the question being asked by perplexed leaders of the petition drive against the Midwestern Bookstore. These leaders say they are frustrated by lack of action by city officials despite the 11,000 signatures they have presented to the Midville City Council.

"The Governor said that matters such as this should be handled locally," one woman said, "But now our local officials won't act."

. . . "I can't understand the indifference and inaction of our local officials," she said.

. . . They said that they want the city attorney, through the Council, to establish what the community standards are. "We feel that the 11,000 signatures gives us a good indication that the material being sold by the Midwestern Bookstore is below the standards of the community."

"Many of the councilmen won their seat by far less than 11,000 votes," the women stated. . . .

"The council feels that we are a bunch of busy bodies and if they ignore us long enough we will just go away," the women said. The council has been receiving petitions against the bookstore for the past six weeks.

The women, however, indicated that they would not "just go away." They said they are considering asking community leaders to bring more pressure on the council. They are asking why, if the sale of obscene material has been restricted in Fredburg and Great Falls, nothing has been done in Midville.

"I have always felt the elected officials of the city were supposed to serve the people and legislate their wishes," one of the women said. "Now I'm not so sure." (*Midville News*, March 7, 1969)

Interviews with several elected and law-enforcement officials indicated that most of them were strongly opposed to the kind of materials being sold in the Midwestern Bookstore and to the Midwestern Bookstore itself. However, several of the officials were hesitant to take action against the bookstore, either because they were concerned about the violation of constitutional rights or because the statutes defining pornography or obscenity were ambiguous or ineffective.

On March 9, the *Midville News* printed an editorial intended to help raise funds for the legal defense of those sued by the bookstore. The editorial read in part:

The recent lawsuit filed against a group of citizens by the proprietor and employees of the Midwestern Bookstore involved one factor that has not been given much consideration thus far: legal expense.

Those named in this suit have been acting basically as "agents" for several thousand people in Midville, yet they alone must bear the inconvenience and expense of the lawsuit. That is not right.

It is our suggestion, therefore, that those citizens of Midville who have expressed concern, whether or not they signed a petition, might want to contribute to a legal defense fund for the citizens named in the complaint. If so, we will be glad to serve as a collecting place for contributions.

. . . Even though there was not a single shred of evidence to support such a suit, those sued still face the cost of hiring attorneys to properly defend themselves.

. . . One dollar, $5, $10, $100—whatever you wish to contribute— is vitally important. Yes, the money is needed. But more than that, your own personal commitment and participation will follow your dollars. Many, many have said: "Yes, we are against this pornography in our city, but what can we, as ordinary citizens, do?"

Here is one answer.

The following night, after a regularly scheduled meeting, the Midville city council voted to applaud the *Midville News* defense fund (*Midville News*, March 10, 1969). The city council further made encouraging remarks about the antipornography crusade. One of the councilmen observed that, although the city council had not yet passed an ordinance that would be more severe concerning the sale of pornography, they had nonetheless been effective in the fight against the bookstore. He continued: "We can be a vehicle to forward protests to state and federal officials, and I'd hate to see citizen efforts ended. In fact, I'd like to see the efforts continued and expanded. What we're doing in Midville is much more than is being done in most other communities" (*Midville News*, March 10, 1969).

Additional petitions condemning the bookstore were presented to the council during its March 10 meeting—one from the Midville Deanery Council of Catholic Women's Church Committee and one each from the Handley School PTA, the Optimist Clubs of Midville, and the Zonta Club of Midville.

The Midville city attorney reported to the council concerning his study on the possibility of passing a revised city antipornography ordinance. The current Midville statute prohibited the sale of pornography to minors but made no provisions for the sale of such materials to adults. There was some discussion about the possibility of creating an ordinance for adults and raising the level of fines under the statute.

On March 10, 1969, another Midwestern Bookstore salesclerk, Mr. Reese, was arrested—charged with the sale of pornographic material (*Midville News*, March 12, 1969). A Midvillian had inaugurated the action with the purchase-complaint-arrest tactic previously used by other antipornography crusaders.

The *Midville News* defense fund met with considerable success. The box score (entitled "Defense Fund" and giving the total figure to date), was published in several issues of the newspaper. On March 17, the defense fund had reached $604; March 19, $730; March 20, $861; March 21, $987; March 24, $1,025; and by March 25, $1,225. (The final figure available, on April 3, 1969, set the defense fund at $1,562.)

Petitions, resolutions, and letters concerning the Midwestern Bookstore continued to be received by the city council. It was estimated that by March 25, 1969, 16,000 Midvillians had declared themselves, by signature or by organizational vote, in opposition to pornography and/or the Midwestern Bookstore (*Midville News*, March 25, 1969).

An ICCD bulletin, published in March, 1969, announced that on March 27, Mr. Raymond P. Gauer, the national executive director of Citizens for Decent Literature, who had spoken in Midville the previous October, was coming to Midville for another speaking engagement. The bulletin asked ICCD members to give the organization all merchandising coupons which they received in advertising mail and which they did not redeem for product discounts. The bulletin stated, "We will be able to use them to defray an expense which we anticipate." Whether the anticipated expense was the cost of legal defense was not clear. The bulletin did state that Citizens for Decent Literature would provide legal assistance to those Midville citizens who had been named in the lawsuit by the Midwestern Bookstore. Of further relevance to the lawsuit was the announcement, in the bulletin, that the names of auxiliary members of ICCD would not be released by the organization—"The file of names has been placed in a safe place."

The March ICCD bulletin congratulated the *Midville News* for its efforts in the antipornography campaign and asked ICCD members to "fill the courtroom with concerned citizens" at all hearings and trials concerning the selling of obscene literature. Date and places of the impending trials were detailed.

At a state convention in Major City, the Federation of Women's Clubs elected to file an *amicus curiae* brief in the federal district of Coast Town, supporting the defendants being sued by the Midwestern Bookstore (*Midville News*, March 29, 1969).

As scheduled, on March 27, 1969, Raymond Gauer returned to Midville as a guest of ICCD. He spoke at a luncheon meeting of the Kiwanis Club and at an evening public meeting in a high school auditorium. For the most part, the speeches were similar to the "typical" speech format he had followed in his October, 1968, visit to Midville. He congratulated the citizens on their antipornography crusade and told the evening audience: "The most important thing anyone can do is report a situation in which obscene literature is being sold to those responsible for enforcing the law. A registered complaint shows that this material is below the standards and brings community support to the law" (*Midville News*, March 28, 1969).

Apparently Mr. Gauer, during his March visit, gave advice to Mrs. Roberts and those being sued by the Midwestern Bookstore and pledged legal assistance from the staff of Citizens for Decent Literature. As cited earlier, his October "typical" speech included the comment that lawsuits against CDL itself were taken as indications of success.

On April 23, 1969, Mr. Smith, after a preliminary hearing, was bound over for trial on one of his four charges of selling obscene literature. The judge had ruled that there was reasonable cause to believe such material had been sold by the defendant (*Midville News*, April 23, 1969). The proceedings of the preliminary hearing were illustrative of the testimony given by antipornography crusaders who had implemented the purchase-complaint-arrest strategy and the kind of intense cross-examination they experienced at the hands of a defense attorney specializing in pornography cases. A partial summary of the hearing (from Civil Action File 2980, *People of the State* v. *Mr. Smith*, March 13, 1969) follows:

The charge on the warrant for the arrest of Mr. Smith read "knowing sale of obscene literature." At the beginning of the hearing two motions made by the defense attorney, one to lower the bond for Mr. Smith and the second to disqualify the judge from hearing the case (since he had been named a defendant in the Midwestern Bookstore lawsuit) were denied.

The judge stated: "Let the record also show that on January 27, 1969, the Defendant stood mute before this Court and entered a plea of not guilty and a demand for preliminary examination. Bond had been set in the amount of $10,000."

The first witness, Mrs. Wyatt, was called. She described the visit that she and a friend had made to the Midwestern Bookstore on January 23, 1969. She said that she had entered the back room and selected a magazine, and tried to open the plastic bag that enclosed it. One of the employees of the Midwestern Bookstore stopped her from opening the plastic wrapper. She then bought the book, left the store, and looked at it in her car. She decided that the magazine was "unfavorable material"; so she took it to the police department, put her initials on it for the purpose of identification, and left it with the police. When asked to describe what she had bought, she responded, ". . . just very distasteful in its entirety."

The defense attorney objected to the prosecutor's asking for a description of the material on the grounds that it "called for opinion and conclusion without foundation." The defense attorney made four more objections on the same grounds. The judge responded, "Let's let this testimony go in .... then we'll see if there's any evidence in there which the Court will dismiss."

In answer to questions from the prosecutor, Mrs. Wyatt characterized the book as being obscene, lewd, and lascivious. She said she had engaged in no conversation with Mr. Smith, had paid no admission to enter the back room (ladies were being admitted free to the Midwestern Bookstore at that time), and had obtained the book from the "left-hand center wall."

The prosecutor asked, "Did you go there for the purpose of buying a book and then signing a complaint, or just what was your motivation?" Mrs. Wyatt responded that she had heard about the store at a "club meeting," and "I wanted to go and find out for myself as an individual, and see if it was really as bad as I heard."

Mrs. Wyatt, when taking the book to the police, appeared before a judge and signed a complaint.

Mrs. Wyatt was a housewife, the mother of two children, whose husband worked in Midville. She was attending classes at Midville Valley College. The club of which she was a member was identified as the Junior Women's Club, which she described as a "social organization for the betterment of the community."

The prosecutor asked to have "people's proposed exhibit number one" admitted as evidence. After some exchange between the defense attorney and the prosecutor, the judge ruled to admit the exhibit (the alleged pornographic magazine).

Cross-examination by the defense attorney revealed that Mrs. Wyatt had learned about Midville's problems with pornography from a report given by a club colleague on Raymond Gauer's speech. Mrs. Wyatt stated that her friend "pointed out what kind of literature is filling our cities, and just exactly what Mr. Gauer thought of the Midville Bookstore, and that he felt it was pretty bad."

Mrs. Wyatt stated that she had borrowed money from her companion to make her purchase and that she spent the entire length of her visit in the back rather than the front part of the Midwestern Bookstore.

The defense attorney asked Mrs. Wyatt why she selected the particular book she did. She responded that she wanted to show it to her husband. The defense attorney asked her why the magazine was "distasteful" and she responded that the average person wouldn't appreciate it, and that she thought that she herself was representative of the average person.

> Defense Attorney: ". . . Alright, now what is your definition of distasteful again?"
> Mrs. Wyatt: "Okay, we'll apply all the adjectives; obscene, lewd, lascivious."
> Defense Attorney: "What is obscenity?"
> Mrs. Wyatt: "Obscenity?"
> Defense Attorney: "Yes."
> Mrs. Wyatt: "Something that is obscene would apply—would, uh, appeal to lust."
> Defense Attorney: "What is lust?"
> Mrs. Wyatt: "Lust is lascivious."
> Defense Attorney: "What is lascivious?"
> Mrs. Wyatt: "Lust, lewd."
> Defense Attorney: "Can you give me the, uh, example?"
> Mrs. Wyatt: "What do you mean by example?"
> Defense Attorney: "Of this definition."
> Mrs. Wyatt: "This magazine is an example."
> Defense Attorney: "Here we have a nude woman."
> Mrs. Wyatt: "Well—"

Defense Attorney: "Nudity is obscenity, is that what you're telling us?"

Mrs. Wyatt: "I didn't say nudity is obscenity, it—"

Defense Attorney: "Well, isn't that what we see here?"

Prosecutor: "I'll object, let her complete her answer before you cut her off."

Defense Attorney: ". . . go ahead and complete the answer, I'd like to hear it."

Mrs. Wyatt: "Obscene is what this magazine contains, obscenity."

Defense Attorney: "Okay, what standard did you apply in making that determination?"

Mrs. Wyatt: "Oh, my criterion of the average individual in the average community."

Defense Attorney: "I see, average individual in an average community. Is that the sole criterion to you in making this determination?"

Mrs. Wyatt: "Yes, sir."

Defense Attorney: "Did you read that thing in its entirety?"

Mrs. Wyatt: "I'm sorry, there's nothing to read."

Defense Attorney: "Well, did you look at each and every picture?"

Mrs. Wyatt: "Yes, sir."

Defense Attorney: "Did any of those pictures appeal to your prurient interests?"

Mrs. Wyatt: "Yes, sir."

Defense Attorney: "They did, which one?"

Mrs. Wyatt: "All of them."

Defense Attorney: "All appealed to your prurient interests?"

Mrs. Wyatt: "Yes, sir."

Defense Attorney: "What is prurient interest?"

Mrs. Wyatt: "Lustful, lewd interest."

Defense Attorney: "A lustful, lewd interest, who told you this?"

Mrs. Wyatt: "No one told me."

Defense Attorney: "Where did you read it?"

Mrs. Wyatt: "Maybe Webster's dictionary?"

Defense Attorney: "Let me ask you this, as a result of your prurient interest having been aroused, were you driven to any lustful deeds or thoughts?"

Mrs. Wyatt: "Thoughts, perhaps."

Defense Attorney: "What were they?"

Mrs. Wyatt: "Well, I've forgotten them, I've just—"

Defense Attorney: "Oh, you could not have forgotten them, this was just—"
Prosecutor: "I'll object to the Defense Attorney arguing with the witness, this isn't a badgering game, it's cross-examination."
The Court: "I think I will sustain the objection."
Defense Attorney: "Was this an important occasion?"
Mrs. Wyatt: "Was what an important occasion?"
Defense Attorney: "Well, you marched down to this bookstore, then from there to the Police Department after you made a purchase, and up here to the Court House to give a complaint and warrant for somebody's arrest."
Mrs. Wyatt: "It was an occasion."
Defense Attorney: "Have you ever done this before?"
Mrs. Wyatt: "No."
Defense Attorney: "First time?"
Mrs. Wyatt: "Yes, sir."
Defense Attorney: "Ever done it since?"
Mrs. Wyatt: "No, sir."
Defense Attorney: "Quite a momentous occasion in your life, wasn't it?"
Mrs. Wyatt: "Pardon?"
Defense Attorney: "I say it was quite a momentous occasion in your life."
Mrs. Wyatt: "It wasn't a very pleasant one."
Defense Attorney: "Wasn't pleasant, alright. Now you say you don't recollect these lustful thoughts which were aroused in your mind?"
Mrs. Wyatt: "No, sir."
Defense Attorney: "Well, did these lustful thoughts relate to sex?"
Mrs. Wyatt: "I'm sorry, I just—I've tried to forget the whole thing."

.   .   .   .

Defense Attorney: "Now, you never did get around to taking this magazine home to your husband, did you?"
Mrs. Wyatt: "Uh, actually, I purchased two of them."
Defense Attorney: "Oh, did you take that one home to your husband?"
Mrs. Wyatt: "Yes, sir."
Defense Attorney: "Same type?"
Mrs. Wyatt: "No, sir."
Defense Attorney: "Same content?"

Mrs. Wyatt: "Yes, sir."
Defense Attorney: "You still have it?"
Mrs. Wyatt: "No, sir."
Defense Attorney: "Do you know that for a fact?"
Mrs. Wyatt: "I don't think he has it, I don't know what happened, if we burned it or what."

. . . .

Defense Attorney: "Now, how many times have you gone through this magazine in its entirety?"
Mrs. Wyatt: "Maybe three times."
Defense Attorney: "Three different occasions?"
Mrs. Wyatt: "Oh, not three different occasions, I went through it three times. I couldn't believe it."
Defense Attorney: "You found it so enjoyable you went through it three times?"
Mrs. Wyatt: "I wouldn't say it was enjoyable, I just couldn't believe my eyes, and I wanted to make sure they weren't deceiving me."
Defense Attorney: "You leafed through it three times, is this correct?"
Mrs. Wyatt: "Yes."
Defense Attorney: "Show us how, please."
Prosecutor: "May the record show that she's turning the pages while she appears to be looking at the object."
Defense Attorney: "You've taken some sixty-three seconds to do so, is this correct?"
Mrs. Wyatt: "I didn't time myself."
Defense Attorney: "Would that be about correct?"
Mrs. Wyatt: "If that's how long it took."

. . . .

Prosecutor: ". . . Does the Court want an opportunity to examine the book before motions, or prefer to wait?"
The Court: "Will you give me—how many seconds was that, Mr. Defense Attorney?"
Defense Attorney: "Sixty-three, Your Honor."
The Court: "Give me sixty-three seconds."
Prosecutor: "Alright . . ."
(Civil Action File 2980, March 13, 1969)

The defense attorney moved for dismissal of the charges against Mr. Smith; the prosecutor moved to have the matter bound over to the circuit court (the preliminary hearing was being held in a Midville district court). After deliberation the Midville district court judge ruled in favor of the prosecution. ICCD members were pleased by the court ruling; the ultimate outcome of Mr. Smith's trial, however, and the outcome of other trials would be disappointing to ICCD members.

Mr. Baker, the owner of the Midwestern Bookstore, came to trial on April 28, 1969, to answer charges of having violated the Midville city tax statute. The jury found him guilty, and he was sentenced to a five-hundred-dollar fine and ninety days in jail, the maximum penalty under the city ordinance. The sentence was suspended (*Midville News*, April 29, 1969).

In other legal action, Mr. Martin had for some time been attempting to be released from the Robbins County Jail, where he was serving a nine-month term for conviction on three charges of the sale of obscene literature in Great Falls (near Midville). (Mr. Martin previously had been found guilty of selling obscene literature by the Hamilton circuit court and had been jailed for ten days, as reported in Chapter 2.) On May 2, 1969, he was released from prison, while the state court of appeals considered his conviction (*Midville News*, May 2, 1969).

While Mr. Martin had been in jail, Mrs. Roberts had written him a lengthy letter, indicating that she was praying for him, and had sent him a religious (scapular) badge. Mr. Martin responded to her on January 29, 1969. The letter reflected some of the feelings shared by bookstore employees who had experienced the purchase-complaint-arrest strategy:

> I just received your letter and now I would like to tell you like it is.
> It isn't me who is mixed up. It's people like you. The business
> I am in is protected just like the business you're in. The only
> difference is you have a hard time getting people in your place of
> business. I don't have the trouble plus I will admit I make money at
> it. If I didn't I wouldn't be in it. I don't do this for my health.
> As far as the courts go they are more crooked than the worst crooks
> for they take an oath to uphold the law. How would you like to be
> sitting in jail for what you just sent me. So you see you are protected
> also.
>   Maybe I did not want what you sent me but you forced upon me.
> That is one thing I don't have to do. People even pay to buy my
> material. You can't even give yours away. Take the prayer you said

for me and apply it to the Vietnam war. Why don't you write the president and tell him that you prayed to end the war. I will say you are the only one who had the guts to sign the name of all the righteous people who have written me. All of the ones so far are nothing but a bunch of hypocrates [sic]. How about you? You could have saved this stamp and try to straighten out your own town of Midville. How many bingo games has the church put on lately? I am sending your Green Skapular [sic] back. Give it to someone who will believe this rot. Maybe you should use it. I have touched it now so you will probably have to burn it.

In May, Miss Strong, the Midwestern Bookstore salesclerk who had been arrested on January 29, was released from charges and bond when the citizen who had filed the complaint (following the purchase-complaint-arrest tactic), the Reverend Mr. Lewis, refused to testify against her in court. Mr. Lewis stated : "My efforts are best aimed at getting the people who are at the root of the sale of pornography. . . . I could see no purpose in inflicting a $10,000 fine on this woman" (*Midville News*, May 16, 1969). He added that his action was not a statement of sympathy for the Midwestern Bookstore and was not an attempt on his part to be dropped as a defendant in the bookstore lawsuit (he had been so named). "If my name is dropped from the suit," Mr. Lewis stated, "I will file another complaint against the store" (*Midville News*, May 16, 1969).

The other Midwestern Bookstore employees who had been arrested, Mr. Thomas (January 28), Mr. Reese (March 10), and Mr. Smith (January 23, January 29, February 6, February 25), were free on bond ($10,000 for each offense) and were awaiting court action. To the great disappointment of ICCD members and many other Midvillians, on June 17, 1969, the first charge of selling obscene literature against Mr. Smith was dismissed. The judge cited a precedent in the state which had been similar to Mr. Smith's case and which had been dismissed (*Midville News*, June 18, 1969). Subsequently, all the charges against all of the arrested Midwestern Bookstore employees were dismissed.

ICCD and the Antipornography Statute

On March 24, 1969, State Representative Travis introduced an antipornography bill into the state house of representatives. The bill was quite similar to the Midville city ordinance, passed by the city council on August 22, 1968. The proposed state statute, like the Midville ordinance, was very similar to a New York statute which had been held constitutional by the Supreme Court. It included the court's criteria for the legal test of pornography (see Preface) and was concerned only with the availability of pornography to minors. Representative Travis's bill called for an increase in maximum fines for first-offense violations against the antipornography statute from one thousand to ten thousand dollars.

The *Midville News* (March 25, 1969) reported that "a sharp legislative battle appears ahead for two anti-pornography bills introduced in the House." The second bill was sponsored by Representative Frank and sought to set additional penalties for the sale of pornography to minors. It received far less publicity and support than Representative Travis's bill—his was the focus of attention for ICCD.

The *Midville News* article of March 25 stated:

> There is considerable feeling in the legislature for doing something to curb commercial traffic in pornographic material, but there also is a view among a number of legislators that any such restriction would be censorship or an abridgement on freedom of the press.
>
> "I'm afraid those supporting the bill are going to get caught between those wanting an all-out witch hunt and those who want anything to be sold," one legislator said. "There should be some fireworks." (*Midville News*, March 25, 1969)

Members of ICCD were concerned with the formulation of the state bill; several of them had attended house hearings and had written a number of letters to legislators. Those items in the bill which weren't satisfactory to members were described in detail in a June 25, 1969, *Midville News* article:

> A bill sponsored by three Midville area legislators to govern the dissemination of pornography was criticized today by a group of citizens as a "watered down piece of legislation."
>
> The bill also was blasted by a national decency spokesman as "trap legislation" which could protect smut peddlers.
>
> Spokesmen for Inter-Denominational Citizens Council for Decency, Inc., said House Bill 2959, dealing with pornography,

would be "worse than the laws presently on the books" if passed
with its present wording.

The legislation also was criticized by Raymond P. Gauer, national
director for Decent Literature, Inc.

. . . In a letter to the Midville decency group, Gauer said: "Do
you realize that if this legislation passes the famous Midwestern
Bookstore will, in effect, have a legal license to operate?

"This concern for juveniles plays right into the hands of the por-
nographer," said Gauer. "Certainly we are concerned for
juveniles—but legalizing pornography for adults doesn't protect
them."

. . . Inter-Denominational representatives said they met
Thursday with the House Committee on Judiciary to examine the
bill closely with its sponsors.

The group asks that the word "primarily" be eliminated from a
sentence in the first section of the bill. This section now reads:

"Any material or performance is 'lascivious,' if it is primarily
devoted to detailed descriptions or detailed narrative accounts of
sexual excitement, sexual conduct or sadomasochistic abuse."

Decency spokesmen said they felt any film or material with any
amount of pornographic descriptions should be considered
"lascivious."

They also ask legislators to delete the word minor from the
section which reads:

". . . . It is presented in such a manner to exploit lust for commercial gain and would appeal to a minor's prurient interest."

In another section of the bill dealing with definition of a
"lascivious performance," the citizens ask that "an audience made
up primarily of minors," be changed to read "with minors present
or containing minors."

They also ask that the following clause be added:

"No exhibitor may employ any person under the age of 18 years
to work on the premises during the showing of a production which
a minor could not attend as a patron because of its contents. Proof
of age resting upon the exhibitor."

One of the major criticisms of the bill by Midville decency
members is the section dealing with the proof of possession of
pornographic material.

The House bill stipulates that "proof of possession of six or more
identical copies of any pornographic or lascivious material is prima

facie evidence of possession with the intent to disseminate for pecuniary gain."

Inter-Denominational members ask that "two or more copies" be used as the definition for possession of literature and one copy for films, sound recordings, tape and wire recordings.

"Under the present bill a store could carry just five copies of a piece of material and not be subject to the proof of possession clause in this bill," said a decency spokesman. "This is ridiculous— especially since film showers rarely have more than one copy of the movie they are using."

Spokesmen say with their suggested changes the bill will have some "teeth" to deal with pornography distributors. Without the changes, however, they say the bill will be worse than present state statutes. (*Midville News*, June 25, 1969)

The letter from Mr. Gauer referred to in the *Midville News* article had been mailed to Mrs. Roberts on June 16, 1969, in response to her letter to him earlier in the month. Mrs. Roberts had sent Mr. Gauer a copy of House Bill 2959 and mentioned her concern about a few specifics of the bill. Mr. Gauer's letter had agreed with Mrs. Roberts's dissatisfactions and apparently raised an issue which Mrs. Roberts herself and her colleagues had not considered—specifically, the problems obtaining when legislation restricts sales of pornographic materials to minors but not to adults. Almost all of the contents of that letter were repro- duced in the June 25 *Midville News* article.

A second letter from Mr. Gauer to Mrs. Roberts, dated June 24, 1969, advised her about amendments to the bill which apparently had been sponsored by lobbyists for publishers and distributors. Mrs. Roberts had sent him the amendments and solicited his advice.

The influence of Mr. Gauer upon Mrs. Roberts and her colleagues in ICCD and, through the *Midville News*, upon the citizens of Midville was considerable and consistent. Mr. Gauer's letters to Mrs. Roberts addressed her by first name and were signed with Mr. Gauer's first name.

The American Civil Liberties Union sent a memorandum to legis- lators voicing its opposition to House Bill 2959, indicating that the ACLU "opposes any restraint under obscenity statutes on the right to create, publish or distribute materials to adults or the rights of adults' to choose the materials they read or view" (*Midville News*, June 2, 1969). The ACLU further claimed that "this legislation, if enforced, would require us to close our museums, libraries, movie houses, publishing companies and every other form of cultural activity under the threat of portraying something which the court might find 'harmful to minors'" (*Midville News*, June 2, 1969).

Representative Travis, sponsor of the bill, reacted to the ACLU's statement: "I am pretty upset with this stand by the Civil Liberties Union. . . . The bill I introduced is aimed at the commercial distribution of pornography. The Civil Liberties Union, in its memorandum to the legislators, would seem to defend the commercial sales of filth. If this is in fact their position, I can do nothing else but vigorously oppose them" (*Midville News*, June 2, 1969).

Ironically, then, the bill was opposed both by ICCD and by ACLU, though for very different reasons. ICCD apparently had urged the formulation of House Bill 2959 and had become increasingly opposed to some of the wording of the bill (emphasis upon minors) after Mrs. Roberts had consulted Mr. Gauer and CDL. In late June, 1969, the bill failed to pass the house of representatives. Both ACLU members and ICCD members reported that they were happy with the bill's failure.

The mobilization-for-action stage of the Midville antipornography crusade was, as one ICCD member put it, "winding down." The purchase-complaint-arrest tactic had been effective in getting police action against the Midwestern Bookstore and its employees, but none of them had been convicted for the sale of obscene materials. That tactic probably would have continued, but the million-dollar lawsuit filed by the Midwestern Bookstore considerably immobilized those citizens who were most prone to take such action. The attempt to "toughen" the state antipornography statute had become complex and difficult and at least temporarily had been stalled. It was at this point that our research observation of ICCD and the Midville antipornography crusade ended. When we left Midville, ICCD leaders and active members were concerned about the lawsuit, exhausted from their intensive efforts, and somewhat demoralized. They avowed, however, as illustrated by Mrs. Roberts's comment, that they had been "set back, but not stopped." With regard to the efficacy of the strategy of direct action against the Midwestern Bookstore, Mrs. Roberts, seconded by her colleagues, observed: "Maybe that bookstore will stay open, but the decent people in this town have gone on record about how they feel and what they can do if they want to, and everybody knows it. We showed them where we stand." The symbolic demonstration of decency action was, to the Midville antipornography crusaders, at least as important as the utilitarian impact of that action.

Southtown

The Uprising for Decency Rally

By 6:30 P.M. on Monday, April 7, 1969, Mr. King and the subcommittee chairmen of Uprising for Decency were scurrying about the stage and the floor of the Municipal Auditorium, making last-minute preparations for the rally. They seemed quite excited and talked nervously among themselves as they centered the speaking podium, arranged chairs on the stage, tested the microphone, stationed distribution centers for petitions and postcards, and so on. Mr. King continually was being questioned by his colleagues, by newspapermen, and by interested spectators and participants, who had already begun arriving in considerable numbers. He calmly fielded the questions, and, though admittedly nervous with the hope that "everything would come off all right," he efficiently directed the last-minute details.[3]

By 7:30 P.M., approximately 2,500 persons were seated in the audience, waiting for the proceedings to begin. At 7:00 P.M. the Ben Hur Shrine Band, in wildly colorful Shrine uniforms, had assembled on the stage and had begun playing spirited music. The stage was bedecked with red, white, and blue bunting and containers of multihued flowers. A large Uprising for Decency banner hung from the main balcony of the auditorium; the walls were decorated with red, white, and blue crepe paper and with Uprising for Decency posters. The members of the UFD Security Committee were wearing red Knights of Columbus jackets.

By the night of the rally, twenty-nine community associations, mostly church-related, youth-serving, or fraternal-service groups, had agreed to support and participate in the Uprising for Decency. (An analysis of those alignees is presented in Chapter 9.) Three other associations which had tentatively agreed to participate along with the others withdrew their names from the rally—two (fundamental religious groups) because they wanted more direct action against the "skin-flicks," one (the Boy Scouts) because they felt it would be better not to be so "public" in strategy.

A few minutes after 7:30 P.M., the band stopped playing and Mr. King took the podium and called the rally to order. The flag was posted by a marching detail of the American Legion, who were wearing matched blue uniforms, white Sam Brown belts, polished boots, and chrome helmets. They marched in from the rear of the auditorium in two separate files and converged on the stage, where they posted the colors. The audience recited the Pledge of Allegiance and, accompanied by the Shrine Band, sang the national anthem.

Mr. King then called upon a priest, a chaplain of the Knights of Columbus council, who gave a brief invocation. Mr. King then introduced State Senator Welles; State Representative and Mrs. Randolph; State Representative Neilsen; the district attorney; Councilman-Elect Williamson; Mr. McIlheny, a candidate in the runoff election for the city council; Councilman-Elect Powers; Councilman-Elect Peterson; Councilman-Elect and Mrs. Stuart; Mr. Jackson, another city council runoff candidate, and Mrs. Jackson; and State Representative Cooper. The audience applauded warmly.

Mr. King then proceeded to read letters from some notables who supported Uprising for Decency: the governor, a U.S. senator, and a U.S. representative. No word had arrived, as had been hoped, from the White House.

Mr. King introduced the first guest speaker of the evening, the Church of Christ minister, who took the podium. (His speech was presented as an example of generalized beliefs in Chapter 4.)

After the minister had concluded, to lengthy applause, Mr. King thanked him "for that very inspiring message." Mr. King then introduced the Catholic layman and attorney who was the executive director of a state Catholic action group. His speech concentrated primarily on the necessity of and strategies for establishing "community standards" by which to judge whether or not materials are "pornographic" and therefore unacceptable. Some of his comments which were particularly relevant to that important point were these:

> The community has a right, a lawful right, even a responsibility, to protect itself from harm and do this by due process of law. . . .
> . . . I know of no better way to determine the standards of the community than through the jury system, wherein members of the community themselves determine whether a given piece of material is patently offensive to that community and without redeeming social value. If on occasion a jury makes a mistake, there is always

a higher court to which we can appeal, so that abuses do not take place. This is the American system, and I know of none better.

So the responsibility, ladies and gentlemen, is ours. The standards of our state and our community are what we make them. No one else can make them for us. Surely, we do not want the standards of our society to be those which are adopted by the publishers and the distributors of material depicting violence, sexual perversion, and human degradation. But their standards will be considered as our standards if we permit it by our silence and our passivity.

(Applause)

. . . I think we can be absolutely certain that if there is really an Uprising for Decency that carries beyond this meeting tonight and gives all our public support to the passage of adequate laws, and then gives all our public support to prosecutors and the courts and to juries who are charged with enforcing the law, then the flood of offensive material will be stopped, and we will no longer need to hang our heads in shame because of what is so frequently displayed for profit in public places in communities across this land. This is our challenge as citizens of a free society.

The attorney received lengthy applause, and Mr. King thanked him. Senator Welles was then introduced by Mr. King and addressed himself specifically to the two antipornography bills he was guiding through the legislature. He stated, in part:

I have introduced into the senate some weeks ago a bill aimed at trying to curb pornographic literature [Senate Bill 661; see Chapter 5]. It's a bill that would provide and give the courts and prosecuting authorities of our counties and state, I believe, the power to take from the newsstands of our cities and towns and communities and our schools what is, as the prior speaker described, offensive to the community morals. The people responsible for distributing the literature can be sent to the penitentiary for ten years, maximum, which is a pretty good deterrence if it can be enforced.

I believe and have enough faith in Congress and in the merchants and citizens of our community that, with a little help, this bill can be passed . . . then the prosecuting attorneys and the attorney general of our state will have the tools to work with that I think will be effective.

I am having a hearing tomorrow in the Jurisprudence Committee at 2:00 P.M. I assume that the committee will get to this bill by about 3:00 P.M. or a little before. I have called some people who are interested in the bill, and they will send representatives to that hearing tomorrow afternoon to demonstrate to the members of the legislature that they are concerned about their own homes and communities. Some of you who feel you can get away from your jobs tomorrow afternoon, we will be glad to have you.

You would think that a bill such as this wouldn't receive opposition, but the purveyors of pornography and obscenity work with devious and underground ways, and they will try to defeat passage of this legislation.

We also have pending in both the house and the senate, a bill aimed at obscene movies [Senate Bill 660; see Chapter 5]. Some of those have been seized in recent weeks by the police department of Southtown. . . . But the laws we have now are not adequate to give the law-enforcing officials and the courts the lasting authority they need.

I will be having a hearing on this bill, too, in the Senate Committee on Jurisprudence. All who can come are welcome to come to this one, too. The gist is to permit the prosecuting attorney to close down and padlock those movie houses who persist in showing pornographic movies.

Mr. King thanked Senator Welles, who was applauded warmly, when he had concluded. Mr. King then introduced, in turn, Representative Randolph and Representative Neilson, both of whom made brief comments in support of "tougher" antipornography legislation. Mr. King then read the Uprising for Decency petition to be signed, and the postcards to be sent to the Motion Picture Association. He informed the audience that the petitions and postcards would be passed out at that time, and everyone should "sign the petition tonight" and "take the postcards home, sign them, and mail them." Mr. King then introduced the third and last major speaker of the evening, the Baptist minister. (Excerpts from that speech were presented as examples of generalized beliefs in Chapter 4.) During his speech, members of the Uprising for Decency Security Subcommittee and their colleagues were distributing petitions and postcards.

By the end of the final speech, 2,286 persons had signed the petition. All five thousand postcards had been handed out to the members of the audience. In the following few days, 530 additional signatures would be acquired on the petition. Mr. King had deliberately begun passing out the petition before the end of the program because he did not want people to leave before they had signed up.

After the Baptist minister had finished his presentation and Mr. King had made sure that all of the petitions had been returned, he thanked everyone present, both those on the program and those in the audience, and formally closed the rally, reminding everyone, "This is just the beginning. Don't forget to support the legislation in every way you can."

As the crowd filed out of the auditorium, Mr. King and his colleagues gathered up their materials and quietly assessed the evening's events. Unanimously, the men felt that the evening had been a great success. They were very happy with the number of officials who had shown up, with the speeches that had been given, and with the audience reaction to the speeches. They were also delighted that there had been no embarrassing moment—no counterdemonstration. They were not completely pleased, however, with the number of people who had turned out for the rally. The estimated total of 2,500 persons was considerably below the various expectations (at different stages during their planning meetings) of 7,000, 5,000, and 4,000. However, as Mr. King pointed out, "I think we can be happy so many people are here, even if it didn't reach our expectations. After all, I'd rather have 2,500 interested people, than 7,000 people who just sit around. I think these people were very interested."

Mr. King felt that a turning point had been passed, but he was not yet sure what it determined. He indicated that he intended to take the petitions to the legislature within a few days, and then "we'll just leave it up to them and see what happens." He looked around at the huge auditorium, then down at the stack of petitions, smiled, and softly said, "I'm glad that's over!"

Postrally Publicity and Events

On April 8, 1969, the day after the Uprising for Decency Rally, four articles relevant to the rally and antipornography activities appeared in local newspapers.

A page-1 article in the *Campus Daily News*, the University newspaper, reported, "Speakers at Rally Uphold Decency." The article read, in part: "Society must express its right and duty to protect itself against obscene literature and films through support of law, 'Uprising for Decency Rally' speakers contended Monday night. A gathering filled half of Municipal Auditorium to participate in the rally sponsored by 27 Southtown civic, church, and educational organizations" (*Campus Daily News*, April 8, 1969). The article then listed the speakers and briefly outlined major points of their speeches. The postcards were described, and the petition "for the purpose of effectively demonstrating to legislators the public sentiment in support of the movement" was outlined.

"Adults and Tots Back Film Decency" was a subheadline on page 1 of the April 8 edition of the *Southtown Globe*. The article read, in part:

> Adult community leaders speaking at an "Uprising for Decency" rally Monday night told a family audience of about 1,500 persons that "all moral restraint has broken down," but many teenagers interviewed at the rally said that youth, not adults, is responsible for turning the tide.
>
> The rally, held in Municipal Auditorium, was called to support legislation to regulate and curb production and sale of lewd films and pornographic material.
>
> Teenagers made up about one-tenth of the audience. Most were parents and many brought their youngsters.
>
> Petitions calling for more stringent laws against obscenity were passed out.
>
> "Petitions don't do any good," a 17-year-old Jefferson Davis High School student said. "Legislators just throw them away."
>
> A 14-year-old Yeats High School girl sitting nearby said "If they had teenagers speaking here, more young people would show up." (*Southtown Globe*, April 8, 1969)

The article then listed the speakers, outlined their speeches, and continued:

> A 14-year-old girl standing in the lobby of the auditorium said that although she is opposed to "real bad movies," she believes that "If some kids want to go to obscene movies, they should be allowed to."
>
> . . . A sophomore at Windsor High School said that he has been "embarrassed" by some downtown movies, and thought "obscene movies" should be stopped altogether.

Most other teenagers said they should "enforce age restrictions on adult movies," rather than eliminating them. And they pleaded for "more general audience" movies.

"At one time, there was nothing but adult and restricted movies in Southtown," . . . a 14-year-old student at Seely Junior High said. "There's no decent movies for kids to see anymore, just Walt Disney movies, and I've seen all of them."

. . . A 17-year-old Central High School junior complained that he "can't take a girl to a movie without some girl coming out half nude."

. . . A junior at Jefferson Davis High said he has walked out of several movies because he considered parts of them obscene. "I just got grossed out," he said. (*Southtown Globe*, April 8, 1969)

On page 2 of the April 8 edition of the *Southtown Globe*, a brief article, under the heading "Panel Plans Smut Sale Bill Hearing" announced the forthcoming Jurisprudence Committee hearing on Senator Welles's Senate Bills 660 and 661.

Also on page 2, and filling at least as many column inches as the page-1 article on the Uprising for Decency Rally, was an article entitled "High Court Assures Right to Obscenity in the Home." The article reported the Supreme Court decision in the case of *Stanley v. Georgia* (1969), and read, in part:

The Supreme Court guaranteed Americans Monday the right to read dirty books or look at dirty movies in the privacy of their homes.

"A state has no business telling a man sitting alone in his own house, what books he may read or what films he may watch," said Justice Thurgood Marshall for the court.

The ruling, an important extension of freedom of thought, forbids states to make mere possession of obscene material a crime—but leaves them free to restrict public distribution.

Marshall said an Atlanta bachelor, Robert Eli Stanley, sentenced to a year in prison because he had three "stag" films at home, was "asserting the right to read or observe what he pleases—the right to satisfy his intellectual and emotional needs in the privacy of his own home."

"Whatever may be the justifications for other statutes regulating obscenity," Marshall said, "we do not think they reach into the privacy of one's own home."

Chief Justice Earl Warren, Justices William O. Douglas, John Marshall Harlan and Abe Fortas joined Marshall's opinion. Justice Hugo L. Black concurred separately . . .

"The Georgia obscenity law, now invalid, was based on the principle that the state should protect individuals and society from literature and films that could spawn antisocial conduct." Marshall said: "We are not certain that this argument amounts to anything more than the assertion that the state has the right to control the moral content of a person's thoughts."

Besides, he said, for the majority, there appears to be little proof that exposure to obscenity leads to deviant sexual behavior or to crimes of sexual violence.

"Given the present state of knowledge," he said, "the state may no more prohibit mere possession of obscenity on the ground it may lead to antisocial conduct than it may prohibit possession of chemistry books on the ground that they may lead to the manufacture of homemade spirits." (*Southtown Globe*, April 8, 1969)

Mr. King was quite disappointed with the newspaper reports of the Uprising for Decency Rally. He thought that the *Southtown Globe* article had "misrepresented who was at the rally and what most people felt about it by emphasizing the teenager audience and quoting only a few of them." He added, "I think the reporter just thought he had a good story in a couple of kids, rather than reporting the feelings of the crowd."

As indicated in earlier chapters, Mr. King wanted to avoid having the rally become just a youth program, because he wanted to gather as many voter signatures as possible on the petitions and thereby to indicate adult support of the antipornography bills pending in the state legislature. Thus, he was considerably disappointed when the major article reporting the rally emphasized the one-tenth of the audience who were young persons.

Mr. King also thought that the teenage quotes selected and presented in print gave the impression of countering some of the "important points made at the rally by the speakers" and "gave the impression that lots of people agree with those [teenagers'] quotes, which is not true." He also felt that there were considerably more than 1,500 persons attending the rally. The management of the Municipal Auditorium, which Mr. King felt "ought to know more about those things," had estimated the attendance to be approximately 2,500. (Our count of those attending the rally agreed with the 2,500-person estimate.)

He wished that there had been more newspaper coverage of the event and that the rally had "gotten more space in the paper." He contrasted the first-page report on the rally with the second-page report on the Supreme Court decision invalidating the Georgia obscenity law and lifting prohibitions for the use of pornography by individual citizens in their private homes. He thought that the fact that the Supreme Court decision had "as much space as we got" was "unfortunate." The content of the Supreme Court article also disturbed Mr. King: "It was almost as if the article were put in there to debate some of our speakers." As the reader can observe, Supreme Court Justice Marshall was quoted as denying the proven validity of the relationship between the use of pornography and social pathology and as dismissing the argument that citizens should protect individuals and society from obscene literature and films—arguments that were central in the rally speeches. Reflecting upon the newspaper coverage, Mr. King philosophized, "Oh well, we got a lot of signatures on the petitions, and that's what counts." There had been virtually no opposition to Uprising for Decency. Mr. King reported that he had received no "crank phone calls and no verbal or written criticisms."

Following the rally, a negative letter to the editor, under the title "Decency Rally" appeared in the *Southtown Globe*. The letter read:

To the Editor:

The rally "Uprising for Decency" which is sponsored by various religious and civic groups of Southtown is a confession by these organizations that they consider themselves unable to convince people by rational means (i.e., by the use of rational persuasion) that lewd films and pornographic materials are worthless and that to patronize them is to waste one's time and money. It is most unfortunate that these religious groups, which preach peace, demand the violent and forcible suppression (by legislation to regulate and curb production and sale of lewd films and pornographic materials) of the products of those whose activities they violently disapprove.

Until pornographers FORCE others to purchase their wares such violent suppression is immoral and unjustified. Moral decency and uprightness cannot be promoted by calling for suppression carried out by the state in the form of "legal" controls. (*Southtown Globe*, April 10, 1969)

The local "underground newspaper," *The Voice*, ran at least three articles that strongly opposed Uprising for Decency and related anti-pornography activities. An article on April 16, describing Senate Bills 660 and 661, commented: "We can guess who this bill was aimed at with no sweat at all" and indicated that the bills "ignore completely the constitutionality issue of specifically defining obscenity, . . . [and] allow a judge to determine for himself what should be considered harmful."

A longer article in a May issue of *The Voice* specifically reported the activities of the Uprising for Decency Rally:

Decency Desist!

Decency Rallies seem to be the latest rage among the unregenerate Victorian set these days. Rearing its pristine head down in Florida, only a few days elapsed until the fad popped up on Southtown in the wake of great press play and predictions of attendance in the thousands. Teenagers seem to be the prime target of these extravaganzas. The local press confidently proclaimed that thousands of decent Southtown teenagers would show up and put in their bit for morality. These, no doubt, were to be the "vast majority" of clean living youth that we're always told about between stories on youth rebellion and dope.

I didn't make it down to catch the performance; I'm allergic to decency, anyway. But, the newspaper stories the next day justified my faith in the basically indecent nature of American youth. Fifteen hundred folks showed up; not a lot of them turned out teen-aged. A lousy 150 decent teenagers out of the thousands in Southtown. Shit, man, we're gonna win.

One 14-year-old, quoted by the paper, lamented the fact that the only movies in town that weren't restricted in admission were Walt Disney flicks—and she'd already seen all of them. The solution, of course, is to abolish the restrictions.

In the long run, the decency set is doomed to extinction. Not only cultural radicals and freaks, but also the main cultural stream has left them behind. Puritanism is simply out. (*The Voice*, May 7, 1969)

The April and May articles in *The Voice* neatly demonstrated the perceived differences in life styles and the status battles between those life styles, from the alternative rather than the traditional point of view. Proponents of the alternative life styles, like those representing the more traditional, often couched their arguments in such terms as "the main cultural stream" and "we're gonna win."

In June, *The Voice* editorialized on "pornography":

A serious thought for the week for those morally outraged mothers and loyal, patriotic super-citizens who see maximum legislation as the way to protect youth from the corruption of obscene material. Denmark has experimented with legalizing all forms of pornography for adults and found sales declined. Minister of Justice Knud Thestrup based his effort to legalize pornography on the assumption (confirmed by a commissioned 2 year study) that public interest in pornography is mostly "the result of curiosity about what is forbidden."

Hardest hit are the "porno" shops who are now asking $8.50 a reel for skin flicks that sold for $40 last year. Said one "legalization is killing business. . . ." Police statistics show a 25% decrease in sex crimes for 1967 when the ban on books but not on pictures had been lifted. Nor does children's contact with obscene material seem to have increased. According to Rektor Ole Barfoed, headmaster of one of Copenhagen's largest grammar schools, children are simply not interested. "This so called altruism about protecting the children is often just a false way adults have of saving themselves from embarrassment." (*The Voice*, June 12, 1969)

Interestingly, the most vehement postrally criticism of Uprising for Decency came, as Mr. King stated, from "within the ranks." Some of the Church of Christ and Baptist Church members, and even some of Mr. King's colleagues in the Knights of Columbus, felt that the rally should have concentrated more upon youth and had young speakers. They did not think that enough attempt had been made to get greater attendance at the rally from among Southtown's young persons. The publication *Churchweek* praised Southtown for "joining the list of cities whose youths have taken a stand against obscenity, as they held a gigantic rally Monday night in Municipal Auditorium" (April 11, 1969).

Mr. King steadfastly continued to believe, however, that it was important to concentrate on "adults, because they vote, and could sign the petitions. Look what is happening to the legislation, and how much support it's receiving, and how rapidly it's moving in committee."

On April 10, 1969, the Uprising for Decency petitions were presented by Mr. King to Senator Welles. He in turn immediately introduced them as supporting evidence during committee meetings and floor discussions on Senate Bills 660 and 661. The committee members, according to Senator Welles, were "unanimously impressed with the petitions." There was virtually no opposition to the bills, and only minor amendments were offered for discussion.

Following the rally, general interest in Uprising for Decency rapidly fell off. Mr. King reported that he received only "an occasional phone call" from individuals whose organizations had aligned with Uprising for Decency. By and large the only persons who manifested continuing interest in the course of the legislation were some of the chairmen of the UFD subcommittees, the Knights of Columbus councils, the speakers at the rally, and ministers of the two large church groups that had been involved in the development of UFD from its beginning (the Southtown Baptist Association and the Michael Road Church of Christ).

Mr. King himself maintained at least weekly, and sometimes daily, contact with the state capitol, "to keep my eye on the progress of the bills and do what I could until they passed." He felt that when the governor signed Senate Bills 660 and 661, UFD would have "accomplished its major goal."

Mr. King felt that the senate bills were "our bills" and that the members of UFD in effect "wrote those bills" and would be responsible for getting them through the legislature. Mr. King and some of his colleagues attended committee meetings and hearings for bills 660 and 661, and some of the UFD members offered testimony in support of the measures.

On April 9, 1969, newspaper articles in the *Campus Daily News* and the *Southtown Globe* reported the successful emergence of Senate Bills 660 and 661 from the Jurisprudence Committee. In the *Campus Daily News* article, Senator Welles, the sponsor of the bills, was quoted as saying: "The parents of this state have just reached the limit of tolerance, and are demanding that we pass some sort of laws to keep this material out of the hands of juveniles."

Senator Welles himself reported in a mimeographed letter to his constituents:

> Among other good things, the Easter season brought a renewal of faith in basic human decency, I thought. First, on Easter Monday, some 3,000 people closed out the holidays with a Southtown rally

in behalf of good taste—not filth—in reading matter and
entertainment. Then, on Tuesday a Senate committee readily
approved my bills to impose needed controls on the flow of
obscenity to young people. . . .

At the Southtown rally and at the committee hearing, I was
impressed with the quiet good sense people are bringing to bear on
this matter of pornography. They are attacking it, not in an
emotional manner, but with effective determination. ("State Affairs:
A Capitol Report," April 11, 1969)

Mr. King reported that, following the rally, donations from groups
participating in Uprising for Decency "trickled in." The Independent
Auto Repair Shop Association had, as indicated above, donated $150
for the Easter Sunday rally ad. In addition, $182 had been donated to
the rally fund by nine of the twenty-nine participating groups—leaving
a balance of approximately $218 unpaid (which the Knights of Colum-
bus subsequently would pay).

On April 18, 1969, Senate Bill 661 passed the senate with little or no
opposition and was referred to the house for deliberation (*Southtown
Globe*, April 19, 1969).

On April 24, 1969, an article from the Associated Press appeared in
the *Southtown Gazette*, as follows:

AUDIENCE TO BLAME FOR FILMS?

Denver (AP)—The spokesman for America's movie industry,
former presidential aide Jack Valenti, says there is no shortage of
family films, "just a shortage of family audiences."

Valenti, in Denver for a special screening of the movie "Goodbye
Columbus," said there was "hypocrisy in American audiences,"
and added that the public has the "greatest civil right in the world
to stay out of the movies."

Valenti said he was opposed to "censorship at any level" and
said the judgment of a censor was "personal and subjective, not like
the judgment of the law."

Mr. King and his colleagues reported that they had had "no feedback
at all" concerning the postcards mailed to Mr. Valenti. Perhaps the
reason was that no return addresses had been printed on the postcards. Mr. King did, however, get some inquiries from people in other
states who had heard about the rally, the petitions, and the postcards,
and wanted advice about how to set up organizations in their own

communities. Mr. King said that he had responded with a long letter to each of the inquiries.

Concerning community reaction to the antipornography endeavors, Senator Welles was quoted as saying: "I have had mail from all over our state thanking me for bills I am sponsoring on drug abuse, pornography, law enforcement and air and water pollution. . . . People are deeply concerned over these and similar problems—especially those that affect the health and well-being of young people. They expect positive action to deal with them" (*Southtown Globe*, April 25, 1969).

The senate, again with little or no opposition, passed Senate Bill 660 on April 30, 1969. Senator Welles commented that he thought the passing of the bill, which named movie theaters showing alleged pornographic films as disorderly houses, would give law-enforcement officers "a more effective approach than in trying to stop the objectionable movie itself from being shown" (*Southtown Gazette*, April 30, 1969).

President Nixon's May 2 request that Congress develop new laws to combat sending of unsolicited pornographic literature in the U.S. mails was printed in detail on page one of the May 3 issue of the *Southtown Globe-Gazette*. On May 8, Congressman Peak, who represented Southtown's district in the U.S. House of Representatives, was quoted at length in the newspaper, agreeing with President Nixon and demonstrating his support for the formulation of stricter legislation (*Southtown Globe*, May 8, 1969).

A May 27 article in the *Southtown Globe* reported that "thirty or forty Southtowners this week" had received unsolicited advertisements for pornographic materials, which themselves were pornographic, in the mail. The article described for the reader how he or she could "dam up the flood of obscene mailings" by filling out a "pandering form" at the post office. The submission of the form would result in a "prohibitive order" to the company that mailed the literature, forbidding it to mail any more such material to the complainant.

Mr. King and his colleagues were aware of the publicity concerning pornographic materials in the mail but did not feel it was appropriate to get Uprising for Decency going again with that issue. Mr. King continued, as he said, to "ride herd" on Senate Bills 660 and 661 and emphatically repeated, "These are my only concerns at the moment. If they do not pass, then the rally and all our efforts were for nothing."

Mr. King had no basis for concern. Senate Bill 661 passed both the senate and the house and was signed into law by the governor on May 22, 1969. Senate Bill 660 was passed by both the senate and the house and signed by the governor on June 12, 1969, to go into effect within ninety days.

Both Senate Bills 660 and 661 proceeded through the legislative process in what both Mr. King and Senator Welles felt was record time. The speedy passage was considered by both Mr. King and Senator Welles to be in good part the result of UFD's demonstration of support for the legislation.

The history of Senate Bill 660 was as follows:

March 14, 1969—filed with the secretary of the senate
April 29, 1969—read for the third time, and passed by a *viva voce* vote
April 30, 1969—sent to the house
May 30, 1969—read for the third time in the house and passed by a nonrecorded vote
May 30, 1969—returned to the senate
May 31, 1969—signed by the Chair of the senate
June 2, 1969—signed by the Speaker of the house
June 12, 1969—signed by the governor, to go into effect within ninety days

The history of Senate Bill 661 was as follows:

March 14, 1969—filed with the secretary of the senate
April 18, 1969—read for the third time and passed by a recorded vote—25 ayes, 0 nays
April 21, 1969 sent to the house
May 8, 1969—returned from the house with amendment
May 8, 1969—senate concurred on the house amendment by a vote of 31 ayes, 0 nays, *viva voce*
May 13, 1969—signed by the Chair of the senate
May 13, 1969—signed by the Speaker of the house
May 22, 1969—signed by the governor, to take immediate effect

The amendment to Senate Bill 661 changed the definition of *minor* from age sixteen years to age seventeen years.

Once Senate Bills 660 and 661 had been passed, Mr. King stated, with some relief, that "the job of Uprising for Decency is over." The subcommittee structure and other aspects of the ad hoc antipornography organization were dissolved.

Uprising for Decency Does Not Rise Again

In May and June, two "controversial" films were shown in Southtown without difficulty. The first, in May, was *The Killing of Sister George*, which had received the attention of antipornography crusaders in several other cities and several other states. The *Campus Daily News* reviewed the film and in the last paragraph of the review stated: "Many people will find that George and Alice are the kind of people their parents warned them about. Maybe it's George's way of fighting the population explosion without the pill; maybe it's time for an emergency meeting of the Southtown Anti-Smut League. Audience reaction ought to be interesting" (May 2, 1969).

Mr. King reported in an interview that some of the Baptist participants in UFD said they wanted to revitalize the ad hoc organization and "get some picks and axes and go down and break up the theater that was showing *The Killing of Sister George*." Mr. King disagreed with "this kind of activity" and felt that it would "accomplish nothing." He added, again repeating his consistent perspective, that "picketing, demonstrating, and that stuff really doesn't do any good." He reminded the Baptists that "what you have to do is bring about legislative change, and that's what we're doing, and that's what the purpose of this is all about."

Candidly, he felt that the position of the Baptists on the issue of *The Killing of Sister George* was "somewhat hypocritical. One minute they wanted to take axes and go chop down the theater, and the next minute they say they want to go see the picture, to see if it's really as bad as they've heard it is. I can't understand that. If you go see it, no matter what your reason, you still have to pay for it, and you support the film and the theater." He added, "One of the ministers who wants to picket said that nothing would really be accomplished about lewd films until somebody went to jail for the cause. I don't believe in that, either."

In early June, the Avalon Theater scheduled a one-night preview of the film *I Am Curious (Yellow)*. The preview was intended by the management to find out community interest and whether or not "we could show it in Southtown." A few days earlier, a theater in another part of the state which was showing the film had been burned to the ground, and there was evidence of arson apparent (*Southtown Globe*, June 13, 1969).

The film was announced in Southtown by considerable newspaper publicity and was shown—without legal incident or police action. Nor did Mr. King or his colleagues become actively involved in opposing the showing of the film. In fact, Mr. King commented, "I hope nobody will do anything foolish about the picture. Pickets or things like that will just give the film more publicity. We've just got to wait until the laws begin to get implemented."

The preview showing of *I Am Curious (Yellow)* was without legal incident, as noted. However, shortly after the film began, a cloud of smoke from a powerfully putrid "stink bomb" (apparently hydrogen sulfide) spread throughout the packed theater (patrons had paid $5.50 for admission). Gasping and choking, about two-thirds of the audience left. One-third of the audience remained (including our two research observers) and, according to one patron, "toughed it out" until the completion of the film, by which time the smoke had dissipated and the odor had abated somewhat.

Following the completion of the film, some of the audience members gathered in the lobby and outside the theater to discuss what had occurred. There was considerable speculation about who had planted the stink bomb. Some of the persons felt that it was "rednecks in the audience, who were angry because the picture wasn't really a stag film." Others argued that "antismut nuts" had tried to interrupt the showing of the film. Still others felt that it was merely a publicity stunt instigated by the theater manager, in the hope that the newspapers would "give it a play," thus guaranteeing the continuing run of the film at the Avalon Theater. There was no report at all of the incident in the local newspaper. The Avalon Theater did subsequently have an extended booking of the film.

Mr. King was relatively certain that the stink bomb was a publicity stunt, and he cited that incident to confirm his belief that harrassment of businessmen showing such films actually plays into their hands. Furthermore, he felt that if such activity was conducted deliberately by citizens opposed to the film, that activity was really against the law. He referred again to the inconsistency of breaking the law as a tactic for establishing new law.

Consistent with his careful approach to legal procedure, Mr. King had checked over the UFD petitions before he submitted them to the senate committee. He found one petition that had been machine-duplicated six times, and the original and six copies (with about ten names each) were included in the pile of petitions. He commented:

> I caught these before they were sent in. It would not have been a good thing for us to do, because it would have made us look bad. Somebody got heated up and thought they could help out the cause this way. That would have done us a lot more harm than good; it was exactly the kind of thing that we should avoid doing. One unfortunate act like this, one illegal or unethical move, and all the rest of our intentions suffer. I sent in the original copy of the petition and pulled out the duplicates, of course.

Mr. King reviewed the goals of Uprising for Decency. He felt that the ad hoc antipornography organization had accomplished, without doubt, its major goal—that of getting legislative change. He thought the goal of getting the community involved in the problem of lewd films had also been accomplished. The companion goal, that of putting pressure on the movie industry to provide better family film entertainment, was, in his opinion, problematically accomplished. Five thousand postcards had been taken by the participants at the UFD rally, and "a lot of people told me they had sent them in," but Mr. King had no adequate way of judging how many actually had been sent in and what impact they had had.

On the whole, Mr. King was very satisfied with the job he and his colleagues had done and with the impact of UFD. He strongly felt that there was no need to perpetuate the antipornography organization, since "there's no point in keeping it alive after the job is done. Sometimes organizations like these begin to have a life of their own and have to look around for issues to fight, and one by one the issues become more and more weak and more and more distant from the original goals. I don't think we should let that happen to Uprising for Decency."

When Mr. King was informed that some recent decisions in state courts had provided precedents invalidating, or at least weakening, the impact of Senate Bills 660 and 661, he responded: "No, I don't think the law is as good as it should be, but the important thing is we got our say in and got the law passed so quickly." He was of the opinion that the symbolic aspects of the antipornography crusade and the public demonstration of opposition to pornography were at least as important as the actual law itself.

When Mr. King was asked in an interview whether he thought his interest in antipornography activities was church-related, citizen-related, or parent-related, he replied that he thought it was "a combination of all three." "Primarily," he reflected, he was "acting as a citizen who was disturbed with the issue of lewd films in Southtown. My approach was a political approach, rather than a crusading approach. I wanted to see diversity of groups in Uprising for Decency, so it wouldn't look like we were a bunch of crazy crusaders."

Early in June, 1969, Mr. King was asked by the state administrative offices of the Knights of Columbus to take the chairmanship of the KC Statewide Pornography Committee. In an interview he commented that he was not certain that he would take the job. "Frankly," he said, "I'm tired. Uprising for Decency took an awful lot of hours each day, and I was going to meetings during the evening almost every night." He added, "On the other hand, it would be quite a challenge, and I think a worthwhile task. I'll have to look at it more closely and see what the leadership is going to be like at the top level. Every year there's a change in KC leadership, and sometimes it is quite different."

Mr. King was referring to the liberal or conservative orientation of the Knights of Columbus leadership. He considered himself to be relatively liberal as compared to some KC officers, especially on the issue of pornography and obscenity. Some of them wanted to "wage total war" and did not agree with the efficacy of Mr. King's strategy of directed legislative change.

Subsequently, Mr. King did take the appointment, and at the conclusion of our research observation he was serving actively in the capacity of chairman of the Knights of Columbus State Pornography Committee.

However, mobilization for action of Uprising for Decency in Southtown was finished.

Discussion

Gusfield (1963:20) observed that the power of the Antisaloon League, a central moral crusade organization in the temperance movement, was sometimes astounding. He was referring primarily to the Antisaloon League's ability to pressure the passing of national legislation and to their control over local and state elections. ICCD and UFD certainly did not have the power of the Antisaloon League, but their ability to implement changes, whether primarily utilitarian or symbolic in impact, was impressive. The mobilization for action implemented by ICCD and UFD involved influential community leaders, politicians at various levels of government, educators, health officials, clergy from diverse religious denominations, representatives from a wide array of community voluntary associations, local press, radio, and television, and significant numbers of additional community citizens.

Smelser noted that the norm-oriented movement "begins with slow, searching behavior" and "accelerates into a period of supercharged activity" (1962:299). Both ICCD and UFD began with tentative action, probing for community support. The actual mobilization for action of ICCD and UFD was indeed supercharged, particularly that of ICCD. By March, 1969, ICCD had gathered delegates from or associated with thirty-one Midville voluntary associations (representing a membership of over sixteen thousand persons), had issued over eight thousand ICCD auxiliary membership cards, and had acquired the signatures of eleven thousand Midvillians on petitions protesting the Midwestern Bookstore. The manager and employees of the bookstore had been arrested several times each (with one employee accumulating a total of forty thousand dollars in bail bonds) as a result of the intensive implementation of the purchase-complaint-arrest strategy. ICCD members had written protest letters and sent petitions to local and national leaders (including the President); had distributed antipornography literature and pamphlets; had lobbied and testified on behalf of antipornography statutes; and, as Mrs. Roberts summarized, had unrelentingly continued to "phone-phone-phone-phone and write-write-write-write."

UFD's mobilization for action was more modest, given its leaders' narrower definition of decency and the lesser intensity of the prerequisite value-added stages. Nonetheless, UFD mobilization was impressive. From the meeting in late February, 1969 (when the leaders decided to hold the decency rally), until May, 1969, UFD, with a total budget of only $550, gathered representation from twenty-nine Southtown voluntary associations, attracted 2,500 persons to the decency rally, distributed five thousand postcards to be mailed to the Motion Picture Association asking for more family film entertainment, and acquired over 2,800 adult signatures on a petition calling for legislator support of two state antipornography bills. UFD, having accomplished its goals, summarily disbanded after the rally; some UFD leaders and members subsequently lobbied and testified for the statutes until June, 1969, when they were passed.

In his discussion of norm-oriented movements, Smelser (1962:296) quoted Schlesinger (1950:52), who had outlined five steps put into operation during the mobilization of a social movement. All five of these steps were manifested in both ICCD and UFD. The first step involves the choosing of an "imposing" designation for the activity. Interdenominational Citizens' Council for Decency and Uprising for Decency were imposing titles. The term *decency* is both symbolically pregnant (in differentiating life styles) and vague enough, as Smelser (1962:299) stated, "to encompass a wide variety of grievances" and to attract a large membership. Second, it is important for the movement to obtain a list of "respectable" names as members and patrons. ICCD's membership included some of the most respectable names in Midville. Similarly, UFD, particularly at the decency rally, included a roster of prominent and respectable Southtowners. Third, it is necessary for the movement to acquire the services of a secretary and an adequate corps of assistants. Both ICCD and UFD were able to draw upon their own voluntary memberships for organizational expertise and assistance. Fourth, a band of popular lecturers must be commissioned and set forth as agents on the wide public. ICCD utilized local speakers of state and local prominence and imported such luminaries as the executive director of Citizens for Decent Literature. UFD included popular and skilled speakers in its decency rally. Fifth, the press must be put into operation. The *Midville News* elaborately publicized the Midwestern Bookstore, ICCD, and antipornography activities. In Southtown, the press took notice of UFD and its activities, but only in noneditorial announcements or reports.

ICCD had already formally existed since 1965 and gave promise of continuing to operate with greater or lesser zeal. UFD existed for only five months altogether. Smelser (1962: 302) noted that the history of a norm-oriented movement can be described as a pattern of discarding one particular tactic which is ineffective (or becoming so) and choosing another, potentially more effective tactic. UFD did not follow that pattern, since the first tactic (nonetheless norm-oriented) was successful in accomplishing the goals. ICCD's history, however, showed a series of activities and strategies (described in Chapters 2 and 5). The broader and vaguer mandate of ICCD's bylaws encompassed concern with a wide array of problems associated with the maintenance of decency. Having such an array guarantees failure in one sense, observed

Smelser (1962:305), since accomplishment can never fulfill total expectation. As one Midville antipornographer exclaimed resolutely, "Our work is never done!"

Both the purposes and the methods of ICCD were broad and at a high level of abstraction—"to safeguard the standards of decency in the community in the field of entertainment" and "to establish a community conscience concerning decency," "through education on the many-faceted problems of decency" and "through encouraging the legal enforcement of our present laws and those laws which may be enacted to further decency." Essentially, those stated goals and methods provided nearly unlimited options for strategies, tactics, and targets. The goals and strategies of UFD, as verbally stated by Mr. King and his colleagues during meetings, were more specific: to pursue "orderly, rational, to the point, and by all means legal" community support for more family entertainment and stronger antipornography laws. (The relation of specificity of goals to the organizational structure and duration of ICCD and UFD will be discussed in Chapter 9.)

The goals and strategies of both ICCD and UFD, however, did reflect the short-circuited generalized belief that normative reconstitution or implementation involving a specific target would resolve structural strain at both higher and lower levels of abstraction.

The difference in the breadth of goals and the kinds of strategies enacted by ICCD and UFD reflected differences in the styles of the two leaders, Mrs. Roberts and Mr. King. Mr. King steadfastly refused (not without difficulty) to let the focus of UFD expand beyond pornography and associated legal change. (If possible, he would have liked to have restricted the goal even further, to apply only to film entertainment.) Mr. King eschewed direct action against businesses perceived to be dealing in pornography. Mrs. Roberts, in contrast, engaged in several kinds of action toward the resolution of several kinds of perceived problems: homosexuality, venereal disease, drugs, prostitution, morally neglected children, and so on. Furthermore, she did not eschew, but even encouraged, direct action against the Midwestern Bookstore.

Smelser noted that, once the value-added sequence has been established for the first four stages, "the only necessary condition that remains is to bring the affected group into action. . . . In this process of mobilization the behavior of leaders is extremely important" (1962: 17).[4] The leadership style of Mrs. Roberts was free-swinging, and she tended aggressively to pursue her chosen action at any level of organization or with any individual. Consequently, some of her actions seemed to be less than cautious. Mr. King, on the other hand, was consistently controlled in his activities concerning the antipornography crusade. He appeared never to decide on a course of action without first exploring the implications and potential impact of that action—checking, for example, with legal or legislative representatives. Consequently, he gave the impression of being cautious in his leadership, though he was not considered timid. Perhaps the clearest example of the difference between the two leaders could be seen in Mrs. Roberts' involvement in the purchase-complaint-arrest strategy against the Midwestern Bookstore and her subsequently being named as a principal in the bookstore's million-dollar conspiracy lawsuit. Mr. King, on the other hand, had counseled participants in UFD to avoid the purchase-complaint-arrest strategy because of what he perceived to be the potential for constitutional and legal repercussions. Smelser suggested: "The leader who is most important in the phase of active mobilization focuses on a set of strategies and tactics—to form a new political party; to influence existing parties; to stage a march or other kind of demonstration; to influence legislatures by conventional lobbying or letter-writing; to engage in "direct action" such as boycotts, lock-outs, or sit-ins; to educate the public; and so on" (1962:298).

Mrs. Roberts, during the mobilization for action of ICCD, concentrated primarily on direct action, with a secondary intention to influence legislatures and educate the public. Mr. King, during the mobilization for action of UFD, concentrated on conventional lobbying and letter-writing, in an attempt to influence legislatures and the movie industry, and implemented, secondarily, a demonstration of community support through the decency rally. In Killian's (1964:437, 447) terminology, a more restrictive set of norms (compared with those of ICCD) had been developed by Mr. King and his colleagues for the conduct of UFD mobilization for action.

ICCD became an entity in itself, and Mrs. Roberts subordinated her other activities to the responsibility of leadership (though secretary-treasurer of ICCD, she often worked in the capacity of chairperson and vice-chairperson). On the other hand, although Mr. King was the principal leader of UFD, he viewed that role as temporary and never saw himself as more than an active member of the Knights of Columbus who was for the moment involved in a transitory occasion of community action.

It seemed as though the antipornography activity had become a way of life for Mrs. Roberts. The dominant role in her life, other than that of housewife and mother, seemed to be that of moral crusader. In contrast, for Mr. King the role of moral crusader was ancillary to his more dominant role of active and rewarded member of the Knights of Columbus. It was clear that Mr. King had been instrumental in the development of the antipornography crusade in Southtown primarily because he felt that his role as chairman of the Community Action Committee of the local Knights of Columbus council called for it. Both Mrs. Roberts and Mr. King were "moral entrepreneurs," as Becker (1963:147–163) labeled such individuals—Mrs. Roberts more in the crusading-reformer sense of the term, Mr. King more in the rule-enforcer or intensifier sense of the term. (The relation of leadership style to the organizational structure and other characteristics of ICCD will be discussed further in Chapter 9.)

The direct-action tactic employed by ICCD in Midville, though norm-oriented (in the sense of being designed to implement existing laws) was considerably more hostile than the legislative-change goals of UFD (although ICCD also attempted to implement legislative change). Smelser (1962:227) commented that it was not unusual for outbursts of hostility to be associated with social movements. Norm-oriented beliefs, as suggested by the hierarchical nature of the components of action, include at least some element of hostile belief—norm-oriented movements have specific targets, the removal, restriction, or punishment of which are taken, by the short-circuiting process, to be the means whereby structural strain will be ameliorated. "When such hostile outbursts occur in the development of these movements depends, however, on other factors, especially conduciveness, strain, and social control" (Smelser 1962:227). We have already reported that the structural conduciveness, structural strain, generalized beliefs, and precipitating factors were more intense and severe in Midville than in Southtown. We have also reported the generalized beliefs in Midville to have been more sharply short-circuited to a specific target, the Midwestern Bookstore. Though the Avalon and Bijou theaters in Southtown could have become specific targets for short-circuiting, the leadership orientation of Mr. King interfered with pressures for such short-circuiting, forcing the process to remain focused on the goal of legislative change.

Smelser suggested that, "when all avenues of agitating for normative change are perceived to be closing or closed, moreover, dissatisfaction tends to find an outlet in a value-oriented movement or in expressions of hostility" (1962:284). ICCD had a considerably longer history than UFD, which history included disappointments with attempts for normative change. Yet ICCD was not about to undertake a value-oriented movement (to move up the hierarchy of the components for action), since it justified its existence in terms of society's basic values. A movement down the mobilization series was in order—an enactment of more hostile norm-oriented action. Similarly, Turner and Killian observed that "certain kinds of opposition so narrow the range of tactics available to a movement that it has no alternative other than to adopt effective means irrespective of their immediate consonance with the values of the movement" (1957:373). Thus ICCD, though espousing the importance of democracy and freedom, undertook action which was perceived, at least by some Midvillians, as an infringement upon democracy and freedom.

Both ICCD and UFD also manifested the lower elements in the Smelser hierarchy of the components of action—panic (flight from existing norms or impending normative change) and craze (plunge to establish new means) (1962:271). However, the natural histories clearly reveal that ICCD manifested those elements more intensely than UFD.

Gusfield (1963:610) distinguished between assimilative reform and coercive reform. In the former, the crusader looks upon the individual who deviates from his life style warmly, with compassion, and as though he has been led astray through no fault of his own. The intent of assimilative reform is to convince the deviant to modify his errant ways and to conform to the dominant life style embraced by the crusader. Coercive reform results when the crusader is threatened by the increasing strength of institutions and groups whose life style differs from his. The issue of prestige and power is resolved through status politics, usually the passing of a law or some other kind of activity which restricts the activities of the deviants, or at least through the passing of legislation which symbolically indicates that the behavior of the deviants is in disfavor and is less prestigeful than that of the crusader (Gusfield 1963:7). Temperance crusaders, according to Gusfield (1963:86), came to the conclusion that societal normative systems could not be depended upon, without prodding or revising, to restrict alcohol and what it represented. Nor was it enough to ask or convert citizens. Laws had to be passed; saloons had to be closed.

The Midville and Southtown Conporns came to similar conclusions regarding pornography and what it represented. Mr. King and Mrs. Roberts had, earlier in their careers as antipornography crusaders, attempted assimilative reform in the control of pornography. Mrs.

Roberts had engaged in attempts to convince drugstore and grocery store owners to "clean up their racks"; Mr. King had done the same before he moved to Southtown. Those earlier attempts at assimilative reform had been for the most part successful; their later attempts, because of the breakdown of informal controls (resulting from the Supreme Court decisions) had not been successful. ICCD members, particularly Mrs. Roberts, felt those failures at assimilative reform more deeply than UFD members. Consequently (and as a result of other aspects of the value-added stages), both ICCD and UFD, in their mobilization for action, engaged in coercive reform—ICCD more than UFD. A further event intensifying the coercive reform in Midville (described above as a precipitating factor) was Raymond Gauer's advice to Midvillians: "One thing that doesn't work is to go around to the guys in the community selling this kind of stuff and say, 'How about being a nice guy and get rid of your dirty books'."

Turner (1970:146) suggested that there are three major alternative strategies available to social movements: persuasion, bargaining, and coercion. The choice of movement strategies is determined by the movement's overall goals, by its concern for constituency values, by its pursuit of support from external publics, and by the degree of its involvement with the entity upon which it hopes to have impact. Turner's use of the term *coercion* is similar to Gusfield's description of coercive reform and Smelser's depiction of hostile action. ICCD employed coercion as a movement strategy; UFD tended more toward a strategy of persuasion. We shall return, in depth, to Turner's argument in Chapter 9, when we address the organizational characteristics of the antipornography crusades.

ICCD's and UFD's mobilization for action indeed had a normative impact upon some people, some organizations, and some activities. Many of the mobilization events were dramatic, were publicly proclaimed, and seized the attention of significant components of the community for some time. But how utilitarian, how effective were those events? After the crusade, the availability of family film entertainment in Southtown did not increase (in fact, it decreased), "skin-flick" theaters soon numbered four instead of two (and all began to show "action" films in addition to the usual run of "skin-flicks"), and four "adult" bookstores opened for business. After the crusade in Midville, the Midwestern Bookstore not only continued to operate but is reported to have opened two new branches. Even the legislative changes appeared not to be utilitarian. Those antipornography statutes or ordinances considered or implemented in Southtown and Midville were concerned with *minors*, and only scarcely, if at all, modified the patronage of "adult" bookstores or theaters. Furthermore, the state statutes supported by UFD and the city ordinance supported by ICCD were challenged in higher courts.

Following Gusfield, it seems tenable that the greatest gains accrued to the Midville and Southtown antipornography crusades were symbolic rather than utilitarian (see also Turner and Killian 1972:48; Klapp 1972:339–381). Wasby (1965), in his legal analysis of an antipornography crusade in Portland, Oregon, similarly indicated the symbolic nature of a resulting local antipornography statute. He quoted the mayor of Portland as stating, "The ordinance has not been passed with the thought in mind of undertaking any immediate prosecution," and Wasby himself observed that "the newest anti-obscene literature ordinance had not been used formally" (1965:128–129). This is not meant to indicate that ICCD and UFD participants were entirely satisfied with the utilitarian impact of their mobilization for action. Rather, it seems to have been at least as important, and at least as satisfactory, to have "showed them where we stand."

It may have been that the Conporns were forced to be content with symbolic accomplishments, with token normative restructurings, with a symbolic defense of their life style. The constrictions placed upon them by the standing Supreme Court decisions perhaps made more utilitarian normative restructuring impossible. Gusfield (1963:23) observed that, when instrumental activities fail, symbols serve nicely as substitute goals for more utilitarian aims. The entire Prohibition movement, having resulted essentially in utilitarian failure, nonetheless provided temperance crusaders with satisfactions (the amelioration of status discontent) derived from symbolic victories ("It was our law they had to violate") (see also Smelser 1962:303–304).

Though local antipornography crusades and Conporns may have been satisfied with symbolic conquests, it remains to be seen whether those satisfactions will be enough in the future. Changes in the context of the value-added stages may lead to norm-oriented antipornography crusades which are more demanding of utilitarian impact. It is quite clear that, no matter what local antipornography crusades are content with, national antipornography organizations, such as Citizens for Decent Literature, will not be satisfied with symbolic crusades only (although their activities still manifest defense of traditional as opposed to alternative life styles and still reflect status discontent). As reported above, Raymond Gauer, the executive director of Citizens for Decent Literature, was disappointed with the antipornography statute initially supported by Mrs. Roberts and ICCD. It dealt only with minors, and he accurately assessed that such a statute modification would change little, if anything, in the availability of sexually explicit materials in Midville. Though he did not say so in these terms, he gave indication that the passing of that statute, as written, would be at best a symbolic gesture. At that time Citizens for Decent Literature (which fits the characteristics of a *professional* social movement organization as described by McCarthy and Zald 1973) was pressing hard for legal changes at the local, state, and federal levels which would *work* in eliminating or at least severely restricting the availability of pornography in American communities.

Chapter 7

Social Control: "Decency Cannot Be Stopped!"

Midville

It appeared in Midville that relatively few components of social control mitigated the community's potential for an antipornography crusade, narrowed the range of strategy and tactics available to ICCD, or delimited the characteristics of ICCD's mobilization for action. What social controls did impinge upon ICCD primarily emerged after the mobilization for action began. ICCD's activities, especially those against the Midwestern Bookstore, were almost totally supported overtly, covertly, or through indifference by law-enforcement agencies; health, educational, and religious institutions; the media; and several local, state, and national government officials.

The tactics of ICCD sometimes were modified by the concern of Mrs. Roberts and her colleagues that they would be labeled "little old ladies in tennis shoes," cranks, members of the "lunatic fringe," and so on. That this concern operated only sometimes as social control was the result of Mrs. Roberts's and her colleagues' increasing tendency to define pejorative labels as coming from the enemy they opposed and as first-order evidence that their antipornography efforts were striking home. On some occasions, Mrs. Roberts and ICCD members identified verbal abuse as part of the role of any righteous activist: "We are people who refuse to be brainwashed by such propaganda or intimidated by such snide salutations as dirty-minded, ignorant, do-gooders, busybodies, snoops, etc. We wear those titles as proudly as Christ wore his crown of thorns."

The rulings of the Supreme Court on pornography and obscenity served, in a limited fashion, as a component of social control and *perhaps* to some degree mitigated antipornography activity in Midville. The "perhaps" should be emphasized. Although the Supreme Court's mandate to protect the rights of the free press and individual liberty encouraged some of the ICCD members to be more cautious in their actions, and although Midvillian judges drew upon Supreme Court interpretations to dismiss pornography charges against employees of the Midwestern Bookstore, such legal-social controls ultimately served as precipitating factors generating the direct action against the Midwestern Bookstore (i.e., the purchase-complaint-arrest strategy).

Customers of the Midwestern Bookstore, some students, a few liberal theologians, and members of such organizations as the American Civil Liberties Union represented opposition to ICCD. (The comments of the ACLU representative in the public pornography debate were presented in Chapter 5, as were the critical comments of Councilman Wood concerning the Midville antipornography crusade and the critical letters to the editor concerning the *Midville News* exposé. However, opposition to ICCD was seldom publicly expressed, and when it was (as in the case of the ACLU representative and Councilman Wood), the response from the majority was swift and severe. As one person, who would have liked to have more strenuously opposed ICCD's actions but chose not to, summarized in an interview, "It is impossible to take a position opposed to what amounted to vigilante activity without seeming or being made to seem opposed to God, America, angels, and innocent children." Disagreement with the purposes or even the methods of ICCD implied, according to the Conporns, disagreement with nearly every traditional and sacred basic value in society.

The *Midville News* initially served as an agent of social control. During the prototypical stages of ICCD, the newspaper staff did not pay much attention to Mrs. Roberts and the emerging leadership of the antipornography crusade. That staff felt that Mrs. Roberts and her colleagues were concerned with relatively inconsequential issues such as "girlie" magazines and rather innocuous "risqué" published materials. Subsequently, however, the *Midville News* ceased to be an agent of social control and became, through its exposé of the Midwestern Bookstore, a precipitating factor. Interestingly, the *Midville News* itself felt some social-control pressures from individuals in the community who disagreed with either the content or the intent of the newspaper's exposé of the bookstore. The cancellation of subscriptions and angry letters to the editor (although the negative letters were in the minority) resulted in the cancellation of the last of a series of four intended articles on the Midwestern Bookstore.

Following the *Midville News* exposé, Councilman Wood again expressed a critical opinion concerning the antipornography crusade. Specifically, he disagreed with the activity of the *Midville News* in the crusade and was quoted in a news story as saying:

> The News has harangued the people and encouraged them to ignore the law. This is a question for the courts to decide, and they have already made their decision.
>
> The News is calling for vigilante action and I believe The News has abused its right of free speech. The people who are going to court are the victims of The Midville News vigilantism.
>
> I'd hate to be put in the position where it looks like I'm defending pornography, but I think this is the first step toward totalitarian government and is the first step toward the loss of our rights as individuals. We can't say we want to shut down a business just because we don't like it. (*Midville News*, March 10, 1969)

Three days later, five Omicron College students picketed the *Midville News*, protesting what they said was "free speech for the Midville News but not for the Midwestern Bookstore" (*Midville News*, March 14, 1969). The students carried signs which read, for example, "The Supreme Court says the books the Midwestern Bookstore sells are within the law!" and "Why have laws if the people who administer them don't follow them?" The students themselves commented, according to the article: "The News is unfair. . . . They slanted their stories to tear down the guy in the Bookstore. They didn't give the other side of the story"; "Most students nowadays are against someone bothering someone when there is no need to bother them. No one has the right to bother a bookstore; if someone wants to read a book it is their business not the News' or anyone else's business." The students indicated that they did not represent any particular group, but that there "are a lot of Omicron students who feel the way we do" (*Midville News*, March 14, 1969). Apparently another group of about twelve students arrived the same day, picketed, and similarly protested the *News* exposé of the bookstore.

On March 16, 1969, the *Midville News* printed an editorial answer to Councilman Wood and the picketing students. The editorial read, in part, as follows:

> . . . this has to be one of the most puzzling aspects of the entire dispute over the filth and garbage being distributed in Midville by

the Midwestern Bookstore. It is perfectly alright for them to sell this material, it is argued, because of freedom of the press.

But for The Midville News to show the people of Midville what that material is, that's abuse of freedom of the press!

Somehow we just can't grasp the distinction. Why don't we, this newspaper, have a constitutional guarantee to report to our readers what is taking place at the Midwestern Bookstore?

Why are we less protected than it is?

This is the reasoning that seems to be sweeping American thought today: The philosophy of a free press was established to protect the purveyor of pornography. The newspaper that tries to reveal the depths of depravity involved and takes an editorial stand against it is guilty of persecution, not reporting.

What kind of rationale is this?

Forgotten in last week's attacks on this newspaper was the role that we have played.

From the very beginning we emphasized editorially that we had no desire to impose our standards on this community. At the request of concerned citizens, our reporters investigated the type of material being sold at the Midwestern Bookstore.

They were absolutely shocked. So were we.

Our first "mental" decision was an unwritten apology to those citizens who had been "pestering" us to do something about that bookstore. We had, subconsciously perhaps, written them off as "busy bodies" and "do-gooders"—a bunch of women who didn't have anything better to do with their time. For even having thought of that, after seeing the type of material the Midwestern Bookstore dealt in—we were ashamed.

Our next step was a long and considered study of how to go about reporting this story, so that others would not give it the brush-off we had. It was our conclusion that only by giving the general public a sample of the type of material the book store handled could the people really know what was going on.

We were able to print only a faint shadow of the substance—yet our reports shocked this community to the core. That shock is ebbing now, and maybe some find themselves thinking we were only talking about a lot of nude pictures. They should not!

It must be emphasized that The Midville News has not persecuted the Midwestern Bookstore. The News gave an honest report of the type of operation it was—and this report has never been challenged.

The wave of revulsion and action against the bookstore came from the people—not us.

It has been citizens who volunteered to obtain warrants to bring the bookstore into court . . . we have never encouraged vigilante action, nor would we tolerate it.

This community has a right to be proud of the restraint of those citizens who are participating in the campaign—and don't forget, more than 11,000 have specifically voiced their protest against the Midwestern Bookstore through petitions that it be closed. Every step along the way has been taken through legal channels . . . and that's the way it should be. . . .

. . . we wish we could take credit for what these Midville citizens have done, but the credit is theirs . . . and more power to them!

The Lawsuit

As mentioned above, on February 27, 1969, the *Midville News* reported that a one-million-dollar civil suit had been filed in Coast Town federal court by Mr. Baker, owner of the Midwestern Bookstore, charging that there had been a conspiracy to violate his civil rights. According to the article: "The suit asks that the defendants be restrained and enjoined from further action against the store. The suit did not request an immediate show-cause hearing and allows the defendants to file an answer to the charges within 20 days." (*Midville News*, February 27, 1969).

Those named in the conspiracy suit were Mr. and Mrs. Morgan, Mr. and Mrs. Steel, Mrs. Wyatt, the Reverend Mr. Lewis, and the Reverend Mr. Wheeler, all of whom had engaged in the purchase-complaint-arrest tactic; the Midville prosecuting attorney; the chief of the Midville police department; a Midville district judge who was at that time conducting hearings on the charges brought against the Midwestern Bookstore employees; Mr. Grey, former Midville chief assistant prosecutor; Mrs. Roberts, secretary-treasurer of ICCD; and Mrs. Stark, president of the Midville Junior Women's Club. Mrs. Roberts stated that she had no knowledge of the litigation "other than what I have seen on television concerning the suit, because I have been home with the flu" (*Midville News*, February 27, 1969).

Mr. Baker, joined in the action by Mr. Smith, Miss Strong, and Mr. Thomas, three of the arrested Midwestern Bookstore employees, alleged that the actions of the sued individuals and organizations (ICCD and the Midville Junior Women's Club) had by their purchase-complaint-arrest tactic violated the plaintiffs' "rights and freedom of the press (First Amendment) and due process of law (Fourteenth Amendment)" (*Midville News*, February 27, 1969).

The brief filed by the plaintiff's attorney alleged conspiracy among the defendants, as follows:

> That Plaintiffs allege it to be a fact that commencing in January of 1969 or thereabouts, the Defendants herein did conspire with one another and did set out and upon a concerted course of action under color of state law. . . . to deprive Plaintiffs and each of them of rights guaranteed to them under the First and Fourteenth Amendments to the United States Constitution and more particularly their right to engage in a legal occupation, that is the operation of a retail bookstore and employment therein, and their rights of free speech and expression involved in the sale of books and magazines guaranteed under the First Amendment." (Civil Action File 2980, February 26, 1969)

The brief consecutively presented allegations intended to support the complaint of conspiracy, including a detailed description of the purchase-complaint-arrest tactic; an argument that the ten-thousand-dollar bonds set for the Midwestern Bookstore sales clerks who were arrested were "in violation of the rights . . . under the Eighth Amendment to the United States Constitution prohibiting excessive bonds"; an argument that the arrest of Mr. Baker for a minor tax infraction and the setting of a ten-thousand-dollar bond constituted a violation of Eighth Amendment rights and further evidence of conspiracy.

The brief described the loss in revenue allegedly caused the Midwestern Bookstore by the activities of the defendants:

> That prior to the activities of the Defendants as herein above set forth, the sales of said bookstore approximated Ten Thousand ($10,000.00) Dollars per month; that since that time sales have been reduced to approximately Two Thousand ($2,000.00) Dollars per month all as a result of the activities of the Defendants herein, said activities having caused the patrons and customers of the Plaintiff . . . to refuse to enter the store for fear that they too would be arrested and harassed by the police and the Defendants herein, all of which has resulted in certain of the Plaintiffs having lost their

employment and the Plaintiff. . . [Baker]. . . having been deprived of his constitutional right to engage in the business of the sale of magazines. (Civil Action File 2980, February 26, 1969)

The brief argued that there was no pornographic material actually involved, under recent Supreme Court decisions:

That Plaintiffs further allege that section 2 [of the State statute—that dealing with the definition of pornography] is violative of the interpretative decisions of the United States Supreme Court regarding the test for determination of obscenity and as more particularly laid down in the cases of *Roth-vs-United States* (1957), *Jacobellis-vs-Ohio* (1964), and *Memoirs-vs-Massachusetts* (1966).

Alternatively, Plaintiffs allege that said statute as applied to them is unconstitutional on the basis of *Redrup-vs-New York* (1967), and in violation of rights granted by the First and Fourteenth Amendments and further that the magazines alleged in the criminal complaints to be obscene . . . are not obscene as a matter of law. (Civil Action File 2980, February 26, 1969)

The brief concluded by asking for an injunction against the defendants' activities, a court rendering of the state statute section as unconstitutional, a relief of excessive bonds upon the plaintiffs, a restraining of the enforcement of the alleged unconstitutional provision of the state statute, and compensatory punitive and exemplary damages not to exceed one million dollars to be assessed against the defendants.

The defense attorney's argument was that no action had been taken, as alleged by the plaintiff's attorney, "under color of state law," since for action to be taken as such, "there must be a misuse of power possessed by virtue of state law and made possible only because the wrongdoer was clothed because of authority of state law." Based upon that argument, the defense attorney stated that there therefore could be no conspiracy "inasmuch as no action had been taken by them [the defendants] under color of state law" (Civil Action File 2980, March 14, 1969).

In his motion for summary judgment, the defense attorney pleaded:

It is fundamental law that a citizen has a right to petition the government for redress of grievances (Amendment 1, Constitution of the United States).

In this case, these defendants made miscellaneous purchases of materials offered for public sale at the bookstore owned and operated by the plaintiff. . . .

Thereafter, upon reviewing their respective purchases each defendant felt the purchased material to be objectionable. Accordingly, complaint to such effect was made to the Midville County Prosecutor's office for his determination, acting as the chief legal enforcement officer of Midville County. (Civil Action File 2980, March 14, 1969)

Concerning the constitutionality of the antipornography statute, the defense attorney stated simply, "It is fundamental law that a statute is presumed to be constitutional until declared otherwise." He concluded his brief: "*Defendants contend that as a matter of law*, any damages sustained by plaintiffs as a consequence of the warrants issuing, are not the result of any unlawful or wrongful act on behalf of these defendants, inasmuch as their initial complaints were lawfully made" (Civil Action File 2980, March 14, 1969).

In Coast Town federal court, on Tuesday, May 20, 1969, the proceedings of the civil action formally began. The first act of the defense attorneys was to request dismissal. The first act of the plaintiffs' attorneys was to ask the court to restrain and enjoin the defendants from further action against the Midwestern Bookstore. A three-member federal court panel sat in judgment (*Midville News*, May 20, 1969).

The plaintiffs' motion for an injunction was denied; the defense request for a dismissal/summary judgment was denied. The *Midville News* article describing the court proceedings reported, in part:

Through the hearing, each judge questioned attorneys about the aspect of a conspiracy on the part of persons in the fight against the store. Proof of a conspiracy would be vital to the plaintiff's claim for damages, attorneys admitted, but the judges only asked questions and did not indicate, except by the call for depositions . . . and interrogatives . . . , if they believed such a conspiracy existed.

[One of the judges] . . . did say "The requiring of excessive bail (in the tax and literature warrants) fits into the picture of a conspiracy."

. . . The panel's decisions mean:

—That the persons who signed criminal complaints against the three employees of the store are still involved in the $1,000,000 civil action;

—That [the Midville] Prosecuting Attorney . . . , [the] Midville

Police Chief . . . , the Midville Junior Women's Club, and the Interdenominational Citizens' Council for Decency are still named in the suit;
—That police can still take citizen complaints against the store and the Prosecutor's office can still issue warrants;
—That further action in the civil suit will rest on depositions and interrogatives from persons involved on both sides of the case and that the case may or may not be tried depending on how far [the plaintiffs' attorney] wishes to press the action;
—That the judges refused to rule on the constitutionality of the state statute under which the employees are being prosecuted and would require that the statute be tested on an individual basis rather than in principle. (*Midville News*, May 21, 1969)

The panel of judges did grant the defense attorney's request for dismissal of the suit against the Midville district judge who had been named as one of the defendants in the suit. When we left Midville early in July, 1969, after our period of research observation, the conspiracy lawsuit was still in progress, and no additional key events had taken place. Clearly, however, the lawsuit had served as a significant element of social control, curtailing at least some of the more direct antipornography activities of ICCD. Yet most of the Midville Conporns saw the legal action as only a temporary setback. "Satan's servants can put barriers in our way," observed a Conporn minister, "but in the final judgment decency cannot be stopped."

One year later, the court ruled a stipulated dismissal of the lawsuit. The plaintiffs and defendants, as stated in the court record, had "amicably settled their differences," and the dismissal was "with prejudice and without cost." The "with prejudice" phrase meant that the lawsuit was dead and could not be heard again in another court. Informal sources reported that the plaintiffs (the bookstore) had agreed to pay court costs and the defendants (the crusaders) had agreed to cease direct action against the bookstore. Both sides claimed victory.

Southtown

In Southtown several components of social control relevant to the development of Uprising for Decency appeared to be operating before mobilization for action. The presence of the state capitol (with its model of due process as the way to maintain normative control) and the university population (as a potentially effective opponent if aroused unduly) were influential social-control mechanisms.

UFD did receive some support from the community, in particular from several notable state and local government officials, from law-enforcement agencies, and from church and civic groups. However, the Southtown support was markedly less than that manifested in Midville (where even an Action for Decency Day could be proclaimed). The media cooperated with UFD, but not (as in Midville) to the extent of serving as a massive precipitating factor.

Relatively little reactive opposition against UFD developed in Southtown. The general community response was indifference.

An article in the March 27, 1969, issue of the *Southtown Globe* reported an incident of opposition to one of the antipornography bills being considered in legislative committee. The article read:

> Opponents of a bill designed to regulate the showing of so-called obscene movies said Wednesday "the measure was nothing but a pure censorship bill."
>
> The bill . . . would allow any city in the State to adopt a motion picture review board. The board would issue licenses to local exhibitors and would have final say over what movies those exhibitors could show.
>
> Roger Sebastian, Attorney for the State Council of Motion Picture Organizations, told the House Urban Affairs Committee the bill was an attempt at "outright censorship." (*Southtown Globe*, March 27, 1969)

The bill discussed in the article did not emerge successfully from the committee. Mr. King and his colleagues had, however, taken notice of the opposition.

The April, 1969, "Central State Chapter News," a mimeographed newsletter of the American Civil Liberties Union, reported briefly that "our State's 'obscenity' legislative proposals are being watched." Interviews with active members of the Southtown chapter of the ACLU revealed that Uprising for Decency was a matter of concern for their chapter but that they were more concerned with the "legislative outcome" than the "citizens organizing and meeting, which is everybody's right." The local chapter of the ACLU had, during the month of April, distributed a pamphlet to their members entitled "Obscenity and Censorship: Two Statements of the American Civil Liberties Union," which had been prepared by the national office.

By far the most important component of social control restraining Uprising for Decency was internal, rather than external—the leadership style and orientations of Mr. King and several of the UFD subcommittee chairmen. Mr. King was a pragmatic, task-oriented, and cautious leader, who was able, with the support of his cadre, to govern the specificity of the goals and the legality of the tactics of UFD. He surrounded himself with legal, public-relations, and other experts who served as components of social control. On numerous occasions, as indicated in the previous chapters, Mr. King opposed deviations from UFD's single-minded pursuit of legislative change. He successfully warded off attempts to have UFD implement the purchase-complaint-arrest strategy; expand the decency rally to include marches; boycott movie theaters in general; picket the "skin-flicks"; broaden the goals of UFD to include other issues, such as drugs; and exploit the press for "splashy" publicity or "exposés." He steadfastly refused to allow the Avalon and Bijou theaters to become targets for direct anti-pornography action.

As an officer of the Knights of Columbus, Mr. King was keenly aware of the kind of image that organization strove to maintain—as he expressed it, that image included "gentlemanly" and "rational" deportment. He did not wish the Knights of Columbus, or himself or any of his colleagues, to be stereotyped as censors, radical rightists, or wild-eyed reformers. Consequently, Mr. King's social role as a Knight and as a businessman dependent upon community respect served as an element of social control for his own behavior and, through him, for UFD.

Another important element of social control impinging upon UFD was the awareness that Mr. King and his colleagues had of the potential for development of a countermovement or counterdemonstration, either from among the university students or from the movie industry. The carefully phased publicity campaign conducted by UFD was deliberately constructed not only to maximize the peaking effect toward increased rally attendance but also to avoid forewarning possible opponents. It was not that Mr. King and his colleagues were afraid of opposition as such. However, they concurred that ill-timed opposition would muddy the issue for the purposes of legislative change.

Consequently, the element of internal social control within UFD and the associated choice of strategies for the antipornography crusade created a situation in which, unlike the experience of ICCD in Midville, significant elements of reactive social control did not emerge. Had a purchase-complaint-arrest strategy been employed by UFD, had other forms of direct action been taken against the "skin-flicks," at least some of the reactions of components of the community might have been similar to those in Midville. The manager of the Avalon Theater, for example, indicated in an interview that he was "ready to call in his lawyers if anybody starts to really harass me."

Discussion

In Gusfield's analysis of moral crusaders (1963:32–35), a crucial aspect of the relation of social control to the emergence and style of collective behavior is the crusaders' perception of their influence over institutional constraints on the behavior of others, of influence over the agents of social control themselves. That is, did the potential crusaders feel that their life style was effectively protected and valued by individuals and agencies who had the potential or responsibility for social control over deviants? Further, did the potential crusaders feel that they had the opportunity to exert their will upon or express their discontent with other persons or groups who overtly threatened the prestige of the traditional life style? As mentioned in earlier chapters, the participants in ICCD and UFD (more so in ICCD) had pressing concerns regarding the efficacy of local agencies of social control to deal with issues of pornography and issues of law and order. The stance of the Supreme Court, the relative ineffectiveness of the local police, the breakdown of informal controls over businesses which might sell pornography were evidence of the weakening of social control. The perception of those weaknesses articulated with other perceived threats to life style, combined with conditions generating status discontent, and contributed to the mobilization of a symbolic crusade.

Gusfield (1963:212) described some of the self-imposed limitations upon temperance crusaders in their pursuit of Prohibition. They did not want their behavior to be volatile to the point of encouraging reaction from organized opposition. Furthermore, they did not want their legislative actions to have unwanted side effects—for example, the increasing of taxes—which would put them in national disfavor. Lastly, the temperance crusaders were somewhat constrained by the impact of their philosophical position that righteousness really should not need much enforcing. Gusfield (1963:129) also noted that the temperance crusaders hoped to avoid being stereotyped as "queers," "old fogeys," "frousy fanatics," or other such types and sometimes modified their behavior accordingly.

The Conporns, more so in Southtown than in Midville, also expressed anxieties about the potential for organized opposition, the unwanted side effects of their activities, and the disadvantages of being negatively stereotyped. UFD in Southtown shaped its strategies and tactics with careful consideration of those factors; ICCD, accurately perceiving greater community support, tended to be considerably less concerned about opposition, side effects, or negative labeling.

Smelser observed that social control, the final value-added stage of collective behavior, "arches over all the others. Stated in the simplest way, the study of social control is the study of those counter-determinants which prevent, interrupt, deflect, or inhibit the accumulation" of the other value-added stages (1962:17). Smelser divided social controls into those which, existing prior to the emergence of a form of collective behavior, mitigate conduciveness and strain, and those which are implemented only after the collective behavior has emerged. The latter controls "determine how fast, how far, and in what direction the episode will develop" and are manifested by the behavior of such agencies of social control as "the police, the courts, the press, the religious authorities, the community leaders, etc." when they are confronted by potential or actual collective behavior (1962:17).[1]

Except for the lawsuit, ICCD experienced relatively few significant elements of social control (concerning antipornography activity) before or after mobilization for action. The police, the press, and many community leaders overtly supported the goals, strategies, and tactics of ICCD. Those goals and orientations (to protect decency in the community) were so broad that they barely channeled the kinds of action which could result in the mobilization stage of the crusade. The ICCD leadership called for a "wide-open" attack on pornography. The advice from Raymond Gauer and the Midville prosecuting attorney concerning the purchase-complaint-arrest strategy essentially lifted social control on direct action against antipornography targets. In Turner's (1970) terminology, a new norm for the character of collective behavior had emerged—one which allowed a greater degree of hostility to be demonstrated. Smelser noted that agencies of social control could determine the duration and severity of an episode of collective behavior by the kind of "avenues of behavior—e.g., hostile expression, norm-oriented protest" they attempted to close off or leave open (1962:384).

In the case of UFD, the presence of the potentially reactive university and the due-process model of state government served as effective premobilization crusade controls. But the most important UFD social control was internal—the leadership style of Mr. King—a style which constricted the UFD goals, strategies, and tactics. UFD was not allowed, by internal leadership control, to engage in hostile direct action against business targets. (See Lewis 1972:95 for an analysis which calls attention to the importance of internal social control.) Furthermore, the goal of UFD was deliberately restricted to focus only upon orderly legislative change in antipornography statutes. The differences between ICCD and UFD in leadership characteristics and the result of those differences suggest that leaders not only are influential in determining what a social movement will do (the usual point of analysis) but also actively determine what the movement will not do. In Chapter 9 we shall describe how differences between ICCD and UFD in organizational characteristics were associated, as an element of social control, with the quality of crusade activity.

Referring to the hierarchy of the components of action, Smelser observed: "We might note that certain types of social control operate as an intermediary between . . . short-circuited collective episodes and orderly social change" (1962:73). The social-control characteristics of Mr. King's leadership style significantly served to interfere with the short-circuiting process potentially operating in the antipornography crusades. Mr. King would not allow the "skin-flick" theaters to become targets for direct action. The short-circuiting process could jump only from strain (status discontent, threats to life style) to a demand for normative restructuring or implementing, concerning pornography in general (calling for passage of new laws or the more vigorous application of old laws). Mr. King stopped the strain from being short-circuited directly to the Southtown "skin-flicks." In Midville, on the other hand, Mrs. Roberts allowed, even encouraged, the short-circuiting process to jump from strain to normative restructuring and then directly to the Midwestern Bookstore. The leaders of symbolic crusades, consequently, can intervene (and perhaps manipulate) the short-circuiting process among the components of action.

The operation of social control, the last value-added stage in Smelser's framework, indeed shaped the style of the Midville and Southtown antipornography crusades. Relative to Midville and ICCD, the greater degree of social control impinging upon UFD prior to mobilization combined with the lesser degree of structural conduciveness and strain, the lesser focus of generalized beliefs, and the lesser impact of precipitating factors to produce a more orderly, more careful, less hostile, and more limited norm-oriented movement.

Both ICCD and UFD were faced with another important aspect of social control, from the Gusfield perspective. As noted in Chapter 6, given the Supreme Court rulings extant at that time, there was actually little that antipornography crusades could do to encourage new statutes which would restrict the availability of pornography for adults. Nor did direct action against target dealers result in much more than inconvenience to them (perhaps even aiding them by the attendant publicity). Essentially, the Supreme Court rulings had implemented a social control which rendered the efforts of antipornography crusades more symbolic than utilitarian. For the most part, the crusaders both in Midville and Southtown knew that—but persisted. For the time being, a symbolic crusade was sufficient to reaffirm their life style.

Chapter 8

Conporns versus Proporns

Chapters 2–7 have described in detail the natural histories of ICCD in Midville and UFD in Southtown. This chapter will present and analyze selected individual characteristics of the participants in the antipornography crusades, that is, the Conporns, and compare those characteristics with those of Proporns and Controls. Essentially, this chapter will attempt to answer, at least partially, the question, "What kinds of people became involved in the antipornography crusades?" The hypotheses concerning the individual characteristics of Conporns stated in Chapter 1 will be tested. We shall discuss, first, general characteristics; second, the manifestations of status inconsistency; and, third, the manifestations of political trust and political efficacy. The data will be interpreted further as they apply to theoretical formulations concerning status discontent, resistance to change, and motivations for participation in social movements.

The individual characteristics of the Conporns, Proporns, and Controls were assessed by a structured questionnaire, assembled by the research staff. Although only one week was available for the preparation and distribution of the questionnaire, it was pretested on a small group of thirty university students, and at least the most apparent sources of measurement error were eliminated. The questionnaire was first administered in Southtown (January–February, 1969) and subsequently in Midville (June–July, 1969). A few modifications among the items were made in transition from Southtown to Midville; but, except where noted, the questionnaires were functionally equivalent in the two cities. A copy of the questionnaire is presented in the appendix.

As mentioned in Chapter 1, the questionnaire was administered to eighty-five Conporns (forty-nine in Southtown and thirty-six in Midville). The sample of Conporn respondents was drawn by using a "snowball" technique—that is, by reference from the members of the antipornography group. Since we had ready access to Southtown, the snowball procedure could be pursued with relative leisure, and we are confident that the entire universe of active and central crusade participants in that city was interviewed. The snowball technique in Midville, on the other hand, was more hurriedly employed. Furthermore, the million-dollar suit against the Midville crusade had named some of the Conporns as defendants. After consultation with their lawyers, we decided not to directly interview seven defendants who were most closely connected with ICCD. We also elected not to interview two other Conporns who expressed hesitancy because of the possibility of their being involved in the lawsuit. We were, however, able to gather relevant information concerning the defendants indirectly, through interviews with their colleagues. Consequently, we are content that the Midville Conporns we interviewed were representative of the universe of Conporns and nearly exhausted that universe.

A total of fifty-one Proporns were interviewed (twenty-six in Southtown and twenty-five in Midville), all of whom were contacted via the snowball technique. We asked Conporn leaders in both communities to name those individuals they felt were most opposed to their antipornography activities. Individuals who had been named in the newspapers as speaking out against antipornography endeavors in their respective communities were also approached. As with the Conporns, the snowball referral process for Proporns in both Midville and Southtown became circular toward the end of the interviewing period (multiple renominations occurred), and we were confident that we had interviewed most of the individuals who were actively opposed to the antipornography crusades.

Only two of the available Conporns (and none of the Proporns) refused to be interviewed. However, some of the respondents chose not to answer certain items in the questionnaire which they thought too personal. Their choices were honored.

Since we intended to match the Controls with the Conporns (at least roughly) in as many variables as possible, samples of the potential Control respondents were drawn from the residential neighborhoods in which the Conporns lived. In Southtown, each interviewed Conporn was located on sections of the city tax maps. From all of the addresses in the limited zone of blocks surrounding each Conporn's address, a potential Control respondent and two alternates were selected by use of a table of random numbers. Similar maps were not available in Midville; so the address of each Conporn was located in the city directory, and the resident listed three spaces above the Conporn was isolated as a potential Control. The residents listed three places below were named as Control alternates. Letters were sent to each of the potential Control respondents, briefly explaining, in general terms, the nature of the research project and indicating that a member of the research staff would subsequently phone to establish an appointment for an interview. The letter and follow-up phone-call procedure was relatively successful in Southtown (approximately 60 percent response rate), and interviews were completed with thirty-eight Controls. The attempt in Midville, however, was not very successful (30 percent response rate), because of time restrictions, concern on the part of the potential respondents about the highly publicized lawsuit, and the timing of the interview (Fourth of July weekend). As a result, the Midville Control group numbered only twelve respondents, enough to be, at best, only illustrative. The majority of the Conporns in Southtown were male heads of households; therefore an attempt was made to interview Controls who were also male heads of households. Most of the Midville Conporns were female, but no female Controls could be acquired for sex-matching.

Interviews were conducted with respondents in their homes or places of work. Wherever possible, male staff members interviewed male respondents, and female staff members interviewed female respondents. The average time for each interview was approximately one hour.

The completed questionnaires were coded according to predetermined and empirically derived categories by a team of coders. Coefficients of coder agreement were .80 or better, with inconsistencies subsequently corrected by discussion toward consensus. The coded data were punched on IBM cards, and frequency counts were derived by computer analysis.

Given the fact that the Conporns and Proporns were assumed to *be* the available populations for study, while the Controls were only a rough sample of their population, and given the diverse measurement levels of the questionnaire scales and items, we have elected not to compute tests of statistical significance of differences. We acknowledge that this decision enhances the likelihood that we have taken undue interpretive liberties with the data.

General Characteristics

Demographic Characteristics (Table 1)

Most of the Southtown Conporns were male; in Midville, females slightly outnumbered males. The differing sex ratios reflected the kinds of voluntary associations from which leaders, cadre, and participants in the antipornography effort, at least initially, were drawn. In South-town, the parent organization of UFD had been a local Knights of Columbus chapter, an all-male group. The leaders of UFD were all male; the speakers at their meetings and rallies were also all male. The key leaders of ICCD were members of Catholic women's groups in the community. Consequently, they tended at least initially to recruit cadre and participants from among colleagues in other women's groups. There was in ICCD, however, a significant number (nearly half) of actively participating males. Most importantly, it can be seen that antipornography activists are not necessarily "little old ladies in tennis shoes." As seen in the case of UFD, the crusades can be popu-lated predominantly by males. Even in ICCD, where women were the key leaders, males were significantly represented among Con-porns.

Most of the Southtown and Midville Proporns were male. Those initially named (the basis of the snowball sampling) by Conporns as being opposed to their activities were all men—lawyers, officers of

TABLE 1. *Demographic Characteristics*

| Characteristic | Midville | | | Southtown | | |
	Conporns N=36	Proporns N=25	Controls N=12	Conporns N=49	Proporns N=26	Controls N=38
Female (%)	53	36	0	22	19	16
Mean age	48	36	48	41	37	41
Religion:						
Catholic (%)	25	20	25	31	4	11
Protestant (%)	58	40	75	68	44	86
None (%)	8	36	0	0	38	3
Attend church once or more per week (%)	71	24	50	74	19	58
Population where reared:						
500,000 or less (%)	89	84	75	94	65	87
100,000 or less (%)	67	60	50	61	42	71

Characteristic	Conporns N=36	Midville Proporns N=25	Controls N=12	Conporns N=49	Southtown Proporns N=26	Controls N=38
Occupation:						
Professional or technical (%)	42	72	42	31	69	42
Managers, official, and proprietors, except farm (%)	31	12	17	33	4	24
Craftsmen and foremen (%)	6	0	8	8	0	5
Mean monthly family income	$946	$874	$832	$956	$1,060	$982
Median formal education	some college	some grad. school	some college	some college	some grad. school	some college
Presently married (%)	81	76	100	94	73	89
Median length of present marriage	21–25 years	11–15 years	16–20 years	16–20 years	11–15 years	16–20 years
One or more previous marriages (%)	0	14	17	11	30	9
Median number of children	3	2	2	3	2	2
If married, would prefer single life (%)	0	12	0	2	8	0
Feel children really a nuisance more than a pleasure (%)	19	56	8	10	35	21

Note: The percentages of some characteristics do not total 100 percent because other smaller response categories are not included. Occupation is that of respondent if employed; of head of household otherwise.

the ACLU, university professors. There were very few female Proporns, probably at least in part because of the greater potential for role conflict and for intense negative reaction from others. As one of the female Proporns reported: "If you're willing, as a woman, to take a public stand against the crusaders, you have to be willing to accept the reactions of not just a few people who see you as being a lot less than a 'lady' by their definition of the term."

Nearly all of the Controls were men, since we deliberately attempted to interview heads of households in the randomly drawn residences proximate to those of the Conporns. The differences in sex ratios between Conporns and Proporns can be defended by the fact that those ratios represented, in Midville and Southtown, the social reality. However, the Controls, as heads of households, do not adequately match the Conporns in sex ratio. Consequently, we remind the reader again that, though the Controls will be seen to be similar in many characteristics to the Conporns, and some tentative conclusions can and will be drawn, for the most part comparisons between Controls and Conporns (and Proporns) are best considered to be primarily illustrative.

As hypothesized, the mean age of the Conporns was higher than that of the Proporns. The mean age of the Controls was identical to that of the Conporns.

Most of the Conporns were members of Protestant religions, primarily Baptist, Lutheran, Methodist, Presbyterian, and Church of Christ. The Conporns leaders *all* were Catholics. The Conporn orientation to religion was primarily conservative, fundamentalist, and dogmatic. Over one-third of the Proporns in both Midville and Southtown declared that they were affiliated with no organized religion. Many Proporns who classified themselves as Protestants or Catholics reported only nominal membership; several Proporns classified themselves as Unitarians. Thus, as hypothesized, Conporns more often than Proporns were affiliated with organized religion. More of the Controls than the Conporns were Protestant.

As hypothesized, Conporns in both Midville and Southtown were more religiously active, as defined by church attendance, than Proporns. By far the majority of Conporns attended church at least once a week. Nearly half of the Proporns rarely or never attended church. The Controls' frequency of church attendance was approximately midway between that of the Conporns and Proporns.

Conporns, as hypothesized, tended to be reared in smaller towns or cities than Proporns, although the differences in Midville were relatively small. Similarly Conporns tended to be reared in smaller towns or cities than Controls, although the relationship is clearer in Midville than in Southtown.

Proporns more often were engaged in professional and technical occupations than Conporns, as hypothesized. Conporns were often white-collar workers, middle-management people, and small independent businessmen. The Controls were more similar in occupational classification to Conporns than they were to Proporns, although there were more white-collar workers, middle-management people, and small independent businessmen among Conporns than among Controls.

Conporns, Proporns, and Controls in both Midville and Southtown had family incomes which placed them in the middle economic bracket. There is no clear pattern of income differences among the three groups, but it is important to note that all of them fall in the middle economic bracket. As hypothesized, Conporns had less formal education than Proporns. The Conporns' educational level was identical to that of the Controls.

More Conporns than Proporns were presently married; moreover, Conporns had been married for a longer period of time and had more children. More of the Proporns than the Conporns had been

TABLE 2. *Political and Participatory Characteristics*

| | Midville | | | Southtown | | |
Characteristic	Conporns N=36	Proporns N=25	Controls N=12	Conporns N=49	Proporns N=26	Controls N=38
Very interested in politics (%)	45	64	25	59	77	45
Participate in precinct meetings (%)[a]	28	40	17	—	—	—
Donate money to political campaigns (%)[a]	42	64	42	—	—	—
Donate time to political campaigns (%)[a]	50	88	33	—	—	—

Characteristic	Midville			Southtown		
	Conporns N=36	Proporns N=25	Controls N=12	Conporns N=49	Proporns N=26	Controls N=38
Follow campaign in news- paper (%)[a]	91	92	83	—	—	—
Vote in local elections:						
Always (%)	83	72	83	0	0	16
Fre- quently (%)	11	16	17	98	92	68
Vote in national elections:						
Always (%)	86	88	100	0	0	16
Fre- quently (%)	8	4	0	98	96	79
Political preference:						
Democrat (%)	11	60	33	61	77	63
Republi- can (%)	56	8	42	29	0	16
Inde- pendent (%)	31	32	25	10	23	18
Political orientation:						
Conserva- tive (%)	56	4	42	69	0	71
Liberal (%)	36	92	50	22	89	18
Moderate (%)	8	1	8	8	11	10
Mean number of community or- ganizations in which a member	3.9	3.0	1.8	2.6	4.0	1.5
Serving as of- ficers in the com- munity organ- izations (%)	78	42	33	50	45	42

Note: The percentages of some characteristics do not total 100 percent because other, smaller response categories are not included.

[a]Asked in Midville only.

divorced. If they were married, more of the Proporns than Conporns indicated that they would prefer single life and felt that children really were a nuisance more often than a pleasure. Thus, as hypothesized, Conporns had more established families (they were older), and seemed to have a greater satisfaction with orientation toward the family than the Proporns. In general, the Controls were more similar to Conporns than to Proporns.

Political and Participatory Characteristics (Table 2)

Proporns were more interested in politics than were Conporns, but Conporns were considerably more interested in politics than were Controls. In Midville (where the questions were asked), Proporns more often than Conporns participated in precinct meetings and donated money or time to political campaigns. Both Conporns and Proporns in Midville generally engaged in those activities considerably more than Controls. In Midville nearly all Conporns and Proporns followed political campaigns in the newspaper, again more often than Controls. Nearly all of the respondents always or usually voted in local and national elections. There is some slight indication that Conporns were more faithful to that activity, especially at the local level, than Proporns. The voting percentages also indicate that Midvillians in general seemed to vote more regularly than Southtowners—a finding which fits the overall voter statistics for the two communities (see Chapter 2).

Proporns more than Conporns in both cities reported affiliation with the Democratic party; Conporns more than Proporns reported affiliation with the Republican party. Party membership was, however, very much influenced by the regional ideologies predominant in the party. Regardless of affiliation, the majority of Conporns were, as hypothesized, conservative; nearly all of the Proporns were liberal. Controls tended to be more like Conporns than Proporns in political orientation.

Proporns and Conporns in both Midville and Southtown belonged to more community organizations than Controls and more often were officers in those organizations. The finding concerning membership in community organizations indicates (as do the Midville data on involvement in political activities) the greater involvement of Conporns and Proporns, as compared with Controls, in community affairs.

TABLE 3. *Social-Psychological Characteristics*

| | Midville | | | Southtown | | |
Characteristic	Conporns N=36	Proporns N=25	Controls N=12	Conporns N=49	Proporns N=26	Controls N=38
Powerlessness	1.82	2.61	2.61	2.25	2.09	2.41
Normlessness	0.75	1.84	1.20	0.63	1.48	0.97
Alienation	1.38	2.32	2.05	1.60	1.85	1.84
Authoritarianism	2.06	1.32	2.40	2.62	0.80	2.49
Religiosity	3.95	2.44	4.00	4.45	2.02	4.04
Traditional family ideology	2.56	1.54	3.25	3.27	1.23	2.97
Political intolerance	2.47	0.34	2.45	3.11	0.38	2.85
Dogmatism	2.22	1.78	2.52	2.93	1.74	2.46
Traditional attitude toward sex	2.41	1.69	2.60	2.80	1.49	2.72
Approval of censorship	3.15	1.45	2.89	3.25	1.47	3.17

Note: All scores are means, with a range of 0–6, derived from seven-position Likert response options. The higher the mean score, the greater the intensity of the characteristic.

Social-Psychological Characteristics (Table 3)

In Midville, Conporns felt less powerless than Proporns, who were quite similar to Controls. In Southtown, Proporns felt slightly less powerless than Conporns, who in turn felt slightly less powerless than Controls. Powerlessness is a feeling of impotence to influence the course of events in society.[1] Conporns were less normless than Controls, who in turn were less normless than Proporns. Normlessness is a feeling of not being closely bound by the norms or rules of society.[2] Conporns were less alienated than Controls, who in turn were less alienated than Proporns. As used in this study, alienation is a syndrome combining feelings of normlessness and powerlessness, a sense of impotence to influence the course of events in society and a feeling of not being closely bound by the norms of society.[3] In general these results differ from our hypotheses, which stated that Conporns would be more alienated (i.e., more powerless and normless) than Proporns in the face of what they perceived to be threatening changes in societal values and norms. However, it appears that Conporns had a clear view of societal norms, were content with them, and, relatively, did not feel powerless in resisting the processes of social change. The results are reasonable if one considers that both Midville and Southtown were conservative communities, where Proporns, not Conporns, were the minority and the deviants. Proporns appeared to be even more in the minority in Midville than in Southtown, which may at least in part account for the greater feelings of powerlessness among the Midville Proporns. In retrospect, it is not surprising that Proporns in both cities felt more normless than either Conporns or Controls. In general they perceived the rules of society and especially those predominant in their community to be either unacceptable or archaic, and in need of change.

As hypothesized, Proporns in both Midville and Southtown were less authoritarian than either Conporns or Controls. Authoritarianism is a syndrome of antidemocratic tendencies at the personality level.[4]

Conporns, as hypothesized, manifested more religiosity than Proporns, a finding in keeping with their greater membership in organized religion and greater religious activity as indicated by church attendance. Religiosity is a favorable attitude toward religious beliefs and a willingness to accept doctrinaire statements and values concerning religion.[5] Proporns also reported less religiosity than Controls, who were not remarkably dissimilar from Conporns.

Proporns, as hypothesized, were less inclined toward a traditional family ideology than Conporns. Traditional family ideology is a global measure of autocratic attitudes toward family relations.[6]

Political tolerance is a degree of respect for the civil rights of radical and liberal nonconformists, even though the respondent may be suspicious or disapproving of their opinions.[7] As hypothesized, Conporns were less politically tolerant than Proporns; they also tended to be somewhat less politically tolerant than Controls.

Proporns were less dogmatic than Conporns, as hypothesized. They also were less dogmatic than Controls. Dogmatism is a relatively closed cognitive orientation of beliefs and disbeliefs about reality, organized around a central set of beliefs about absolute authority which, in turn, provide a framework for patterns of intolerance and qualified tolerance of others.[8]

Proporns had a less traditional attitude toward sexual activities than Conporns, as hypothesized. Traditional attitude toward sex is a favorableness toward traditional norms for sexual behavior.[9] Proporns, consequently, tended to view sexual activity in a less religious, less normatively rigid, and somewhat hedonistic framework.

Conporns were, as hypothesized, more approving of censorship than Proporns. Approval of censorship was defined as a positive attitude toward it, drawn from considerations of the moral, legal, and political implications of an argument surrounding censorship.[10]

In the selected social-psychological characteristics, Controls were more like Conporns than they were like Proporns. In some cases, however, Controls were more pronounced in a given characteristic than Conporns. In Midville, Controls were higher than Conporns in powerlessness, normlessness, alienation, authoritarianism, religiosity, traditional family ideology, dogmatism, and traditional attitudes toward sex. In Southtown, the pattern of findings generally shows Controls to be located, on measures of given characteristics, somewhere between Conporns at the higher end and Proporns at the lower end. It is likely that the small sample size of the Midville Controls accounts for some of the reversals in the response distributions.

Women in the general population, it has been reported, tend to be more inclined toward restricting the availability of pornography than men (Commission on Obscenity and Pornography 1970:49). We found there to be no remarkable differences between male and female Conporns in the social-psychological characteristics (including approval of censorship). If anything, the men tended to be slightly more severe. In general, there were no remarkable differences between male and female Conporns in any of the attitudinal variables we assessed. Any inclination to explain the more volatile and expressive Midville crusade as having been influenced by "female characteristics" is unwarranted.

Southtown Conporns were higher on nearly all the social-psychological characteristics than Midville Conporns (powerlessness, alienation, authoritarianism, religiosity, traditional family ideology, political intolerance, dogmatism, traditional attitudes toward sex, and approval of censorship). Yet, as indicated by the natural histories of the anti-

pornography crusades, ICCD in Midville conducted the far more intense crusade. If one were to have anticipated the intensity of the
crusades from the social-psychological characteristics alone, one might
have predicted that UFD in Southtown, rather than ICCD, would have
manifested the most intense activity. It is plausible to suppose that
structural and situational characteristics, rather than social-psychological characteristics, accounted for the differences between the two
crusades. We shall address this problem further in the discussion of
general characteristics below.

Sex Education and Contact with Pornography (Table 4)

Proporns were more prone than Conporns or Controls to discuss sex
at least occasionally in the total family setting. The difference between
Conporns and Proporns in tendency to talk at least occasionally with
their own children about sexual matters was inconsistent in the two
studies. It was clear, however, that Conporns and Proporns more
often than Controls tended to talk at least occasionally with their children about sexual matters. Proporns more than Controls and Controls
more than Conporns talked frequently with their spouses about sexual
matters. Nudity in their own homes was more casually treated by Proporns than by Conporns and Controls. These findings are consistent
with Conporns' greater traditional family ideology and traditional
attitudes toward sex, as reported in the section on social-psychological
characteristics, and support the hypotheses concerning those Conporn
orientations.

There was no clear pattern of differences, as was hypothesized, between Conporns and Proporns in completion of courses in sex education. In Southtown, Proporns more often had such courses, but not
in Midville. Both Conporns and Proporns in Midville and Southtown
did participate in sex education courses more than Controls.

Among the Midville respondents, Proporns more often than Controls and Controls more often than Conporns reported having been
exposed to pornography when they were children. Of those Midvillians who indicated exposure to pornography as children, Conporns more than Controls and Controls more than Proporns reported
that their parents had reacted punitively if they knew about the exposure. Midvillian Proporns were less restrictive or punitive than Controls, who in turn were less restrictive or punitive than Conporns if
they discovered that their own children had seen pornography.

TABLE 4. *Sex Education and Contact with Pornography*

| | Midville | | | Southtown | | |
Characteristic	Conporns N=36 (%)	Proporns N=25 (%)	Controls N=12 (%)	Conporns N=49 (%)	Proporns N=26 (%)	Controls N=38 (%)
Sex at least occasionally is a topic of general family discussion	65	82	60	68	70	67
Talk at least occasionally with own children about sexual matters	72	70	33	71	85	60
Talk frequently with spouse about sexual matters	24	57	33	24	37	26
Casual attitude toward nudity and some actual open nudity in home	38	83	33	38	84	43
Have had a school course in sex education	28	28	17	29	46	11
Exposed to pornography as a child[a]	42	76	50	—	—	
Own parents punitive if they found out respondent saw pornography as a child[a]	71	33	67	—	—	—
Restrictive or punitive when discover own children have seen pornography[a]	59	24	50	—	—	—

[a]Asked in Midville only.

Perceptions and Definitions of Pornography and Assumed Correlates (Table 5)

When asked to define pornography, Proporns more than Conporns gave relativistic ("eye of the beholder") and cynical ("any movie John Wayne is in") responses. Conporns more than Proporns gave definitions which included religious judgments, the presence of nudity, the presence of "abnormal" sexual content (sadomasochism, lesbianism, homosexuality, adultery), and the presence of stimuli which offended esthetic sensibilities. Several Conporns and Proporns included

TABLE 5. *Perceptions and Definitions of Pornography and Assumed Correlates*

	Midville			Southtown		
	Conporns N=36	Proporns N=25	Controls N=12	Conporns N=49	Proporns N=26	Controls N=38
Characteristic	(%)	(%)	(%)	(%)	(%)	(%)
Definitions of pornography:						
Nudity	8	0	8	20	11	42
Sexual activity	11	4	17	10	11	8
Profit motive	36	12	25	12	23	16
Abnormal sexuality	11	8	17	29	1	3
Relativistic definitions	0	36	0	2	39	5
Unattractive, vulgar	17	12	8	12	4	13
Religio-moral affront	17	8	8	12	4	8
Cynical response	0	20	8	0	8	0
Don't know	0	0	8	2	0	5
Have only heard about or have not seen or read what they feel to be:						
Pornographic movies	33	8	13	19	14	11
Pornographic books	71	56	25	64	24	65
Pornographic magazines	17	16	25	31	8	29

	Midville			Southtown		
Characteristic	Conporns N=36 (%)	Proporns N=25 (%)	Controls N=12 (%)	Conporns N=49 (%)	Proporns N=26 (%)	Controls N=38 (%)
Judgments concerning the effects of pornography:						
Encourages violence	22	4	8	18	0	3
Encourages crime	6	0	0	8	0	5
Encourages sexual deviance	11	4	8	6	8	8
Causes undue sexual arousal	25	0	0	8	8	13
Interferes with family sex education	19	8	33	33	12	29
Degrades and debases individual	14	8	0	25	4	21
No significant effect	0	52	17	0	46	16
Positive effects	0	16	8	0	19	3
Don't know	3	8	25	2	4	3
Feel *Playboy* is pornographic	55	4	71	69	20	75
Feel organized crime is connected with pornography:						
Very much	53	12	42	57	0	45
Somewhat or indirectly	37	16	50	27	61	45
Feel communism is connected with pornography:						
Very much	31	0	17	14	0	11
Somewhat or indirectly	33	4	33	43	23	37

Characteristic	Midville			Southtown		
	Conporns N=62[a] (%)	Proporns N=43[a] (%)	Controls N=20[a] (%)	Conporns N=114[a] (%)	Proporns N=43[a] (%)	Controls N=72[a] (%)
Judgment concerning kinds of people who produce pornography:						
Religio-moral	13	0	5	11	0	11
Ideological	3	0	0	3	2	1
Psycho-diagnostic	76	72	70	68	60	62
Socioeconomic level	0	5	0	0	5	4
Occupation	2	12	0	4	26	6
Social role	3	12	15	13	7	14
Don't know	3	0	10	3	0	1

Characteristic	Midville			Southtown		
	Conporns N=83[a] (%)	Proporns N=50[a] (%)	Controls N=22[a] (%)	Conporns N=127[a] (%)	Proporns N=54[a] (%)	Controls N=98[a] (%)
Judgment concerning kinds of people who use or are attracted to pornography:						
Religio-moral	7	2	5	9	0	1
Ideological	1	0	0	0	0	0
Psycho-diagnostic	61	54	55	56	50	50
Socioeconomic level	18	12	14	21	17	28
Occupation	1	0	0	0	4	3
Social role	9	32	14	13	28	14
Don't know	2	0	14	0	2	3

Characteristic	Midville			Southtown		
	Conporns N=89[a] (%)	Proporns N=58[a] (%)	Controls N−36[a] (%)	Conporns N=118[a] (%)	Proporns N=51[a] (%)	Controls N−92[a] (%)
Judgment concerning how those attracted						

to or using
pornography
differ from
respondent:

Religio-moral	43	36	58	46	16	36
Ideological	0	0	3	0	0	0
Psycho-diagnostic	48	48	19	40	53	44
Socioeconomic level	1	2	8	7	0	7
Occupation	0	0	3	0	0	0
Social role	0	0	3	1	0	0
Not different	2	14	0	3	26	5
Don't know	7	0	6	5	6	8

	Midville		Southtown	
	Conporns N=36 (%)	Proporns N=25 (%)	Conporns N=49 (%)	Proporns N=26 (%)

Judgment concerning how the community at large feels about respondent's position on the pornography issue:

Apathetic	11	16	8	8
Disagree	6	60	0	58
Agree partly	31	20	35	12
Agree strongly	47	0	53	0
Don't know	6	4	4	23

	Midville		Southtown	
	Conporns N=48[a] (%)	Proporns N=53[a] (%)	Conporns N=75[a] (%)	Proporns N=39[a] (%)

Judgment concerning what groups in the community oppose the respondent's point of view on pornography:

Religio-moral	13	11	13	10
Ideological	21	13	16	15
Psychodiagnostic	15	19	24	33
Socioeconomic level	17	9	1	0
Occupation	8	13	21	0
Social role	10	8	4	0
Organizational affiliation	10	25	19	33
Specific individuals	6	2	1	8

Note: The percentages of some characteristics do not total 100 percent because of rounding.
[a]Total number of multiple responses.

in their definitions of pornography the specification that the producer had contrived to include deliberately titillative content and thereby hoped to profit financially from the sale of the material. The definitions of pornography reported by Conporns, Proporns, and Controls were impressively diverse, in keeping with the general finding of other studies that there is no universal standard among people or in the law for a definition of pornography.[11] Conporns, as individuals who had committed themselves to action concerning the problem of pornography might have been expected to have given more precise and consensual definitions of the term. Similarly, Proporns, who had publicly taken a stand against the action of the Conporns, might have been expected to give more precise and consensual definitions. Proporns' definitions were somewhat more precise than those of Conporns, inasmuch as sizeable percentages of the Proporn definitions fell within the relativistic and cynical categories.

Virtually all of the respondents were able to give examples of what they felt to be pornographic movies or films. Conporns more than Proporns tended to identify pornographic films by type, referring specifically to "art" films, "skin-flicks," or "X-rated" films. Some of the Conporns felt that commercial movies in general were pornographic. Those Conporns who gave examples according to the content of the film indicated that such films contained nudity or sex activity (centered around coitus or coituslike motions). Those Proporns who gave examples of pornographic films by content generally specified sadomasochistic or violent activity. Conporns more often than Proporns identified what they felt to be pornographic books or magazines by type ("best sellers," "paperbacks," "men's magazines," "girlie magazines," etc.). Proporns again often specified violence when giving examples of pornographic books or magazines by content. Proporns and Conporns differed in the diversity of examples of pornographic films, books, and magazines and in the degree to which the examples were negatively judged. Ranging from *Camelot* to *The Lustful Turk* (movies), from *Grapes of Wrath* to *Bitches in Heat* (books), and from *Life* to *Screw* (magazines), Conporn examples were always associated with stated disapproval. Proporns, on the other hand, presented examples of pornography in a rather clinical fashion. That is, they seldom expressed disapproval (except when such materials involved violence or were poorly produced) and often indicated that they were specifying the type or content of materials that other people (not themselves) would consider pornographic. Those patterns were consistent with the patterns of responses made by Proporns and Conporns concerning definitions of pornography—a diversity in definitions would be expected to be associated with a diversity in examples; a negative or relativistic definitional focus would be expected to be associated with negatively or relativistically interpreted examples.

Other studies have demonstrated that persons who are older, less educated, and more religiously active are more likely to judge a given film, book, or magazine to be pornographic (Commission on Obscenity and Pornography 1970:30). As shown in Table 1, Conporns were older, had less formal education, and were more religiously active than Proporns. Females as a group have been reported to be more severe than males as a group in their judgments concerning what is pornographic (Commission on Obscenity and Pornography 1970:46). There were larger percentages of females among the Conporns than among the Proporns, but the difference in proportions was not marked.

Remarkably, relatively high percentages of Conporns and Proporns reported never having seen a pornographic film or read a pornographic book or magazine. The elevated percentages among the Proporns can be explained by the fact that many of them denied that any film, book, or magazine was pornographic (taken to be a value judgment); therefore they could not have seen or read pornographic material, since there was no such thing. But the elevated percentages among Conporns were intriguing. Nearly all of them had opinions, expressed by type or content, concerning what such movies, books, and magazines were. Indeed they had committed themselves to the expenditure of considerable time and resources as active participants in antipornography crusades. Apparently much of their knowledge concerning pornographic materials was hearsay from significant others. It is generally the case that those persons who are older, less educated, and more active in religious affairs, as were the Conporns, have relatively less experience with erotic materials (Commission on Obscenity and Pornography 1970:147). The tendency, if one is opposed to antipornography activity, is to suggest that Conporns did not really understand the issue and were utterly confused while fighting it. But brief interviews with only a few Conporns quickly revealed that Conporns were, in their own view, quite certain about the issue and, in their actions, not at all confused. Indeed, in interviews they often stumbled in their attempts to define pornography or obscenity, were diffuse in their presentation of examples of such materials, and even might not have seen such materials. However, they were *convinced* that they knew what pornography was, even if reduced to the ultimate subjective position of saying, as did Justice Stewart, "I know it when I see it" (*Jacobellis* v. *Ohio*)—or, in the case of some Conporns, "I would know it if I saw it."

As hypothesized, pornography was believed by Conporns to be related causally to many kinds of social and individual pathology, including crimes of sex and violence, general crimes, sexual aberrations, undue sexual arousal, self-abasement and self-abuse, juvenile delinquency, dropping out of school, marriage failure, drug addiction, venereal disease, and rejection of religion. The judgments of Controls were similarly diverse and largely negative, though some of them, unlike Conporns, were of the opinion that there were positive effects or no significant effects from exposure to pornography. Interestingly, relatively large percentages of Conporns and Controls felt that pornography interfered with the family's prerogative to educate children concerning sexual matters, especially concerning *values* for specific kinds of sexual behavior or restrictions. The majority of Proporns were convinced that exposure to pornography either had no significant effects or had positive effects (educational, recreational, tension-releasing). It has been pointed out in other studies that individuals who, like Proporns, are relatively better educated, younger, and less religiously active tend less to associate exposure to pornography with socially undesirable effects (Commission on Obscenity and Pornography 1970:193–194).

Large percentages of Conporns and Controls (Controls more) felt that *Playboy* magazine (in its pre–pubic-hair era) was pornographic, thus giving some indication of relative judgments of pornography. Those few Proporns who judged *Playboy* to be pornographic assessed its exploitative qualities, rather than its sexual contents, as obscene.

Relatively large percentages of Conporns were certain that organized crime was very much involved with the production of pornography. Several Controls were similarly convinced. Many of the other respondents, including some Proporns, thought organized crime was somewhat or indirectly associated with the production and distribution of pornography. Many Conporns and somewhat fewer Controls thought that Communism was very much, or at least somewhat or indirectly, associated with the production of pornography. Very few Proporns had that opinion.

Conporns harshly judged individuals who produced pornographic materials for sale. Some Conporns labeled the producers in religio-moral terms, as being immoral, atheistic, or irresponsible. The majority of the respondents assessed the producers of pornography in psycho-diagnostic terms. Conporns, and to a lesser extent, Controls, diagnosed producers as being mentally ill, deviant, perverted, lacking in self-respect, psychopathic, and so on. Proporns also diagnosed producers of pornography, but their judgments were less severe, labeling the makers as being immature, having different tastes (from Proporns), and being ignorant. Several Proporns described pornography producers simply as businessmen, engaged in an occupation which wasn't very admirable but was legitimate. Most of the Conporns and Proporns indicated that producers of pornography were making a considerable amount of money at their trade. That observation, according to the report of the Commission on Obscenity and Pornography (1970:7) was incorrect. Even more disturbing to some of the Conporns than the alleged financial profit was the relative ease with which producers could operate and the kinds of status-enhancing individuals or groups (such as the Supreme Court) who seemed to be directly or indirectly legitimizing the producer.

The relatively few Conporns who classified persons who were attracted to or used pornography in religio-moral terms labeled them as atheists, agnostics, those who had "lost the faith," or adherents to weak religions. When Conporns classified users according to socio-economic level, inevitably they labeled them as "lower-class" types; Controls similarly judged users to be "lower-class" but more often cited persons who were out of the labor force (adolescent or unemployed). When Conporns referred to users by social role, they generally labeled them as males, illiterates, bums, misguided youths, college students, or military personnel. Controls identified them by social role as males or students; Proporns using the category of social role saw users as single males but indicated no other pattern of role characteristics.

Most of the respondents described the users or those attracted to pornography in psychodiagnostic terms. Conporns saw the users as being mentally ill, sexually troubled, deviant, anomic, insecure, and looking for illicit sexual stimulation. Controls substantially agreed with Conporns in psychodiagnostic categories but were a little less negatively oriented, concentrating primarily upon judgments of insecurity and immaturity. Proporns, on the other hand, diagnosed users as being average, healthy, but perhaps in some cases curious, immature, and frustrated. Conporns' general negative evaluation of users of pornography was tempered with charity and included a sense of obligation to protect such people, somehow, from the pandering of pornography producers. Proporns did not express that feeling of protectiveness, no doubt because many of them thought that pornography did not negatively affect the users or that there was yet no good evidence to demonstrate that it did. Proporn diagnoses concerning moral well-being or psychological health were much less negatively stated than those of Conporns.

If data concerning patrons of adult bookstores and adult movie theaters are taken as indices of the kinds of individuals who are attracted to or who use pornographic materials, the estimation of Conporns and, to a lesser extent, Controls was considerably in error. As noted in Chapter 3, studies of such persons indicate that they "may be characterized as predominantly white, middle class, middle aged, married males, dressed in business suits or neat casual attire, shopping or attending the movie alone" (Commission on Obscenity and Pornography 1970:25).

When comparing themselves to those attracted to or using pornography, many respondents described the differences in religio-moral terms. Conporns and, to a lesser extent, Controls thought themselves to be more religious, more Christian, more moral, more self-disciplined, and to have had better home backgrounds. Proporn religio-moral statements essentially were relativistic—they felt they had a different, but not necessarily better, value system than did users of pornography. Many of the respondents assessed differences between themselves and users of pornography in psychodiagnostic terms. Conporns and, with less intensity, Controls felt themselves to be better adjusted sexually, to be more normal, to have better mental health and family life, and not to have the need to be attracted to or the inclination to be excited by pornography. Proporns perceived themselves to be in a better state of mental health, in so far as they were better adjusted sexually, to have different interests than users, and to prefer the "real thing" (sexual activity) rather than pictorial or literary depictions of such activity. A few Proporns indicated that they enjoyed pornography but, unlike the users, did not seek it out. Some Proporns felt that there were no significant differences in characteristics between themselves and the users of pornography, except for the involvement in the use of pornography.

A large majority of Conporns in both Midville and Southtown perceived the community at large to agree with their position on the pornography issue. The majority of Proporns in both cities perceived the community essentially to be in disagreement with them. Both perceptions were, as the natural history data (Chapters 2–7) indicate, correct. Proporns indeed had minimal support for the more liberal position they held with regard to restricting or censoring alleged pornography.

When asked what groups or individuals in the community opposed their point of view on pornography, respondents gave a diverse assortment of assessments. Conporns typified their opponents according to characteristics which were religio-moral (atheists, agnostics, etc.), ideological (radicals, hippies, etc.), socioeconomic (lower class), occupational (professors, profit-oriented businessmen, etc.), related to social role (young persons, students, criminals, etc.), organizational (ACLU, local universities and colleges, liberal churches, etc.), and psychodiagnostic. Conporns diagnosed their opponents as being misguided, afraid of legitimate authority, unpatriotic, enslaved by pornography, stupid, psychopathic, and so on. Proporns typified their opponents according to characteristics which were religio-moral (religious fanatics), ideological (radical rightists, ultraconservatives), socioeconomic (the epitome of the middle class), occupational (ministers, priests, especially conservative ones), related to social role (housewives, community "do-gooders"), organizational (John Birch Society, PTA, Daughters of the American Revolution), and psychodiagnostic. Proporns' psychodiagnostic assessment of opponents to their perspective included opinions that they were rigid, hypocritical, sexually troubled, bigoted, close-minded, mentally ill, chronically dissatisfied, and so on.

In total, 58 percent of the Conporns included among those they perceived to be disagreeing with them what they labeled as radicals, hippies, young people, college students, and professors—the "modernists" who espoused alternative life styles.

Discussion

The questionnaire data with only a few exceptions support the hypotheses concerning differences in general characteristics between Conporns and Proporns. Conporns in both Midville and Southtown manifested general characteristics which, though markedly different from those of Proporns, were only in a few instances different from those of Controls. Based upon the relative differences among the respondents, a tentative profile of Conporns can be suggested.

Conporns were middle-aged, tended to have been reared in smaller towns than Proporns, were religiously oriented and religiously active. They often were employed in nonprofessional white-collar or small-business occupations, had at least some college experience, had achieved material comfort, and easily fell within the range of middle-class affluence. Conporns had been married for several years, had several children, had a stable marriage history, and were satisfied with and oriented toward marriage and family life. Many of the Conporns were men, contrary to the common stereotype of antipornography activists as women.

Gusfield (1963:84–85) noted that active members of the temperance movement in the late nineteenth century were not marginal to the "American way of life." On the contrary, they belonged to major churches (fundamentalist), and were quite middle-class in every way. The life style they embraced represented a model of the legitimate and dominant definition of respectability.

Conporns were similar to the status discontents participating in temperance crusades described by Gusfield—relatively rural, middle-class, middle-aged, politically active, religiously active, family oriented, and conservative. The similarities in these characteristics are shared not only by Conporns and temperance crusaders but also by individuals who tend (without taking action) to define sexually explicit materials as pornographic.[12]

Though similar to Conporns in socioeconomic level and therefore in middle-class membership, Proporns tended to be well educated, young, not oriented toward family or religion, reared in larger cities, employed in professional occupations, politically active, and politically liberal. The similarity between Conporns and Proporns in socioeconomic status, linked with the striking differences in most of their other characteristics, highlights the interpretation that not economic but value orientations were the source of opposition between the two groups.

Compared with Controls, Conporns were more often Catholic, more religiously active, more often reared in smaller towns, less often employed in professional occupations, more family oriented, and more politically active. Conporns and Controls were similar in several of the characteristics we have discussed, indicating that Conporns, not Proporns, were more representative of the community at large. Essentially it was not the Conporns but the Proporns and what they represented that affronted the modal community perspective.

Compared with Controls, both Conporns and Proporns were significantly more engaged in community activities. As the natural-history presentation indicated, Proporns had not taken as much action supporting their perspective as had Conporns. Most Proporns interviewed reported that they were waiting until the question of pornography became significantly involved in the local courts, at which time they would do whatever they could to assist in the winning of court cases supporting civil liberties. For the most part, Proporns refused to, as one summarized, "fight book-burners in their own emotional trenches, before the rationality of law entered."

Contrary to expectations, Conporns, in comparison with the other two respondent groups, did not feel a pervasive sense of powerlessness, normlessness, or alienation. Indeed, they felt very much a part of American society, as they defined it, and were basically satisfied with what they perceived to be the dominant societal values and norms. However, their views of those values and norms tended to be somewhat rigid, as indicated by their relatively high scores on authoritarianism and dogmatism. Similarly, they tended to be intolerant of individuals whose political values were different from theirs—particularly if that difference was in a radical or liberal direction. Conporns maintained traditional and restrictive views of sexual behavior and favored censorship to promote and to protect those views. Several of these characteristics of Conporns were similar to characteristics of persons observed to be active in various change-resisting or radical-right protest groups.[13]

Proporns, in contrast, were considerably less authoritarian, dogmatic, politically intolerant, and traditional in their view of family and sexual behavior. They opposed censorship for any purpose. In these characteristics Proporns were similar to individuals observed to be participants in change-supporting or radical-left protest groups.[14]

Compared with Conporns, Proporns felt more powerless, normless, and alienated in their communities. Both the natural-history and questionnaire data, which showed great similarities between Conporns and Controls, indicated that conservatism and traditionalism prevailed in the political, educational, economic, and religious institutions of both Midville and Southtown. The fact that Proporns were uncomfortable with conservatism and traditionalism no doubt significantly contributed to their feelings of distance from and powerlessness within their communities. Conporns, on the other hand, accurately believed that the norms and values predominant in their communities (and the society at large) for the most part were akin to theirs and that they could effectively counter threats to those norms and values by political, legal, or direct action.

As reviewed in Chapter 1, Gusfield (1963:88) pointed out that individuals who have built their self-concepts on traditional values and who conduct their everyday behavior according to traditional norms are vulnerable to the inevitable processes of social change in modern societies. Change upsets old hierarchies, develops new collective aspirations, and challenges long-established values and norms with potential obsolescence. When the individual is threatened with the impact of social change upon his self-concept, especially upon the prestige and respect he has enjoyed and has come to expect as associated with his espousal of traditional values and norms, he will resist both the change and those he perceives to be the agents of change. Such individuals, according to Gusfield, are concerned about the status of a style of life into which they have been socialized, and they will strive to preserve, defend, or enhance the power and prestige of that style (1963:3). One method of defending one's style of life is to engage in a symbolic crusade against the perceived threat and against individuals whose style of life differs and whose actions are threatening. In contemporary American society, countercultures and cross-cultural pressures are challenging traditional values and norms concerning education, religion, authority, war, work, marriage, children, patriotism, and sexual behavior. The symbolic crusade is a means of demonstrating, of reaffirming, the universality and power of traditional values, and it offers an avenue of dissent. That dissent can effectively be conducted by focusing on a specific moral issue. Gusfield has described alcohol as such an issue. We suggest that the natural-history and questionnaire data presented thus far demonstrate that pornography served as such an issue. The behaviors of Conporns described in the natural histories of ICCD in Midville and UFD in Southtown articulate with the general characteristics of Conporns. Actions taken to defend traditionalism, to defend a conservative life style, articulate well with the specific measures of traditionalism and conservatism. Conversely, actions taken to oppose conservative and traditional behaviors articulate well with specific measures of antitraditionalism and liberality. Discussion of the remaining characteristics of Conporns and Proporns will further substantiate that articulation.

At this point, it is important to note that the consideration of general characteristics *alone*, especially social-psychological characteristics alone, although associated with crusade behaviors, was not enough to predict the intensity of those behaviors. Most certainly, Conporns and Proporns consistently were different on a number of important characteristics, but several social and situational factors accounted for the participation of those persons in Conporn or Proporn activities: recruitment contact by friends, memberships in voluntary associations which by charter or inclination found pornography a challenging issue, and so on. The natural histories of ICCD and UFD demonstrate the kinds of situational factors which attracted specific individuals into participation, either as Conporns or as Proporns. In Chapter 9 we shall discuss in detail the patterns of recruitment processes as influencing who would or would not become a Conporn.

If social-psychological characteristics alone were taken as predictors of the shape or intensity of the antipornography crusades in Midville and Southtown, one could be misled. (This assumes, of course, that those characteristics were the same *prior* to participation in the crusades and were not grossly modified by participation.) As compared with Midville Conporns, Southtown Conporns were more conservative, more authoritarian, more powerless, more religious, more traditional in family ideology, less politically tolerant, more dogmatic, more traditional in their view of sex, and more approving of censorship. One would think, therefore, that UFD in Southtown would have conducted the more intense, more volatile, more demanding, and more hostile crusade. As the natural histories indicate, the opposite was the case—ICCD in Midville conducted the more severe crusade. The social-psychological characteristics, therefore, though perhaps indicative of the general pool of individuals from whom crusade participants might have been recruited and though perhaps generally articulating with the intentions of crusade behavior (defense of life style and demonstration of status discontent), do not in themselves determine crusade characteristics. The social-psychological characteristics and the kinds of pressures that social change may bring to bear concerning them are only a part of the overall process of the evolution of a crusade—they are primarily a part of two stages of the value-added processes toward crusade emergence, structural strain and the growth and spread of a generalized belief. Other components within those two stages and characteristics of the other stages (structural conduciveness, precipitating factors, mobilization for action, and social control) interact with social-psychological characteristics, in some cases being influenced by them and in some cases overriding them. Conporns indeed may be (and we argue are) status discontents, but that label cannot be affixed to them on the basis of measured social-psychological characteristics alone. It can be affixed only after a consideration of those measured characteristics, the kinds of changes and stresses which impinge upon the characteristics, and the perceptions of the changes and stresses by the involved individuals. Given those criteria, it can be predicted that other persons displaying similar characteristics, similar situational determinants, and similar perceptions will also be status discontents who are likely to engage in status politics.[15]

Primarily because the courses were not available to them while they were going to school, most of the Conporns had not had formal sex education. They tended to have had no exposure to pornography as children, to have been treated punitively by their parents if exposure did take place and was discovered, and, in turn, to be restrictive or punitive with their own children who had been exposed to pornography. Conporns and Proporns, considerably more than Controls, tended to discuss sexual matters with their own children. Apparently, both Conporns and Proporns were sensitized to sexual issues and to the importance of sharing information with their children. The content of such talks and the associated moral imperatives, however, were quite dissimilar. Conporns seemed somewhat restrictive about discussing sexual matters with their spouses and about nudity in their homes.

Conporns were unable to provide consensual definitions of pornography, despite the fact that they had committed themselves to its opposition (some of them being involved up to forty hours a week in active crusading). The definitions given were diverse, including pronouncements of religious judgments, indictments of the profit motive, and condemnation of specific sexual behavior or "abnormality." Essentially, Conporns' definitions of pornography were value judgments contrasting their traditional set of accepted values and norms with those manifested in various elements of social change. Though the language of social movements is often obtuse and abstract, we interpret the Conporn diversity of definitions to manifest the diversity of changes about which they were concerned and to demonstrate the argument that pornography was, for the Conporns, a summary symbol for status discontent.

Despite the fact that some Conporns had never seen what they would define as pornographic movies and had never read what they would define as pornographic books or magazines, nearly all of them expressed highly negative judgments concerning the effects of pornography, the people who produced it, and the people who were attracted to or used it. Those judgments were diverse, intense, and value-laden—a pattern similar to that of the Conporn definitions of pornography. Often the judgments were made in a fashion which juxtaposed the Conporn life style, as the respondents saw or lived it, with alternative life styles (alternative values, norms, roles).

Proporns' definitions of pornography and their judgments concerning its effects, producers, and users were somewhat less diverse than Conporns' but still rather diverse and not less intense or less value-laden. Proporns, too, were speaking to pornography less as a single issue than as a symbolic representation of an alternative value/norm/role complex—one opposed to that of the Conporns.

Many of the Conporns believed that organized crime and/or a Communist conspiracy were connected with the production and distribution of pornography. That finding supported Gusfield's (1963) and Hofstadter's (1967) assertion that moral crusaders generally manifest belief in a theory of conspiracy. Most social movements, regardless of orientation, incorporate attributions of conspiracy into their generalized beliefs. Many Conporns (not incorrectly) also saw university people, liberals, and radicals (proponents of the modernist alternative life style which threatens Conporns) as an active part of that same conspiracy. Such modernists were *the* opponents, according to most Conporns, of their antipornography efforts. The vast majority of the people in their communities were, according to Conporns, "right-thinking" and supportive of the crusades.

The characteristics we have described for Conporns can be seen on the one hand to reflect and on the other hand to influence the components of action as specified by Smelser. The demographic, political, social-psychological, and perceptual characteristics described, summarized as traditional and conservative, can be seen to reflect or influence values, norms, roles and rewards, and situational facilities. The values themselves are traditional and conservative, shape the rules and regulations which implement and maintain them, pattern the roles and rewards by which and for which individuals are to live up to them, and orient the skills, knowledge and techniques which allow the individual to live up to them. Structural strain can exist for the individual and for the system at any one of the component levels. We have noted in the natural histories of ICCD in Midville and UFD in Southtown that Conporns in general were worried about threats to their basic values by social change and particularly by the increasing presence and growing prestige of alternative life styles. Conservatism and traditionalism were, as they perceived it, threatened. The rules and regulations, the laws which protected those basic values, seemed to be weakening. The rewards associated with the Conporns in acting the "right" way, especially the prestige associated with that dedication, seemed to be diminishing. Predictability of events in and feelings of control over day-to-day life had been challenged for the Conporns, as had been the veracity of their knowledge and the utility of their skills. In other words, as we have summarized it, the life style of the Conporns had been threatened (life style including the values, norms, roles and rewards, and situational facilities which they cherished). Individual characteristics we have described (as measured by structured questionnaires), operating in the natural-history setting we have detailed (as organized according to the value-added stages), merge to demonstrate the emergence of status discontents (Conporns) who took action (antipornography crusades) to defend the prestige and power of their style of life.

Status Inconsistency

It was hypothesized in Chapter 1 that Conporns would tend toward an over-rewarded status-inconsistency pattern of higher income and lower education and/or lower occupation. In contrast, Proporns would tend toward an under-rewarded status-inconsistency pattern of lower income and higher education and/or higher occupation.

The status variables of education, occupation, and income were dichotomized into *high* and *low* status categories at the median of the response distribution. The *high* category for education was *college graduate or more*; the *low* was *some college or less*. The *high* category for occupation was *professional, technical or kindred*; the *low* was *all other occupations*. The *high* category for income was *$1200.00 or more monthly family income*; the *low* was *less than $1200.00 monthly family income*. Since all of the respondents were Anglo, ethnicity was not a relevant status variable in this study. For the purpose of the analysis of status inconsistency we have merged the Midville with the Southtown Conporns and the Midville with the Southtown Proporns. Eighteen Conporns and seven Proporns preferred not to divulge information concerning one or more of the status variables; consequently, the respondents numbered 111 for the purposes of the present analysis (sixty-seven Conporns; forty-four Proporns).

Table 6, which presents the percentage of Conporns and Proporns among respondents within each status pattern, shows that Conporns were markedly more represented than Proporns among the over-rewarded status inconsistents. In fact, all but one of the over-rewarded status inconsistents were Conporns. Conporns were especially numerous in the most over-rewarded status pattern (high income, low education, low occupation). Taken by itself, this finding can be interpreted to support the hypothesis that Conporns would tend toward a status inconsistency pattern of high income and low education and/or low occupation.

The hypothesis that Proporns would tend toward an under-rewarded status pattern of low income and high education and/or high

TABLE 6. *Percentage of Conporns and Proporns among Respondents within Each Status Pattern*

Status Patterns			Configuration	Conporns (N=67)	Proporns (N=44)	Totals (N=111)
Occupa-tion	Income	Educa-tion				
High	High	High	High consistent	29.6% (8)	70.4% (19)	100.0% (27)
High	Low	High	Under-rewarded	42.3% (11)	57.7% (15)	100.0% (26)
High	Low	Low	Under-rewarded	71.4% (5)	28.6% (2)	100.0% (7)
Low	Low	High	Under-rewarded	50.0% (5)	50.0% (5)	100.0% (10)
High	High	Low	Over-rewarded	100.0% (3)	0.0% (0)	100.0% (3)
Low	High	High	Over-rewarded	100.0% (5)	0.0% (0)	100.0% (5)
Low	High	Low	Over-rewarded	92.9% (13)	7.1% (1)	100.0% (14)
Low	Low	Low	Low consistent	89.5% (17)	10.5% (2)	100.0% (19)

occupation was not, as shown in Table 6, consistently supported. The most under-rewarded status pattern (low income, high education, high occupation) did contain a substantial majority of Proporns. But the other two under-rewarded patterns contained either an equal number of Conporns and Proporns or more Conporns than Proporns.

Table 7, which presents the distribution of Conporns, Proporns, and all respondents over all status patterns, demonstrates clearer support for the greater Conporn than Proporn tendency toward over-rewarded inconsistency and the greater Proporn than Conporn tendency toward under-rewarded inconsistency. Table 8 summarizes the findings in Table 7 according to configuration of status patterns. That Table shows

TABLE 7. *Distribution of Conporns, Proporns, and All Respondents over All Status Patterns*

Status Pattern			Configuration	Conporns (N=67)	Proporns (N=44)	All Respondents (N=111)
Occupation	Income	Education				
High	High	High	High consistent	11.9% (8)	43.2% (19)	24.3% (27)
High	Low	High	Under-rewarded	16.4% (11)	34.1% (15)	23.4% (26)
High	Low	Low	Under-rewarded	7.5% (5)	4.5% (2)	6.3% (7)
Low	Low	High	Under-rewarded	7.5% (5)	11.4% (5)	9.0% (10)
High	High	Low	Over-rewarded	4.5% (3)	0.0% (0)	2.7% (3)
Low	High	High	Over-rewarded	7.5% (5)	0.0% (0)	4.5% (5)
Low	High	Low	Over-rewarded	19.4% (13)	2.3% (1)	12.6% (14)
Low	Low	Low	Low consistent	25.4% (17)	4.5% (2)	17.1% (19)

Note: Percentages may not total 100 percent because of rounding.

TABLE 8. *Summary of Distribution of Conporns, Proporns, and All Respondents over All Status Configurations*

Status Configuration	Conporns (N=67)	Proporns (N=44)	All Respondents (N=111)
High consistent	11.9% (8)	43.2% (19)	24.3% (27)
Under-rewarded	31.3% (21)	50.0% (22)	38.7% (43)
Over-rewarded	31.3% (21)	2.3% (1)	19.8% (22)
Low consistent	25.4% (17)	4.5% (2)	17.1% (19)

Note: Percentages may not total 100 percent because of rounding.

most clearly of the three Tables the greater tendency of Conporns than Proporns toward over-rewardedness and the greater tendency of Proporns than Conporns toward under-rewardedness.

Tables 6, 7, and 8 also highlight other important Conporn and Proporn status patterns. Notable percentages of Conporns were low status consistents; notable percentages of Proporns were high status consistents. Nearly one-third of the Conporns were *under*-rewarded status inconsistents (the same percentage as those who were *over*-rewarded.) There was an uneven but nonetheless diverse distribution of status configurations among Conporns and, to a lesser extent, among Proporns. Conporns were fairly well distributed among high and low consistents and among under-rewarded and over-rewarded inconsistents. Proporns were more narrowly clustered among high consistents and under-rewarded inconsistents.

When the distributions of status patterns and configurations were analyzed separately for Midville and Southtown, the results were the same as when the data from the two cities were analyzed as pooled.

Discussion

The Conporn status-inconsistency pattern of over-rewardedness and the Proporn pattern of under-rewardedness tended to substantiate the arguments of Curtis (1970), Eitzen (1970*a*), Geschwender (1967; 1968),

Hunt and Cushing (1970), Lipset (1959), Rush (1967), and Trow (1958) concerning the types of status inconsistency manifested by individuals favorably inclined toward, or having membership in, conservative (over-rewarded) or liberal (under-rewarded) groups. However, several Conporns were either under-rewarded inconsistents or status consistents (the over-rewarded, under-rewarded, and consistent configurations each accounted for approximately one-third of the Conporns). The status patterns of the Conporns were by no means as homogeneous as we had hypothesized. Nor were the status patterns of the Proporns as homogeneous as we had hypothesized. It seems reasonable to assume that the over-rewarded Conporns could be defending their over-rewardedness against the threat of change by engaging in a symbolic crusade against such change (with pornography as the summary symbol for the change). It also seems reasonable to assume that the under-rewarded Proporns would like to see change in society which would remedy their condition of under-rewardedness. But what of the under-rewarded status inconsistents among the Conporns? What of the low consistents among the Conporns and the high consistents among the Proporns?

It has already been shown (see Table 1) that Conporns differ from Proporns in median level of formal education and in representation among higher occupational categories. The data presented in Tables 6, 7, and 8 also suggest the salience of education and occupation, independently of status inconsistency or consistency, in differentiating between Conporns and Proporns. Conporns tended to have lower levels of formal education and to be in lower status occupations than Proporns. But there were some Conporns who were in the high-status categories of education and/or occupation. There were some Proporns who were in the low-status categories of education and/or occupation.

Though the findings provided partial support for our hypotheses concerning over-rewarded Conporns and under-rewarded Proporns, the data more generally indicated a diversity of status inconsistency and consistency configurations among both Conporns and Proporns. The results tend to support the argument of some researchers that the perception of status threat is a more significant variable in the determination of change-encouraging or change-discouraging behavior than configurations of status inconsistency or consistency.[16] Perception of the same status threat may exist among individuals whose status configurations are quite diverse. Individuals who share the same status configuration may have quite diverse perceptions of a specific status threat. Over-rewarded status inconsistents may resist change which they perceive to be a status threat; they may encourage change which they perceive to be status enhancing. Under-rewarded status inconsistents, high status consistents, and low status consistents similarly may resist or encourage change, depending upon their perceptions of status threat.

The finding of a diversity of status configurations among Conporns and Proporns also tends to support the view that participants in social movements are not necessarily a homogeneous lot (Turner and Killian 1972). They can be involved in the movement for differing reasons, often quite disparate, which may or may not include or be related to such social or social-psychological factors as status consistency or inconsistency. But we cannot dismiss the fact that Conporns claimed the bulk of the over-rewarded status configuration and Proporns claimed the bulk of the under-rewarded status configuration.

The processes of status patterns and the processes of status threat, as perceived, might usefully be subsumed within Gusfield's concept of status discontent and within Smelser's concept of structural strain. Status discontent is generated when an individual's prestige is less than he or she expects as someone who has pledged to enact and maintain a traditionally prestigeful style of life. The term *style of life*, according to Gusfield, includes the system of values, customs, and habits distinctive to a particular status group, as perceived by the individual. Regardless of whether individuals are over-rewarded status inconsistents, under-rewarded status inconsistents, or status consistents, they have enacted and are maintaining a style of life which it is likely they will defend against loss of approval, respect, admiration, or deference (i.e., prestige). Gusfield's concept of status discontent can, therefore, be used conceptually to include the operation of perceived status threats in a context of status inconsistency; to represent concern with social power, privilege, and prestige; and to relate those factors directly to participation in symbolic crusades. The concept can, consequently, include, as mentioned by Olsen and Tully in their critique of the status-inconsistency literature, a variety of independent variables, such as one's social power, privilege, and prestige (1972).

Status inconsistency might also be included as one of the components of structural strain among Smelser's value-added stages, as suggested by Geschwender (1968). Status inconsistency most probably could be interpreted as a structural strain operating within the role or reward element of the components of action. Thus, for some individuals, perceived status inconsistency, in the usual definition of the term, could be an important source of strain contributing to the value-added evolution toward collective behavior (e.g., participation in a symbolic crusade). We have argued earlier that status discontent as a manifestation of perceived threat to life style can and does operate among all four elements of the components of action: values, norms, roles or rewards, and situational facilities. Thus perceived status inconsistency can conceptually become a part of status discontent, operating most specifically at the level of roles and rewards. Status inconsistency becomes, then, one possible type of perceived status threat, one kind of structural strain, in the entire value-added sequence. In and of itself, status inconsistency is not enough to engender participation in the symbolic crusade or, more generally, in a social movement.

Geschwender (1967) has argued that status inconsistency generates cognitive dissonance and that in order to resolve the dissonance the individuals will shift to increasingly complex forms of reduction behavior. Placing the status-inconsistency concept within the broader framework of status discontent and within the framework of the value-added stages (as structural strain at the level of roles or rewards) provides a conceptual mechanism for demonstrating the shifting to more complex forms of dissonance reduction. If the individual is significantly influenced, to the point of strain, by a perception of status inconsistency, he or she, depending upon the context of structural conduciveness and the types of operating social control, may strive to resolve the inconsistency (or defend the inconsistency or the consistency) by engaging in a craze, a hostile outburst, a norm-oriented social movement, or a value-oriented social movement. The persons thus can move up the components of action if unsatisfied at any particular level. Of course the other value-added stages—generalized belief, precipitating factors, and elements associated with mobilization for action—must also have operated.

Placing the concept of status inconsistency in the broader scheme of status discontent and the value-added stages might help answer Orum's (1974) call for a framework which shows the linkage among status inconsistency, psychological strain, and the belief in or participation in social movements.

Political Efficacy and Political Trust

The natural-history data revealed that, though both ICCD in Midville and UFD in Southtown manifested an orientation toward constraint (both sought to influence the availability of alleged pornographic materials in the community by introducing new disadvantages to the commercial sellers of such materials), ICCD clearly manifested the more direct, harassing, immediate, and thus more severe constraining behavior. According to the Gamson (1969) proposition, therefore, the hypothesis stated in Chapter 1 can be sharpened as follows: Conporns in Midville would report a higher degree of political efficacy and a lower degree of political trust than Conporns in Southtown.

The structured questionnaire administered to Conporns contained items which we have taken to operationalize the variables under consideration. There are four items concerned with *political efficacy*: (a) frequency of voting in local elections; (b) frequency of voting in national elections; (c) number of community voluntary associations in which a member; (d) satisfaction rank given to participation in community affairs (when compared with religious activities, family relationships, recreational activities, and career or occupation). Gamson (1969) advised that in order to test hypotheses about the operation of trust and efficacy, one needs independent measures of the two variables. He cited Paige's (1968) measure of political efficacy, namely a measure of political information, as being uncontaminated by trust but quite highly related to efficacy. The questionnaire administered to Conporns contained no items which would measure political information. However, voting in local and/or national elections often has been taken as an index of political efficacy (see, for example, Campbell et al. 1960). Similarly, membership in community voluntary associations and satisfaction with participation in community affairs have been shown to be related to indices of personal and political efficacy.[17] Two items on the questionnaire are concerned with *political trust*: (a) belief that the person who is elected really makes a difference in the way we live (Nettler 1957); (b) belief that in this complicated world of ours the only way we can know what is going on is to rely on leaders or experts who can be trusted (Rokeach 1960). Gamson (1969) indicated that Paige's measure of political trust was a straightforward question concerning the degree to which his respondents felt that they could trust the local government. No such direct question was asked of the Conporns, but the two items stated above seem to have face validity as indices of political trust. The items are similar to some in the Political Cynicism Scale, and political cynicism is reported to measure the extent to which one is contemptuously distrustful of politicians and the political process (Agger, Goldstein, and Pearl 1961).

As shown in Table 9, and as hypothesized, Midville Conporns reported higher political efficacy and lower political trust than Southtown Conporns.

Discussion

Though the measures of political efficacy and political trust we used were ad hoc and did not fully explore or operationalize the concepts of political efficacy and political trust as discussed by Gamson (1968),[18] the results suggest support for Gamson's proposition concerning the relation of political efficacy and political trust to mobilization for citizen action. Since most of the Conporns considered themselves to be politically conservative (see Table 2), and since the political behavior in which the Conporns engaged was conservative in nature (that is,

TABLE 9. *Political Efficacy and Political Trust among Midville and Southtown Conporns*

	Midville Conporns N=36	Southtown Conporns N=49
Political efficacy		
Frequency of voting in local elections: always (%)	83	0
Frequency of voting in national elections: always (%)	86	0
Number of community voluntary associations in which a member (mean)	3.9	2.6
Satisfaction rank given to participation in community affairs: third or better among other activities (%)	33	14
Political trust		
Belief that the person who is elected to office really makes a difference in the way we live (%)	69	82
Belief that in this complicated world of ours the only way we can know what is going on is to rely on leaders or experts who can be trusted (%)	41	64

change-resistant rather than change-advocating), the findings suggest that Gamson's proposition has application to citizen action that is to the right as well as that which is to the left of political center.

Gamson (1969) described the lack of political trust among Blacks who participated in riot activity. Political mistrust is relatively easy to understand among Blacks, who, as a minority group systematically discriminated against within the political system, have seldom been part of and have not had much reason to trust that system. But what about Conporns? They were Anglo, middle-class, dramatically traditional, politically efficacious, very typical and powerful Americans quite active in and accepted by the political system. Why should there be any political mistrust among the Conporns? Why should there be a disparity between their political efficacy and their political trust?

As we have argued, Conporns were status discontents. The traditional life style with which they were comfortable and to which they were committed was increasingly being challenged by social change. Conporns felt strongly that the prestige and power of their style of life was being undermined and was not being represented, particularly in the mass media, as viable. The issue of pornography had become, for the Conporns, a suitable summary symbol of the challenges and changes and a focus for resistance to them.

In Southtown and especially in Midville, the Conporns perceived and reported political officials at the federal, state, and local levels, including the police, to be generally unable or unwilling to deal "toughly" with the problem of pornography and what it symbolized to them. The Conporns were generally disappointed and disillusioned with the actions of social control agencies within the political system to safeguard the power and prestige of their style of life, as exemplified by the ineffectiveness with which pornography was controlled nationally and locally. Disillusionment and even anger were particularly marked concerning the Supreme Court and its then recent decisions dealing with such basic issues as prayer, criminal behavior, integration, and, of course, pornography. Gamson commented, "A loss of trust in authorities may have the consequence of increasing the resources of interest groups by making the necessity of using them to influence authorities more apparent to their constituency" (1969:8). He further wrote, "The decline of trust has the effect of encouraging groups to demand explicit fulfillment of the government's obligations to them" (1969:5). Conporns had experienced a loss of trust in the political system concerning the intention and/or effectiveness of that system to guarantee the prestige and power of their style of life. Consequently they felt strongly that they should take action themselves to "right the wrong." That action included efforts to influence authorities to deal more dramatically and effectively with the problem of pornography, efforts to revise segments of the political system (laws), and, in Midville, direct action against the Midwestern Bookstore.

Midville Conporns manifested more political efficacy and less political trust than Southtown Conporns, and ICCD took a more blatant and constraining antipornography action than UFD. The natural-history data indicate that the Midville Conporns had a greater reason for low political trust. Their state antipornography statute had been struck down as unconstitutional, the informal pornography arrangement between the local police department and community businesses which sold books and magazines had eroded, and the Midwestern Bookstore noticeably affronted their sensibilities, despite the awareness of the police.

Gamson's formulation and data suggest that the "have-nots" (those groups having relatively less power, status, or economic well-being) manifest a lack of political trust when they perceive the political system as not supporting their potential to "have"; and, if politically efficacious, they will engage in *change-oriented* action which can be considered left of political center. Our findings concerning the Conporns suggest, in the Gamson framework, that "haves" (those groups having relatively more power, status, or economic well-being) manifest a relative lack of political trust when they perceive the political system as not defending their position of "having" against threats from impending change (in values, norms, roles, or rewards); and they will, if politically efficacious, engage in *change-resistant* action which can be considered right of political center. (For another study which tests Gamson's proposition concerning political efficacy and political trust, see Michener and Zeller 1972.)

As suggested by Gamson (1968) and as we hypothesized, Midville Conporns reported a lower mean score of powerlessness (1.82) than Southtown Conporns (2.25)—a finding which fits with the greater sense of political efficacy among Midville Conporns. Furthermore, Midville Conporns reported a higher mean score of normlessness (0.75) than Southtown Conporns (0.63)—a finding which fits with the lesser degree of political trust among Midville Conporns.

The variables of political efficacy and political trust articulate with the differences in the degree of constraint employed by ICCD and UFD, but those variables do not alone explain the differences in tactics. Although, at the mean, the Midville Conporns felt more politically efficacious and expressed less political trust than the Southtown Conporns, several of the individual Midville Conporns did not fit that pattern. Similarly, several of the Southtown Conporns felt more politically efficacious and less politically trustful than some of the Midville Conporns. Like status inconsistency and other social-psychological variables we have discussed, the ratio of political efficacy to political trust does not fully explain the participation of the Conporns or the shape of their crusades. Those concepts can, however, be usefully integrated with broader frameworks which attempt to describe and explain the development of political protest.

Gusfield's concept of status discontent can be seen to include, for the individuals so labeled, a concern that the agents of social control (including political officials and the political system) are inadequately protecting the integrity and prestige of their life styles. Furthermore, status discontents, as described by Gusfield, strongly feel that they have the potential to do something which will either mobilize the agents of social control or modify them so that they will be more effective for protective purposes. If that strategy should fail, status discontents may continue to be convinced of their efficacy to take direct action, outside of the agents of social control, to protect their prestige and its attendant power.

Gusfield distinguished between assimilative reform and coercive reform in the symbolic crusade. By assimilative reform the status discontent attempts to convince the deviant to conform to the life style embraced by the crusader. By coercive reform the status discontent engages in crusade activities which are more characterized by hostility and force. The crusade may begin with an emphasis upon assimilative reform, but if the crusaders perceive the individuals and groups whose life style differs from and threatens theirs to be increasing in strength, despite crusade efforts, the strategy may shift to coercive reform. The perceived growing strength of the enemy may be associated with a perception of continuing unwillingness or inability of political officials or the political system to control that enemy, and this may decrease political trust. Thus the operation of political trust can be seen to be part of the process of status discontent.

Political efficacy and political trust can conceptually be made a part of the Smelser framework. Both efficacy and trust are situational facilities among the components of action (Smelser 1962:30). They contribute to the individual's confidence in the social system in which he operates and in his own ability to control significant aspects of his environment. Thus, among the value-added stages, discrepancies between political efficacy and political trust can be interpreted as engendering structural strain at the level of situational facilities. Furthermore, elements of strain concerning political trust can engender strain at the components-of-action levels of roles (the behavior of public officials) and norms (the effective operation of laws). The ratio between political efficacy and political trust can, therefore, be considered one *among* conditions of structural strain which contribute to the emergence of the collective behavior. Expressions of political efficacy and political trust can also become part of the generalized beliefs concerning the source of the strain, the specifics of the strain, and the kind of action that should be taken (and can be taken) to ameliorate the strain. If political officials or the political system are believed to be ineffective in solving the problems, then it may be decided to somehow modify the behavior of those officials or the operation of that system, or it may be decided to act relatively independently of the officials or the system. We have seen that part of the generalized belief of the Conporns was that the police were ineffective in implementing or unwilling to implement measures which would control pornography. Conporns also were convinced that statutes concerning pornography, given the limitations imposed by the Supreme Court, were ineffective in dealing with the control of pornography. Furthermore, Conporns believed that they had the ability and the resources to affect the officials and the system. Thus part of the generalized belief of Conporns, or at least of several Conporns, included overt considerations of their own mistrust of the effectiveness of political officials or the political system and a positive judgment concerning their own potential to act effectively. In UFD, the generalized belief contained significantly more components of trust in legal procedures—UFD members pursued a course of legal change. In ICCD, the generalized belief contained less trust of the legal system (although not an abandonment of that system) and influenced a course of action which was more constraining, more direct, more tinged with hostility, and ultimately in itself charged with being illegal.

The degree of constraint manifested by the ICCD and UFD could have been influenced by the ratio of political efficacy to political trust, but only in tandem with other elements of structural strain and generalized belief. The differences between the tactics of ICCD and UFD could have been influenced by differences in that ratio, but again only in tandem with the other differences in the value-added stages we have described.

There are also a number of organizational variables related to the kind of tactics elected by the antipornography crusades, including the impact of the reaction of the community to early crusade efforts. We shall consider those variables in the next chapter.

Chapter 9

Organizational Characteristics of the

Antipornography Crusades

In Chapter 8 we considered the individual characteristics of the participants in the antipornography crusades. We interpreted those characteristics within the broader framework of Gusfield's concept of status discontent and Smelser's value-added stages for collective behavior.

The natural histories of ICCD in Midville and UFD in Southtown revealed the fact that the crusades were carried out by ad hoc organizations, specifically assembled to deal with the perceived problem of pornography and what it represented. Furthermore, the ad hoc organizations were populated by individuals who themselves were members of other community voluntary associations, more permanent and formal in nature. UFD, for example, was started by another community organization—the Knights of Columbus.

We shall now discuss in greater detail the organizational characteristics of the antipornography crusades as such. What were the key characteristics of the organizations, and how did those characteristics interact? How did the melding of organizational characteristics influence the direction taken by the crusades, their successes, and their duration? What were the kinds and consequences of leadership styles, membership satisfactions, community reactions, and stated organizational goals? What impact did integration of the antipornography organization with other voluntary associations in the community have upon the shaping of the crusades?

To answer these questions, which have been stated as hypotheses in Chapter 1, we shall present comparative (Midville and Southtown) natural-history and questionnaire data relevant to, first, the growth, decay, and change of the antipornography organizations; second, the operation of the antipornography organizations in multiorganizational fields; and, third, the determinants of crusade strategy. Some of these organizational characteristics and operations were described as elements of structural conduciveness (Chapter 2) in the value-added process. Several other of these organizational characteristics and operations were described within the context of crusade mobilization for action (Chapter 6) in the value-added process. It is of course in the latter stage, mobilization for action, that the organizational characteristics of the social movement become most analytically salient.

Organizational Growth, Decay, and Change

The pattern of interrelationships contained within the Zald-Ash (1966) propositions which we have established as hypotheses (Chapter 1) can conveniently further be summarized under four headings, all of which are general organizational variables: exclusiveness of the membership requirements; leadership characteristics; origin of the organization; and organizational goals. We shall discuss, in turn, each of these organizational variables and the propositions it represents.

Exclusiveness of Membership Requirements

Zald and Ash (1966:330–331) distinguished between social movement organizations which are primarily *inclusive* in membership requirements and those which are *exclusive*. The inclusive organization requires of its members minimum levels of commitment and activity, a short indoctrination period or none at all, and a pledge of general support without specific duties; and it allows members the opportunity to divide their time among other organizations as they see fit. The exclusive organization, on the other hand, makes much heavier demands. It expects greater time commitment and assumes that members' participation will permeate all aspects of their lives. The exclusive organization tends to demand a lengthy indoctrination period and the members' submission to the organization's discipline. Zald and Ash suggest that some social movement organizations may have both sets of characteristics and that the cadre of leaders may be exclusive while the membership recruitment strategy is more inclusive. The leadership cadres of both the ICCD and UFD were exclusive. All the key leaders of UFD were members of the same men's religious fraternal organization. They directed the antipornography organization from its beginning to its termination, with no changes in leadership personnel. All the ICCD leaders were associated with religious or public service organizations, and replacements in that leadership cadre were made by the cadre members themselves and not by the general membership.

Considering the exclusive-inclusive characteristics on a continuum, the membership recruitment strategy of UFD was considerably more exclusive than that of ICCD. UFD implemented a more highly selective procedure both for members and for supporting voluntary associations. This procedure was marked by calculated interpersonal and interorganizational contacts rather than mass advertising; the use of formal committee structures for membership recruitment; strategies and techniques which demanded congruent representative postures from the memberships; and an expectation that individual members would pledge time for specific tasks and would maintain the integrity of the organizational boundaries. Consequently, the membership of UFD manifested greater homogeneity in age, income, and education than the ICCD membership (we shall discuss this in detail in the next section of this chapter, concerning multiorganizational fields).

We conclude that UFD was more exclusive in orientation than ICCD. The Zald-Ash propositions which establish exclusiveness as an independent variable yield, therefore, a set of hypotheses. Compared with ICCD, Uprising for Decency, since it was more exclusive in orientation, would: show greater stability of organizational goals; be less susceptible to pressures for organizational maintenance; have fewer incidences of coalitions or mergers; have schisms; have a leadership which focused on mobilizing the membership for tasks; have a longer life span.

During its period of operation UFD pursued the single, unchanging goal of influencing the passing of stricter state antipornography statutes. Once that goal was accomplished, there was no longer any pressure for organizational maintenance, and the group disbanded. ICCD, on the other hand, had been maintained formally for five years before the crusade and is still operating, thus indicating successful pressures for organizational maintenance. There appeared to be considerable goal transformation within ICCD—attempts to "clean up" newsracks, to modify television programing, to regulate local carnivals, to lower the community V.D. rate, to increase night illumination of the streets, to restrict the business operations of the Midwestern Bookstore. Though these activities, described in the natural histories, may be consistent with the overall ICCD goal of maintaining decency in the community, the degree of transformation by diversity was far greater than that of UFD.

A merger, according to Zald and Ash (1966:335–336), takes place when movement organizations combine to the point of loss of previous organizational identity. A coalition results when movement organizations pool results and coordinate plans, while keeping distinct organizational entities. UFD did not engage in either a merger or a coalition with any other movement organizations. ICCD did not effect a merger, but it did enter into a coalition with a nationally established movement organization, Citizens for Decent Literature (CDL). ICCD formally affiliated with CDL and invited visits from CDL leaders, and Midville Conporns were in contact with that organization for strategic advice concerning antipornography activities and for legal advice concerning the Midwestern Bookstore lawsuit.

We have no information which would indicate schisms among the ICCD membership. However, as noted in Chapters 2 and 6, the UFD leadership was questioned by delegates of six participating voluntary associations. Representatives of four of the associations withdrew affiliation because they perceived the antipornography strategy (the rally) to be too flamboyant. Representatives of the remaining two associations challenged the antipornography strategy and argued for more direct and dramatic forms of protest (rather than the orderly procedures toward legislative change advocated by the leadership). Subsequently, the latter two challenging voluntary associations resigned from UFD, with the intention (never realized) of launching their own more direct crusade against pornography.

The leadership style of UFD was more oriented toward mobilizing the membership for specific tasks than that of ICCD. Mr. King steadfastly and determinedly kept the Southtown Conporns focused upon the single goal of legislative change. That change was to be encouraged by petitions supporting antipornography bills currently under consideration by the state legislature. UFD was structured to facilitate that task, and each voluntary association or individual participant was expected to contribute toward the accumulation of petition signatures, primarily by working to guarantee a large attendance at the decency rally. The UFD leadership cadre was divided into specific task-oriented committees, each of which was to accomplish some specific aspect of preparation for the rally and was to recruit assistants from among the pool of Conporns. The key leader, Mr. King, carefully protected the boundaries of UFD, refusing to let it become part of any other decency crusade either in or beyond the community. The leadership style of ICCD, on the other hand, tended to be more articulating. That is, the leadership cadre was less concerned with maintaining the organizational boundaries and, as pointed out above, was willing to affiliate with other decency crusades and social movement organizations. Mrs. Roberts encouraged a diversity of membership goals and was less concerned with the assignment and coordination of specific membership tasks.

The remaining hypothesis drawn from the propositions concerning exclusiveness, unlike those discussed thus far, does not seem to be supported. The more exclusive UFD did *not* have a longer life span than ICCD. In fact, the life span differences were dramatic: five months for UFD as opposed to ICCD's eight years and continuing. At first glance, the reason for the failure to support this hypothesis seems to be an inconsistency in the Zald-Ash propositional scheme. If a social movement organization tends to be insulated by exclusive membership requirements, states one of the propositions we have already discussed, it is less susceptible to pressures for organizational maintenance (or general goal transformation) (Zald and Ash 1966:332). Consequently, it would seem to follow that the exclusive movement organization would be less susceptible to perpetuation—that is, it would have a *shorter* life span. But the Zald-Ash proposition we now discuss seems to state precisely the opposite: "Inclusive organizations are likely to fade away faster than exclusive organizations; the latter are more likely to take on new goals" (Zald and Ash 1966:334). We conclude, however, that this apparent difference can be accounted for by the operation of significant intervening variables, alluded to by Zald and Ash themselves, which interact with exclusiveness and life span.

The degree to which the social movement organization employs purposive as opposed to solidary incentives to obtain compliance from members is one such intervening variable. Purposive incentives are those which center around value fulfillment; solidary incentives center around prestige, respect, or friendship. It can reasonably be assumed that those organizations emphasizing purposive incentives will be less prone to pressures for organizational maintenance, since the goals based upon such incentives will have greater potential for tangible and terminating attainment. Those organizations emphasizing solidary incentives will be more prone to self-perpetuation, since member rewards are not necessarily based upon the conclusive attainment of specific organizational goals. The discussion of the characteristics of UFD thus far suggests that, compared with ICCD, it emphasized purposive incentives. This observation was supported by interview data: 44 percent of the Midville Conporns reported that they had joined ICCD at the urging of friends who already were members; only 25 percent of the Southtown Conporns gave that reason for joining UFD. As one of the parts of a compound proposition, Zald and Ash posit that those social movement organizations which employ solidary incentives are less likely to vanish than those which employ purposive incentives. The ICCD and UFD cases seem to support that statement. More importantly, the ICCD and UFD results suggest that the *degree* of organizational preference for solidary or purposive incentives can interact with (and perhaps overshadow) exclusiveness in determining the life span of a social movement organization.

Differences in the orientation and power of the key leaders of ICCD and UFD also complicated the relation between exclusiveness and life span. Mr. King sweepingly determined the characteristics of UFD, including its exclusive orientation, its dependence upon purposive incentives, *and* its termination upon the accomplishment of its specific goal. Mrs. Roberts manifested a style more generative of an inclusive orientation, solidary incentives, and the perpetuation of ICCD, with the mercurial goal of community decency. Thus leadership style, as we shall discuss further, can significantly restructure the relationships among organizational variables and outcome. Propositional statements notwithstanding, leaders can influence exclusive organizations to be short-lived.

Leadership Characteristics

Zald and Ash observed that leadership characteristics are more crucial to the development and style of a social movement organization than of other complex organizations. More specifically, they argued, "Because the situation of the movement organization is unstable, because the organization has few material incentives under its control, and because of the non-routinized nature of its tasks, the success or failure of the movement organization can be highly dependent on the quality and commitment of the leadership cadre and the tactics they use" (1966:338; see also Blumer 1951). In our opinion, almost all of the Zald-Ash propositions depend for validity and continuity upon holding

constant the intervening variable of leadership style. This is particularly true if the social movements are small rather than large and in early
rather than late phases of development. In UFD the perspective and
style of Mr. King significantly influenced the exclusiveness of the
organization, its goal specificity and task orientation, its short duration, its utilization of purposive incentives, avoidance of coalitions
or mergers, and its legally oriented strategies and tactics. In ICCD,
the perspective and style of Mrs. Roberts significantly influenced the
relative inclusiveness of the organization, its goal diffuseness and
articulating orientation, its long duration, its utilization of solidary
incentives, its entrance into coalitions, and its strategy and tactics of
direct action.

Two discrete leadership variables are included among the Zald-Ash
propositions we are considering: task-oriented versus articulating
leadership style and routinization of charisma. We have already discussed the hypothesized relation between leadership styles and organizational exclusiveness.

Neither Mrs. Roberts of ICCD nor Mr. King of UFD was replaced
during our period of observation. Both leaders seemed to manifest
considerable charisma, as demonstrated by their ability to recruit the
affiliation of like-minded individuals and like-oriented voluntary associations. The charisma manifested by Mrs. Roberts, however, was
relatively more emotional, more overtly religious, and noticeably more
dramatic. Mr. King tended more toward a hybrid variety of charisma,
perhaps typical in modern organizational forms, which has been called
bureaucharisma (Zurcher 1967:416). That leadership attribute is an ad-
mixture of enthusiastic and contagious commitment and a knowledge
of, experience with, and practical ability in the use of organizing and
organizational techniques. Consequently, we suggest that although
the charismatic leadership of ICCD and UFD leaders did not appear
to routinize, the greater bureaucharisma of Mr. King created a functional difference between the two organizations—a difference paralleling varying degrees of routinization of charisma. Thus, two hypotheses can be derived from the proposition. Since it manifested a
relatively greater degree of bureaucharisma, UFD would: manifest
conservative tendencies in the dominant organizational core; experience the emergence of radical splinter groups.

The leadership cadre of UFD, from its onset and throughout its
life span, insisted upon the well-ordered and cautious pursuit of legislative change. The leaders wanted at all costs to avoid being labeled

as extremists. All the organizational and leadership characteristics discussed thus far testify to that conservative orientation. On the other hand, the leadership cadre of ICCD was more free-wheeling in its style. The relative lack of caution of ICCD leaders is perhaps best indicated by the fact that they encouraged and participated in tactics which invited a million-dollar lawsuit.

In our discussion of schisms, we mentioned that four voluntary associations, disapproving of the orientation of the leadership, withdrew from UFD. After their resignation, representatives of the two groups who felt that the orientation was too conservative met in order to organize direct action (picketing) against the Southtown "skin flicks." Though their plans were not implemented and their actions cannot be considered the formulation of operating radical splinter groups, we were not aware of even this degree of splintering in ICCD.

Supporting the Zald-Ash proposition, we conclude that in the anti-pornography organizations the routinization of charisma (or the presence of bureaucharisma, a functional counterpart) was associated with conservative tendencies in the dominant organizational core and with the emergence of potentially radical splinter groups.

Origin of the Organization

According to the Zald-Ash propositions, those movement organizations which have been created by other organizations tend to disband following goal achievement. UFD was created by a men's religious fraternal organization. ICCD was founded by twelve persons, all of whom were active members of community organizations or agencies but who acted as individual citizens in forming ICCD. The propositions suggest the hypothesis that UFD, originated by another organization, would be likely to terminate following success. This hypothesis was supported. We have already reported that UFD was dissolved as soon as the antipornography statutes were passed. ICCD, on the other hand, continues to exist.

The question of success or goal achievement is linked conceptually and operationally both to the specificity of the goals and to the member-incentive structure. The more goal-specific and purposive movement organization, such as UFD, essentially has a tangible success target—either the antipornography statutes would be passed or they would not. The goal-diffuse and solidaristic movement organization, such as ICCD, has broad and somewhat unreachable success criteria.

When is a community sufficiently decent? When are the solidaristic needs of the participants satisfied?

It seems reasonable to assume that, when a parent organization deliberately establishes and directs a movement organization, it does so with a task in mind. The movement organization from the onset is goal-specific and purposive. Thus the created movement organization should have greater potential for success (and failure), since its performance criteria are more clearly delineated.

As a corollary to this proposition, Zald and Ash suggested that a movement organization will be more likely to establish new goals if it has its own member-recruiting and fund-raising support base. ICCD, incorporated and not dependent upon a parent organization, had its own card-carrying members and fairly well developed fund-raising system. ICCD was able to raise money for guest speakers, pamphlets, seminars, newspaper advertisements, and so on. UFD, without its own member base and dependent upon the parent organization, was able to accumulate, by voluntary contributions, only enough money to rent an auditorium for the rally and to print and distribute posters and flyers announcing the rally.

Organizational Goals

Two of the Zald-Ash propositions distinguish between movement-organization goals which are aimed at changing individuals and those which are aimed at changing society. Those organizations which are oriented more toward people-changing goals are postulated to be less susceptible to pressures for organizational maintenance, more stable in organizational goals, and longer in duration.

Zald and Ash (1966:331) stated that those movement organizations with religious affiliations tended to have people-changing goals. Many of the ICCD and UFD leaders and participants were affiliated with or were representatives of church-related groups. Thirty-two percent of the community voluntary associations affiliated with ICCD were church-related. Fewer (24 percent) of the UFD affiliates were church-related. ICCD seemed to have been more oriented toward changing people than UFD. ICCD leaders sponsored a number of lectures, seminars, and mailings intended to educate people about the dangers of pornography and other threats to decency. They utilized the mass media and public meetings primarily to apprise fellow citizens of the existence of pornography in the area, to recruit them for membership, and, it seems, to make believers of them. ICCD's strategy of direct action against the Midwestern Bookstore focused on the individual owners and employees of the store. UFD utilized public meetings and to some extent the mass media, but primarily to gather petitions signed by voting adults in support of antipornography legislation. Its strategy of influencing legislative change was intended more to change society (or at least the community) than to change the behavior of any specific individuals.

From these propositions three hypotheses can be drawn. Since it manifested a greater orientation toward people-changing goals, ICCD, compared with UFD, would: be less susceptible to pressures for organizational maintenance; have more stability of organizational goals; be longer in duration.

Only one of the three hypotheses was supported. ICCD was relatively longer in duration. However, ICCD did *not* manifest less pressure for organizational maintenance or more stability of organizational goals. We suggest that these hypotheses were not supported because of the significant operation of other variables, namely, leadership orientation, goal specificity, and incentive structure. The ICCD pursuit of people-changing goals can be seen to be linked with leader-encouraged goal diffuseness and solidary incentives. The opinions, attitudes, and behavior of nonmembers were to be changed to become more like those which were shared and mutually rewarded by the members—that is, more decent. But decency, as we have discussed above, is a diffuse goal capable of many and transforming subgoals. The movement organization which attempts to convince people to be more decent almost guarantees itself a continuing crusade, self-maintenance, and a myriad of tasks.

In another proposition, Zald and Ash postulated that those movement organizations which have specific goals are likely to cease operations following goal achievement. That proposition, we conclude, has already been supported by the interpretation of findings pertinent to the other propositions.

Discussion

The Zald-Ash propositions which we have considered have been generally supported by data from the natural histories and questionnaires. Exclusiveness of membership requirements was associated with resistance to pressures for organizational maintenance, stability of organizational goals, schisms, task-oriented leadership style, and an avoidance of coalitions and mergers. The routinization of charisma (or the functionally equivalent bureaucharisma) was associated with conservative tendencies in the dominant organizational core and the emergence of radical splinter groups. The antipornography organization created by another organization ceased operation following goal achievement. The antipornography organization utilizing solidary membership incentives and having diffuse and people-changing goals had a relatively long life span. The propositions stating that exclusiveness would be associated with a relatively long life span and that people-changing goals would be associated with less pressure for organizational maintenance and more stability of goals were not supported. That lack of support, however, can be explained by the overriding operation of other variables, especially leadership orientation, goal specificity, and incentive structure.

In the conclusion of their own paper, Zald and Ash stated: "Our focus has been on organizational change, and we have examined the sequence from the environment and sentiment base to goals and structure rather than from goals *to* structure. But, the organizational leadership's commitment to a set of goals may also influence the structure" (1966:340). Our discussion of the antipornography-organization data tended to support that speculation even more than it did the propositions as such. Throughout our analysis we have indicated what we feel to have been the crucial impact of leadership style (particularly the degree of task orientation), of organizational goals (particularly the degree of specificity), and of membership incentives (particularly the degree of purposiveness) upon virtually all of the organizational characteristics described in the propositions. We conclude that in the small or emerging social movement organization, the variables of leadership orientation, goal specificity, and incentive structure are significant and perhaps overriding independent variables, accounting for much of the variance in other organizational characteristics. In the national and more firmly established social movement organizations which Zald and Ash considered in their propositions, those three factors may be relatively less salient as antecedent variables.

In summary, we have demonstrated that ICCD in Midville, with the leadership of Mrs. Roberts oriented toward goal diffuseness and solidary incentives, manifested the following characteristics: expressive orientation; charisma; radicalism in strategies and tactics; inclusiveness in membership recruitment; heterogeneity of membership characteristics; mergers or coalitions with other social movement organizations; fewer schisms; a long duration; susceptibility to pressures for organizational maintenance; goal transformation; person-changing goals; and absence of any parent organization.

In comparison, UFD in Southtown, with the leadership of Mr. King oriented toward goal specificity and purposive incentives, manifested the following characteristics: task orientation; bureaucharisma; conservativeness in strategy and tactics; exclusiveness in membership recruitment; homogeneity of membership characteristics; failure to form mergers or coalitions with other social movement organizations; schisms; a short duration, terminated upon goal attainment; resistance to pressures for organizational maintenance; lack of goal transformation; society-or-community-changing goals; and existence of a parent organization.

The difference between ICCD and UFD can be articulated with the Smelser value-added stages. Some of the organizational characteristics (e.g., existence of a parent organization, potential leaders, potential antipornography organization), can be seen from the natural histories to have been operating as structural conduciveness to the emergence of the antipornography crusade. The organizational roles of Mrs. Roberts and Mr. King were also seen, at least in part, to contribute to structural strain—the obligation to do something in order to live up to role expectations. The conviction that the way to deal with the problem of pornography was to create an antipornography organization, the understanding of what shape that organization was to take, and the anticipation of the tactics the organization was to use were part of the generalized belief. Turner observed that the rumor process, which is one of the key generating processes for generalized belief, "itself creates an organization, with at least the beginnings of differentiation into roles" (1964:403). The leaders of the antipornography organizations, operating according to the generalized belief, created in part significant precipitating factors, which served to reinforce organizational goals and intended tactics. The recruitment styles, the kinds of membership rewards, the tendency toward schism/merger/coalition, and the organizational duration all were elements of mobilization for action. Those elements were significantly influenced by the other organizational elements manifested in the earlier value-added stages, especially leadership style. As has been mentioned, Zald and Ash and Smelser noted the impact that leadership can have upon the emergent social movement.[1] As we have seen, leadership style also serves as an element of social control, restricting or expanding movement strategies and tactics.

We have noted in the natural histories that ICCD had a more hostile and direct form of mobilization for action than UFD. The Midville Conporns' generalized belief had evolved over time to include a greater content of hostility, though that crusade was still norm-oriented. The dramatic nature of the value-added stages in Midville, the greater intensity of the events within those stages, and consequently the greater perceived threat to life style yielded the more severe crusade. The organizational style of the ICCD can be taken to have served the more volatile generalized belief of the Midville Conporns and to reflect the greater intensity of premobilization events in Midville.

What organizational form will emerge to serve the needs of status discontents? The pattern reflected by ICCD? The pattern reflected by UFD? Both crusades were the actions of status discontents, individuals attempting to reaffirm the prestige and power of their life style. UFD's more purposive and goal-specific norm orientation and organizational structure was successful in that the goal of revised antipornography statutes was attained. ICCD's solidary, goal-diffuse, and more hostile orientation and organizational structure was successful in allowing participants affectively and expressively to engage in direct action (after other less hostile remedies had failed). Both the ICCD and UFD organizational forms allowed status discontents to express at least symbolically the viability and virility of their life style. The type of organization that will emerge to meet the needs of status discontents will be the type which best reflects the processes of the value-added stages.

Though the influence of leadership and premobilization goals cuts across the value-added stages leading to the emergence of a social movement, those elements are *among* other elements in the stages which shape the form and the processes of the movement organization.

Nelson (1974), analyzing premovement factors in the Southern civil rights movement, argued for the importance of the relation between the "clients" of the movement-to-be and the external environment preceding the emergence of that movement. Dickson (1968) observed the impact of organization response to environmental pressure in a norm-oriented movement concerning marijuana laws. We have noted in the natural histories the effect of community reaction upon the evolution of the antipornography crusade. In the next two sections of this chapter we shall address some of those environmental elements as they impinged upon and influenced the antipornography crusades in Midville and Southtown.

The Multiorganizational Field

Both antipornography organizations were enmeshed in multiorganizational fields, as hypothesized in Chapter 1. ICCD in Midville had ties with thirty-one other community voluntary associations; UFD in Southtown with twenty-nine. Table 10 shows the types of organizations with which ICCD and UFD were linked—mostly youth-serving, church-related, or fraternal-service organizations. The pattern of alignment manifested the interests, goals, and audiences shared by ICCD and UFD and the components of their multiorganizational fields. Both ICCD and UFD openly declared their intention to protect youth from the influences of pornography, to defend decency and faith against pornography, and, by crusading against "smut," to serve the community and its citizens. Those declarations and the ideologies and strategies they represented appealed to the interests of youth-serving, church-related, and fraternal-service organizations. The data in Table 10 show the network of the multiorganizational field on the *organizational level*, by presenting the alignment patterns of the components.

Table 11 presents the network of the multiorganizational field on the *individual level*, by presenting affiliation patterns of Conporns. Ninety-four percent of the Southtown and 89 percent of the Midville Conporns were affiliated with one or more community organizations. The multiple affiliations of Conporns were concentrated primarily among fraternal-service, civic-political, and youth-serving organizations. The orientations of these organizational types again were compatible with crusade orientations, this time on the individual level. Table 11 also shows that, compared with the Babchuk and Booth (1969) Nebraska random sample, Conporns were over-represented in affiliations with fraternal-service, civil-political, and youth-serving organizations, about equally represented in church- and job-related organizations, and under-represented in recreational organizations— perhaps not an atypical pattern for the potential or actual Conporn.

The differences between the organizational and individual patterns within the ICCD and UFD multiorganizational fields invite interpreta-

TABLE 10. *Classification of Other Community Organizations Aligned with the Antipornography Organizations*

	Categories of Organizations[a]							
	Job-Related	Church-Related	Recreational	Fraternal-Service	Civic-Political	Youth-Serving	Other	Total
ICCD in Midville	3.2% (1)	32.3% (10)	0.0% (0)	19.4% (6)	3.2% (1)	41.9% (13)	0.0% (0)	100.0% (31)
UFD in Southtown	3.4% (1)	24.1% (7)	0.0% (0)	20.7% (6)	10.3% (3)	34.5% (10)	6.9% (2)	100.0% (29)
ICCD and UFD	3.3% (2)	28.3% (17)	0.0% (0)	20.0% (12)	6.6% (4)	38.3% (23)	3.3% (2)	100.0% (60)

[a]Adapted from Babchuk and Booth (1969).

tion. Fraternal-civic and youth-serving organizations tended to operate both on the organizational level (they were aligned with ICCD and UFD) and on the individual level (ICCD and UFD members were affiliated with them). Church-related organizations tended to operate primarily on the organizational level and civic-political organizations on the individual level. The goals and strategies of ICCD and UFD apparently so appealed to some fraternal-service and youth-serving organizations that they became both alignment and recruitment sources. Church-related organizations were willing to align with ICCD and UFD as entities but were less a source of active members (although they were a source of leadership). Civic-political organizations were less willing (perhaps to protect a tax-exempt status) to align as entities but were good sources for recruitment. The data in Table 11 are at best suggestive, and differences might be completely accounted for by some artifact of multiple membership. But the problem is interesting enough to encourage future research which might draw on the distinction between individual and organizational levels in analyses of multiorganizational fields and their implications, especially as to motivations for and functions of alignment or affiliation.

Though both ICCD and UFD were enmeshed in multiorganizational fields, UFD was the more closely integrated with its field. The list of thirty-one organizations reported to be aligned with the ICCD shortly after it incorporated was almost entirely different from the list of petition and resolution presenters during the crusade against the Midwestern Bookstore.[2] Many of the original ICCD alignees (upon whom we base our organizational analyses) were inclined to take a "low profile" concerning the crusade after the retaliatory bookstore lawsuit. But even before the lawsuit, those alignees tended only to lend their organizations' names to ICCD as a token of support, and rarely did they send formal delegates to crusade meetings. Of those alignees who took direct action against the Midwestern Bookstore, most seemed to do so relatively independently of direct or coordinated mandates by ICCD leaders. For example, as noted in Chapter 6, one of the anti-bookstore petition leaders commented that she was not representing ICCD but was just one of a "bunch of citizens" acting.

UFD carefully developed alignment with its multiorganizational field, evolving from eleven alignees at its first public meeting to twenty-nine at the decency rally. All the aligned organizations sent formal delegates to UFD meetings, and these delegates and the organizations they represented acted in concert under the direction of UFD leaders.

TABLE 11. *Classification of Other Community Organizations with Which Conporns Were Affiliated*

	Percentage of Individuals Belonging to One or More Organizations in Each Category							Average Percentage per Category[a]
	Job-Related	Church-Related	Recrea-tional	Fraternal-Service-	Civic-Political	Youth-Serving	Other	
All Conporns (N=85)	21% (18)	24% (20)	15% (13)	54% (46)	47% (40)	42% (36)	7% (6)	30.1% (179/595)
Midville Conporns (N=36)	28% (10)	22% (8)	22% (8)	58% (21)	47% (17)	44% (16)	8% (3)	32.9% (83/252)
Southtown Conporns (N=49)	16% (8)	24% (12)	10% (5)	51% (25)	47% (23)	41% (20)	6% (3)	28.0% (96/343)
Nebraska study (Babchuk and Booth) (N=402)	25% (102)	26% (105)	29% (116)	18% (72)	13% (52)	2% (9)	24% (95)	19.6% (551/2814)

	Percentage of Affiliations in Each Category							Average Number of Affiliations
	Job-Related	Church-Related	Recreational	Fraternal-Service	Civic-Political	Youth-Serving	Other	
All Conporns (N=271)	10% (28)	10% (26)	7% (18)	25% (69)	23% (61)	23% (61)	3% (8)	38.7 (271/7)
Midville Conporns (N=130)	10% (13)	8% (10)	9% (12)	27% (35)	22% (29)	22% (28)	2% (3)	18.6 (130/7)
Southtown Conporns (N=141)	11% (15)	11% (16)	4% (6)	24% (34)	23% (32)	23% (33)	4% (5)	20.1 (141/7)

Note: In order to obtain comparability with the Babchuk and Booth (1969) data for a Nebraska statewide sample of stable (four-year-period) affiliates, the figures in the top part of the table indicate whether an individual belonged to a given type of organization. A single or multiple affiliation within a category would count as 1. In the second half of the table, the units are individual affiliations, and the percentages represent proportions of total affiliations within given types of organizations. All figures are rounded.

ªThe average percentage of individuals per category is determined by dividing the total number of representations by the product of the number of respondents (N) and the number of categories (7).

The greater organizational integrity of UFD and the tighter quality of its relations with the multiorganizational field were evident during the recruiting process. UFD tended to gain members through contact with potentially aligned organizations (who subsequently would send representatives). ICCD followed that pattern too but more than UFD tended to approach individuals directly, rather than organizations or their formal representatives. Whereas UFD tended to recruit on the organizational level of the multiorganizational field, ICCD tended to recruit on the individual level. Seventy-five percent of the Southtown Conporns indicated that direct and official contact from UFD leaders had been responsible for their affiliation; 25 percent indicated contact from "friends." In contrast, 56 percent of the Midville Conporns indicated that direct and official contact from ICCD leaders had been responsible for their affiliation; 44 percent indicated contact from "friends."

The quantity and quality of active member participation in other organizations indicated the greater integration of UFD with its multiorganizational field. As noted above, 94 percent of the Southtown Conporns, as compared with 89 percent of the Midville Conporns, were affiliated with one or more community organizations. Furthermore, 62 percent of the Southtown as compared with 52 percent of the Midville Conporns indicated that they were officers in other community organizations. Twenty-six percent of the Southtown Conporns, as compared with 15 percent of the Midville Conporns, reported that they had belonged to similar ad hoc protest organizations in the past (e.g., antipornography, anti–sex-education, antifluoridation, antialcohol). This finding does not support the common assumption that members of one crusade tend to have been members of many but does indicate another bit of evidence concerning the tighter affiliation network of the Southtown Conporns—more of them had prior experience in ad hoc crusade organizations.

The degree of integration of the antipornography organization with its multiorganizational field should be associated with the degree of goal clarity and specificity. Aligned organizations had to decide to align and thus needed to know the risks and benefits of alignment. UFD was more integrated with its field; and, as the natural-history data indicate (and as discussed in the section on growth, decay, and change in this chapter), it single-mindedly pursued the goal of "tougher" antipornography laws throughout its organizational life span.

ICCD was less integrated with its field, and its goal continued through-out to be a vague and yet perpetual maintenance of community decency.

The closer integration of UFD with its multiorganizational field and its more focused recruitment procedure were reflected in the greater homogeneity of that organization's membership. The average age of Southtown Conporns was forty-one years, with a standard deviation of 9.85 years. The average age of Midville Conporns was forty-eight years, with a standard deviation of 16.02 years. The marked difference in standard deviations shows the greater homogeneity of age among Southtown members. There was similarly greater UFD homogeneity in levels of education and monthly family income. The UFD median categories for both education and income contained larger percentages (41 percent, 77 percent) than the ICCD median categories for educa-tion and income (22 percent, 40 percent). ICCD's greater heterogeneity was not a matter of skewness but the result of more cases at *both* *extremes* of the two distributions. Since levels of education and monthly family income were obtained for range options, standard deviations were not computed.

Previous studies have indicated that membership in complex organ-izations tends to be firmer and more integrated for those who have orderly and successful occupational careers,[3] who have an active in-terest in political activities,[4] and who have such personal attributes as high self-esteem and feelings of fate control.[5] The Southtown Con-porns had been recruited in a more orderly and systematic fashion than the Midville Conporns. They were more completely integrated into UFD, which itself was more closely associated with other com-munity organizations. Consequently, Southtown Conporns should have reflected to a greater degree than Midville Conporns some of the work, political, and personal characteristics cited above. Ninety per-cent of the Southtown Conporns in contrast to 55 percent of Midville Conporns liked their work. Fifty-nine percent of Southtown Conporns in contrast to 44 percent of Midville Conporns were "very interested" in politics. Eighty-one percent of Southtown Conporns felt that elec-tion of a specific person to political office can influence daily life (a rough measure of political trust), in contrast to 69 percent of Midville Conporns.

Thus, the closer integration of UFD with its multiorganizational field paralleled its greater membership homogeneity in age, education, and income, its higher indices of members' integration and satisfaction with work, and its greater degree of member political interest and sense of political trust.

Consistent with the more ordered approach of its recruitment process, the organizational boundary of UFD was less diffuse than that of ICCD. Thirty-one percent of the Midville Conporns indicated that they were not *official* members of the antipornography organization; only 6 percent of the Southtown Conporns so indicated. Similarly, 42 percent of ICCD members could not accurately name their crusade; 20 percent of UFD members could not accurately name theirs. In part, these differences could have been influenced by the hesitancy of Midville Conporns to identify themselves publicly with an organization that was under civil suit. There was also a difference in the degree of complexity of the two names—Midville's InterDenominational Citizen's Council for Decency, Incorporated, undoubtedly was more difficult to remember than Southtown's Uprising for Decency.

Southtown more than Midville Conporns also revealed their greater sense of identification with their antipornography organization by the level of their outreach activities. Ninety-one percent of the Southtown Conporns, as contrasted with 79 percent of the Midville Conporns, talked about crusade activities with nonmembers outside of meetings and other scheduled events. Ninety-four percent of Southtown Conporns, as contrasted with 61 percent of Midville Conporns, were trying to recruit additional crusade members.

More Southtown Conporns (96 percent) could articulate at least one specific crusade goal than Midville Conporns (78 percent), and the judgments of Southtown Conporns were more accurate, given the actual operations of the crusades. Similarly, more Southtown (96 percent) than Midville (81 percent) Conporns could identify a crusade strategy, Southtown Conporns again more accurately identifying the actual strategy of the crusade. Ninety-five percent of Southtown Conporns were optimistic about the potential of the crusade to accomplish its goal; 83 percent of Midville Conporns were optimistic. The same pattern appears in optimism about the degree to which the community supported the crusade (79 percent of the Southtown Conporns perceived support for UFD; 69 percent of the Midville Conporns perceived support for ICCD) and about the future of pornography in the United States (64 percent of the Midville Conporns thought it would increase; 31 percent of the Southtown Conporns so thought). Those perceptions and orientations indicated the greater organizational integrity of UFD and reflect its higher degree of integration with its multiorganizational field.

The differential linkages of ICCD and UFD with their multiorganizational fields and the associated variations in membership and organization characteristics were also associated with both the goal accomplishment and the persistence of the crusade. UFD accomplished its specific goal of legislative change and upon doing so summarily disbanded. The closer association of UFD with the multiorganizational field dramatized its temporariness—basically an organization of organizations, the crusade was only a temporary part of the agenda of other community voluntary associations and organizations. ICCD has yet to accomplish its rather sweeping goal of maintaining decency and continues to operate, though at least temporarily with less vigor. It is less an organization of organizations and has become over time an organizational entity on its own—duly incorporated.

Discussion

As hypothesized in Chapter 1, both ICCD and UFD depended on the recruited support of members and representatives from other like-minded community organizations and were involved to a greater or lesser extent in a multiorganizational field. Compared with ICCD, UFD had closer and more ordered interaction and integration with its multiorganizational fields. Consequently, as hypothesized, it had *greater* recruitment focus, use of organizational rather than extra-organizational contacts, and stability of aligned organizations. UFD was the more homogeneous (in age, education, and income). Its members were more committed to and satisfied with their work. They had a greater interest in politics and a greater sense of political trust. Southtown Conporns were more closely identified with UFD, and they knew more about it—its name, its goals, and its strategies. With this sense of identity went more sharply defined boundaries. Southtown Conporns talked more with outsiders (outreach) and were more optimistic about achieving their goals, gaining community support, and reducing the distribution of pornography. Their aims were more specific, and they were prompter to disband once the goals had been attained.

The findings indicate that the characteristics of the multiorganizational field and the degree to which an antipornography organization is integrated with it are variables perhaps significantly associated with structural and membership characteristics of the organization itself. The findings support the contention that few organizations, unless their purposes include isolation or freedom from exogenous influence or contamination, can operate in an interorganizational void (see McCarthy and Zald 1973). Finally, the findings disclose multiple affiliation career paths for voluntary association members.

The multiorganizational field seems to be an important element in some of the value-added stages of a social movement. The potential that a movement organization has to draw upon the resources and memberships of other community organizations contributes to structural conduciveness. The perceived and actual facility with which the movement organization becomes an organization of organizations can contribute to the spread of generalized belief concerning the proper target and course of action and can even serve as a precipitating factor for more intense mobilization. The multiorganizational field can enhance recruitment and goal attainment, enabling an ordered mobilization for action. Finally, the multiorganizational field can operate as social control, helping to influence the strategy, tactics, and duration of the crusade. We suggest that, for the small or emergent social movement organization, the leader and the specificity/diffuseness of the goals that the leader fosters do significantly influence the use of a multiorganizational field and, consequently, the impact it will have upon the crusade. The presence or absence of such a field, however, becomes a factor in some of the value-added stages.

In the first section of this chapter, we analyzed and synthesized the Zald-Ash (1966) propositions for which we had relevant data. To that synthesis we now can add the multiorganizational field. Closer integration with the multiorganizational field is associated with the other characteristics of the small or emergent movement organization whose leadership is oriented toward goal specificity and purposive incentives.

The manner in which the ICCD in Midville and UFD in Southtown drew upon like-minded individuals and organizations for affiliations and alignments (despite differences between the two antipornography organizations) demonstrates a common defense of a common life style. Status discontents generally tended to call upon other status discontents for help.

The Determinants of Crusade Strategy

As we noted in Chapter 1, Turner (1970) suggested that a social movement organization is influenced toward a persuasive, bargaining, or coercive strategy by the movement's orientation along a strategic-expressive dimension, the values perceived to be held by the constituency, the sensitivity to or dependence upon support from external publics, and the degree of dependence upon and interpenetration with the target group.

Summarizing the Turner propositions, we find that the social movement organization which will tend to elect primarily the persuasive strategy will: be guided by strategic considerations; have a more sophisticated leadership; have more organizational discipline; perceive and espouse constituent values which favor persuasion and preclude coercion; be more dependent upon and have more interpenetration with publics external to the movement organization; be more dependent upon and have more interdependent links with the target group.

On the other hand, the social movement organization which will tend to elect primarily the coercive strategy will: be guided by expressive considerations; have a less sophisticated leadership; have less organizational discipline; use more power than is needed to attain its goal; perceive and espouse constituent values which foster coercion and preclude persuasion; be relatively less dependent upon and have relatively less interpenetration with publics external to the movement organization; be less dependent upon and have fewer interdependent links with the target group.

The natural histories of the ICCD and UFD and their organizational characteristics discussed thus far support the Turner propositions and the hypotheses we have derived from them.

UFD was guided by strategic (purposive) considerations, had a more task-oriented and pragmatic leadership than ICCD, had more organizational discipline, and exercised restraint in the use of what power it had. The leadership perceived and espoused a constituent value for orderly political process and sensitivity to the constitutional rights of pornography dealers. The organization (smaller, publicly weaker, and with less longevity than ICCD) was more deeply concerned about negative public response and was more fully enmeshed in the community multiorganizational field. Finally, the organization focused on the legislature as a target group (for change in antipornography statutes) and had several links to the legislature through the organizational leadership. The natural-history data also indicate that UFD primarily implemented a persuasive strategy (appeal to legislator values), with some secondary emphasis upon the bargaining strategy (explicit and implicit offers of vote support to legislators).

ICCD was guided by expressive (solidaristic) considerations, had a less task-oriented and pragmatic leadership, had less organizational discipline, and used unchecked what power it had. The leadership perceived and espoused a constituent value for direct action against pornography dealers, with little sensitivity for their constitutional rights. ICCD was less concerned about negative public response and was less fully enmeshed in the community multiorganizational field. Finally, ICCD focused on the Midwestern Bookstore as a target for direct action and had no links with it. The natural-history data also indicate that ICCD primarily implemented a coercive strategy (direct action against the bookstore), with some secondary employment of the bargaining strategy (explicit or implicit promise of votes, consumer support, overt praise).

Discussion

The determinants of movement strategy suggested by Turner do seem to be related to the kinds of strategy used by ICCD in Midville and UFD in Southtown. Those determinants can be seen, in the context of the natural-history data, to have been among other important elements throughout the Smelser value-added stages, which influenced the shape of the crusades. The strategic-expressive orientation and the perception of constituency values were elements of generalized belief. We have observed that the key events in the long evolution of the Midville crusade (notably, the failure of usual normative restraints) had generated a more hostile norm orientation among the Midville Conporns, which in general was more attuned to constraint as a strategy. The presence of a responsive public was an element of conduciveness. The degrees of dependence upon or interpenetration with external publics and the target were elements of mobilization for action and social control.

Turner's determinants can also be seen to parallel strategy-related factors discussed by other authors to whom we have given attention. The failing attempt at assimilative reform (Gusfield 1963), along with key precipitating factors (e.g., Raymond Gauer's speech, the newspaper exposé of the Midwestern Bookstore, and the strong community support) encouraged ICCD toward coercive reform. The higher political efficacy and lower political trust (Gamson 1968; 1969) of the Midville Conporns influenced more constraining political behavior in the Midville crusade. The Midvillians had relatively less faith in the usefulness of persuasion as a means of defending their life style.

Zald and Ash (1966) discussed the operation of differences in purposive (strategic) and solidary (expressive) goals in the growth, decay, and change of social movement organizations. We suggest, following our selective synthesis of the Zald-Ash propositions as illustrated with antipornography data, that the persuasive (with secondary bargaining) strategy will be among the characteristics of small or emerging social movement organizations whose leadership is oriented toward goal specificity and purposive incentives. The coercive (with secondary bargaining) strategy will be among the characteristics of small or emerging social movement organizations whose leadership is oriented toward goal diffuseness and solidary incentives. Again, however, the salience of these factors, as part of the value-added stages toward collective behavior, depends upon the characteristics of other elements of the stages and the interaction effects among those elements.

Chapter 10

Conclusions

Brief Summary of the Initial Hypotheses

At the beginning of this book, we hypothesized, following Gusfield (1963), that the antipornography crusades would manifest status politics, escalated to the level of symbolic crusades by the concerted activities of status discontents—individuals who perceived as threatened the prestige and attendant power of the life style to which they were committed. For the crusaders, pornography would have emerged as a summary symbol for threats to that life style. We further hypothesized that the antipornography crusades would be norm-oriented social movements and would manifest the characteristics of such movements as detailed by Smelser (1962). The crusaders would cite acceptance of, commitment to, and concern over "basic societal values" and would act to restore, protect, or create norms in the name of a generalized belief. That generalized belief would call for new laws or regulatory devices concerning pornography, which would be intended to control the "irresponsible" behavior of others who were perceived to be deviants from the established patterns of behavior and thereby were perceived to be threatening social order and basic values. Since the implementation of a norm-oriented social movement includes components of action lower on the Smelser hierarchy, the antipornography crusaders would express and attempt to resolve strains concerning the stability of traditional social institutions (family, religion, education, work, etc.); concerning the rewards they received from enacting roles in those institutions; and concerning the usefulness of their knowledges, skills, and perspectives in predicting the consequences of their own behavior and in controlling significant aspects of the social environment which impinged upon their everyday lives. Similarly, the antipornography crusades as norm-oriented movements would involve elements of hostility (eradication of someone or something responsible for evils), panic (flight from existing norms or impending normative change), and craze (plunge to establish new means). Varying strains on different components of action would yield variation in the operations of the antipornography crusades (e.g., more or less hostility, more or less panic, more or less craze). Finally, the process of short-circuiting as described by Smelser would be apparent in the operation of the crusades. That is, the Conporns, experiencing strains concerning their ability to predict and control their social environment and concerning the prestige they felt should be associated with the enactment of traditional social roles in traditional institutions, would perceive the general source of the strain to be the challenge to basic values and traditions by the enactors of alternative life styles. Pornography, and more concretely certain "adult" bookstores and theaters, would be perceived to represent the alternative life styles and changes and would be labeled dramatically and specifically as the source of evil. The generalized belief would emerge that laws pertaining to pornography, to "adult" bookstores and theaters, were inadequate. If the old laws could be strengthened or otherwise made operational, or new ones introduced, pornography, the bookstores and theaters, and the life styles or changes they represented would be punished, immobilized, damaged, or destroyed. The short-circuiting process would be completed with the belief that the normative changes would once and for all significantly remove or in some way neutralize or offset the original source of strain, the alternative life styles.

We have presented the natural histories of the Midville and Southtown crusades according to the Smelser value-added stages for a norm-oriented social movement, both for convenience of organization and to examine the conceptual and empirical usefulness of the stages. To the natural histories we added data concerning the characteristics of the individual Conporns and the characteristics of the antipornography organizations which directed the crusades.

Brief Summary of the Major Findings

Throughout the preceding chapters we have interpreted the natural-history, individual, and organizational data to support our hypotheses. The Conporns were indeed status discontents, engaged in a symbolic crusade to defend the integrity of their life style. Pornography was a summary symbol for the broader Conporn concerns centered around the impact of social change. The antipornography crusades were norm-oriented movements (and we suggest that all symbolic crusades are norm-oriented movements). Conporns were concerned with other of the components of action, specifically the stability of traditional social institutions, social roles and their attendant rewards, and control over the social environment. In fact, the starting points of Conporn distress were centered in strains concerning control and role prestige. Those concerns did short-circuit with the generalized belief that normative restrictions on pornography dealers and users would abate the broader threat to control and prestige. Both of the crusades did manifest elements of hostile outbursts, of panic, and of craze, though always subsidiary to the primary goal of normative restructure or normative implementation. The Midville crusade clearly was more hostile in nature than the Southtown crusade and manifested more elements of panic and craze, because of factors associated with greater severity and intensity of experiences throughout the value-added stages, which made normative restructuring more difficult to obtain.

The value-added stages did serve well to organize the natural-history data, though assignment of natural-history elements to specific stages was at times quite arbitrary. Several authors[1] have commented that the value-added stages may be useful for descriptively organizing natural-history data but are not very useful for predicting the emergence or development of social movements. Lewis (1972:95) further argued that, even for descriptive purposes, the stages may be best suited only for large sets of data related to an episode of collective behavior.

Conclusions concerning the lack of predictive value for the stages may be influenced by factors which have to some extent been artifacts of research design and research opportunity. Since virtually all studies of social movements have been ex post facto, the data available may not have filled the stages completely enough to have provided a predictive paradigm. Had the Smelser stages been postulated *prior* to the mobilization for action of a social movement, and enough contingencies known, if-then predictions perhaps could have been made concerning the emergence and shape of a given social movement. Also, if *prediction* is defined less in terms of certainty of one-to-one relations and more in terms of probabilities among (or between) sets of alternatives, the stages may be made to possess more predictive value (see Gergen 1973). Finally, each of the stages may need more conceptual detail, more elements, to make increased prediction possible (see Gibbs 1972).

Turner and Killian (1972:254–255) noted the strengths of what they called the "life-cycle" approach to studying social movements. The life-cycle "consists of an idealized series of stages from the origin to the success or other termination of the movement . . . a framework within which the many aspects of a movement can be seen working together —leadership, ideology, tactics, membership, etc.—rather than each being studied separately . . . it provides a framework within which the causes for success can be approached" (1972:252–253). As examples of the life-cycle scheme, Turner and Killian cite Blumer (1951), Dawson and Gettys (1948), Hopper (1950), and Jackson et al. (1960). It can be argued that Smelser (1962) also utilized the life-cycle approach, although he may not agree with that argument.

Citing Cameron (1966), Turner and Killian noted that "The experiences of different movements are much too diverse to make any typical sequence generally valid" (1972:255). They suggested that "efforts to identify and clarify more limited sequences applicable to a restricted range of situations offer greater promise of augmenting our understanding of movement processes" (1972:255).

Turner and Killian further recommended "the concentrated examination of process and contingencies in such situations as the encounter between authorities and a movement whose objectives are not sufficiently specified to permit systematic bargaining, the struggle between romantic and pragmatic adherents to a movement, the struggle for a unity and persistence in a movement when authorities implement part of but not all its goals, and many others" (1972:255).[7]

We have elected to follow the life-cycle (natural-history) scheme in this book, through the use of the Smelser value-added stages. As we have argued above, we feel that each of the stages can and should be conceptually expanded. The expansion would enhance the strength of the life-cycle approach, would provide more of the kinds of limited sequences and restricted range of situations analytically called for by Turner and Killian, and would also make possible increased predictive value of the stages.

Expansion of the Value-Added Stages

We have melded several other conceptual elements with the Smelser stages, both to help us explain the phenomena of antipornography crusades and to experiment with expanding the parameters of the stages. We have suggested that Gusfield's concept of status discontent provides a theoretically and empirically useful addition to the structural-strain stage associated with the emergence of norm-oriented movements. Status discontent conceptually represents a strain which bridges the social (structural) and psychological (perceptual) factors of strain. Furthermore, since the concept is concerned with style of life, it encompasses strain which may impinge upon all four components of action specified by Smelser: values, norms, roles and rewards, and situational facilities. The status discontent is concerned about prestige losses to his or her value system, about the efficacy of norms which implement and protect those values, about the rewards he or she gets as a result of enacting roles in keeping with the values and their protecting norms, and about the control he or she has over maintaining a status quo in which those value, norm, and role specifics continue unambiguously to function.

We have inserted into the structural-strain and generalized-belief stages the conceptual and empirical consideration of several individual characteristics of Conporns, including demographic characteristics, political characteristics, social-psychological characteristics, sex education and contact with pornography, and perceptions and definitions of pornography and assumed correlates. The assessment of those characteristics, especially in the comparisons among Conporns, Proporns, and Controls, revealed more fully the processes generating status discontent and the factors associated with structural strain and generalized belief (especially the interaction between social and psychological factors). Conversely, the placing of individual characteristics of antipornography crusaders into the strain and belief stages demonstrated the pressing fact that the individual characteristics alone did not explain the emergence of variations in the styles of the crusades.

The demographic, political, social-psychological, and perceptual characteristics can be seen to influence strain, when linked with other social factors, at all four levels of the Smelser components of action—values, norms, roles and rewards, and situational facilities. For example, the generally traditional and conservative individual characteristics of the Conporns were part of the process of strain which was manifest in their concern about: threats to their basic values by social change, and particularly by the increasing presence and prestige of alternative life-styes; the weakening of normative systems which implemented and protected those basic values; the lessening of rewards, especially prestige, associated with enacting the "right" way of living; the decreasing certainty of the veracity of their knowledge and the efficacy of their skills in controlling significant aspects of their everyday lives.

The degree or kind of status inconsistency and the ratio of political trust to political efficacy are special aspects of individual characteristics which we suggest should be included primarily within the structural-strain stage. Our findings concerning the differences in status inconsistency between Conporns and Proporns tentatively indicate that there may be patterns of consistency or inconsistency that are associated with participation in or opposition to the crusades. Though our study did not clearly identify those patterns, other studies might. Our findings did indicate, however, that status inconsistency alone is not a sufficient explanation of participation in the crusades and needs to be considered at most as a part of the value-added stages. Also our findings indicated that *perception* of status inconsistency might be more important as a variable than objective status inconsistency, and thus the concept of status inconsistency might usefully be subsumed under the broader concept of status discontent, at least for the analysis of antipornography crusades. Among the Smelser components of action, status inconsistency can conceptually be a part of strain at the level of roles and rewards.

Political efficacy and political trust, we conclude, can be usefully incorporated into the structural-strain stage, transcending into the generalized-belief stage, of the crusades. The crusaders' perceptions of the operation of normative controls within the political system and of their own potential to impose such controls if they are lacking within that system—are important among other factors of strain and belief. Both efficacy and trust are situational facilities among the components of action. They contribute to the individual's confidence in the social system in which he operates and in his own abilities to control his social environment. Thus, among the value-added stages, discrepancies between political efficacy and political trust can be interpreted as engendering structural strain at the level of situational facilities.

We have examined, in the light of data from the antipornography crusades, several propositions concerning the characteristics of social movement organizations. Some of the variables contained within the propositions, we argue, can profitably be incorporated within the Smelser stages. (In fact, perhaps the greatest lacuna in the Smelser framework is the lack of detail concerning the characteristics and the

TABLE 12. *Variables Associated with the Value-Added Stages of the Antipornography Crusades*

Value-Added Stage	Variable
	Individual Characteristics of the Crusaders

Structural conduciveness: S, T, V, W, X, Y, Z, AA, BB, CC, DD, EE, FF, GG, HH, II, JJ	A. Status discontent
	B. Demographic characteristics
	  1. Age
	  2. Religious affiliation
	  3. Religious activity
	  4. Size of place reared
	  5. Occupation
	  6. Income
	  7. Education
	  8. Marital status
	  9. How long married
	  10. Number of children
	  11. Satisfaction with marriage
	  12. Satisfaction with family life

Structural strain: A, B, C, D, G, H, K, CC, DD, EE, FF, GG	C. Political characteristics
	  1. Interest in politics
	  2. Participation in campaigns
	  3. Regularity of voting
	  4. Political party preference
	  5. Political orientation
	  6. Membership in voluntary associations
	  7. Offices in voluntary associations

Growth and spread of a generalized belief: A, B, C, D, E, F, H, I, J, L, T, X, Y, Z, AA, BB, HH	D. Social-psychological characteristics
	  1. Powerlessness
	  2. Normlessness
	  3. Alienation
	  4. Authoritarianism
	  5. Religiosity
	  6. Traditional family ideology

Precipitating factors: I, L, N, O, R, T, BB, HH	E. Sex education and contact with pornography
	  1. Sex as topic of family discussion
	  2. Discussion with children about sex
	  3. Discussion with spouse about sex
	  4. Attitude toward nudity in home
	  5. Course in sex education
	  6. Exposed to pornography as child
	  7. Own parent's reaction to own exposure to pornography
	  8. Reaction to own children's exposure to pornography

Mobilization of the participants for action: I, J, K, L, M, N, O, P, Q, R, S, T, U, V, W, BB, HH	F. Perceptions and definitions of pornography and assumed correlates
	  1. Definition of pornography
	  2. Familiarity with pornography
	  3. Judgment concerning effect of pornography
	  4. Judgment concerning connection of pornography with organized crime
	  5. Judgment concerning association of pornography with Communism
	  6. Judgment concerning the kind of people who use pornography
	  7. Judgment concerning the kind of people who produce pornography
	  8. Judgment concerning how those attracted to pornography differ from self
	  9. Judgment concerning how the community at large feels about own position on pornography

Operation of social control: I, J, K, N, O, P, Q, R, S, T, V, W, BB, HH	

7. Political intolerance
8. Dogmatism
9. Traditional attitude toward sex
10. Approval of censorship

10. Judgment concerning what groups or people in community oppose own point of view on pornography
G. Status Inconsistency
H. Political efficacy and political trust

Organizational Characteristics of the Crusades

I. Leadership style
J. Organizational goals
K. Membership incentives
L. Strategies and tactics
M. Homogeneity of membership
N. Mergers or coalitions
O. Schisms
P. Duration

Q. Pressures for organizational maintenance
R. Goal transformation
S. Existence of parent organization
T. Integration with multiorganizational field
U. Recruitment focus
V. Independence from target group
W. Dependence upon external publics

Characteristics of the Community

X. Degree of conservative orientation among the population
Y. Degree of patriotic orientation among the population
Z. Degree of religious orientation among the population
AA. Degree of community urbanization
BB. Presence of a communication network
CC. Presence of a potential for antipornography organization

DD. Presence of a potential for antipornography leaders
EE. Presence of pornography
FF. Presence of a potential crusade target
GG. Presence of alternative life styles
HH. Presence of a responsive public
II. Presence of channels for modifying norms
JJ. Presence of precrusade antipornography activity

correlates of social movement organizations.) Key variables are style of leadership, kinds of organizational goals, kinds of membership incentives, and degree of integration with the multiorganizational field. Those key variables, as we have noted, were in the case of the antipornography crusades associated with differences in strategies and tactics; membership recruitment processes; relative heterogeneity or homogeneity of membership; schism; mergers or coalitions with other organizations; duration of the crusade; goal-transformation; pressures for organizational maintenance; and the presence of a parent organization. All of those characteristics are usefully incorporated in the mobilization-for-action stage. Some, like opportunity for close integration in the multiorganizational field, the existence of a parent organization, independence from the target group, and dependence upon external publics, will also fit profitably as elements of structural conduciveness and social control. Organizational goals, leadership style, and strategies and tactics reflect the nature of generalized beliefs as a value-added stage; membership incentives reflect the nature of structural strain. Leadership style, strategies, and tactics, mergers or coalitions, schisms, goal transformation, and the degree of integration with the multiorganizational field can operate within the precipitating-factor stage. Leadership style, we have determined, in the antipornography crusades we studied, was an important factor in the value-added stages, influencing their shape and the shape of organizational characteristics generally.

Four of the theorists we have discussed referred specifically to the degree of severity of crusade or movement strategy and tactics as a dependent variable. Gusfield saw coercive reform replace the failing assimilative reform. Smelser described the increase of hostile outbursts against a target by the movement whose primary norm-oriented attempts were frustrated. Gamson reported an increase in constraint strategy as the ratio of political efficacy to political trust widened. Turner noted that coercive movement strategy was associated with more expressive orientation, less sophisticated leadership, more power required to attain goals, more constituent value for coercion, and less linkage with external publics and target groups. The perspectives of Gusfield, Gamson, and Turner can be conceptually linked with Smelser's as organizational variables in the value-added stages of mobilization for action and social control.

All the community characteristics we discussed fit empirically with the structural-conduciveness stage, setting the stage for the potential emergence of the antipornography crusade. A few of the characteristics (presence of a potential for antipornography organization; presence of a potential for antipornography leadership; presence of pornography; presence of a potential crusade target; presence of alternative life styles) also can be usefully assigned to the structural-strain stage. The degree of conservative, patriotic, and religious orientation, degree of urbanization, and presence of a responsive public and a communication network fit with the generalized-belief stage. The presence of a responsive public and a communication network also operate within the precipitating-factor, mobilization and social-control stages.

Table 12 summarizes the variables we employed and demonstrates their primary places among the various value-added stages. The measures which operationalized the variables and the variables' conceptual subcomponents have been described throughout the book.

From Table 12 and from the discussion sections in the preceding chapters, we can summarize the value-added stages and associated variables as they applied to the antipornography crusades. The summary is intended also to present the stages and variables in a predictive mode. That is, we offer our interpretations of and additions to the stages as predictive hypotheses concerning the emergence and development of antipornography crusades. The presentation of the predictive hypotheses is organized according to the order of the value-added stages. However, in the presentation we shall not always follow the order of the variables as listed in Table 12. Some of the variables are listed in more than one stage and in our judgment could be set in a hypothesis better under one stage rather than under other stages. Some of the hypotheses are quite specific; others are quite broad. The differences in explicitness are due to the varying degrees of complexity described by the hypotheses and to the fact that we were able to understand some of the crusade processes more clearly than others.

Predictive Summary of the Value-Added Stages of an Antipornography Crusade

Structural Conduciveness

The community population will contain a significant number of politically conservative individuals.

The community population will contain a significant number of patriotic individuals (in the sense of a traditional view of Americanism).

The community population will contain a significant number of religious individuals (having fundamentalistic or dogmatic religions).

The community population will modally manifest a style of life represented by values, customs, and habits which center around traditionalism and conservatism.

The community will have a relatively recent frontier history and/or a relatively recent increase in urbanization.

Potential leaders and cadre for the antipornography crusade will be present.

A potential target or targets for the crusade will be present.

A multiorganizational field upon which the crusade organization can draw for support will be present.

A communication network (interorganizational networks, the media, voluntary associations) will be present for potential use in the development of a crusade (for recruitment, for task accomplishment).

There will be an existing or potentially existing permanent or ad hoc organization which can direct the crusade.

There will be evidence of an actual or potential degree of independence of the ad hoc organization from the target group.

There will be a possibility to modify norms without modifying values.

There will be possible strategies and tactics by which to affect the normative order.

Interest articulation will be separate from interest aggregation.

There will be evidence that some avenues for normative control might be closing.

There will be evidence of alternative (nontraditional) life styles present in the community.

There will be evidence that the number of individuals electing alternative life styles in the community is becoming greater.

There will be a responsive public in the community which can react to the actions of the antipornography crusade.

Pornography will be present as a potential symbol of status discontent.

There will have been some precrusade antipornography activity in the community.

Structural Strain

The media and other communication sources (the pulpit, voluntary association programs, and newsletters) will report a growing threat to the traditional and conservative American life style, both in society and in the community, as a result of social change.

There will be a real or apparent loss of wealth, power, or prestige associated with the traditional and conservative American life style, both in society and in the community, as a result of social change.

There will be a perception that laws which protect that life style are weakening; recent legislative changes and/or the "failure" of social control agents will have supported that perception.

There will be a perception that status figures in society (the Supreme Court, political figures, theologians, educators, etc.) are according alternative life styles prestige at the expense of the traditional and conservative American life style.

There will be a perception that the number and power of individuals electing alternative life styles is dangerously increasing in the community.

There will be a perception that the balance of power between individuals electing alternative life styles and those electing traditional life styles is becoming ambiguous.

The media or other communication sources will indicate that pornography is becoming more abundant and bolder in the community, as evidenced by the operation of specific businesses making sexually explicit materials available to the public.

The group or groups of potential crusaders in the city will feel the pressure of responsibility to protect themselves, their peers, and their community against challenges to the traditional and conservative American life style.

There will be a perception that the community is one of the last bastions of true Americanism.

There will be evidence of other fears bearing on status dislocation, such as recession and ethnic conflict.

The perceptions and strains at this time in the evolution of the crusade will be ambiguous and vague.

The potential crusaders and their opponents will manifest individual characteristics which are juxtaposed with and conflict with each other (i.e., Conporns versus Proporns); the potential crusaders will possess individual characteristics which manifest the traditional and conservative American life style and are juxtaposed with and conflict with the characteristics of individuals electing alternative life styles. When compared with their opponents, the potential antipornography crusaders will be older; more often affiliated with organized religion; more religiously active; more often reared in smaller towns and communities; less often employed in professional or technical occupations; more often employed in white-collar, middle-management, and small independent business occupations; equally characterized by membership in the middle socioeconomic class; less formally educated; more often presently married; less often previously married; married longer; parents of more children; less inclined to prefer single life; less inclined to think children are a nuisance; less interested in politics; less often members of the Democratic party; more often members of the Republican party; more politically conservative; more often officers in community voluntary associations; less powerless; less normless; less alienated; more authoritarian; more inclined toward religiosity; more inclined toward traditional family ideology; less politically tolerant; more dogmatic; more inclined toward a traditional attitude toward sex; more approving of censorship; more often over-rewarded status inconsistents or low status consistents (while their opponents more often will be under-rewarded status inconsistents or high status consistents); inclined toward a higher sense of political efficacy and a lower sense of political trust.

The potential crusaders will manifest individual characteristics which by and large are similar to those of the majority of the citizens in the city, with the following notable exceptions. The potential crusaders, as compared with the majority of citizens (i.e., Conporns versus Controls), will be more religiously active; more often reared in smaller towns and communities; less often employed in professional or technical occupations; more often employed in white-collar, middle-management, and small independent business occupations; less often previously married; members of more voluntary associations; more often officers in voluntary associations; less powerless; less normless; less alienated; less politically tolerant.

The individual characteristics of the potential crusaders, their perceptions of challenges to the prestige and power of their life style, and the manner in which the individual characteristics and perceived challenges interact will generate a condition of status discontent and its attendant strains among the potential crusaders. Those strains will include concern about: prestige losses to the crusaders' value systems; the efficacy of norms which implement and protect those values; the rewards the crusaders get as a result of enacting roles in keeping with the values and the protecting norms; the control they have over maintaining a status quo in which those value, norm, and role specifics continue to function unambiguously.

Growth and Spread of a Generalized Belief

The potential antipornography crusaders will express beliefs in God; in the dangers of political liberality; in the dangers of Communism; in the dangers of permissiveness; that the United States is experiencing an erosion of basic values and a breakdown of law and order, as a result of unchecked and deleterious social change; that the United States is experiencing an erosion of the traditional and conservative life style, as a result of unchecked and deleterious social change; that the United States is at the present time paralleling the conditions which led to the fall of Greece and Rome; that human nature is essentially weak, especially in younger persons; that modernism (antitraditionalism) is basically dangerous; that they, the potential crusaders, are morally strong and consequently morally responsible; that pornography is causally related to the erosion of basic values, to the challenges to the traditional and conservative American life style, and to wide varieties of other perceived forms of social and psychological pathology; that the laws controlling pornography are ineffective but can be strengthened by statute change, better implemented by social control agents, or significantly bolstered by citizen action; that there is a conspiracy (e.g., of Communists or organized crime) supporting the availability of pornography; that, if pornography is controlled or eliminated, the threat to the traditional and conservative American life style will be mitigated; that action against pornography is necessary, possible, and realistic and that they can effectively carry out such action; that pornography is a symbol of disastrous social changes and dangerous alternative life styles in society and in the community; that concerted action against pornography in the community would be an effective step toward reestablishing or reinforcing basic values and traditional life styles; that concerted action against pornography in the community would punish, immobilize, damage, or destroy the alternative life styles symbolized by pornography; that the pendulum of opinion against pornography is swinging in the direction of the potential crusaders; that most of the people in the community are on the side of the potential crusaders; that there is no middle position on pornography; that the potential crusaders are not vigilantes but responsible citizens engaging in the democratic process and are not infringing upon the civil liberties of their targets; that there is a need to show people where they (the potential antipornography crusaders) stand on the issue and to demonstrate what the real community (or state or national) standards concerning the issue are; that the antipornography action can be taken by a collectivity of persons, or an organization, with explicit goals related to the control of pornography.

The generalized beliefs will contain beliefs that are norm oriented, hostile, hysterical, and wish-fulfilling.

The generalized beliefs will include concerns about the stability of traditional social institutions; the continuity of prestige received as a reward for enacting roles in those institutions; and the usefulness of one's knowledge, skills, and perspectives for predicting the consequences of one's own behavior and for controlling significant aspects of one's own environment.

Sources for generalized beliefs will include newspaper and magazine stories and editorials; speeches and statements by prestigious individuals; conservative political tracts; personal observations; conversations with associates; religious sermons; PTA speeches; other voluntary associations; bulletins and pamphlets from national religious and/or antipornography organizations; and leaders of the local antipornography crusade.

In the early phases of the crusade, the generalized beliefs will be more diffuse and informally communicated than in the later phases of the crusade.

The generalized beliefs will be represented in part by abstractions, which can be shaped by the interactive processes of keynoting, symbolization, and coordination.

The generalized beliefs will manifest the short-circuiting process, skipping from concern for the prestige and rewards associated with a traditional and conservative life style to concern about pornography and to the belief that normative changes attacking pornography would neutralize the life style threat.

The generalized beliefs of the potential antipornography crusaders will be manifested and influenced by the individual characteristics (demographic, political, social-psychological, and related to political efficacy, political trust, and status discontent) included in structural strain above. However, the generalized beliefs will also be influenced by the potential crusaders' experience with, perceptions and definitions of, and assumptions concerning the correlates of pornography. The potential crusaders, when compared with their opponents (i.e., Conporns versus Proporns) will: less often discuss sex in the family; less often talk with spouses about sex; be less casual about nudity among family members; less often have been exposed to pornography as children; more often have had parents who were punitive toward them concerning exposure to pornography; more often be punitive toward their own children's exposure to pornography; have more diverse and judgmental definitions of pornography; more often have never seen pornography; more often report pornography to be related causally to or associated with assorted forms of social and psychological pathology (e.g., marriage failure, juvenile delinquency, erosion of religion, violence, crime in general, rape and other sex crimes, self-abuse, divorce, illegitimacy, drug addiction, perversion, homosexuality, drunkenness, murder, and insanity); more often negatively assess the producers of pornography; more often associate organized crime with pornography; more often associate Communism with pornography; more often negatively assess the users of pornography; more often perceive differences between themselves and users of pornography; more often see community members in agreement with them and not their opponents; more often see individuals in the community opposed to them as modernists.

The potential antipornography crusaders will manifest characteristics which by and large are similar to those of the majority of citizens in the community, with the following notable exceptions. The potential crusaders, as compared to the majority of citizens (i.e., Conporns versus Controls), will: less often have been exposed to pornography as children; more often have had parents who were punitive toward them concerning exposure to pornography; more often be punitive toward their own children concerning exposure to pornography; more often have never seen pornography; more often report pornography to be associated causally or related to assorted forms of social and psychological pathology; more often assess the producers of pornography negatively; more often associate organized crime with pornography; more often associate Communism with pornography; more often negatively assess the users of pornography; more often perceive differences between themselves and users of pornography.

The generalized beliefs will be influenced by shifts in leadership style; organizational goals, strategies, and tactics; multiorganizational fields; communication networks; and the responsiveness or orientation of publics.

Precipitating Factors

Attention will be dramatically called, by a status figure, the media, an event, or some other keynoter or keynoting situation, to the blatant and/or growing presence of pornography in the community.

Attention will be dramatically called, by a status figure, the media, an event, or some other keynoter or keynoting situation, to a specific instance of the alleged relationship between pornography and various forms of social or psychological pathology.

Attention will be dramatically called, by a status figure, the media, an event, or some other keynoter or keynoting situation, to the issue of the growing presence and prestige of alternative life styles in the community.

A status figure, the media, an event, or some other keynoter or keynoting situation will dramatically summarize the problem of pornography by employing or generating highly repeatable and shocking catch words, keynotes, and phrases (e.g., "plain, flat filth").

Attention will be dramatically called, by a status figure, the media, an event, or some other keynoter or keynoting situation, to a specific target or targets in the community which represent the problem of pornography.

The potential antipornography crusaders will experience an instance or instances of change in their prestige and power vis-à-vis alternative life styles generally or the target or targets specifically (e.g., the early successes and failures of the rudimentary antipornography organizations and of individuals who subsequently would become key leaders of the crusades).

The precipitating factors will convince the potential crusaders that their generalized beliefs about pornography, alternative life styles, and social change are correct. They will perceive that they clearly have reason to fear a present threat to their traditional and conservative life style and must act in defense.

Leaders among the potential crusaders will deliberately arrange for precipitating factors which will stimulate the mobilization for action and the actual implementation of the crusade (e.g., the antipornography leaders' manipulation of the press, their staging of meetings and influencing community status figures to serve as precipitating factors).

A status figure, the media, an event, or some other keynoter or keynoting situation will demonstrate to potential crusaders that action against pornography is urgent and must be carried out *now* because delay will disastrously allow the target to gain power and prestige, perhaps irreversibly.

A status figure, the media, an event, or some other keynoter or keynoting situation will encourage the potential crusaders to believe that action against the target can be successful, particularly emphasizing the potential to "put the target in its place."

A status figure, the media, an event, or some other keynoter or keynoting situation will describe in detail a procedure for antipornography action.

Following mobilization of the movement, shifts in leadership style, strategy and tactics, organizational goals, multiorganizational fields, communication networks, the responsiveness of publics, or the emergence of schism, merger, or coalition will serve as precipitating factors which can modify the direction and shape of the movement (this is discussed more fully in the next stage, mobilization of the participants for action).

Mobilization of the Participants for Action

The mobilization for action of the antipornography crusade will be directed by an organization of some kind, either an ad hoc group or a community voluntary association which takes on the task of the crusade as part of its broader mission. The ad hoc organization can become institutionalized and take its place among the array of standing community voluntary associations.

The crusade will be labeled with an imposing title, will be legitimized with a list of status individuals associated with it, will have a rudimentary staff of individuals who run it (leaders and cadre), will utilize flamboyant and popular speakers to present its points to the public and to recruit new members, and will employ the media for its purposes wherever and whenever possible.

The activities of the crusades will include all or some of the following activities: speeches and public meetings, seminars, debates, panels, forums, television programs, radio programs, newspaper interviews, letters to the editors of newspapers and magazines, letters to politicians and to officials at all levels of government, deliberate lobbying with legislators and other politicians, personal and informal approaches to friends and other informal networks, massive phone-call campaigns to spread the word, petitions, initiatives, referenda, direct attempts to influence the target informally to change somehow, direct action against the target to harass or force such change.

The crusade will begin with slow, searching behavior and will accelerate into a period of supercharged activity.

All of the action of the antipornography crusade will be norm oriented, with a greater or lesser degree of hostility and directness determined by conditions in the earlier value-added stages (particularly the degree of success or failure concerning within-the-system attempts at normative change).

The crusade action will also manifest, to a greater or lesser degree as determined by earlier value-added stages, elements of panic and craze.

If the crusade mobilization for action is thwarted in its norm-oriented goals, and if the crusade does not as a result demobilize, it is likely (depending upon the characteristics of the earlier stages and the nature of the obstacles) to engage in action that is more hostile, more hysterical, or more wish-fulfilling in orientation.

The power of the antipornography crusade within the community (its ability to mobilize participants for action, to draw upon community resources, to touch upon the lives of other citizens in the community) will be surprising and sometimes awesome.

The antipornography crusade generally will leave behind it a normative change in the form of a new or modified statute, a new or modified social control agency or organization, or some other form of institutionalized "watchdog" organization.

There will be considerable evidence among the actions and interpretations of success (the mobilization for action of the antipornography crusade) that the symbolic accomplishments of the crusade are at least as important as the utilitarian accomplishments. That is, the demonstration and recognition of the crusaders' power to impose normative controls upon the target will be at least as important to the crusaders as the actual effectiveness of those controls in modifying the behavior of the target.

The style of leadership of the antipornography crusade will have a sweepingly significant impact upon other movement characteristics, particularly upon the characteristics of the crusade organization.

When the leadership of the antipornography crusade is oriented toward goal specificity and purposive incentives (as opposed to goal diffuseness and solidary incentives), the crusade organization will manifest the following characteristics: greater task orientation; greater bureaucharisma; greater conservativeness in strategy and tactics; more exclusiveness in membership recruitment; greater homogeneity of membership characteristics; absence of mergers or coalitions with other social movement organizations; more schisms; a shorter duration or a duration terminated upon goal attainment; greater resistance to pressures for organizational maintenance; absence of goal transformations; more society-changing or community-changing goals; the existence of a parent organization; closer integration with the multiorganizational field; greater recruitment focus; members who are more closely identified with the crusade organization; members who know more about the goals and strategies of the crusade; a crusade organization with more sharply defined boundaries; a more efficient mechanism for member outreach to other persons in the community; members who are more optimistic about gaining community support for the crusade goals, about achieving crusade goals, and about restricting the availability of pornography; a greater organizational orientation toward the use of persuasion (as opposed to coercion) as a crusade strategy; more concern about negative reactions from the community to crusade strategy and tactics; a closer interdependence between the crusade organization and the immediate focus of crusade action; a closer alignment between members' sense of political efficacy and members' sense of political trust.

When the leadership of the antipornography crusade is oriented toward goal diffuseness and solidary incentives (as opposed to goal specificity and purposive incentives), the crusade organization will manifest the following characteristics: greater expressive orientation; greater charisma; greater radicalism in strategies and tactics; more inclusiveness in membership recruitment; greater heterogeneity of membership characteristics; mergers or coalitions with other social movement organizations; fewer schisms; a longer duration; greater susceptibility to pressures for organizational maintenance; goal transformation; more person-changing goals; absence of a parent organization; a looser integration with the multiorganizational field; less recruitment focus; members who are less clearly identified with the crusade organization; members who know less about the goals and strategies of the crusade; a crusade organization with less sharply defined boundaries; a less efficient mechanism of member outreach to other persons in the community; members who are less optimistic about gaining community support for crusade goals, about achieving crusade goals, and about restricting the availability of pornography in the community; a greater organizational orientation toward the use of coercion (as opposed to persuasion); less concern about negative reaction from the community to crusade strategy and tactics; a less close interdependence between the crusade organization and the immediate focus of crusade action; a less close alignment between members' sense of political efficacy and members' sense of political trust.

The antipornography organization will tend to align for crusade purposes with church-related, fraternal-service, and youth-serving community organizations (less so with job-related, recreational, and civic-political community voluntary associations).

Though civic-political organizations will tend not to align with the antipornography crusade, they will be good sources for member recruitment.

Conporns will be over-represented (compared with other community members) in association with fraternal-service, civic-political, and youth-serving voluntary associations. They will be under-represented in job-related and recreational voluntary associations.

The mobilization for action of the antipornography crusade can have such a sweeping impact upon the community (especially if it is a small community) and can involve such a large percentage of the population of the community that the crusade leadership and organization loses control of the antipornography activities. That is, other individuals or groups of individuals may become involved in crusade activities unrelated to or uncoordinated by the crusade organization. In some cases, that phenomenon may be invited by the crusade organization, particularly if the leadership style is oriented toward goal diffuseness and solidary incentives (e.g., in Midville as compared with Southtown).

Operation of Social Control

The antipornography crusade will escalate into more intense and complex mobilization for action if the usual agents for social control are perceived to be unable or unwilling to take effective action which would safeguard the traditional and conservative life style.

The antipornography crusade will escalate into a more intense and complex mobilization for action when the crusade leaders perceive the agents of social control in the community to be supportive of, or at least not opposed to, crusade goals, strategies, and tactics. Those agents of social control will include local politicians, police, media, and community leaders.

The antipornography crusade will escalate into a more intense and complex mobilization for action when the crusade leaders perceive the presence or likely emergence of supporting publics or the absence or likely absence of opposing publics. On the other hand, the perception of the presence or likely emergence of effective opposing groups (e.g., the university in Southtown) will serve as a mechanism of social control, limiting the intensity of the antipornography crusade.

The explicit or implicit definitions that the antipornography crusaders have of themselves as crusaders (e.g., the Southtown leaders' view of themselves as "gentlemanly" Knights of Columbus) will limit the varieties of strategies and tactics that the crusade can utilize. This social-control aspect of perception of self as a crusader will include the relative degree of attempting to avoid pejorative labels—the greater the fear of those labels, the greater the element of social control.

The leaders of the antipornography crusade will serve as major mechanisms of social control. Their leadership styles (particularly their orientation toward goal specificity and purposive incentives or goal diffuseness and solidary incentives) will influence, as a social-control mechanism, the crusade strategy and tactics, duration, and so on, as outlined in the mobilization-for-action summary above.

Social control within the antipornography crusade will: weaken with a shift toward goal-diffuse and solidary-incentive oriented leadership style; strengthen with persuasive and bargaining as compared with coercive organizational strategies and tactics; weaken with pressures for organizational maintenance; weaken with goal transformation; strengthen with crusade mergers or coalitions with other organizations; weaken with increased heterogeneity of membership; weaken with the formation of schisms (although social control within the factions themselves will become more intense); strengthen with greater integration with the multiorganizational field; strengthen with increased interdependence of the crusade with the target group; strengthen with increased dependence of the crusade upon external publics; strengthen with the presence of a parent organization; weaken with increased crusade duration; strengthen with the presence of an effective community communication network.

All the relationships we have presented within the value-added stages, as well as the value-added stages themselves, can be considered predictive hypotheses pertaining to the emergence of an antipornography crusade (as a form of norm-oriented social movement). Furthermore, the differences in direction and degree among the relationships can be predictive hypotheses pertaining to the intensity, shape, and outcome of the crusade (or crusades, if the analysis is comparative). Not all the hypotheses we have offered need be supported for a crusade to emerge. The absence of support for some may be offset by a high level of support for others. Further empirical tests would identify those independent variables that are most salient and the conditions for their salience.

The Question of Generality

To what extent can our findings be generalized to other antipornography crusades, to other symbolic crusades, and to other social movements? We have studied only two antipornography crusades—hardly an impressive sample. Consequently, we advise against straightforward extrapolation of our specific findings to other cases. Also, an N of two is insufficient for us confidently to have *tested* (in the strict sense of the term) the assorted propositions and hypotheses we have presented. So we repeat our warning about conclusions concerning the support (or lack of it) for the propositions and hypotheses.

Essentially, we leave the question of the generality of our findings to the judgment of the reader and, hopefully, to verification by further research. Our cautions now having been given, we are nonetheless confident that a substantial number of our findings would be supported. To facilitate further research we have expressed our findings as a set of predictive hypotheses within an expanded version of the Smelser value-added stages of collective behavior.

In their present form, the predictive hypotheses and expanded stages refer specifically to antipornography crusades. To begin research on or analysis of other cases of antipornography crusades, no modifications of the language of the hypotheses and variables are required. This is not to say that our list of variables and predictive hypotheses is exhaustive of those which could usefully expand the stages or could represent the processes of antipornography crusades. Indeed, the variables and hypotheses we have presented were arbitrary selections based upon our interests and upon what we felt to be the exigencies of the research project.

But what about the application of those variables and hypotheses we did use to other kinds of symbolic crusades? Our study actually has been concerned with a *conservative* symbolic crusade. That is, we have analyzed what we saw to be the change-resisting status politics of individuals, status discontents, who perceived the prestige and power of their traditional and conservative life style to be threatened by the popular ascendance of alternative life styles. Correspondingly, Gusfield's temperance crusade was also a *conservative* symbolic crusade.

It is possible, however, for individuals who are enacting a nontraditional and nonconservative life style to be status discontents and to engage in a symbolic crusade in order to enhance current or indicate potential prestige and power of that alternative life style. Their status politics, when extensive, can be considered a *liberal* symbolic crusade —generally encouraging change rather than resisting it. The encouragement of or resistance to a specific social or technical change depends for both liberal and conservative crusaders upon how the change is perceived to affect life-style prestige and power. Conservative crusaders more often base their prestige and power upon the societal status quo; hence they more often perform change-resisting acts. However, the terms *liberal* and *conservative* are, as used here, time-bound and relative; today's change-urging liberal may become tomorrow's change-resisting conservative. Furthermore, some variant mixture of movement orientation may appear. For example, the anti-pornography efforts of a women's liberation group would be a *liberal* antipornography campaign. In such a case, the overall orientation of the movement dictates the symbolism of the specific target or tactic.

The most direct application of our expanded stages and predictive hypotheses would (after antipornography crusades themselves) be *conservative* symbolic crusades. The terms which refer specifically to pornography in most instances can readily be replaced with terms referring to other potentially symbolic issues; for example, marijuana, abortion, fluoridation, birth control, euthanasia, sex education, homosexuality, women's liberation, the United Nations, penal reform, school busing for integration. The set of variables labeled "Perceptions and Definitions of Pornography and Assumed Correlates" could be changed to "Perceptions and Definitions of Marijuana and Assumed Correlates." The hypothesis "Conporns as compared with Proporns will more often report pornography to be related causally to or associated with assorted forms of social and psychological pathology" can be changed to "Conpots as compared with Propots will more often report marijuana to be related causally to or associated with assorted forms of social and psychological pathology." And so on.

Again, our list of variables and hypotheses is not by any means exhaustive, and a few on the list need considerable reworking to apply to other *conservative* symbolic crusades (e.g., the set of variables titled "Sex Education and Contact with Pornography"). But most of the variables and hypotheses, with only a change in wording from pornography to some other symbolic issue, could be productively applied.

The application of the variables and hypotheses within the expanded stages to *liberal* symbolic crusades calls for more extensive modification but might be useful. A propornography crusade, for example, would be a *liberal* symbolic crusade—change-oriented and implemented by individuals who were enacting relatively nontraditional and nonconservative life styles. The crusade would be attempting to ease or remove legal and other normative restrictions on the availability of pornography. If successful in that endeavor, Proporns would have enhanced the prestige and power of the liberal, civil-libertarian life style at the expense of the traditionalists' conservative life style.

If the case to be studied or analyzed is a propornography crusade, the terms specific to pornography can be retained. The hypotheses concerning organizational characteristics of the crusade can remain the same (with the exception that the Proporn organization will be hypothesized to align for crusade purposes with job-related, recreational, and civic-political community voluntary associations). The directions of the hypotheses concerning characteristics of individual crusaders and characteristics of the community must be considerably reworked —in most cases, revised or reversed in a direction opposite that of the Conporns. For example, "Community population will contain a significant number of politically conservative individuals" should be changed to "Community population will contain a significant number of politically liberal individuals." "There will be evidence that the number of individuals electing alternative life styles in the community is becoming greater" should be changed to "There will be evidence that the number of individuals electing conservative and traditional life styles in the community is becoming greater." "Conporns will be older" should be reversed to "Proporns will be younger." And so on. Throughout the hypotheses, "traditional and conservative" should be changed to "alternative and liberal"; "more" to "less" and vice versa, "anti-" to "pro-," "against" to "for." And so on.

If the *liberal* symbolic crusade is concerned with issues other than pornography (e.g., marijuana, abortion, fluoridation, birth control, euthanasia, sex education, homosexuality, women's liberation, the United Nations, penal reform, school busing for integration), then the hypotheses concerning community and individual characteristics must be revised or reversed, *and* the pornography-specific terms must be replaced with terms suitable to the symbolic issue at hand. For example, "The potential antipornography crusaders will express the belief that if pornography is controlled or eliminated, the threat to the traditional and conservative American life style will be mitigated" should be changed to "The potential promarijuana crusader will express the belief that if marijuana is legalized (or attempts for more restrictive laws are defeated), the threat to nontraditional and nonconservative American life styles will be mitigated." "Conporns more often (than Proporns) will be punitive toward their own children concerning exposure to pornography" should be changed to "Propots less often (than Conpots) will be punitive toward their own children concerning exposure to marijuana." And so on.

Both *conservative* and *liberal* symbolic crusades are the status political acts of individuals who are status discontents attempting to enhance the prestige and power of their life styles. The conservative crusaders tend to be defending a traditional and conservative life style against threats from ascending alternative life styles. The liberal crusaders tend to be urging the general public acceptance of their alternative life styles and to be seeking prestige and power at the expense of traditionalism and conservativeness.

In summary, our list of variables and hypotheses works best in application to other antipornography crusades, and we have presented the list in language that applies to those cases. The variables and hypotheses, with in most cases minor changes in wording, can be made to apply also to *conservative* symbolic crusades in general. Considerable restructuring of the variables and hypotheses is demanded for application to *liberal* symbolic crusades. We have given examples of the restructuring but have not transposed the entire list—because some of the variables and hypotheses may not be transposable; because of the sheer bulk of the lists; because the list is not exhaustive; and because the researcher can best do the transposing in the context of his or her own study.

The usefulness of our findings to an understanding of social movements in general is threefold: (*a*) the conclusion that symbolic crusades are norm-oriented movements adds importantly to the typology of such movements; (*b*) some of the variables and predictive hypotheses (especially those concerned with movement organization) are useful in understanding the processes of all social movements; (*c*) our expansion of the Smelser value-added stages, though not exhaustive, is an example of the kinds of refinement which will recast the stages into a predictive mode.

A few more words of caution are in order. Though the intensive study of small local antipornography crusades affords opportunity for the richness of an in-depth analysis, and although we have placed that analysis in a context of social change, our focus necessarily has been relatively narrow. That is, we could not attempt to acquire data which would *conceptually* link the two local crusades with the extensive efforts of national antipornography organizations and with what might be a national antipornography social movement. Similarly, we could not attempt to acquire data which would locate the crusade broadly enough in what might be a societal trend of resistance or reaction to social change. Such a trend could be expected following the sweeping, change-oriented social movements of the early and mid-sixties. The local antipornography crusades we studied were what Blumer (1951) would have called "specific" social movements—and small ones, at that. Blumer also identified broader, society-wide "general" social movements of which many specific movements are a part (either supporting or resisting). Analyses at that level of abstraction are ultimately necessary if a thorough understanding of the emergence and function of symbolic crusades is to be acquired.

We have argued that the Conporns, in defense of their life style, were at least as satisfied with symbolic as with utilitarian antipornography victories. But a case cannot be made to demonstrate that they actually *preferred* the symbolic successes to those that were utilitarian. It may be that a symbolic victory is better than none at all, when conditions preclude a utilitarian victory—when social change cannot be stopped. We shall return to that speculation in the following chapter, when we discuss the future of antipornography crusades. The point is raised here in order to place it in the context of Blumer's distinction between general and specific social movements and to reinforce our belief in the importance of further research which fits such local phenomena as ICCD and UFD into a larger perspective. It may be that crusaders are willing to accept local accomplishments that are only symbolic, *if they see their efforts as contributing somehow to a national movement which is utilitarian*. Perhaps a symbolic victory is an experience required before effective utilitarian strategies, tactics, or affiliations are implemented. Perhaps the leadership of the national social movement encourages symbolic crusades by local persons, because such crusades generate a support base for national utilitarian efforts. McCarthy and Zald (1973) have described the operation of "professional movement organizations" at the national level and discussed the manner in which they work to mobilize resources necessary to their goals. Might symbolic crusades be one such resource?

In this book, we have wedded ourselves to the idea that challenge to life style can yield status discontent and that status discontent can generate a symbolic crusade. We have bent every effort to make that case and will conclude the book continuing to argue for it. But life style is a complex concept, and there are ways in which it may be threatened other than by loss of prestige, control, or reward. Furthermore, there are ways in which life style may be defended other than by a symbolic crusade or any other kind of social movement. In the press to make our case for status discontent, we do not wish our temporary single-mindedness to be interpreted as arguing for homogeneity either in definition of or response to social change. Nor do we wish to suggest a homogeneity of motivation for participation in social movements, symbolic crusades, or even in ICCD and UFD. It may be that the evidence we gathered and interpreted demonstrates Conporns to have manifested characteristics that made them sensitive to contemporary social change and to have evolved a vocabulary for crusade participation that represented status discontent. Those characteristics and that vocabulary are important phenomena in the emergence and implementation of the crusades. However, they were assessed *after* or *during* crusade participation. Thus we may have hit accurately upon the manner in which the Conporns *justified* their participation, in generalized beliefs, but we did not have data which clearly indicated why each individual became involved in the first place. What natural-history evidence we did present suggests a diversity of reasons for initial individual affiliation—role expectations associated with membership in certain kinds of voluntary associations, friendships, idiosyncratic happenings, and so on. Furthermore, the concept of status discontent, referring as it does to the complex concept of life style, involves a network of values, norms, roles, and situational facilities. Consequently, even within the concept of status discontent, Conporns could have been representing a heterogeneity of patterns of discontent—some having focused their concern around threat to values, some around threat to norms, and so on, fanning throughout a mixture of concerns.

We have limited our interpretations of the data to those theoretical perspectives which, at the time, interested us most. Much of our analysis follows the lead of Weber (1946; 1947), emphasizing the operation of social prestige and status with respect to morality and life style. We think that interpretation is important. But other perspectives might be as productive, or perhaps more productive. The antipornography crusades might be analyzed, following Durkheim (1966), as attempts by citizens to re-establish a collective consciousness disturbed by the behavior of deviants—a disruption of the set of moral precepts which are taken for granted by most of the members of the community (see Kirkpatrick, In Press). The crusades might be analyzed, following Reich (1946), Marcuse (1965), and Ranulf (1938), as social movements which have emerged as false issues, serving to obfuscate the real problems of societal sexual repression or exploitation (see Kirkpatrick 1974). Or the crusades might be analyzed, following Marx (1972) or Dahrendorf (1959), as reflecting more fundamental conflicts between social classes for the possession of productivity or economic control. The Midville crusade might even be described as a specific manifestation of the general movement of women toward liberation and the acquisition of influence. The actions of the crusaders might be interpreted, following Sorokin (1947), as reflections of transitional agonies associated with a societal shift from ideational to sensate orientations. Finally, at least among our suggestions for alternative analysis, the crusades might be reviewed, following Toennies (1964), as struggles to maintain elements of *Gemeinschaft* in a milieu of pervasive *Gesellschaft*. As we mentioned in the preface, we deliberately have included in this book enough of the raw data about the crusades so that the reader can apply whatever alternative perspectives and interpretations he or she chooses.

Chapter 11

After the Crusades: The

Commission Reports,

Conporns Respond, and the

Supreme Court Redeems Itself

The Report of the Commission on Obscenity and Pornography

In October, 1967, Congress established in law the Commission on Obscenity and Pornography, whose purpose was "after a thorough study which shall include a study of the causal relationship of such materials to anti-social behavior, to recommend advisable, appropriate, effective, and constitutional means to deal effectively with such traffic in obscenity and pornography" (Commission on Obscenity and Pornography 1970:1). In January, 1968, President Lyndon Johnson appointed the eighteen commission members, and they began their work, part of which was to let contracts for research concerning pornography. (One of the smaller of the research projects was ours.) In September, 1970, the commission presented its report to the president (Richard Nixon), to the Congress, and to the general public. The commission had reached, based upon its investigation, a set of conclusions (1970:7–81) which included the following:

> Extensive empirical investigation, both by the Commission and by others, provides no evidence that exposure to or use of explicit sexual materials play a significant role in the causation of social or individual harms such as crime, delinquency, sexual or nonsexual deviancy or severe emotional disturbances. . . . Empirical investigation thus supports the opinion of a substantial majority of persons professionally engaged in the treatment of deviancy, delinquency,

and antisocial behavior, that exposure to sexually explicit materials has no harmful causal role in these areas. (p. 58)

Exposure to erotic stimuli appears to have little or no effect on already established attitudinal commitments regarding either sexuality or sexual morality. (p. 29)

. . . many persons become temporarily sexually aroused upon viewing explicit sexual materials and the frequency of their sexual activity may, in consequence, increase for short periods. Such behavior, however, is the sexual activity already established as usual activity for the particular individual. (p. 58)

. . . explicit sexual materials are sought as a source of entertainment and information by substantial numbers of American adults. At times, these materials also appear to serve to increase and facilitate constructive communication about sexual matters within marriage. (p. 59)

The Commission has also taken cognizance of the concern of many people that the lawful distribution of explicit sexual materials to adults may have a deleterious effect upon the individual morality of American citizens and upon the moral climate in America as a whole . . . the Commission has found no evidence to support such a contention. (p. 61)

Several studies show that depictions of conventional sexual behavior are generally regarded as more stimulating than depictions of less conventional activity. (p. 28)

The only experimental study on the subject to date found that continued or repeated exposure to erotic stimuli over 15 days resulted in satiation (marked diminution) of sexual arousal and interest in such material. In this experiment, the introduction of novel sex stimuli partially rejuvenated satiated interest, but only briefly. There was also partial recovery of interests after two months of non-exposure. (p. 28)

. . . more exposure to erotica occurs outside the commercial context and is a social or quasi-social activity. (p. 24)

Patrons of adult bookstores and adult movies may be characterized as predominantly white, middle class, middle-aged, married males, dressed in business suits or neat casual attire, shopping or attending the movie alone. (p. 25)

There is no consensus among Americans regarding what they consider to be the effects of viewing or reading explicit sexual materials. (p. 27)

Public opinion in America does not support the imposition of legal prohibitions upon the right of adults to read or see explicit sexual materials. (p. 59)

A large majority of sex educators and counselors are of the opinion that most adolescents are interested in explicit sexual materials, and that this interest is a product of natural curiosity about sex. They also feel that if adolescents had access to adequate information regarding sex, through appropriate sex education, their interest in pornography would be reduced. (p. 33)

Based upon these and other findings, the Commission on Obscenity and Pornography (1970:53–81) offered (with six commissioners dissenting) a series of recommendations, including: (a) the repeal of federal, state, and local legislation prohibiting the sale, exhibition, or distribution of sexual materials to consenting adults; (b) the implementation of a massive sex education program; (c) the enactment of statutes which would prevent unsolicited advertisements containing potentially offensive sexual materials from being communicated through the mails to persons who do not wish to receive such advertisements; (d) the enactment of statutes which would prohibit the commercial distribution or display for sale of pictorial sexual material to young persons; (e) the gathering of additional factual information, and a continued and open discussion based on that information concerning the issues regarding obscenity and pornography; (f) a continuing involvement of citizens at local, regional, and national levels to aid in the implementation of the commission's recommendations.

The Reaction of the Dissenting Commissioners

Needless to say, the impact of the report was explosive, and controversy was immediate.[1] The controversy was, in fact, intense among the commissioners themselves prior to and during preparation of the report. Among the six commissioners who dissented from the interpretations of the research and subsequent recommendations, two were particularly vociferous: Father Morton Hill, S.J. (a Roman Catholic priest and the president of Morality in Media) and Mr. Charles Keating (a lawyer, the only Nixon appointee to the commission, and the founder of Citizens for Decent Literature). Father Hill (with another commissioner, the Reverend Winfrey Link, a Protestant minister) wrote a dissenting opinion (concurred in by Mr. Keating) which was published within the report (Commission on Obscenity and Pornography 1970:456–578). Mr. Keating wrote a separate dissenting opinion which was also published within the report (pp. 578–700). The dissenting opinions of Father Hill and Mr. Keating, as they appeared in the report and in other publications, are instructive and often parallel the kinds of structural strain and generalized beliefs manifested by the Conporns we have described in earlier chapters. For example, in their report dissent, Father Hill and Mr. Link argued:

> The Commission's majority report is a Magna Carta for the pornographer . . . the conclusions and recommendations in the majority report will be found deeply offensive to Congress and to tens of millions of Americans. . . . [The report] will be quoted ad nauseum by cultural polluters and their attorneys within society.
> (pp. 456–457)

> The basic question is whether and to what extent society may establish and maintain certain moral standards. If it is conceded that society has a legitimate concern in maintaining moral standards, it follows logically that government has a legitimate interest in at least attempting to protect such standards against any source which threatens them. (p. 457)

Father Hill and Mr. Link took particular issue with the then-current item among the legal tests for pornography, that the material must be "utterly without redeeming social value." The majority of the commission had, in their opinion, ignored the inappropriateness of that test. The clergymen summarized their critique:

> In sum, the conclusions and recommendations of the Commission majority represent the preconceived views of the Chairman [law professor William Lockhart] and his appointed counsel [Mr. Paul Bender] that the Commission should arrive at those conclusions most compatible with the viewpoint of the American Civil Liberties Union . . . the policy of the ACLU has been that obscenity is pro-

tected speech. Mr. Lockhart . . . has long been a member of the American Civil Liberties Union. Mr. Bender . . . is an executive of the Philadelphia Civil Liberties Union. . . . The two million dollars voted by Congress have gone primarily to "scholars" who would return conclusions amenable to the extreme and minority views of Mr. Lockhart, Mr. Bender, and the ACLU. (p. 458)

Father Hill and Mr. Link gave their contrasting view (relative to that of the majority of the commissioners) concerning the effects of pornography:

We believe that pornography has an eroding effect on society, on public morality, on respect for human worth, on attitudes toward family love, on culture. . . . We believe it is impossible, and totally unnecessary, to attempt to prove or disprove a cause-effect relationship between pornography and criminal behavior. . . . Pornography is loveless; it degrades the human being, reduces him to the level of animal. . . . We believe government must legislate to regulate pornography, in order to protect the "social interest in order and morality." (pp. 458–459)

The two clergymen pointed to flaws in the design of some of the commission research which was concerned with the effects of pornography and noted some negative effects among the findings which, they argued, did not appear in the majority commission report.

Mr. Keating's dissenting statement paralleled that of Father Hill and Mr. Link. He argued that "our nation is imperiled by a poison [pornography] which is all-pervasive . . . its invidious effect upon individuals and upon nations has been held in reasonable control by law" (Commission on Obscenity and Pornography 1970:578). The commission's recommendation that laws restricting pornography be stricken from the books was, according to Mr. Keating, a "shocking and anarchistic recommendation" made by the commission "in spite of the lessons of history, in spite of the will of the overwhelming majority of the people of this nation, and in spite of the circumstances of our times." He continued, "Such presumption! Such an advocacy of moral anarchy! Such a defiance of the mandate of the Congress which created the Commission! Such a bold advocacy of a libertine philosophy!" (pp. 580–581)

Like Father Hill and Mr. Link, Mr. Keating strongly felt that pornography was related causally to many social and psychological pathol-

ogies. Though the relationships may not be clearly demonstrable by
scientific method, he said, common sense attests to it. He stated, "To
those who believe in God, in His absolute supremacy as the Creator
and Law-giver of Life, in the dignity and destiny which He confirmed
upon the human person, in the moral code that governs sexual activity
—for those who believe in these 'things,' no argument against pornography should be necessary." He added, "One can consult all the experts he chooses, can write reports, make studies, etc., but the fact that
obscenity corrupts lies within the common sense, the reason, and the
logic of every man" (p. 616). Like Father Hill and Mr. Link, Mr. Keating
also felt that the report reflected the value and norm bias of the ACLU.
He contributed a more specific critique of the value orientations of
the researchers who provided the substance of the report (especially
those researchers who assessed the effects of pornography): "Those
'contractors' are, generally speaking, academicians with ivory-tower
views, who have little or no responsibility to anyone or anything,
excepting their own thought processes which go unhoned by the
checks and balances of a competitive, active, real world. And even beyond the contracting academicians, we find a bulk of work done by
their assistants, green graduates, and college students" (p. 584).

The Reaction of Conporns

To the dissenting commissioners we have quoted (two of whom were
Conporns, as we have used the term, by virtue of their active and central participation in antipornography organizations), and to Conporns
throughout the United States, the majority commission report was an
insult—a dismissing of their beliefs, a dramatic devaluing of their life
style. The report told them, under the aegis of scientific research, that
nobody really agrees upon a definition of examples of pornography or
obscenity. Though the Conporns themselves demonstrated little consensus on such definitions or examples, they nonetheless felt firmly
that their idiosyncratic definitions and examples, vague as they may
have been, were sound—and, given their own experiences and applied
to a defense of their own life style, the definitions *were* sound. The report told the Conporns that the kinds of people who produce pornography are not necessarily criminals, depraved, or intent upon seducing
youth—that they are generally not very apt, small businessmen who
don't make a lot of money plying their trade. The majority commission
report informed Conporns that the kinds of people who use pornog-

raphy, as represented by customers in "adult" bookstores and movies, are in several demographic characteristics not unlike the Conporns themselves. Most repulsive of all to Conporns, the report argued that exposure to pornography has few or no negative effects upon individuals—in fact, in several situations, exposure to pornography, according to the research and the opinions of sex educators and counselors, may have educational or other salutary effects. Finally, most people in the country, summarized the report, unlike the Conporns, want the laws restricting pornography from adult use removed.

The Report of the Commission on Obscenity and Pornography was (with the exception of the dissenting commissioners' statements) a further threat to all the Conporns held sacred—a further strain on all the Smelser components of action: values, norms, roles and rewards, and situational facilities. The report challenged the basic values typified by morality, traditionalism, and conservatism. Not only did it further weaken normative control over pornography (and what it symbolized)—it called for almost total removal of normative control. The report denigrated the traditional role enacted by Conporns and robbed that role of prestige and other social rewards. Finally, the report negated the knowledge the Conporns felt they had about causal relations, about the order of their world, and about their power and control in that world. The Report of the Commission on Obscenity and Pornography was, as one of the Conporns we interviewed complained, "an obscenity itself."

The objections of the dissenting commissioners well represented the feelings and complaints about the report among those Conporns we were able to interview after the publication of the report (eighteen, all in Southtown). Throughout their dissenting statements, the commission minority insisted that, the majority report and its evidence notwithstanding, pornography *does* have a deleterious and direct effect upon the individual, the nation, and civilization. Furthermore, it is not at all necessary to demonstrate "scientifically" a relationship between exposure to pornography and social or psychological pathologies in order to take legal or other sanctioning action against it. To the dissenting commissioners, as to the Conporns, pornography is a value issue, symbolically representing a wide array of concerns involving all four components of action. One's position on pornography, given its symbolism, is all or none—one is either for it or against it; there is no marginal position, no "shades of gray," only black or white. Those who are "soft" concerning pornography are depicted as being representatives of a very different, more permissive, and potentially invidious life style—that of the ACLU and the modernists. That depiction included the commissioners who voted with the majority, the commission staff who wrote the report, all of the researchers whose findings supported the majority report, and, of course, all Proporns. (For additional details concerning the viewpoint of the dissenting commissioners, see, in addition to the report, Keating 1971; Hill 1970.) The dissenting commissioners argued for the test or definition which had emerged in the 1957 *Roth* Supreme Court decision: "A thing is obscene if, by contemporary community standards and considered as a whole, its predominant appeal is to the prurient interest." *Roth* allowed arbitrary tests of obscenity to be established locally and left open a wide range of value judgments concerning "prurient interests." It also did not include the criterion "utterly without redeeming social value." The dissenting commissioners particularly were opposed to the latter criterion, which had entered some state statutes, making it almost impossible to obtain convictions. The dissenting commissioners urged, as did some of the Conporns, that the phrase was not to be considered as "law of the land," since it had evolved subsequent to *Roth*, under nonvoting circumstances of the Supreme Court. If one accepts the premise that crusades against pornography are actually defenses against perceived threats to a cherished life style and that pornography is symbolic of those threats, then it is easy to understand how difficult it would be for a Conporn to accept the idea that pornography could *ever* have any "redeeming social value." Pornography as an issue was too closely tied (negatively) with other important value constellations for Conporns to recognize it as anything but evil. Furthermore, it does not stretch the boundaries of cognitive dissonance theory to suggest that a Conporn's acceptance of a positive or even neutral evaluation of pornography would be painfully inconsistent with the life style (and its sacrifices) and with the antipornography activity to which he or she had been committed.

The Reaction of the President, His Administration, and the Senate

Conporns were gratified by the response of President Nixon, Vice President Agnew, and the Senate to the Report of the Commission on Obscenity and Pornography. Mr. Nixon straightforwardly rejected the report (according to some news sources before he had even seen it), with strongly condemnatory language:

I have evaluated that Report and categorically reject its morally bankrupt conclusions and its major recommendations. So long as I am in the White House, there will be no relaxation of the national effort to control and eliminate smut from our national life.

. . . The Commission contends that the proliferation of filthy books and plays has no lasting effect on a man's character. If that were true, it must also be true that great books, great paintings and great plays have no ennobling effect on a man's conduct. Centuries of civilization and ten minutes of common sense tell us otherwise. . . .

. . . The warped and brutal portrayal of sex in books, plays and magazines and movies, if not halted and reversed, could poison the well springs of American and Western culture and civilization. . . .

. . . The pollution of our culture, the pollution of our civilization with smut and filth is as serious a situation for the American people as the pollution of our once-pure air and water. . . .

. . . Pornography is to freedom of expression what anarchy is to liberty; as free men willingly restrain a measure of their freedom to prevent anarchy, so must we draw the line against pornography to protect freedom of expression.

. . . moreover, if an attitude of permissiveness were to be adopted regarding pornography, this would contribute to an atmosphere condoning anarchy in every field—and would increase the threat to our social order as well as to our moral principles. . . .

. . . Smut should not be simply contained at its present level; it should be outlawed in every state in the Union. And the legislatures and courts at every level of American government should act in unison to achieve that goal. . . .

. . . American morality is not to be trifled with, the Commission on Pornography and Obscenity [sic] has performed a disservice, and I totally reject its Report. (*Southtown Globe-Gazette*, October 25, 1970; also in *Weekly Compilation of Presidential Documents* 6 (November 2, 1970):1454–1455).

Mr. Nixon's comments almost directly paralleled several of the speeches and other public statements of the Midville and Southtown Conporns. (They also almost directly paralleled several of the statements publicly made by Citizens for Decent Literature and Morality in Media.) His observations clearly represented the Conporns' generalized belief concerning pornography and what it symbolized and reaffirmed the prestige of their life style. "The President understands," boasted a Southtown Conporn, "and he won't let us down."

Similarly damning statements rejecting the majority commission report were made by the vice president, the attorney general, the postmaster general, and the White House press secretary.

The Conporns were also gratified by the Senate's depiction of the commission report as "marshmallow-headed thinking" and its sixty-to-five vote for a resolution to reject all the report's major findings and to condemn it. The sponsor of the resolution, Senator John McClellan, commented:

> I feel that if we allow and encourage the flow of obscene material, there will be no stopping these sex offenders. This filth is stimulating them, they feed on it and the Commission would guarantee that they have their fill. . . .
>
> . . . I do not think that the Senate should allow this report—which would substitute hedonism for morality—to stand unchallenged. (*Southtown Globe*, October 14, 1970)

Senator John Stennis commented: "The Report gives the impression that the majority of the Commission have essentially given up on human nature and are prepared to accept a very cynical view of an inherent good in the human soul" (*Southtown Globe*, October 14, 1970).

Summarizing his critique of the report, Senator Harry Byrd emphatically stated that "this outrageously permissive Commission shows how far this Nation has traveled down the road of moral decadence" (*New York Times*, October 4, 1970).

The Reversal by the Burger Supreme Court

The rejection of the commission report by President Nixon, his administration, and members of Congress heartened the Conporns. But it was not until June, 1973, that a major norm-oriented victory would be evident to them. In that month, the Burger Supreme Court, by a vote of five to four (*Miller*, 1973; *Paris Adult Theater*, 1973), revised the legal test for pornography. (See Preface for a full statement of the test.) The new decision removed as a criterion the "utterly without redeeming social value" qualification, and emphasized strongly the force of "contemporary community standards" as a test. The "community" was more precisely defined as not that of the nation as a whole but those of individual states and localities (*New York Times*, June 24, 1973).

Those two issues (redeeming social value and community standards) had been, as we have noted, particularly sore points with Conporns —both reflected life-style challenges; both interfered with normative controls. Citizens for Decent Literature had specified the removal of "redeeming social value" and the emphasis on local community standards (with jury determination of such standards on a case-by-case basis) as key legislative lobbying points. Now, in 1973, Conporns had won their case with the Supreme Court—at least with the Supreme Court that had four Nixon appointees on it. "The Supreme Court Justices are wearing black robes again," smiled a Southtown Conporn, "and not black hats."

But how utilitarian had the Supreme Court reversal actually been in restricting the availability of pornography? According to several lawyers and prosecutors, confusion lay ahead in the implementation of the ruling. In particular, the definition of what was a "community" seemed quite problematical, as was who would determine what is "prurient," "patently offensive," and "serious" (*New York Times*, June 24, 1973). By September, 1973, a burst of raids and arrests had been made involving "adult" bookstores and theaters. But there had been very few prosecutions and no successful prosecutions (*Southtown Globe-Gazette*, September 1, 1973; September 9, 1973). Not only was the definition of "community" causing problems, but the Supreme Court mandate that state laws had to be specific in their definitions of pornography was in some states not met, causing appellate courts to be divided on whether present laws applied or not. Furthermore, several of the state laws concerning pornography currently included the "utterly without redeeming social value" test in their statute language. Thus the Supreme Court modification could not be applied, since current state laws took precedence. Ironically, one of the states that was unable to implement the Supreme Court ruling was the state of which Southtown was capital. Uprising for Decency, in its successful 1970 bid to "toughen" the state's antipornography statutes, had supported bills which included the "social value" phrase in their language, in order to assure maximum constitutionality. But, starting in 1973 and continuing to this writing, throughout the United States, including Southtown, there were legislative procedures being implemented to bring state antipornography statutes into accord with the new Supreme Court ruling.

Despite the continuing confusion concerning legal tests for pornography and the consequent limitation upon the utilitarian, pornography-limiting aspects of the new tests, Conporns have been rewarded by the Supreme Court reversal. Revered, status-giving persons have attested to the validity and viability of the Conporn life style. At least some of the pornographers, and what they symbolized, have been forced temporarily to become a bit more cautious, a bit less blatant. And, even if the new pornography test is not yet (if ever) fully operative, it is nonetheless *their* test, from the perspective of Conporns, as was Prohibition from the perspective of temperance crusaders, and corresponds to *their* life style.

Another dimension of the Supreme Court decision and the current vagueness of its implementation is the new potency and legitimacy it gives to the purchase-complaint-arrest strategy, as, for example, employed by the Midville crusaders. "Adult" bookstores and theaters are now more vulnerable than ever to direct citizen action; and, even if convictions are not the result, their businesses may be tied up for long periods of time during exploratory legal determination. As of early 1975, though there has been a marked escalation of action against such businesses, nearly all of it has been conducted by the police—not by Conporns. "Their law" has been passed—their life style symbolically supported. The usual agencies of social control have a new weapon against the "deviants," and it will take time before the efficacy of that weapon can be evaluated.

The Future

But what if the new Supreme Court modifications are not able to be effectively implemented, and pornography continues, with perhaps a few temporary slowdowns, to be available? What if the Supreme Court were to reverse itself again (and there are legal system pressures upon the court to do so from book publishers, movie producers, and the ACLU)? Would the Conporns take up the crusade again? If the value-added stages were operative, they would indeed. But structural strain must be experienced, a generalized belief concerning pornography or pornographers must be held, a precipitating factor must emerge, and social control must be at least permeable. The mere occurrence of failure of the Supreme Court ruling might be a precipitating factor but would not be enough, in itself (without the other stages), to encourage crusading anew.

And what of the impact of the antipornography crusades upon society, upon the process of safeguarding "basic values" against change? In effect, the temperance crusaders, though effective in influencing normative restriction at least temporarily upon drinking behavior, actually did little to stop the growing acceptance of alcohol as socially approved. Will that also be the case with pornography? Will societal values concerning sexual behavior move toward greater permissiveness and pornography generally be accepted or at least tolerated for those who choose it? If so, what then has been the function of the symbolic crusade against pornography, in a context of social change? One interpretation would be that participation in the crusade allows individuals whose life style is being threatened to reinforce that style and yet not to interfere lastingly or significantly with social change. This interpretation assumes a kind of "escape-valve" process as one reaction to social change and its attendant dislocations.[2]

Of course as social-change processes continue, there will emerge new sources of status discontent—new "deviants," new alternative life styles, and new challenges to "basic values." Alcohol is no longer a suitable summary symbol for status discontent and a symbolic crusade. Pornography may have, with the Supreme Court action, hit its high mark as a summary symbol. It may not for much longer be operative as a key factor in generalized belief (thus diminishing the possibility of antipornography crusades). But there are other potential symbols available—marijuana, abortion, homosexuality, euthanasia, and so on—and still other potential symbols loom on the horizon—alternative marriage or mating arrangements; alternative, non-achievement-oriented work patterns; variations from the traditional educational processes; extrauterine conception; chemically stimulated intellectual and emotional states; genetic manipulation for the production of specific physiological and behavioral characteristics—the list can be extensive. So long as social change impinges upon the prestige and power of a central life style (in American society as presently structured), it is likely that there will be symbolic crusades in service of that prestige, power, and centrality. The Supreme Court's recent emphasis on local community standards for the determination of what is pornographic may be a dramatic precedent, facilitating the expression of status discontent and escalating the possibilities for symbolic crusades. If there can be a determination of the dominant local standards for pornography, why not for marijuana use, abortion, homosexuality, and so on? Why not for the dominant local life style? The Supreme Court may have made symbolic crusades a more important part of American society than ever.

Appendix: The Structured Questionnaire

Community Action Study

_____

_____

(case number)

_____   _____

(interviewer name)   (date)

1. Sex: 0   Male
            1   Female

2. Age: (Years)

3. Religious preference:
                    0   Roman Catholic
                    1   Baptist
                    2   Lutheran
                    3   Methodist
                    4   Presbyterian
                    5   Church of Christ
                    6   Jewish
                    7   Other (specify)
                    8   None

4. About how often do you attend church worship services?
                    0   Two or more times a week
                    1   Once a week
                    2   Two or three times a month
                    3   Once a month
                    4   Two to ten times a year
                    5   Once a year
                    6   Rarely or never

5. How large was the town or city you lived in most of the time when you were growing up?

        0 Up to 2,499 people
        1 2,500 to 24,999 people
        2 25,000 to 49,999 people
        3 50,000 to 99,999 people
        4 100,000 to 499,999 people
        5 500,000 and over

6. What state did you live in most of the time when you were growing up?

6a. How long have you lived at your present address?

7. The main occupation of the respondent or (if not employed) the head of the household:

_____

        (Kind of work done and duties involved)

8. For whom do you (or head of household) work?

        0 Self-employed
        1 Private business or industry
        2 Government or school
        3 Nonprofit organization

9. About how many hours a week do you (or head of household) work?

        (Hours)

10. How would you say you like the work you do?

        0 Dislike extremely
        1 Dislike somewhat
        2 Indifferent
        3 Like somewhat
        4 Like extremely

11. Did you ever wish you had gone into another field?

        0 Yes
        1 No

12. Is there some other employment you would rather have?

  0 Yes

  1 No

13. Give the total monthly income for the entire family:

  0 Below $400

  1 $400 to $599

  2 $600 to $799

  3 $800 to $999

  4 $1000 to $1199

  5 $1200 to $1399

  6 $1400 to $1599

  7 $1600 or more

14. How interested are you in politics?

  0 Not at all

  1 Very little

  2 Somewhat

  3 Very much

14a. Do you participate in precinct meetings?

  0 Yes

  1 No

14b. Have you donated money to political campaigns?

  0 Yes

  1 No

14c. Have you donated time to political campaigns?

  0 Yes

  1 No

14d. Do you follow the campaigns in the newspaper?

  0 Yes

  1 No

15. What is your political preference?

    0 Democrat
    1 Republican
    2 Independent

16. Do you consider yourself conservative or liberal?

    0 Conservative
    1 Liberal

17. Please list the organizations to which you belong (e.g., professional, service, religious, social, political, civic, etc.).

18. How often do they schedule meetings?

19. How often do you attend their meetings?

20. Are you an officer of the organization?

21. Rank the following activities in the order that they give you the most satisfaction.

    0 Career or occupation
    1 Leisure time recreational activity
    2 Family relationships
    3 Religious beliefs and activities
    4 Participation in community affairs

22. Please indicate your highest level of education:

    0 Some grade school
    1 Completed grade school
    2 Some high school
    3 Completed high school
    4 High school plus other (not college) training
    5 Some college
    6 Completed college
    7 Some graduate work
    8 Graduate degree

23. Are you now married?

0 Yes
1 No

23z   have you ever been pregn.

IF YES:

23a. How long have you been married?   (Years)

23b. Have you been married before?
    If yes, how many times?   (Number)

23c. How many children do you have? (Itemize by sex and age.)

INTERVIEWER READ: We would now like to ask your opinion
on statements that have been made by various people around the
country. Please indicate whether you AGREE VERY MUCH,
AGREE ON THE WHOLE, AGREE A LITTLE, ARE UNDE-
CIDED, DISAGREE A LITTLE, DISAGREE ON THE WHOLE,
or DISAGREE VERY MUCH with each statement.

0	1	2	3	4	5	6
Agree Very Much	Agree on the Whole	Agree a Little	Undecided	Disagree a Little	Disagree on the Whole	Disagree Very Much

Alienation*

Powerlessness

24. Sometimes I have the feeling that people   0 1 2 3 4 5 6
    are using me

25. There is little or nothing that I can do   0 1 2 3 4 5 6
    toward preventing a major shooting war.

*This and subsequent headings identifying social-psychological items have
been added for the reader's convenience. They do not appear in the actual
questionnaire. Some items have been worded so as to reverse Likert answers
and break response set. Computer analysis treated all Likert responses so
that the higher the mean scale score is, the greater is the intensity of the
characteristic assessed.

26. We are just so many cogs in the machin- 0 1 2 3 4 5 6
ery of life.

Normlessness

27. Everything is relative, and there just 0 1 2 3 4 5 6
aren't any definite rules to live by.

28. With so many religions around, one 0 1 2 3 4 5 6
doesn't know which to believe.

Authoritarianism

29. The most important thing to teach 0 1 2 3 4 5 6
children is absolute obedience to their
parents.

30. Any good leader should be strict with 0 1 2 3 4 5 6
people under him in order to gain their
respect.

31. A person who has bad manners, habits, or 0 1 2 3 4 5 6
breeding can hardly expect to be liked
by decent people.

32. The businessman and the manufacturer 0 1 2 3 4 5 6
are much more important to society
than the artist and the professor.

33. There are two kinds of people in the 0 1 2 3 4 5 6
world: the weak and the strong.

Religiosity

34. The Church has done as much as any 0 1 2 3 4 5 6
existing social institution to combat
modern evils.

35. Those people to whom God has revealed 0 1 2 3 4 5 6
himself have been subject to delusions.

36. The soul is a mere supposition, having no better standing than a myth.　　0 1 2 3 4 5 6

37. Organized religion has acted as a powerful agency in the development of social justice.　　0 1 2 3 4 5 6

38. Since the findings of modern sciences have left many things unanswered, we must accept the concept of God.　　0 1 2 3 4 5 6

39. Without the Church, there would be a collapse of morality.　　0 1 2 3 4 5 6

Traditional Family Ideology

40. A child should not be allowed to talk back to his parents or else he will lose respect for them.　　0 1 2 3 4 5 6

41. There is hardly anything lower than a person who does not feel a great love, gratitude, and respect for his parents.　　0 1 2 3 4 5 6

42. A woman whose children are messy or rowdy has failed in her duties as a mother.　　0 1 2 3 4 5 6

43. A child who is unusual in any way should be encouraged to be more like other children.　　0 1 2 3 4 5 6

44. Some equality in marriage is a good thing, but by and large, the husband ought to have the main say-so in family affairs.　　0 1 2 3 4 5 6

Political Intolerance

45. An admitted Communist should not be allowed to make a speech in the community.　　0 1 2 3 4 5 6

46. Books written against churches and re- 0 1 2 3 4 5 6
    ligion should be taken out of public
    libraries.

47. Communists should not be allowed to 0 1 2 3 4 5 6
    teach at state universities.

48. How often do you vote in local elections?
        0 Always
        1 Frequently
        2 Sometimes
        3 Rarely
        4 Never

49. How often do you vote in national elections?
        0 Always
        1 Frequently
        2 Sometimes
        3 Rarely
        4 Never

For the following statements, please indicate whether you
AGREE VERY MUCH, AGREE ON THE WHOLE, AGREE A
LITTLE, ARE UNDECIDED, DISAGREE A LITTLE, DIS-
AGREE ON THE WHOLE, or DISAGREE VERY MUCH.

0	1	2	3	4	5	6
Agree	Agree	Agree	Undecided	Disagree	Disagree	Disagree
Very	on the	a		a	on the	Very
Much	Whole	Little		Little	Whole	Much

Dogmatism

50. In this complicated world of ours, the 0 1 2 3 4 5 6
    only way we can know what is going on is
    to rely on leaders or experts who can be
    trusted.

51. My blood boils whenever a person stub- 0 1 2 3 4 5 6
    bornly refuses to admit he's wrong.

52. There are two kinds of people in this world: those who are for the truth and those who are against the truth.   0 1 2 3 4 5 6

53. Most people just don't know what's good for them.   0 1 2 3 4 5 6

54. Of all the different philosophies which exist in this world, there is probably only one which is correct.   0 1 2 3 4 5 6

55. Most of the ideas which get printed nowadays aren't worth the paper they are printed on.   0 1 2 3 4 5 6

56. The highest form of government is democracy and the highest form of democracy is a government run by those who are most intelligent.   0 1 2 3 4 5 6

57. The main thing in life is for a person to want to do something important.   0 1 2 3 4 5 6

58. I'd like it if I could find someone who would tell me how to solve my personal problems.   0 1 2 3 4 5 6

59. Man on his own is a helpless and miserable creature.   0 1 2 3 4 5 6

Traditional Attitude toward Sex

60. People who have too much sex before marriage do not make good marriage partners.   0 1 2 3 4 5 6

61. First of all, sex is for fun.   0 1 2 3 4 5 6

62. Sexual intercourse without marriage is unnatural.   0 1 2 3 4 5 6

63. Being too preoccupied with sex is a sign of being mentally unbalanced.   0 1 2 3 4 5 6

64. Most people can't control what they do sexually, as it is a matter of how strong the sex drive is.   0 1 2 3 4 5 6

65. Most men talk about love but are really only interested in sex.   0 1 2 3 4 5 6

66. It is possible to have intimate loving relations without sex.   0 1 2 3 4 5 6

67. People who have too much sexual experience have difficulty being faithful to just one person.   0 1 2 3 4 5 6

68. The man is ultimately responsible for the consequences of sexuality (e.g., pregnancy).   0 1 2 3 4 5 6

The following are statements made by people around the country about censorship. Please indicate whether you AGREE VERY MUCH, AGREE ON THE WHOLE, AGREE A LITTLE, ARE UNDECIDED, DISAGREE A LITTLE, DISAGREE ON THE WHOLE, or DISAGREE VERY MUCH with each one.

Approval of Censorship

69. I doubt if censorship is wise.   0 1 2 3 4 5 6

70. A truly free people must be allowed to choose their own reading and entertainment.   0 1 2 3 4 5 6

71. We must have censorship to protect the morals of young people.　0 1 2 3 4 5 6

72. The theory of censorship is sound, but censors make a mess of it.　0 1 2 3 4 5 6

73. Only narrow-minded Puritans want censorship.　0 1 2 3 4 5 6

74. The whole theory of censorship is utterly unreasonable.　0 1 2 3 4 5 6

75. Until public taste has been educated, we must continue to have censorship.　0 1 2 3 4 5 6

76. Many of our greatest literary classics would be suppressed if the censors thought they could get away with it.　0 1 2 3 4 5 6

77. Everything that is printed for publication should first be examined by government censors.　0 1 2 3 4 5 6

78. Plays and movies should be censored but the press should be free.　0 1 2 3 4 5 6

79. Censorship has practically no effect on people's morals.　0 1 2 3 4 5 6

80. Censorship is a gross violation of our constitutional rights.　0 1 2 3 4 5 6

81. Censorship protects those who lack judgment or experience to choose for themselves.　0 1 2 3 4 5 6

82. Censorship is a very difficult problem and I am not sure how far I think it should go.　0 1 2 3 4 5 6

83. Censorship is a good thing on the whole   0 1 2 3 4 5 6
    although it is often abused.

84. Education of the public taste is prefer-   0 1 2 3 4 5 6
    able to censorship.

85. Human progress demands free speech   0 1 2 3 4 5 6
    and free press.

86. Censorship is effective in raising moral   0 1 2 3 4 5 6
    and aesthetic standards.

87. Censorship might be warranted if we   0 1 2 3 4 5 6
    could get reasonable censors.

88. Morality is produced by self-control,   0 1 2 3 4 5 6
    not by censorship.

89. What is the attitude towards nudity in your home?
     0 Very casual, much nudity
     1 Casual, some nudity
     2 Concerned that people are prop-
      erly covered
     3 Very concerned that people
      are properly covered

90. How often is sex the topic of general family conversation?
     0 Frequently
     1 Occasionally
     2 Seldom
     3 Never

91. How often do you talk to your children individually about sexual matters?

                   0 Frequently
                   1 Occasionally
                   2 Seldom
                   3 Never

92. How often do you and your spouse talk about sexual matters?

                   0 Frequently
                   1 Occasionally
                   2 Seldom
                   3 Never

93. Have you ever given your children books or pamphlets on sexual subjects?

                   0 Yes
                   1 No

94. How do you handle things which you feel your children shouldn't read or see?

95. Are your children now receiving or have they ever received formal sex education?

                   0 Yes
                   1 No

96. Have you yourself ever attended a school that offered a course on sex education?

                   0 Yes
                   1 No

97. If yes, did you ever take the course?

                   0 Yes
                   1 No

98. Were you ever exposed to pornography as a child? How much? In what ways were you exposed to it?

99. How did your parents react when they learned of your exposure to pornography when you were a child?

100. What is your general position on censorship?

101. How does the community at large feel about your position on the pornography issue?
   - 0 Apathetic
   - 1 Disagree with you
   - 2 Agree partly
   - 3 Agree strongly
   - 4 Agree no matter what

102. What groups or people in the community tend to agree with you?

102a. Why do you think they agree?

103. What groups or people in the community tend to disagree with you?

103a. Why do you think they disagree?

104. Are you associated with the antiobscenity organization here in town?
   - 0 Official member
   - 1 Directly associated
   - 2 Indirectly associated
   - 3 Not associated
   - 4 Opposed

IF MEMBER OR ASSOCIATED, OR KNOWS ABOUT THE
ORGANIZATION (MAY BE OPPOSED TO ORGANIZATION),
ASK:

105. Could you tell me the name of the antiobscenity organization here in town?

106. Who do you see as the key or most influential members in this group?

107. What are the goals of this organization?

108. How exactly do you expect to accomplish these goals?

109. How many of these goals do you really think will come about?
    0 All or most
    1 Some
    2 Few
    3 None

FOR DECENCY CRUSADE PARTICIPANTS ONLY. IF NOT,
GO TO QUESTION 119.

110. How many meetings of the group have you attended?

111. What are the reasons you joined this organization?

112. Do you hold an office in this organization?
    0 Yes
    1 No

113. Are you on committees?
    0 Yes
    1 No

114. Are you trying to get additional members for this group?
    0 Yes
    1 No

115. How often do you talk about the organization and its activities and goals outside the meetings, e.g., to business associates?

0   Quite a bit
1   Sometimes
2   Rarely
3   Never

116. How many similar organizations do you belong to *now*?

117. Have you been involved in similar activities or groups or activities having to do with the issue of pornography or censorship in the past?

0   Yes
1   No

117a. If yes, what were they?

(IF 111 ANSWERED, GO TO 119)

118. Exactly how did you get involved in the present activity?

119. Will you give us a definition of pornography or obscenity? Is there a difference between "obscenity" and "pornography"? If so, what is it?

120. Can you give us some examples of what you feel are pornographic movies or films? Are they completely or partially obscene? (If partially, what parts, activities, language?) Have you seen them or did someone tell you about them? If nothing is obscene, would you put restrictions on any kinds of movies or films?

121. Can you give us examples of what you feel to be pornographic books? Are they completely or partially obscene? (If partially, what parts, activities, language, etc.?) Have you read them?

122. Now about magazines. Which ones do you feel to be obscene?

IF NOT MENTIONED, ASK: Is *Playboy* obscene?

123. Now about TV. Are there any programs you feel to be obscene? What is your position on censorship of certain programs, language, etc.?

124. What kinds of people do you think make pornography?

125. Do you think organized crime is connected with pornography?

     0 Very much
     1 Somewhat or indirectly
     2 Not at all

126. Do you think communists are connected with pornography?

     0 Very much
     1 Somewhat or indirectly
     2 Not at all

127. What kinds of people are attracted to or use pornography?

128. What are the effects of pornography?

129. In what ways are you different from those who are attracted to or use pornography? If respondent does not differ, ask him how he differs from people who join decency crusades.

130. Is there a sexual revolution going on? IF YES: Is pornography related to this? IF YES: How is the present sexual scene different from when you were young? (Causes and examples)

131. What do you see as the future of obscenity and pornography in the nation? (Will it increase, more and more reaction against it, etc.?) (Ask about major events, awareness of any recent legislation, etc.)

132. Do you believe that pornography is a social problem? If yes, how serious is it as compared with other social problems?

133. Is there anything we haven't touched upon that you feel is important for us to know?

INTERVIEWER CHECK:

1. Was respondent receptive?
   0 Yes
   1 No

2. How cooperative was the respondent?
   0 Very cooperative
   1 Somewhat cooperative
   2 Somewhat uncooperative
   3 Very uncooperative

3. What questions did the respondent have difficulty with?

4. Did respondent seem embarrassed?
   0 Yes (On questions   )
   1 No

5. Did respondent feel or indicate that he felt you were "on his side"?
   0 On his side
   1 Neutral
   2 On other side

Notes

1. Introduction: Theoretical Aspects of Antipornography Crusades

1. Aberle 1966; Ash 1972; Blumer 1939; 1951; 1957; Brown 1965; Cameron 1966; Evans, ed. 1969; Gusfield 1968; 1970; Heberle 1951; 1968; Killian 1964; King 1956; Klapp 1972; Lang and Lang 1961; McLaughlin 1969; Milgram and Toch 1969; Park 1927; 1934; Park and Burgess 1924; Pinard 1971; Smelser 1962; 1968; Turner and Killian 1972; Wilson 1973.

2. Feldman and Thielbar, eds. 1972; Gintis 1972; Gordon 1973; Kanter and Zurcher, eds. 1973; Keniston 1968; Laing 1967; Reich 1970; Roszak 1969; Slater 1970; Yablonsky 1968.

3. We use the words *hypothesis* and *test* throughout the book, with full realization that several of our assessments are more explorations of patterns of relations than tests of specific hypotheses. Furthermore, we are aware that our mode of assessment often shifts between, and sometimes merges, the verificational and analytical approaches to research design (see Zetterberg 1965). Given our intention to synthesize assorted levels of data drawn from diverse sources and to weave that synthesis into a natural-history framework, we do not feel remiss in using whatever mode of assessment best helps interpret the data at hand.

4. For other studies using and critiquing the value-added scheme see Brown 1965; Fendrich and Pearson 1970; Hundley 1966; Lewis 1972; Milgram and Toch 1969; Oberschall 1968; Quarantelli and Hundley 1969. Thorough general critiques of the Smelser theory are provided by Berk 1974a; 1974b; Brown and Gouldin 1973; Currie and Skolnick 1970; Manning 1971; Pfautz 1963.

5. See Abcarian and Stanage 1965; Adorno et al. 1950; Apter 1964; Barker 1963; Bell 1961; Bell, ed. 1955; 1963; Bittner 1963; Chesler and Schmuck 1963; Dean 1961; Dicks 1950; Eitzen 1970b; Ferkiss 1962; Fromm 1941; Gerth 1940; Gusfield 1963; Hoffer 1951; Hofstadter 1954; 1955; 1967; Hunt and Cushing 1970; Kerr 1952; Kirkpatrick 1949; Krout and Stagner 1939; Ladd 1966; Lasswell 1930; Levinson and Huffman 1955; Lipset 1955; 1959; 1960; 1963; Lipset and Raab 1969; 1970; McClosky 1958; McCormack 1950; Polsby 1963; Reich 1946; Riley and Pettigrew 1969; Ringer and Sills 1952–1953; Rohter 1967; 1970; Rokeach 1960; Rush 1967; Trow 1958; Walzer 1965; Wolfinger et al. 1964.

6. Bauman 1968; Brandmeyer 1965; Broom and Jones 1970; Goffman 1957; Kelly and Chambliss 1966; Kenkel 1956; Laumann and Segal 1971; Lenski 1954;

1956; 1966; 1967; Olsen and Tully 1972; Portes 1970*a*; 1970*b*; Ringer and Sills 1952–1953; Segal 1969; 1970; Segal and Knoke 1968; Smith 1969.

7. Eitzen 1970*a*; Hunt and Cushing 1970; Lipset 1959; 1963; 1967; Riley and Pettigrew 1969; Rohter 1970; Rush 1967; Trow 1958.

8. Fauman 1968; Treiman 1966.

9. Blalock 1967*a*; Bloombaum 1964; Fenchel, Monderer, and Hartley 1951.

10. Demerath 1965.

11. Curtis 1970; Dohrenwend 1966; Geschwender 1967; Jackson 1962; Jackson and Burke 1965; Martin 1965; Meile and Haesse 1969; Parker 1963.

12. Berelson, Lazarsfeld, and McPhee 1954; Lane 1959; Lazarsfeld, Berelson, and Gaudet 1944.

13. Geschwender 1968; Orum 1974.

14. Chiricos, Pearson, and Fendrich 1970; Marx 1969; Pinard 1969; Surace and Seeman 1967.

15. Adams 1953; Brandon 1965; Exline and Ziller 1959; Sampson 1963.

16. Brandmeyer 1965; Broom and Jones 1970; Kelly and Chambliss 1966; Kenkel 1956; Laumann and Segal 1971; Olsen and Tully 1972; Orum 1974; Portes 1970*a*; 1970*b*; Surace and Seeman 1967.

17. Geschwender 1968; Jackson 1962; Segal 1969; Segal and Knoke 1968; Smith 1969; Treiman 1966.

18. Bauman 1968; Bloombaum 1964; Brandon 1965; Chiricos, Pearson, and Fendrich 1970; Curtis 1970; Dohrenwend 1966; Eitzen 1970*b*; Hunt and Cushing 1970; Lane 1959; Martin 1965; Meile and Haesse 1969; Parker 1963.

19. Berelson, Lazarsfeld, and McPhee 1954; Demerath 1965; Eitzen 1970*b*; Jackson and Burke 1965; Lazarsfeld, Berelson, and Gaudet 1944; Rohter 1970; Sampson 1963.

20. Blalock 1965; 1966; 1967*b*; 1967*c*; Hyman 1966; Jackson and Curtis 1968; Kasl 1969; Mitchell 1964; Robinson and Shaver 1969.

21. Bauman 1968; Bloombaum 1964; Brandon 1965; Chiricos, Pearson, and Fendrich 1970; Curtis 1970; Hunt and Cushing 1970; Kelly and Chambliss 1966; Mitchell 1964; Segal 1969.

22. Anderson and Dynes 1973; Dickson 1968; Gusfield 1955*b*; 1957; 1963; King 1956; Lipset 1950; Messinger 1955; Myers 1971; Nelson 1967; 1971; Rudwick and Meier 1970; Warburton 1967; Zald and Denton 1963.

23. Several other authors have discussed the analysis of collective behavior as it articulates with or is part of institutional or organizational structure. See, for example, Brown and Gouldin 1973; Couch 1968; 1970; Dynes and Quarantelli 1968; Janowitz 1964; McPhail 1969; Oberschall 1973; Pfautz 1963; Turner 1964; Weller and Quarantelli 1973.

24. Broyles 1964; Gurlach and Hine 1970; Gusfield 1957; Holtzman 1963; Lipset 1950; McCarthy and Zald 1973; Messinger 1955; Turner 1967; Ware 1970; Zald 1970; Zald and Denton 1963.

25. Couch 1970; Kerckhoff, Back, and Miller 1965; Morrison and Steves 1967; Pinard 1969; Smith 1966; Weiss 1963.

26. Bell 1957; Bruce 1971; Erbe 1964; Freedman and Axelrod 1952; Hagedorn and Labovitz 1968a; 1968b; Hastings 1954; Maccoby 1958; Mizruchi 1960; Rose 1959; Vorwaller 1970; Wilenski 1961.

27. At the time we were conducting the research for the Commission on Obscenity and Pornography (1969–1970), there was widespread publicity concerning antipornography efforts and considerable conflict between Conporns and Proporns nationally. There were not infrequent instances of Conporns and Proporns being harassed by anonymous, insulting telephone calls and letters. We concluded, with the staff of the commission, that it would be best to disguise as much as feasible the cities, specific organizations, and pertinent individuals involved in the crusades we were studying.

28. Our procedures for gathering the natural-history data were guided by Adams and Preiss, eds. 1960; Becker 1958; Bruyn 1966; Filstead, ed. 1970; Gold 1958; Gottschalk, Kluckhohn, and Angell 1945; Gusfield 1955a; Junker 1960; McCall and Simmons 1969; Taylor, Zurcher, and Key 1970; Vidich, Bensman, and Stein, eds. 1964; Webb et al. 1966; Zurcher 1970. Our procedures for developing the structured questionnaire, for gathering the interview data, and for content-analyzing responses to open-ended items were guided by Bonjean, Hill, and McLemore, eds. 1967; Cannell and Kahn 1968; Gorden 1969; Holsti 1969; Kahn and Cannell 1957; Moser and Kalton 1972; Robinson and Shaver 1969.

29. Several collective-behavior theorists, notably Smelser, have been criticized for representing a "managerial," "establishment," social-control bias in favor of the status quo and opposed to social change. For examples of such critiques, see Berk 1972; 1974a; 1974b; Bramson 1961; Brown and Gouldin 1973; Currie and Skolnick 1970; Skolnick 1969.

2. Structural Conduciveness: "A Little Slice of Real America"

1. These and other descriptive Midville data were drawn from the *Greater Midville Chamber of Commerce Statistical Data Sheet*, 1969, and from the 1960 U.S. Census.

2. These and other descriptive Southtown data were drawn from *Basic Data: Southtown and Central County 1969; High Points in Southtown's History*, 1969; and the 1960 U.S. Census.

3. Structural Strain: "Changes Are Raging out of Control!"

1. Establishment of pornography as a summary symbol for a broad range of

challenges to life style will become more apparent in the discussion of generalized beliefs in Chapter 4.

2. For detailed descriptions of "adult" bookstore patrons, see Commission on Obscenity and Pornography 1970:157–160; Finkelstein 1971; Kutschinsky 1971; Massey 1971; Nawy 1971; Winick 1971.

3. The distribution of patrons in the Avalon and Bijou theaters conformed to general findings concerning attendance at "adult" movie theaters, given variations in the ethnic makeup of the communities. See, for example, Commission on Obscenity and Pornography 1970:160–162; Massey 1971; Nawy 1971; Winick 1971.

4. We use the term *strain* to indicate disequilibrium, inconsistency, or conflict among the components of social structure *and* to indicate the psychological stress which may be experienced by individuals who perceive the disequilibrium, inconsistency, or conflict.

4. Generalized Beliefs: "Pornography Is Leading Us to the Fall of Rome!"

1. See also Blumer 1939; Shibutani 1966; Turner and Surace 1956.

2. In our opinion, the process of short-circuiting is not unique to social movements but is operative in much highly institutionalized behavior as well. Nor do we feel that short-circuiting is necessarily irrational. It may be quite rational in the context of its occurence, though pronounced irrational by those who reject or are not familiar with that context. For arguments relevant to the issue of rationality-irrationality in collective behavior, see Berk 1974a; 1974b; Berk and Aldrich 1972; Bohannon 1958; Brissett 1968; Dynes and Quarantelli 1970; Oberschall 1968; Smith 1968; Turner and Killian 1972; Wanderer 1968; 1969.

6. Mobilization for Action: "We Showed Them Where We Stand!"

1. These and subsequent announcements concerning the visit of "representatives" from the Commission on Obscenity and Pornography were to create an interesting initial problem for us, in our efforts to study the Midville antipornography crusade. Some of the Conporns seemed to have the impression that we were a team of crack FBI troops who had been sent in by J. Edgar Hoover, or at least by Spiro Agnew, once and for all to crush the infamous Midwestern Bookstore. Some of the Proporns initially assumed that we were at least hyperliberal super-Naders who had come to Midville in order to put the Conporns in their place. More than a few of the Controls we contacted seemed to be afraid that we were actually lawyers who were conniving to involve them somehow in the million-dollar lawsuit the bookstore had lodged

against the Conporns. We immediately had to rectify those expectations and were able to do so by citing our research role.

We were less successful in overcoming the assumption of the management and employees of the Midwestern Bookstore that we were, at best, John-Birch-oriented social scientists who had been contracted by the Conporns to gather information which would help drive the bookstore out of business. On our first day of attempts to interview Midwestern Bookstore personnel, we somewhat naïvely walked into the store, smilingly introduced ourselves, and with our by now (we thought) quite polished approach asked the supervising male employee if we could interview him. He leaned back in his chair and pointedly responded, "I want no part of the bullshit from a bunch of quacks." (We had some difficulty coding that response.) We asked him what he meant, and he pointed to the questionnaires we were holding. We told him that he was mistaken if he thought we were part of the antipornography organization, to which he responded, simply, "Bullshit!" We suggested that we were interested in getting his opinions about the antipornography activity, to which he responded: "We don't want our opinions registered. We don't give a shit what happens. . . . We just want to be left alone." At that point, we took our leave. The man we had attempted to interview was Mr. Smith, who (as noted in the narrative) was under heavy bail bond, was a witness for the plaintiff in the lawsuit, and understandably wanted to be left alone. Subsequently, however, we were able to interview two of the bookstore employees informally.

2. In an attempt to learn something about the characteristics of those individuals who were affiliated with but not active members of ICCD, we decided to send a brief questionnaire by mail to a random sample of one hundred persons from among the list of eight thousand ICCD auxiliary members. The questionnaire contained items inquiring about demographic characteristics, attitudes, etc., and essentially was an abbreviated version of the field questionnaire. Over a period of thirty days, we received fifty responses, but very few of them were usable for the purpose of comparing the respondents with the Conporns and Proporns. Most of the questionnaires were incomplete, and many had editorial comments which, though interesting, were not responsive. One returned interview advised us, for example: "Why are you asking me all these questions? Ask Jesus Christ. He's got the answers." Another warned us that we had better hurry up and finish our study, and the commission had better hurry up with its report, because the end of the world was only a few weeks away. Another respondent simply suggested, "Why don't you stop studying this stuff and go out and get laid!" We concluded that the latter probably was *not* a Conporn.

3. Two weeks prior to the rally, UFD leadership had generously given us permission to administer a one-page questionnaire to all the individuals in the audience. Our intention was simply to assess the demographic characteristics of the audience members, their other voluntary associations, how far they had

traveled to the rally, how they had been recruited, and so on—information of that kind did not exist in the literature. With lack of foresight, we included two items in the short questionnaire which had to do with attitudes toward religion and sexual behavior. Those items were objected to on the night of the rally by some of the rally organizers. Rather than force the issue and jeopardize our rapport with the Conporns, we withdrew the questionnaire and lost the opportunity.

4. See also Gusfield 1963:76, 80–81, 88–93, 124–125, 129–131, 149–152; Lang and Lang 1961:522–523; Nelson 1971; Roche and Sachs 1965.

7. Social Control: "Decency Cannot Be Stopped!"

1. For other discussions of social control in collective behavior, see Janowitz 1968; Lang and Lang 1961; Smith 1968; Turner and Killian 1972; Westley 1957.

8. Conporns versus Proporns

1. Dean 1961; Neal and Rettig 1963; measured in this study by a three-item short form of the Dean (1961) Powerlessness Scale developed by Straus and Nelson (1960).

2. Dean 1961; Neal and Rettig 1963; measured in this study by two items of the three-item short form of the Dean Normlessness Scale developed by Straus and Nelson (1960).

3. Dean 1961; derived by summing Powerlessness and Normlessness scale scores.

4. Adorno et al. 1950; measured in this study by five items from the six-item Sanford and Older (1950) short form of the Adorno Authoritarianism Scale.

5. Kirkpatrick 1949; measured in this study by six items selected randomly from the twelve-item Kirkpatrick Religiosity Scale.

6. Levinson and Huffman 1955; measured in this study by five items selected randomly from the twelve-item short form of the Levinson and Huffman Traditional Family Ideology Scale.

7. Stouffer 1955; measured in this study by a three-item short form of the Stouffer Political Intolerance Scale developed by Straus and Nelson (1960). This measure lacks assessment of tolerance for conservative nonconformists.

8. Rokeach 1960; measured in this study by a ten-item short form of the Rokeach Dogmatism Scale, developed by Trodahl and Powell (1965).

9. Institute for Sex Research 1968; measured in this study by nine items selected from the Institute for Sex Research Traditional View of Sex Scale.

10. Rosander and Thurston 1931; measured in this study by the twenty-item (Form B) Rosander and Thurston Attitude toward Censorship Scale.

11. Bender 1971; Byrne and Lamberth 1971; Commission on Obscenity and Pornography 1970:43, 45, 250; Katzman 1971; Kronhausen and Kronhausen 1959; 14–24; Mosher 1971; Wallace, Wehmer, and Podany 1971.

12. See, for example, Commission on Obscenity and Pornography 1970:30; Gallup Poll 1969; Katzman 1971; Reed and Reed 1970; Wallace, Wehmer, and Podany 1971.

13. See, for example, Abcarian and Stanage 1965; Bell 1955; Hofstadter 1967; Ladd 1966; Lipset 1955; Lipset and Raab 1969; Rohter 1967; Trow 1958; Wolfinger et al. 1964.

14. See, for example, Bittner 1963; Flacks 1967; Krout and Stagner 1939; Lipset and Wolin, eds. 1965; McCormack 1950; Peterson 1968; Surace and Seeman 1967; Watts and Whittaker 1966; Westby and Braungart 1966.

15. For other arguments concerning the importance of placing considerations of general individual or social-psychological characteristics of protest movement participants into the broader social context, see Marx 1969:198–204; Orum 1974; Turner and Killian, 1972:247–251; Zygmunt 1972. Smelser (1962), of course, presents the same argument.

16. See, for example, Bloombaum 1964; Brandon 1965; Chiricos, Pearson, and Fendrich 1970; Curtis 1970; Fauman 1968; Hunt and Cushing 1970; Kelly and Chambliss 1966; Mitchell 1964; Segal 1969.

17. See, for example, Curtis and Zurcher 1971; Erbe 1964; Hagedorn and Labovitz 1968a; Maccoby 1958; Rose 1959; Teele 1967; Vorwaller 1970.

18. See also Easton 1965; Lipset 1960; Parsons et al. 1961.

9. Organizational Characteristics of the Antipornography Crusades

1. See also Lang and Lang 1961; Nelson 1971; Roche and Sachs 1965; Turner and Killian 1957; 1972.

2. In order to distinguish between organizational and individual-level linkages, the former is referred to as an *alignment* and the latter as an *affiliation*, with the focal units being designated, respectively, as *alignees* and *affiliates*.

3. Bruce 1971; Vorwaller 1970; Wilenski 1961.

4. Erbe 1964; Freedman and Axelrod 1952; Hastings 1954; Maccoby 1958.

5. Bell 1957; Hagedorn and Labovitz 1968b; Mizruchi 1960; Rose 1959.

10. Conclusions

1. Berk 1972; Lang and Lang 1961; Lewis 1972; Manning 1973; Milgram and Toch 1969; Pfautz 1961; Quarantelli and Hundley 1969; Turner and Killian 1972.

2. Other discussions pertinent to the analysis of collective behavior phe-

nomena as developing processes include Brissett 1968; Fisher 1972; McPhail 1972; Manning 1973; Pfautz 1961; Swanson 1970.

11. After the Crusades: The Commission Reports, Conporns Respond, and the Supreme Court Redeems Itself

1. For further comment on the Report of the Commission on Obscenity and Pornography, see Clor 1971; Johnson 1971; Rist 1973; Wilson 1971.

2. See Gluckman 1963:110–136; Klapp 1972:162–212; Turner and Killian 1972:424–425.

Bibliography

Abcarian, G., and S. M. Stanage
   1965 "Alienation and the Radical Right." *Journal of Politics* 27 (November): 776–796.
Aberle, D.
   1966 *The Peyote Religion among the Navajo*. Chicago: Aldine.
Adams, R. N., and J. J. Preiss, eds.
   1960 *Human Organizational Research*. Homewood, Ill.: Dorsey.
Adams, S.
   1953 "Status Congruency as a Variable in Small Group Research." *Social Forces* 32 (October):16–22.
Adorno, T., E. Frenkel-Brunswik, D. J. Levinson, and R. N. Sanford
   1950 *The Authoritarian Personality*. New York: Harper and Row.
Agger, R. E., M. N. Goldstein, and S. A. Pearl
   1961 "Political Cynicism: Measurement and Meaning." *Journal of Politics* 23 (August):477–506.
Almond, G. A.
   1960 "Introduction: A Functional Approach to Comparative Politics." In *The Politics of the Developing Areas*, edited by idem and J. S. Coleman, pp. 16–50. Princeton: Princeton University Press.
Anderson, W. A., and R. R. Dynes
   1973 "Organization and Political Transformation of a Social Movement: A Study of the 30th of May Movement in Curacao." *Social Forces* 51 (March). 330–341.
Apter, D. E., ed.
   1964 *Ideology and Discontent*. New York: Free Press.
Ash, R.
   1972 *Social Movements in America*. Chicago: Markham.
Babchuk, N., and A. Booth
   1969 "Voluntary Association Membership: A Longitudinal Analysis." *American Sociological Review* 34 (February):31–45.
Barker, E. N.
   1963 "Authoritarianism of the Political Right, Center, and Left." *Journal of Social Issues* 19 (April):63–74.
Barton, A. H., and P. F. Lazarsfeld
   1969 "Some Functions of Qualitative Analysis in Social Research." In *Issues*

in Participant Observation: A Text and Reader, edited by G. J. McCall and J. L. Simmons, pp. 163–205. Reading, Mass.: Addison-Wesley.

Bauman, K. E.
   1968 "Status Inconsistency, Satisfactory Social Interaction, and Community Satisfaction in an Area of Rapid Growth." *Social Forces* 47 (October): 45–52.

Becker, H. S.
   1958 "Problems of Inference and Proof in Participant Observation." *American Sociological Review* 23 (December):652–660.
   1963 *The Outsiders: Studies in the Sociology of Deviance*. New York: Free Press.

Bell, D.
   1961 "Status Politics and New Anxieties: On the 'Radical Right' and Ideologies of the Fifties." In *The End of Ideology*, edited by idem, pp. 103–123. New York: Free Press.

Bell, D., ed.
   1955 *The New American Right*. New York: Criterion.
   1963 *The Radical Right*. New York: Doubleday.

Bell, W.
   1957 "Anomie, Social Isolation and Class Structure." *Sociometry* 20 (June): 105–116.

Bender, P.
   1971 "Definition of 'Obscene' under Existing Law." In *Technical Reports of the Commission on Obscenity and Pornography*, II, 5–27. Washington, D.C.: Government Printing Office.

Berelson, B., P. F. Lazarsfeld, and W. McPhee
   1954 *Voting*. Chicago: University of Chicago Press.

Berk, R. A.
   1972 "The Controversy surrounding Collective Violence: Some Methodological Notes." In *Collective Violence*, edited by J. Short and M. Wolfgang, pp. 112–118. Chicago: Aldine-Atherton.
   1974a *Collective Behavior*. Dubuque, Iowa: W. C. Brown.
   1974b "A Gaming Approach to Crowd Behavior." *American Sociological Review* 29 (June):335–373.

Berk, R. A., and H. E. Aldrich
   1972 "Patterns of Vandalism during Civil Disorders as an Indicator of Selection of Targets." *American Sociological Review* 37 (October):533–547.

Bittner, E.
   1963 "Radicalism and the Organization of Radical Movements." *American Sociological Review* 28 (December):928–940.

Blalock, H. M.
   1965 "Theory Building and the Statistical Concept of Interaction." *American Sociological Review* 30 (June):374–380.
   1966 "The Identification Problem and Theory Building: The Case of Status Inconsistency." *American Sociological Review* 31 (February):52–61.

1967a "Status Inconsistency, Social Mobility, Status Integration and Structural Effects." *American Sociological Review* 32 (October):790–801.
1967b "Tests of Status Inconsistency Theory: A Note of Caution." *Pacific Sociological Review* 10 (Fall):69–74.
1967c "Status Inconsistency and Interaction: Some Alternative Models." *American Journal of Sociology* 73 (November):305–315.
Bloombaum, M.
1964 "Mobility Dimension in Status Consistency." *Sociology and Social Research* 48 (April):340–347.
Blumer, H.
1939 "Collective Behavior." In *An Outline of the Principles of Sociology*, edited by R. E. Park, pp. 221–280. New York: Barnes and Noble.
1951 "Collective Behavior." In *New Outline of the Principles of Sociology*, edited by A. M. Lee, pp. 167–222. New York: Barnes and Noble.
1957 "Collective Behavior." In *Review of Sociology*, edited by J. Gittler, pp. 127–158. New York: Wiley.
Bohannon, P.
1958 "Extra-Processual Events in Tiv Political Institutions." *American Anthropologist* 60 (February):1–12.
Bonjean, C. M., R. J. Hill, and S. D. McLemore, eds.
1967 *Sociological Measurement: An Inventory of Scales and Indices*. San Francisco: Chandler.
Booth, A., and N. Babchuk
1969 "Personal Influence Networks and Voluntary Association Affiliation." *Sociological Inquiry* 39 (Spring):179–188.
Bradburn, N. M., and Caplovitz, D.
1965 *Reports on Happiness*. Chicago: Aldine.
Bramson, L.
1961 *The Political Context of Sociology*. Princeton: Princeton University Press.
Brandmeyer, G.
1965 "Status Consistency and Political Behavior: A Replication and Extension of Research." *Sociological Quarterly* 6 (July):241–256.
Brandon, A. C.
1965 "Status Congruence and Expectations." *Sociometry* 28 (September): 272–288.
Brissett, D.
1968 "Collective Behavior: The Sense of a Rubric." *American Journal of Sociology* 74 (July):70–78.
Broom, L., and F. L. Jones
1970 "Status Consistency and Political Preference: The Australian Case." *American Sociological Review* 35 (December):989–1001.
Broom, L., and P. Selznick
1968 "Collective Behavior." In their *Sociology*, Ch. 8. New York: Harper and Row.

Brown, M. and A. Gouldin
   1973 *Collective Behavior*. Pacific Palisades, Calif.: Goodyear.
Brown, R.
   1965 "Collective Behavior and the Psychology of the Crowd." In his *Social Psychology*, Ch. 14. New York: Free Press.
Broyles, J. A.
   1964 *The John Birch Society: Anatomy of Protest*. Boston: Beacon.
Bruce, J. M.
   1971 "Intergenerational Occupational Mobility and Participation in Formal Associations." *Sociological Quarterly* 12 (Winter):46–55.
Bruyn, S. T.
   1966 *The Human Perspective in Sociology: The Methodology of Participant Observation*. Englewood Cliffs, N. J.: Prentice-Hall.
Butler v. *Michigan*
   1957 352 U.S. 380.
Byrne, D., and J. Lamberth
   1971 "The Effect of Erotic Stimuli on Sex Arousal, Evaluative Responses, and Subsequent Behavior." In *Technical Reports of the Commission on Obscenity and Pornography*, VIII, 41–67. Washington, D.C.: Government Printing Office.
Cain v. *Kentucky*
   1970 397 U.S. 319.
Cameron, W. B.
   1966 *Modern Social Movements: A Sociological Outline*. New York: Random House.
Campbell, A., P. E. Converse, W. E. Miller, and D. E. Stokes
   1960 *The American Voter*. New York: Wiley.
Campbell, A., G. Gurin, and W. E. Miller
   1954 *The Voter Decides*. Evanston, Ill.: Row, Peterson.
Cannell, C. F., and R. L. Kahn
   1968 "Interviewing." In *The Handbook of Social Psychology*, edited by G. Lindzey and E. Aronson, II, 526–595. Reading, Mass.: Addison-Wesley.
Chesler, M., and R. Schmuck
   1963 "Participant Observation in a Super-Patriot Discussion Group." *Journal of Social Issues* 19 (April):18–30.
Chiricos, T. G., M. A. Pearson, and J. M. Fendrich
   1970 "Status Inconsistency, Militancy and Black Identification Among Black Veterans." *Social Science Quarterly* 51 (December):572–586.
Clor, H. M.
   1969 *Obscenity and Public Morality: Censorship in a Liberal Society*. Chicago: University of Chicago Press.
   1971 "Science, Eros, and the Law: A Critique of the Obscenity Commission Report." *Dusquesne Law Review* 10 (Fall):63–76.

Commission on Obscenity and Pornography
1970 *The Report of the Commission on Obscenity and Pornography*. Washington, D.C.: Government Printing Office.
1971 *Technical Reports of the Commission on Obscenity and Pornography*. 9 vols. Washington, D.C.: Government Printing Office.
Couch, C. J.
1968 "Collective Behavior: An Examination of Some Stereotypes." *Social Problems* 15 (Winter):310–322.
1970 "Dimensions of Association in Collective Behavior Episodes." *Sociometry* 33(4):457–471.
Currie, E., and J. H. Skolnick
1970 "A Critical Note on Conceptions of Collective Behavior." *Annals of the American Academy of Political and Social Science* 391 (September):34–45.
Curtis, R. L.
1970 "Status Inconsistency: A Theory of Perception and Effects." Unpublished. University of Texas, Austin.
Curtis, R. L., and L. A. Zurcher
1971 "Voluntary Associations and the Social Integration of the Poor." *Social Problems* 18 (Winter):339–357.
Dahrendorf, R.
1959 *Conflict in Industrial Society*. Stanford: Stanford University Press.
Davis, C.
1968 *Bitches in Heat*. Cleveland, Ohio: Classics Library.
Dawson, C. A., and W. E. Gettys
1948 *An Introduction to Sociology*. New York: Ronald Press.
Dean, D. G.
1961 "Alienation: Its Meaning and Measurement." *American Sociological Review* 26 (October):753–758.
Demarath, N. J.
1965 *Social Class in American Protestantism*. Chicago: Rand-McNally.
Dicks, H. V.
1950 "Personality Traits and National Socialist Ideology." *Human Relations* 3:111–154.
Dickson, D. T.
1968 "Bureaucracy and Morality: An Organizational Perspective on a Moral Crusade." *Social Problems* 16 (Fall):143–156.
Dohrenwend, B. P.
1966 "Social Status and Psychological Disorder." *American Sociological Review* 31 (February):14–35.
Durkheim, E.
1966 *The Division of Labor in Society* (1893). Reprint. New York: Free Press.
Dynes, R. R., and E. L. Quarantelli
1968 "Group Behavior under Stress: A Required Convergence of Organiza-

tional and Collective Behavior Perspectives." *Sociology and Social Research* 52 (July):416–429.

Easton, D.

1965 *A Systems Analysis of Political Life*. New York: Wiley.

Eitzen, D. S.

1970a "Status Inconsistency and Wallace Supporters in a Midwestern City." *Social Forces* 48 (June):493–498.

1970b "Social Class, Status Inconsistency and Political Attitudes." *Social Science Quarterly* 51 (December):602–609.

Elkin, F.

1960 "Censorship and Pressure Groups." *Phylon* 25 (Spring):71–80.

Erbe, W.

1964 "Social Involvement and Political Activity: A Replication and Elaboration." *American Sociological Review* 29 (April):198–215.

Evans, R. R., ed.

1969 *Readings in Collective Behavior*. Chicago: Rand-McNally.

Exline, R. V., and R. C. Ziller

1959 "Status Congruency and Interpersonal Conflict in Decision-Making Groups." *Human Relations* 12 (May):147–162.

Fauman, F. J.

1968 "Status Crystallization and Interracial Attitudes." *Social Forces* 47 (September):53–60.

Feldman, S. D., and G. W. Thielbar, eds.

1972 *Life Styles: Diversity in American Society*. Boston: Little, Brown.

Fenchel, G. H., J. H. Monderer, and E. L. Hartley

1951 "Subjective Status and the Equilibration Hypothesis." *Journal of Abnormal and Social Psychology* 46 (October):476–479.

Fendrich, J. M., and M. A. Pearson

1970 "Alienation and Its Correlates among Black Veterans." *Sociological Symposium* 4 (Spring):55–85.

Ferkiss, V. C.

1962 "Political and Intellectual Origins of American Radicalism, Right and Left." *Annals of the American Academy of Political and Social Science* 344 (November):6.

Festinger, L.

1957 *A Theory of Cognitive Dissonance*. Evanston: Row, Peterson.

1964 *Conflict, Decision and Dissonance*. Stanford: Stanford University Press.

Filstead, W. J., ed.

1970 *Qualitative Methodology*. Chicago: Markham.

Finkelstein, M. M.

1971 "Traffic in Sex Oriented Materials, Part I: Adult Bookstores in Boston, Massachusetts." In *Technical Reports of the Commission on Obscenity and Pornography*, IV, 99–154. Washington, D.C.: Government Printing Office.

Fisher, C.
1972 "Observing a Crowd." In *Research on Deviance*, edited by J. Douglas. New York: Random House.
Flacks, R.
1967 "The Liberated Generation: An Exploration of the Roots of Student Protest." *Journal of Social Issues* 23 (Winter):52–75.
Freedman, R., and M. Axelrod
1952 "Who Belongs to What in a Great Metropolis?" *Adult Leadership* 1 (November):6–9.
Fromm, E.
1941 *Escape from Freedom*. New York: Farrar and Rienhart.
Gallup Poll
1969 *Gallup Opinion Index, Report Number* 49 (July):16–24.
Gamson, W. A.
1968 *Power and Discontent*. Homewood, Ill: Dorsey.
1969 "Political Trust and Its Ramifications." Paper presented at the meeting of the Southwestern Sociological Association, Dallas.
Gergen, K. J.
1973 "Social Psychology as History." *Journal of Personality and Social Psychology* 26 (May):309–320.
Gerth, H.
1940 "The Nazi Party: Its Leadership and Composition." *American Journal of Sociology* 45 (January):517–541.
Geschwender, J. A.
1967 "Continuities in Theories of Status Consistency and Cognitive Dissonance." *Social Forces* 46 (December):160–171.
1968 "Status Inconsistency, Social Isolation, and Individual Unrest." *Social Forces* 46 (June):477–483.
Gibbs, J. P.
1972 *A Mode of Formal Theory Construction*. New York: Dryden.
Gintis, H.
1972 "Activism and Counter-Culture: The Dialectics of Consciousness in a Corporate State," *TELOS* 12 (Summer):42–63.
Ginzburg v. *United States*
1966 383 U.S. 463.
Gluckman, M.
1963 *Order and Rebellion in Tribal Africa*. New York: Free Press.
Goering, O. J., J. B. McLaird, and W. E. Coates
1969 "The 'Candy' Controversy: A Study in Community Censorship." Paper presented at the meeting of the Southern Sociological Society, New Orleans.
Goffman, I. W.
1957 "Status Consistency and Preference for Change in Power Distribution." *American Sociological Review* 22 (June):275–281.

Gold, R. L.
1958 "Roles in Sociological Field Observations," *Social Forces* 36 (March): 217–223.
Gorden, R. L.
1969 *Interviewing: Strategy, Techniques and Tactics*. Homewood, Ill.: Dorsey.
Gordon, F.
1973 "A Class Analysis of Radical Student Movements." *The New Scholar* 4 (Fall):5–16.
Gottschalk, L., C. Kluckhohn, and R. Angell
1945 *The Use of Personal Documents in History, Anthropology and Sociology*. New York: Social Science Research Counsel.
Greer, S., and P. Orleans
1962 "The Mass Society and Parapolitical Structure." *American Sociological Review* 27 (October):634–646.
Gurlach, L., and V. Hine
1970 *People, Power and Change: Movements of Social Transformation*. New York: Bobbs-Merrill.
Gusfield, J. R.
1955a "Field Work Reciprocities in Studying a Social Movement." *Human Organization* 14(3):29–33.
1955b "Social Structure and Moral Reform: A Study of the Women's Christian Temperance Union." *American Journal of Sociology* 61 (November):221–232.
1957 "The Problems of Generations in an Organizational Structure." *Social Forces* 35 (May):323–330.
1963 *Symbolic Crusade: Status Politics and the American Temperance Movement*. Urbana: University of Illinois Press.
1968 "The Study of Social Movements." In *Encyclopedia of the Social Sciences*, edited by D. L. Sills, XIV, 444–452. 2d ed. New York: Macmillan and the Free Press.
1970 *Protest, Reform, and Revolt: A Reader in Social Movements*. New York: Wiley.
Hagedorn, R., and S. Labovitz
1968a "The Differential Political Activity of Participants in a Voluntary Association." *American Sociological Review* 23 (October):524–532.
1968b "Occupational Characteristics and Participation in Voluntary Associations." *Social Forces* 47 (September):16–27.
Hastings, P. K.
1954 "The Non-Voter in 1952: A Study of Pittsfield, Massachusetts." *Journal of Psychology* 38 (Fall):301–312.
Heberle, R.
1951 *Social Movements: An Introduction to Political Sociology*. New York: Appleton-Century-Crofts.
1968 "Types and Forms of Social Movements." In *Encyclopedia of the Social*

Sciences, edited by D. L. Sills, XIV, 438–452. 2d ed. New York: Macmillan and the Free Press.

Hill, M.
1970 "Pornography Report Labeled Shoddy." Interview of Hill by Philip Nobile. *National Catholic Reporter* 6 (October):1, 10–11.

Hoffer, E.
1951 *The True Believer*. New York: New American Library.

Hofstadter, R.
1954 "The Pseudo-Conservative Revolt." *American Scholar* 24 (Winter): 9–27.
1955 *The Age of Reform*. Cambridge: Harvard University Press.
1967 *The Paranoid Style in American Politics*. New York: Vintage.

Holsti, O. R.
1969 *Content Analysis for the Social Sciences and Humanities*. Reading, Mass. Addison-Wesley.

Holtzman, A.
1963 *The Townsend Movement*. New York: Bookman Associates.

Hopper, R. D.
1950 "The Revolutionary Process: A Frame of Reference for the Study of Revolutionary Movements." *Social Forces* 28 (March):270–279.

Hoyt v. *Minnesota*
1970 399 U.S. 524.

Hundley, J. R.
1966 "A Test of Theories in Collective Behavior: The National Farmers Organization." Ph.D. dissertation, Ohio State University.

Hunt, L. L., and R. G. Cushing
1970 "Status Discrepancy, Interpersonal Attachment and Right Wing Extremism." *Social Science Quarterly* 51 (December):587–602.

Hyman, M. D.
1966 "Determining the Effects of Status Inconsistency." *Public Opinion Quarterly* 30 (Spring):120–129.

Institute for Sex Research
1968 "A Scale for Traditional Attitudes toward Sex." Unpublished questionnaire. University of Indiana, Bloomington.

Jackson, E. F.
1962 "Status Consistency and Symptoms of Stress." *American Sociological Review* 27 (August):469–480.

Jackson, E. F., and B. J. Burke
1965 "Status and Symptoms of Stress: Additive and Interactive Effects." *American Sociological Review* 30 (August):556–564.

Jackson, E. F., and R. F. Curtis
1968 "Conceptualization and Measurement in the Study of Social Stratification." In *Methodology in Social Research*, edited by H. M. Blalock and A. B. Blalock, pp. 112–154. New York: McGraw-Hill.

Jackson, M., E. Peterson, J. Bull, S. Monsen, and P. Richmond
  1960 "The Failure of an Incipient Social Movement." *Pacific Sociological Review* 3 (Spring):35–40.
Jacobellis v. *Ohio*
  1964 378 U.S. 184.
Janowitz, M.
  1964 "Converging Theoretical Perspectives." *Sociological Quarterly* 5 (Spring): 113–132.
  1968 *Social Control of the Escalated Riot*. Chicago: University of Chicago Press.
Johnson, H.
  1960 *Sociology: A Systematic Introduction*. New York: Harcourt, Brace.
Johnson, W. T.
  1971 "The Pornography Report: Epistemology, Methodology and Ideology." *Dusquesne Law Review* 10 (Winter):190–219.
Junker, B. H.
  1960 *Field Work: An Introduction to the Social Sciences*. Chicago: University of Chicago Press.
Kahn, R. L., and C. F. Cannell
  1957 *The Dynamics of Interviewing: Theory, Technique and Cases*. New York: Wiley.
Kanter, R. M., and L. A. Zurcher, eds.
  1973 *Alternative Institutions. Journal of Applied Behavioral Science* 9 (May).
Kasl, S.
  1969 "Status Inconsistency: Some Conceptual and Methodological Considerations." In *Measures of Occupational Attitudes and Occupational Characteristics*, edited by J. Robinson et al., pp. 377–396. Ann Arbor, Mich.: Survey Research Center.
Katzman, M.
  1971 "The Relationship of Socio-Economic Background to Judgments of Sexual Stimulation and Their Correlation with Judgments of Obscenity." In *Technical Reports of the Commission on Obscenity and Pornography*, IX, 1–8. Washington, D.C.: Government Printing Office.
Keating, C. H.
  1971 "The Report That Shocked the Nation." *Readers Digest* (January):2–6.
Kelly, K. D., and W. J. Chambliss
  1966 "Status Consistency and Political Attitudes." *American Sociological Review* 21 (June):375–382.
Keniston, K.
  1968 *Young Radicals: Notes on Committed Youths*. New York: Harcourt, Brace and World.
Kenkel, W. F.
  1956 "The Relationship Between Status Consistency and Political-Economic Attitudes." *American Sociological Review* 21 (June):365–368.

Kerckhoff, A. C., K. W. Back, and N. Miller
1965 "Sociometric Patterns in Hysterical Contagion." *Sociometry* 28 (March): 2–15.

Kerr, W. A.
1952 "Untangling the Liberalism-Conservatism Continuum." *Journal of Social Psychology* 35:111–125.

Killian, L. M.
1964 "Social Movements." In *Handbook of Modern Sociology*, edited by R. E. L. Farris, pp. 426–456. Chicago: Rand-McNally.

King, C. W.
1956 *Social Movements in the United States*. New York: Random House.

Kirkpatrick, C.
1949 *Religion and Humanitarianism: A Study of Institutional Implications*. *Psychological Monographs* 63.

Kirkpatrick, R. G.
1974 "Moral Indignation and Repressed Sexuality." *Psychoanalytic Review* 61 (Spring):141–149.
In Press "Collective Consciousness and Mass Hysteria: Collective Behavior and Anti-Pornography Crusades in Durkheimian Perspective." *Human Relations*.

Klapp, O. E.
1972 *Currents of Unrest: An Introduction to Collective Behavior*. New York: Holt, Rinehart and Winston.

Kluckhohn, C.
1951 "Values and Value-Orientations." In *Toward a General Theory of Action*, edited by T. Parsons and E. A. Shils, pp. 388–434. Cambridge: Harvard University Press.

Kronhausen, E., and P. Kronhausen
1959 *Pornography and the Law*. New York: Ballantine Books.

Krout, M. H ., and R. Stagner
1939 "Personality Development in Radicals: A Comparative Study." *Sociometry* 2:1–46.

Kutschinsky, B.
1971 "Pornography in Denmark: Studies on Producers, Sellers and Users." In *Technical Reports of the Commission on Obscenity and Pornography*, IV, 263–288. Washington, D.C.: Government Printing Office.

Ladd, E. C.
1966 "The Radical Right: The White-Collar Extremism." *South Atlantic Quarterly* 65 (Summer):314–324.

Laing, R. D.
1967 *The Politics of Experience*. London: Penguin.

Lane, R. E.
1959 *Political Life*. Glencoe, Ill.: Free Press.

Lang, K., and G. Lang
  1961 *Collective Dynamics*. New York: Crowell.
Lasswell, H. D.
  1930 *Psychopathology and Politics*. Chicago: University of Chicago
  Press.
Laumann, E. O., and D. R. Segal
  1971 "Status Inconsistency and Ethnoreligious Group Membership as Determinants of Social Participation and Political Attitudes." *American Journal
  of Sociology* 77 (July):36–60.
Lazarsfeld, P. F., B. Berelson, and H. Gaudet
  1944 *The People's Choice*. New York: Duell, Sloan and Pearce.
Lenski, G. E.
  1954 "Status Crystallization: A Non-Vertical Dimension of Status." *American Sociological Review* 19 (August):405–413.
  1956 "Social Participation and Status Crystallization." *American Sociological
  Review* 21 (August):458–464.
  1966 *Power and Privilege: A Theory of Social Stratification*. New York: McGraw-
  Hill.
  1967 "Status Inconsistency and the Vote: A Four Nation Test." *American
  Sociological Review* 32 (April):298–301.
Levinson, D. J., and P. E. Huffman
  1955 "Traditional Family Ideology and Its Relation to Personality." *Journal
  of Personality* 23:251–273.
Lewis, J. M.
  1972 "A Study of the Kent State Incident Using Smelser's Theory of Collective Behavior." *Sociological Inquiry* 42 (Spring):87–96.
Lipset, S. M.
  1950 *Agrarian Socialism*. Berkeley: University of California Press.
  1955 "The Sources of the Radical Right." In *The New American Right*, edited
  by D. Bell, pp. 166–234. New York: Criterion.
  1959 "Social Stratification and Right-Wing Extremism." *British Journal of
  Sociology* 10 (December):1–38.
  1960 *Political Man: The Social Bases of Politics*. Garden City, N. J.: Doubleday.
  1963 "Three Decades of the Radical Right: Coughlinites, McCarthyites, and
  Birchers." In *The Radical Right*, edited by D. Bell, pp. 373–446. New York:
  Doubleday.
  1967 "Political Sociology." In *Sociology*, edited by N. J. Smelser, pp. 483–499.
  New York: Wiley.
Lipset, S. M., and E. Raab
  1969 "The Wallace Whitelash." *Trans-action* 7 (December):23–35.
  1970 *The Politics of Unreason: Right Wing Extremism in America, 1790–1970*.
  New York: Harper and Row.
Lipset, S. M., and S. S. Wolin, eds.
  1965 *The Berkeley Student Revolt*. Garden City: Doubleday.

Long, N. E.
   1958 "The Local Community as an Ecology of Games." *American Journal of Sociology* 64 (November):251–261.
McCall, G. J., and J. L. Simmons
   1969 *Issues in Participant Observation: A Text and Reader*. Reading, Mass.: Addison-Wesley.
McCarthy, J. D., and M. N. Zald
   1973 *The Trend of Social Movements in America: Professionalization and Resource Mobilization*. Morristown, N. J.: General Learning Press.
McClosky, H.
   1958 "Conservatism and Personality." *American Political Science Review* 52 (March):27–45.
Maccoby, H.
   1958 "The Differential Political Activity of Participants in a Voluntary Association." *American Sociological Review* 23 (October):524–532.
McCormack, T. H.
   1950 "The Motivation of Radicals." *American Journal of Sociology* 56:17–24.
McLaughlin, B.
   1969 *Studies in Social Movements: A Social Psychological Perspective*. New York: Free Press.
McPhail, C.
   1969 "Student Walkout: A Fortuitous Examination of Elementary Collective Behavior." *Social Problems* 16 (Spring):441–445.
   1972 "Theoretical and Methodological Strategies for the Study of Individual and Collective Behavior Sequences." Urbana: University of Illinois, mimeographed.
Manning, R. O.
   1971 "A Critical Analysis of Contemporary Collective Behavior Theory." *Social Forces* 4 (Summer):99–106.
   1973 "Fifteen Years of Collective Behavior." *Sociological Quarterly* 14 (Spring): 279–286.
Manual Enterprises, Inc. v. *Day*
   1962 370 U.S. 478.
Marcuse, H.
   1965 *Eros and Civilization*. Boston: Beacon Press.
Martin, W. T.
   1965 "Socially Induced Stress: Some Converging Theories." *Pacific Sociological Review* 8 (Spring):63–64.
Marx, G. T.
   1969 *Protest and Prejudice: A Study of Belief in the Black Community*. New York: Harper and Row.
Marx, K.
   1972 *Capital: A Critical Analysis of Capitalistic Production*, Vol. 1 (1867). Reprint. Moscow: Progress Publishers.

Massey, M. E.
1971 "A Market Analysis of Sex-Oriented Materials in Denver, Colorado, August, 1969—A Pilot Study." In *Technical Reports of the Commission on Obscenity and Pornography*, IV, 3–98. Washington, D.C.: Government Printing Office.
Meile, R. L., and P. N. Haesse
1969 "Social Status, Status Incongruence and Symptoms of Stress." *Journal of Health and Social Behavior* 10 (September):237–244.
Memoirs v. *Massachusetts*
1966 383 U.S. 413.
Messinger, S. L.
1955 "Organizational Transformation: A Case Study of a Declining Social Movement." *American Sociological Review* 20 (July):3–10.
Michener, H. A., and R. A. Zeller
1972 "A Test of Gamson's Theory of Political Trust Orientation." *Journal of Applied Social Psychology* 2 (April–June):138–156.
Milgram, S., and H. Toch
1969 "Collective Behavior: Crowds and Social Movements." In *The Handbook of Social Psychology*, edited by G. Lindzey and E. Aronson, IV, 507–610. Reading, Mass.: Addison-Wesley.
Miller v. *California*
1973 93 Supreme Court Reporter 2607.
Mishkin v. *New York*
1966 383 U.S. 502.
Mitchell, R. E.
1964 "Methodological Notes on a Theory of Status Crystallization." *Public Opinion Quarterly* 28 (Summer):315–325.
Mizruchi, E. H.
1960 "Social Structure and Anomia in a Small City." *American Sociological Review* 25 (October):645–654.
Morrison, D. E., and A. D. Steves
1967 "Deprivation, Discontent, and Social Movement Participation: Evidence on a Contemporary Farmer's Movement, The NFO." *Rural Sociology* 32:414–434.
Moser, C. A., and G. Kalton
1972 *Survey Methods in Social Investigation*. 2d ed. New York: Basic Books.
Mosher, D. L.
1971 "Psychological Reactions to Pornographic Films." In *Technical Reports of the Commission on Obscenity and Pornography*, VIII, 255–312. Washington, D.C.: Government Printing Office.
Murphy, T. J.
1963 *Censorship: Government and Obscenity*. Baltimore: Helicon Press.

Myers, F.
1971 "Civil Disobedience and Organizational Change: The British Committee of 100." *Political Science Quarterly* 86:92–112.
Nawy, H.
1971 "The San Francisco Erotic Market Place." In *Technical Reports of the Commission on Obscenity and Pornography*, IV, 155–224. Washington, D.C.: Government Printing Office.
Neal, A. G., and S. Rettig
1963 "Dimensions of Alienation Among Manual and Non-Manual Workers." *American Sociological Review* 28 (August):599–608.
Nelson, H. A.
1967 "The Defenders: A Case Study of an Informal Police Organization." *Social Problems* 15 (Fall):127–147.
1971 "Leadership and Change in an Evolutionary Movement: An Analysis of Change in the Leadership Structure of the Southern Civil Rights Movement." *Social Forces* 49 (March):353–371.
1974 "Social Movement Transformation and Pre-Movement Factor-Effect: A Preliminary Inquiry." *Sociological Quarterly* 15 (Winter):127–142.
Nettler, G.
1957 "A Measure of Alienation." *American Sociological Review* 22 (December): 670–677.
Oberschall, A.
1968 "The Los Angeles Riot of 1965." *Social Problems* 15 (Winter):322–341.
1973 *Social Conflict and Social Movements*. Englewood Cliffs, N. J.: Prentice-Hall.
Olsen, M. E., and J. C. Tully
1972 "Socioeconomic-Ethnic Status Inconsistency and Preference for Political Change." *American Sociological Review* 37 (October):560–574.
Orum, A. M.
1972 *Black Students in Protest: A Study of the Origins of the Black Student Movement*. Arnold and Caroline Rose Monograph Series. Washington, D.C.: American Sociological Association.
1974 "On Participation in Political Movements: A Critique of Existing Theories and a Modest Proposal Toward a New One." *Journal of Applied Behavioral Science* 10 (April–June):181–207.
Paige, J. M.
1968 "Collective Violence and the Culture of Subordination." Ph.D. dissertation, University of Michigan.
Paris Adult Theater v. *Slaton*
1973 93 Supreme Court Reporter 2628.
Park, R. E.
1927 "Human Nature and Collective Behavior." *American Journal of Sociology* 32 (March):733–741.

1934 "Collective Behavior." In *Encyclopedia of the Social Sciences*, II, 631–633. 1st ed. New York: Macmillan.

Park, R. E., and E. W. Burgess
1924 *Introduction to the Science of Sociology*. 2d ed. Chicago: University of Chicago Press.

Parker, S.
1963 "Comment on Status Consistency and Stress." *American Sociological Review* 28 (February):131–132.

Parsons, T.
1951 *The Social System*. Glencoe, Ill.: Free Press.

Parsons, T., and E. A. Shils, eds.
1951 *Toward a General Theory of Action*. Cambridge: Harvard University Press.

Parsons, T., E. Shils, R. D. Naegele, and J. P. Pitts
1961 *Theories of Society*. New York: Free Press.

Peterson, R. E.
1968 "The Student Left in American Higher Education." *Daedalus* 97 (Winter):293–317.

Pfautz, H. W.
1961 "Near Group Theory and Collective Behavior: A Critical Reformulation." *Social Problems* 9 (Fall):167–174.
1963 "Review of Neil J. Smelser, Theory of Collective Behavior." *Social Research* 30 (Winter):541–546.

Pinard, M.
1969 "Processes of Recruitment in the Sit-In Movement." *Public Opinion Quarterly* 33 (Fall):355–369.
1971 *The Rise of a Third Party*. Englewood Cliffs, N. J.: Prentice-Hall.

Polsby, N. W.
1963 "Toward an Explanation of McCarthyism." In *Politics and Social Life*, edited by N. W. Polsby, R. A. Dentler, and P. A. Smith, pp. 809–824. Boston: Beacon.

Portes, A.
1970a "Leftist Radicalism in Chile: A Test of Three Hypotheses." *Comparative Politics* 2 (January):251–274.
1970b "On the Logic of Post-Factum Explanations: The Hypothesis of Lower-Class Frustration As the Cause of Leftist Radicalism." Paper presented at the meetings of the Rural Sociological Society, August, Washington, D.C.

Quarantelli, E. L., and J. R. Hundley
1969 "A Test of Some Propositions about Crowd Formation and Behavior." In *Readings in Collective Behavior*, edited by R. R. Evans, pp. 538–554. Chicago: Rand-McNally.

Ranulf, S.
1938 *Moral Indignation and Middle Class Psychology*. Copenhagen: Levin and Munksgard.

Redrup v. *New York*
1967 386 U.S. 767
Reed, J. P., and R. S. Reed
1970 "Profile of the Student Censor: A Research Note on Pornography."
Sociological Symposium 5 (Fall):53–59.
Reich, C. A.
1970 *The Greening of America*. New York: Random House.
Reich, W.
1946 *The Mass Psychology of Fascism*. New York: Orgone Institute Press.
Riley, R. T., and T. F. Pettigrew
1969 "Relative Deprivation and Wallace's Northern Support." Paper presented at the annual meeting of the American Sociological Association, San Francisco.
Ringer, D. B., and D. L. Sills
1952–1953 "Political Extremists in Iran: A Secondary Analysis of Communication Data." *Public Opinion Quarterly* 16 (Winter):689–701.
Rist, R. C.
1973 "Polity, Politics, and Social Research: A Study in the Relationship of Federal Commissions and Social Science." *Social Problems* 21 (Summer): 113–128.
Robinson, J. P., and P. R. Shaver
1969 *Measures of Social Psychological Attitudes*, pp. 21–23. Ann Arbor, Mich.: Survey Research Center, Institute for Social Research.
Roche, J., and S. Sachs
1965 "The Bureaucrat and the Enthusiast: An Exploration of the Leadership of Social Movements." *Western Political Quarterly* 8 (June):248–261.
Rohter, I. S.
1967 "Radical Rightists: An Empirical Study." Ph.D. dissertation, Michigan State University.
1970 "The Genesis of Political Radicalism: The Case of the Radical Right." In *Learning About Politics: A Reader in Political Socialization*, edited by R. Sigel, pp. 626–651. New York: Random House.
Rokeach, M.
1960 *The Open and Closed Mind*. New York: Basic Books.
Rosander, A., and L. L. Thurston
1931 "Scale of Attitudes toward Censorship." In *The Measurement of Social Attitudes*, edited by L. L. Thurston, scale no. 28. Chicago: University of Chicago Press.
Rose, A. M.
1959 "Attitudinal Correlates of Social Participation." *Social Forces* 37 (March): 202–205.
Roszak, T.
1969 *The Making of a Counter-Culture: Reflections on the Technocratic Society and Its Youthful Opposition*. Garden City, N. Y.: Anchor Books.

Roth v. *United States*
1957 354 U.S. 476
Rudwick, E., and A. Meier
1970 "Organizational Structure and Goal Succession: A Comparative Analysis of the NAACP and CORE, 1964–1968." *Social Science Quarterly* 51 (June): 9–24.
Rush, G. B.
1967 "Status Consistency and Right-Wing Extremism." *American Sociological Review* 32 (February):86–92.
Sampson, E. E.
1963 "Status Congruence and Cognitive Consistency." *Sociometry* 26 (June): 146–162.
Sanford, F. H., and H. J. Older
1950 *A Short Authoritarian-Egalitarian Scale*. Progress Report No. 6, ser. A. Philadelphia: Institute for Research and Human Relations.
Schlesinger, A. M.
1950 *The American as Reformer*. Cambridge: Harvard University Press.
Segal, D. R.
1969 "Status Inconsistency, Cross Pressures and American Political Behavior." *American Sociological Review* 34 (June):352–359.
1970 "Status Inconsistency and Party Choice in Canada: An Attempt to Replicate." *Canadian Journal of Political Science* 3 (September):471–474.
Segal, D. R., and D. Knoke
1968 "Social Mobility, Status Inconsistency and Partisan Realignment in the United States." *Social Forces* 47 (December):154–158.
Shibutani, T.
1966 *Improvised News*. Indianapolis: Bobbs-Merrill.
Skolnick, J. H.
1969 *The Politics of Protest*. Washington, D.C.: Government Printing Office.
Slater, P.
1970 *The Pursuit of Loneliness: American Culture at the Breaking Point*. Boston: Beacon Press.
Smelser, N. J.
1962 *Theory of Collective Behavior*. New York: Free Press.
1968 *Essays in Sociological Explanation*. Englewood Cliffs, N.J.: Prentice-Hall.
1969 "Theoretical Issues of Scope and Problems." In *Readings in Collective Behavior*, edited by R. R. Evans, pp. 89–94. Chicago: Rand-McNally.
1972 "Some Additional Thoughts on Collective Behavior." *Sociological Inquiry* 42 (Spring):97–103.
Smith, D. H.
1966 "A Psychological Model of Individual Participation in Formal Voluntary Organizations: Application to Some Chilean Data." *American Journal of Sociology* 72 (November):249–266.

Smith, T.
1969 "Structural Crystallization, Status Inconsistency, and Political Partisanship." *American Sociological Review* 34 (December):907–921.
Smith, T. S.
1968 "Conventionalization and Control: An Examination of Adolescent Crowds." *American Journal of Sociology* 74 (September):172–183.
Sorokin, P.
1947 *Society, Culture, and Personality.* New York: Harper and Row.
Stanley v. *Georgia*
1969 394 U.S. 557.
Stouffer, S.
1955 *Communism, Conformity and Civil Liberties.* New York: Doubleday.
Straus, M. A., and J. I. Nelson
1960 *Sociological Analysis: An Empirical Approach through Replication.* New York: Harper and Row.
Surace, S. J., and M. Seeman
1967 "Some Correlates of Civil Rights Activism." *Social Forces* 46 (December):197–207.
Swanson, G. E.
1970 "Toward Corporate Action: A Reconstruction of Elementary Collective Processes." In *Human Nature and Collective Behavior,* edited by T. Shibutani, pp. 124–144. Englewood Cliffs, N.J.: Prentice-Hall.
Taylor, J. B., L. Zurcher, and W. Key
1970 *Tornado: Community Response to Disaster.* Seattle: University of Washington Press.
Teele, J. E.
1967 "Correlates of Voluntary Social Participation." *Genetic Psychology Monographs* 76 (August):165–204.
Toch, H.
1965 *The Social Psychology of Social Movements.* New York: Bobbs-Merrill.
Toennies, F.
1964 "Community and Society: Gemeinschaft and Gesellschaft." In *Social Change,* edited by A. Etzioni and E. Etzioni, pp. 64–72. New York: Basic Books.
Treiman, D.
1966 "Status Discrepancy and Prejudice." *American Journal of Sociology* 71 (May):651–664.
Trodahl, V. C., and F. A. Powell
1965 "A Short Form Dogmatism Scale for Use in Field Studies." *Social Forces* 44 (December):211–214.
Trow, M.
1958 "Small Businessmen, Political Tolerance, and Support for McCarthy." *American Journal of Sociology* 64 (November):270–281.

Turk, H.
1970 "Inter-Organizational Networks in Urban Society: Initial Perspectives and Comparative Research." *American Sociological Review* 35 (February):1–19.

Turk, H., and M. J. Lefcowitz
1962 "Towards a Theory of Representation between Groups." *Social Forces* 40 (May):337–341.

Turner, R. H.
1964 "Collective Behavior." In *Handbook of Modern Sociology*, edited by R. E. L. Faris, pp. 382–425. Chicago: Rand-McNally.
1967 "Types of Solidarity in the Reconstituting of Groups." *Pacific Sociological Review* 10 (Fall):60–68.
1970 "Determinants of Social Movement Strategies." In *Human Nature and Collective Behavior*, edited by T. Shibutani, pp. 145–164. Englewood Cliffs, N.J.: Prentice-Hall.

Turner, R. H., and L. M. Killian
1957 *Collective Behavior*. Englewood Cliffs, N.J.: Prentice-Hall.
1972 *Collective Behavior*. 2d ed. Englewood Cliffs, N.J.: Prentice-Hall.

Turner, R. H., and S. J. Surace
1956 "Zoot-Suiters and Mexicans: Symbols in Crowd Behavior." *American Journal of Sociology* 62 (July):14–20.

Twomey, J. E.
1955 "The Citizens Committee and Comic-Book Control: A Study of Extra-governmental Restraint." *Law and Contemporary Problems* 20 (Autumn):621.

Vidich, A. J., J. Bensman, and M. R. Stein, eds.
1964 *Reflections on Community Studies*. New York: Wiley.

Vierick, P.
1955 "The Revolt against the Elite." In *The New American Right*, edited by D. Bell, pp. 91–116. New York: Criterion Books.

Vorwaller, D. J.
1970 "Social Mobility and Membership in Voluntary Associations." *American Journal of Sociology* 75 (January):481–495.

Walker v. *Ohio*
1970 398 U.S. 434.

Wallace, D., G. Wehmer, and E. Podany
1971 "Contemporary Community Standards of Visual Erotica." In *Technical Reports of the Commission on Obscenity and Pornography*, IX, 27–88. Washington, D.C.: Government Printing Office.

Wallis, R.
1972 "The Dilemma of a Moral Crusade." *New Society* 21 (July):69–72.

Walton, J.
1967 "The Vertical Axis of Community Organization and the Structure of Power." *(Southwestern) Social Science Quarterly* 48 (December):353–368.

Walzer, M.
1965 *The Revolution of the Saints*. Cambridge: Harvard University Press.

Wanderer, J.
  1968 "1967 Riots: A Test of the Congruity of Events." *Social Problems* 16 (Fall):
  193–198.
  1969 "An Index of Riot Severity and Some Correlates." *American Journal of
  Sociology* 74 (March):500–505.
Warburton, T. R.
  1967 "Organization and Change in a British Holiness Movement." In *Patterns of Sectarianism*, edited by B. Wilson, pp. 106–137. London: Heineman.
Ware, C.
  1970 *Woman Power: The Movement for Women's Liberation*. New York: Tower
  Publications.
Warren, R. L.
  1967 "The Inter-Organizational Field as a Focus for Investigation." *Administrative Science Quarterly* 12 (December):396–419.
Wasby, S. L.
  1965 "Public Law, Politics, and the Local Court: Obscene Literature in Portland." *Journal of Public Law* 14(1):105–130.
Watts, W., and D. Whittaker
  1966 "Free Speech Advocates at Berkeley." *Journal of Applied Behavioral Science* 2 (January):41–62.
Webb, E. J., D. T. Campbell, R. D. Schwartz, and L. Sechrest
  1966 *Unobtrusive Measures: Non-Reactive Research in the Social Sciences*. Chicago: Rand-McNally.
Weber, M.
  1946 "Class, Status, and Party." In *From Max Weber*, translated and edited by
  H. Gerth and C. W. Mills, pp. 180–196. New York: Free Press.
  1947 *Theory of Social and Economic Organization*. Translated by A. M. Henderson and T. Parsons. New York: Oxford University Press.
Weiss, F. R.
  1963 "Defection From Social Movements and Subsequent Recruitment to
  New Movements." *Sociometry* 26 (March):1–20.
Weller, J., and E. L. Quarantelli
  1973 "Neglected Characteristics of Collective Behavior." *American Journal of
  Sociology* 79 (November):665–685.
Westby, D. L., and R. Braungart
  1966 "Class and Politics in the Family Backgrounds of Student Political
  Activists." *American Sociological Review* 31 (October):690–692.
Westley, W. A.
  1957 "The Nature and Control of Hostile Crowds." *Canadian Journal of Economic and Political Science* 23 (February):33–41.
Wilenski, H. L.
  1961 "Orderly Careers and Social Participation: The Impact of Work History
  on Social Integration in the Middle Class." *American Sociological Review* 26
  (August):521–539.

Wilson, J.
1973 *Introduction to Social Movements*. New York: Basic Books.
Wilson, J. Q.
1971 "Violence, Pornography, and Social Science." *The Public Interest* 22 (Winter):45–61.
Winick, C. A.
1971 "Some Observations of Patrons of Adult Theatres and Bookstores." In *Technical Reports of the Commission on Obscenity and Pornography*, IV, 225–244. Washington, D.C.: Government Printing Office.
Wolfinger, R. E., B. K. Wolfinger, K. Prewitt, and S. Rosenhack
1964 "America's Radical Right: Politics and Ideology." In *Ideology and Discontent*, edited by D. Apter, ch. 7. New York: Free Press.
Yablonsky, L.
1968 *The Hippie Trip*. New York: Pegasus.
Zald, M. N.
1969 "The Structure of Society and Social Service Integration." *Social Science Quarterly* 50 (December):557–567.
1970 *Organizational Change: The Political Economy of the YMCA*. Chicago: University of Chicago Press.
Zald, M. N., and R. Ash
1966 "Social Movement Organizations: Growth, Decay and Change." *Social Forces* 44 (March):327–341.
Zald, M. N., and T. Denton
1963 "From Evangelism to General Service: On the Transformation of the YMCA." *Administrative Science Quarterly* 8 (June):214–234.
Zetterberg, H. L.
1965 *On Theory and Verification in Sociology*. 3d ed. Totawa, N.J.: Bedminster Press.
Zurcher, L. A.
1967 "Functional Marginality: Dynamics of a Poverty Intervention Organization." *(Southwestern) Social Science Quarterly* 48 (December):411–421.
1970 *Poverty Warriors: The Human Experience of Planned Social Intervention*. Austin: University of Texas Press.
Zygmunt, J. F.
1972 "Movements and Motives: Some Unresolved Issues in the Psychology of Social Movements." *Human Relations* 25 (November):449–467.

Index